In Defence of Religious Schools and Colleges

It is often argued that religious schools and colleges promote intolerance, divisiveness, and fanaticism and that they violate the principle of academic freedom. Some writers also suggest that economic support for religious schools by the state violates the principle of the separation of church and state. Elmer Thiessen provides a philosophical defence of religious schools and colleges against these and other standard objections. He concludes with the radical proposal that a pluralistic educational system will better prepare students for citizenship in pluralist liberal democracies than a monopolistic state-maintained school system. Placing his argument within the context of liberal-democratic values, Thiessen gives concrete examples of objections to religious schools and offers practical suggestions that follow from the philosophical treatment of the problem.

In Defence of Religious Schools and Colleges bridges the gap between philosophical argument and educational practice. It will be of interest not only to philosophers and educational theorists but also to practitioners in education. Academics, policy makers, political theorists, teachers, administrators, and parents – those who object to religious schools and colleges and those who find themselves trying to answer the objections – will benefit from reading this book.

ELMER JOHN THIESSEN teaches philosophy at Medicine Hat College and is the author of *Teaching for Commitment: Liberal Education, Indoctrination, and Christian Nurture.*

In Defence of Religious Schools and Colleges

ELMER JOHN THIESSEN

McGill-Queen's University Press
Montreal & Kingston · London · Ithaca

© McGill-Queen's University Press 2001
ISBN 0-7735-2177-1 (cloth)
ISBN 0-7735-2221-2 (paper)

Legal deposit third quarter 2001
Bibliothèque nationale du Québec

Printed in Canada on acid-free paper

This book has been published with the help of a grant from the
Humanities and Social Sciences Federation of Canada, using funds
provided by the Social Sciences and Humanities Research Council
of Canada. Funding has also been received from Medicine Hat College.

McGill-Queen's University Press acknowledges the financial support of the
Government of Canada through the Book Publishing Industry
Development Program (BPIDP) for its activities. It also acknowledges the
support of the Canada Council for the Arts for its publishing program.

Canadian Cataloguing in Publication Data

Thiessen, Elmer John, 1942-
    In defence of religious schools and colleges
    Includes bibliographical references and index.
    ISBN 0-7735-2177-1 (bound) – ISBN 0-7735-2221-2 (pbk.)
    1. Religious education – Philosophy. 2. Pluralism. 3. Liberalism – Religious
    aspects. I. Title.
    LC368.T442001   371.07′01   C00-901493-4

This book was typeset by Typo Litho Composition Inc.
in 10/12 Baskerville.

Contents

Acknowledgments

I have benefited from opportunities to try out earlier versions of the arguments of this book at a variety of conferences and seminars in Canada, the USA, and the UK.

I am thankful for the valuable comments made by Alvin M. Schrader, who read an earlier draft of chapter 9, and Perry L. Glanzer, who read earlier drafts of chapters 1, 6, 12, and 13.

My thanks go to the administration and the Board of Medicine Hat College, who granted me a sabbatical in 1993–4 to work on this project. They have also provided some research funds over the past few years, as well as a grant for publication. I would also like to thank Rory Mahony and Elaine Chapman of the Visual Communications Department for their technical help in producing the illustrations.

Portions of this book have appeared previously in somewhat different form and are here used with permission. The relevant papers are as follows:

– "A Defence of a Distinctively Christian Curriculum." *Religious Education* (80) 1 (Winter, 1985): 37–50.
– "Educational Pluralism and Tolerance." *Journal of Educational Thought* (21) 2 (August, 1987): 71–87. Copyright © 1985/1999 by the University of Calgary.
– "Independent/Private/Religious Schools and the Question of Rights to Choose a Child's Education." *Proceedings of the Far Western Philosophy of Education Society* (1988): 119–28.

– "Christian Nurture, Indoctrination and Liberal Education." *Christian Librarian* (34) 2 (1991): 40–9; and *Spectrum* (23) 2 (Summer, 1991): 105–24.
– "Who Has the Right to Educate?" *Spectrum* (26) 2 (Summer, 1994): 141–55.
– "Liberal Education, Public Schools and the Embarrassment of Teaching for Commitment." In *Philosophy of Education 1995: A Publication of the Philosophy of Education Society,* ed. Alven Neiman. Urbana, Ill.: Philosophy of Education Society, 1996, 473–81.
– "Fanaticism and Christian Liberal Education: A Response to Ben Spiecker's 'Commitment to Liberal Education." *Studies in Philosophy and Education* (15) 3 (1996): 293–300. With kind permission from Kluwer Academic Publishers.
– "Academic Freedom in the Religious College and University: Confronting the Postmodern Challenge." *Paideusis: Journal of the Canadian Philosophy of Education Society* (11) 2 (1998): 55–72. With permission from the Canadian Philosophy of Education Society.

References to the Bible are from the New International Version of The Holy Bible.

I would like to express my thanks to the editors who helped bring this work to fruition: Aurèle Parisien, editor at McGill-Queen's University Press, who provided good advice and kept up my hope at various stages in the process; Nora Harder, macro-editor, who helped me to better understand myself as a writer, thus making it less painful to condense this work to a manageable size; and copy-editor, Judy Williams, for her careful attention to detail.

My thanks also to my wife, Magdalene, for her ongoing encouragement and help with some tasks related to manuscript production, and finally to Madeleine, Sylvie, and Ariane, who provided welcome diversions to my work. I dedicate this book to them and to any future grandchildren, who I trust and pray will get the kind of schooling they so much deserve.

In Defence of Religious Schools and Colleges

Prologue

I will dare to defend what many people consider indefensible – religious schools and colleges. Implicit in such a defence is an attack against a sacred cow of Western democracies – state-maintained public education, the supposed bulwark of liberal democracy.[1]

This is not a task which I relish because I know strong opposition exists to my viewpoint. Indeed, there was a time when I was strongly opposed to the position I will be arguing in this book. Many of the objections to religious schools which I will attempt to answer in the following chapters are objections which I once raised and vigorously defended. Further reading, reflection, and experience have placed me on the other side of this debate. Integrity and courage require that I defend that which I now consider to be true with regard to religious schools and colleges. Humility and intellectual charity demand that I make this defence with care and with some caution. I also do so with some hesitation, because I still feel the logical pull of arguments from the other side, at times strongly, but not enough to persuade me to change back to my original position. At the heart of the philosophical spirit is a willingness to go where the wind of the argument carries one, as Socrates said so long ago.

A note on my own background will help to explain why I have vacillated on the question of religious schools and colleges. It should also help the reader understand what kind of argumentation to expect in this book. Most of my education took place within a secular context. All of my elementary and secondary education occurred in state-maintained common schools. I should mention a peculiar feature of my early education – my father was my teacher for most of my elementary grades. This was in the days of one-room schools in the Canadian prairies when one teacher taught grades 1–12, and when public schools were still much more Christian than secular! Except for three years spent studying theology at a denominational college, I attended secular universities for my undergraduate and graduate education. My teaching career too has been mainly within a secular context, most of it at Medicine Hat College, a state-maintained institution of higher education. I began my teaching career with a two-year stint at Waterloo Lutheran University (a university Lutheran in name only, which soon after became a secular university – Wilfrid Laurier University). One of my sabbaticals included one semester of teaching at Lithuania Christian College, a daring experiment in Western-style college education in a country with newly gained independence from Soviet domination. But even here, most of the students were not Christian.

Thus, though I defend religious schools and colleges, it needs to be underscored that my academic career has been located primarily within a secular context. I feel deeply indebted to the universities of Saskatchewan, McMaster, and Waterloo for my own intellectual development. But I am also grateful to the Mennonite Brethren Bible College for initiating me into the humanities and for giving me a challenging theological education. Such a background, and my own Christian and Mennonite commitment, have prompted me to explore particularly the relation between religion and education.

This mix between the secular and the religious in my educational background also shapes the approach to be taken in this book. I want to avoid the isolation that often exists between these two realms. This book aims at facilitating dialogue between religious and secular opponents. As one might expect, the objections to religious schools generally arise out of a secular context.[2] In responding to these objections, I want to avoid strictly theological arguments, though I believe this kind of response to be legitimate in its own right and important in certain contexts.[3] There will therefore be little in this book by way of theological argument, although I believe the philosophical arguments I raise are compatible with Christian presuppositions, and I will point this out from time to time. Instead, I want to respond to objections against religious schools using arguments that will be accepted by Christians and sceptics alike, as well as adherents to other religious traditions. My approach aims specifically at bridging language and worldview barriers.[4] Interest in what I have to say in this book should therefore not depend on one's religious commitment or lack of it.

There is perhaps one final point of clarification that should be made in this introduction. Exactly what is it that is being defended in this book? I am defending religious schools and colleges generally. I am arguing for the *principle* or the *idea* of religious schools and colleges in pluralistic liberal democracies. Different countries have differing arrangements in accommodating such schools, as will be shown in the first chapter. In Canada, for example, there are Roman Catholic schools which are fully funded by the state and are viewed by many as "public" schools. Then there are independent religious schools, some of which get partial government funding while others get none. The central objective of this book is to defend all these schools regardless of how they are funded, though my preferences with regard to the funding question will become clear when I deal with economic concerns in part 4. But this is incidental to the main thrust of this book.

It should also be noted that it is not my intent to provide a blanket defence of all existing religious schools and colleges. Again, my intent is to defend the principle of religious schooling, although as my argument proceeds, I will also be clarifying what is and what is not acceptable in religious schools and colleges in pluralistic liberal democracies.

OBJECTIONS AND OBJECTIVES

There are a variety of standard objections raised against religious schools and colleges. For example, such schools promote intolerance and divisiveness, it is maintained. Many critics question the parents' alleged right to bring a child up in their own religion. The committed nature of religious colleges is also thought to violate the principle of academic freedom, leading to indoctrinative teaching which in turn fosters religious fanaticism. The central objective of this book is to provide a philosophical defence of religious schools and colleges against these and other commonly made objections.[5] The basic thrust of my argument is a general defence of religiously committed schools, although in some of the detailed argumentation and illustrations of my arguments, I will focus on Christian schools. This is because I am more familiar with Christianity and with Christian schools and colleges. However, most of what I have to say can be applied equally well to other types of religious schools and colleges. I will argue that in a pluralistic society, there should be a variety of religious schools (including secular schools).

APPROACH TO BE TAKEN

In concluding this prologue, it might be well to give the reader some idea of the general parameters of the argument in this book and the approach to be taken. I have already pointed out my central objective – a philosophical defence of religious schools and colleges.

In defending religious schools I will be challenging some widely held liberal-democratic values, though it needs to be stressed that it is not my intent to reject these values entirely. Rather, it will be argued that these values have become distorted and require careful reformulation in order to be defensible. My defence of religious schools will therefore be broadly placed within the context of liberal-democratic values, though qualified in important ways.

A philosophical defence of religious schools against various objections raises a broad spectrum of concerns and issues. Such a defence crosses the boundaries of religion, philosophy, politics, economics, epistemology, ethics, and education. This book is therefore interdisciplinary in nature, although it needs to be stressed that the orientation is fundamentally philosophical. Although my argumentation will involve some conceptual analysis, I want to move beyond the sometimes narrow and seemingly futile preoccupation with conceptual clarification which in times past has characterized philosophical writing on educational matters. I want to get at substantive philosophical issues, providing justification for religious schools against various arguments often raised against them.

One unique feature of this book is that each chapter will begin with some concrete historical examples, as found in Canada, the USA, and Great Britain, examples which illustrate the objection to religious schools under consideration. I take this approach because far too often philosophical dialogue occurs in the abstract. I want to show that philosophical debate grows out of concrete situations, some very ordinary, and some not so ordinary.

Another important feature of this book is that each chapter which considers an objection to religious schooling will conclude with some practical implications that follow from the philosophical treatment of the problem under consideration. I want to show that "Ideas Have Consequences," to quote the title of R.M. Weaver's oft-reprinted book (1971). Philosophical ideas have practical consequences and that is why it is sad that in the training (education?) of our teachers today, little attention is being paid to the exploration of the philosophical foundations underlying educational practice. This book will attempt to bridge the gap between philosophical ideas and educational practice. It should therefore be of interest not only to theoreticians but also to practitioners of education.

Philosophical writing is not only often abstract but also, sadly, abstruse. I believe there is no need for the obscurity that colours much philosophical dialogue. The profound can be stated simply. Complexity is often merely a sign of confusion. This volume will, I hope, be characterized by philosophical clarity and simplicity. It should therefore appeal not only to the academic or the philosopher, but also to the educated lay-person, to well-read teachers and parents who rightly demand that profound truth be stated in ordinary language.

One further word about the readership being addressed. Since this is a defence of religious schools against commonly made objections, I hope that both those making the objections and those who often find themselves trying to answer these objections will benefit from reading this book. It is meant to be read by sceptic and believer alike. I would expect that the concluding "practical implications" sections of the middle chapters will be of more interest to the religiously committed, and more specifically to Christians, but even here I expect the liberal-minded sceptic will be looking for more grist for the liberal mill.

Finally, a word or two on the conclusion of the argument of this book. First of all, it needs to be stressed that it is not at all my intention to provide a blanket defence of all religious schools and colleges and everything that goes on in such institutions. I believe the practices of some religious schools deserve criticism, and the practical section of each of the central chapters (i.e. those dealing with specific objections) will spell out areas where I have some concerns. I am rather arguing for the principle of religious schooling.

Each of the middle chapters of this book will attempt to answer one commonly made objection to religious schools. In critiquing these arguments, I will particularly be concerned to uncover some underlying assumptions and to show how these assumptions are problematic. The exercise is really one of deconstruction. This will pave the way for a broader critique of the opposition to religious schooling in the final chapters. Here I will be looking for some common threads to all the objections considered earlier. It is here where I will be suggesting a revision to some widely held liberal democratic values.

My overall argument will be in favour of a system of educational pluralism in contrast to a state-maintained system of common schools, which is the norm in Canada, the USA, and the United Kingdom. Here I am joining others who are calling for a radical restructuring of our system of schooling.[6] However, I want to disassociate myself from the current arguments for, and trends towards, the privatization of schooling, most often rooted in an economic free-enterprise ideology coming from the Right. I believe that the state still has an important role to play in education and my ideal of a system of educational pluralism does not exclude the state from exercising its legitimate role. I believe the state can exercise too much control over schooling, however, and the imposition of a monolithic system of common schooling is one expression of too much control. What the legitimate role of the state is with respect to schooling will become clear in the chapters that follow.

It needs to be stressed at the outset that my argument for this general conclusion will be somewhat tentative, as I am focusing primarily on answering various objections that have been raised against religious schools and colleges and their incorporation as full-fledged members of the educational enterprise. My primary strategy is deliberately a defensive one. Although I will move on to an offensive posture in the final chapter, even there I will not be able to address all the factors that would have to be taken into account in defending a system of educational pluralism and in coming to a final and firm conclusion on this matter. That is the subject of another book.

This prologue began with an expression of some hesitation regarding the objective I am undertaking in this book. I take encouragement from some words written quite some time ago by E.G. West in a book with somewhat similar objectives to my own: "For it is a test of a mature and a free society that in each generation there are sufficient writers prepared to persist with awkward but searching questions and an equally sufficient number of patient individuals willing to consider them" (West 1970, 2).

PART ONE

Introduction

1 Context of Charges against Religious Schools and Colleges

Much of the traditional historiography of urban and public education has indeed claimed that religious schooling has represented undemocratic, sometimes elitist, often "backward" and "divisive" interests – that "old" values are preserved at the expense of the young and their needs.

Ron Goodenow, "Schooling, Identity and Denominationalism: The American Experience"

The purpose of this book is to provide a philosophical response to some common objections to religious schools and colleges. But there is some preliminary work that must be done before I proceed.

In the Prologue I suggested that it is important to place philosophical argument into context. Each of the subsequent chapters (except for the final two) will begin with some concrete historical examples of an objection to religious schools and colleges. There is an even broader kind of contextualization that is required in order to appreciate more fully the thrust of the specific objections being considered. We need to ask why these objections appear to be raised with renewed vigour in our times. And why too a book responding to these objections? In order to answer these questions I need to review some facts and figures regarding religious schools and colleges in a few Western countries where such schools cause considerable debate.

This chapter is unique. It is meant to provide contextual background to the objections considered in subsequent chapters. Careful, detailed analysis of trends, facts, and figures will be involved. For the reader who does not care about such contextualization and who is more interested in getting to the heart of this book – philosophical argument – I would recommend that he or she move directly to chapter 2. While I agree that philosophical argument can, to some extent, stand on its own, it is helpful first to come to an appreciation of the context out of which such argument arises.

Interestingly, there has been a burgeoning of research regarding private and religious schooling in Western countries in the last decade.[1] A decade and a half ago, a Canadian writer commented that "although the pace of inquiry has quickened recently, research in the area of private schooling has not, in fact, been extensive" (Shapiro 1986, 266). And why might this be so? Goodenow has suggested that this failure to study the growth and persistence of religious schools in America has been due to a bias among American educational historians. They preferred to write about the triumphs of public education, which they assumed could overcome "divisive" religious interests. Further, they assumed that state-maintained schools would sooner or later consign religious schools to the junk heap of history, Goodenow maintains (1988, 197–8). Still, religious schools seem to be here to stay. Another reason for the increased research interest in religious schools is their growth and surrounding controversies.

This survey does not aim to provide a detailed analysis of religious schooling in the countries selected for treatment. I offer a more impressionistic approach, highlighting important legislative changes, and identifying significant trends. This survey will also highlight some of the controversies surrounding these legislative changes and trends in religious schooling. Finally, I will set the stage for a practical focus, which will conclude each of the central chapters of this book.

My main focus will be on Canada because that is the country with which I am most familiar. Canada has seen considerable volatility concerning religious schooling, and a summary of recent developments might be of interest to international readers. I will also provide a brief overview of religious schooling in the United States and Great Britain. A treatment of these other countries is included to provide a "check on parochialism" that so often exists in thinking about education (Walford 1989, 3). I also want to signal that the objections to religious schools and colleges considered in this book cross national boundaries. The philosophical argumentation in response to these objections should therefore have international appeal.

CANADA

The present picture of religious schooling in Canada is complex and varied. This complexity is due in part to provincial autonomy respecting school legislation and financing. This complexity in education has been appropriately described as "a patchwork quilt," which some would see as reflecting the patchwork character of Canadian identity (Holmes 1990, 232). Others might instead join Canadian sociologist Reginald Bibby in referring to it as another illustration of "mosaic madness" (Bibby 1990). However evaluated, this variety makes it difficult to provide a summary of religious schooling in Canada without running the risk of oversimplification. I shall try.

Let me begin by describing what was, until very recently, the most unusual arrangement concerning religious schooling in Canada.[2] The province of Newfoundland was the only place in North America that didn't have a public (secular) school system. As in other parts of Canada and the Western world, the first schools in Newfoundland were begun by churches or religious societies. But Newfoundland was unique in having maintained a system of tax-supported church schools for over 150 years. The civil right for various Christian denominations either individually or jointly to conduct their own schools was guaranteed in the British North America Act of 1867. When Newfoundland united with Canada in 1949, this right was confirmed in the Terms of Union, and in 1982 it was included in the Constitution of Canada.[3]

The governance and operation of the educational system in Newfoundland thus came to be shared among a non-denominational Department of Education, the denominational Educational Councils, and denominational school boards. Until recently, Pentecostals, Seventh Day Adventists, and Roman Catholics each operated their own school systems. There was also an Integrated School Board, formed in 1969, eventually representing the Anglican, United, Moravian, and Presbyterian churches and Salvation Army.

From its inception, this arrangement was not without controversy. In 1967 a royal commission recommended that the Department of Education be organized along functional lines rather than according to denominational division, and that the role of the churches in education be changed. Another royal commission was established in 1990, and was again asked to look at the denominational make-up of the schools, and to explore the consolidation of districts and schools as well as the barriers to effective schooling. The final report, published in 1992, advocated a total restructuring of education in Newfoundland. Churches were to be removed from the governance of education, but would still retain an important advisory role through a Denominational Policy Commission. Responding to an overwhelming majority of people surveyed who were not in favour of creating a fully secular approach to education within a uniform school system, the report also recommended that the valued Christian character of schooling be preserved, though in a non-sectarian way. Schools were to be governed by elected non-denominational school boards.

The provincial government committed itself to implementing all of the recommendations of the report, but a long and bitter battle ensued. The Catholic and Pentecostal churches, in particular, refused to make compromises and fought the changes in the provincial House of Assembly, the federal House of Commons, and the Senate. The changes required an amendment of the Constitution of Canada. The provincial government fought back with two referenda, the last one held on 2 September 1997. This time the citizens of Newfoundland were asked to vote on a more radical change, involving a complete severing of church control of schools. An overwhelming majority of voters (over 70 per cent) came down on the side of the government.

The vote was not entirely a surprise. The government was actively involved in campaigning for a "yes" vote. Although Premier Brian Tobin was careful not to attack church leaders for their opposition, his appeal for support was clearly directed towards the idea of a modern secular and pluralist society: "I believe it's time to allow all of our children, of every denomination, to sit in the same classroom, in the same schools, to ride the same bus, to play on the same sports teams, to live and learn together in the same community."[4] After the referendum, the premier called the vote a clear and strong mandate "to end the separation of our children."[5]

In an article describing the intense and often angry debate prior to the referendum, one writer characterized church control of education in Newfoundland as "curiously dated, a quaint anachronism in a secular land."[6] It would seem that this "quaint anachronism" on the North American scene has indeed come to an end. The Newfoundland Catholic Education Association, however, described the changes somewhat differently, alleging that the provincial government planned "to subordinate the rights of religious minorities to the tyranny of the majority."[7] Critics of these changes were predicting attempts to initiate similar constitutional amendments in other provinces which have state-supported religious schools.[8]

Indeed, such changes were recently implemented in Quebec. Historically, Quebec has had a dual confessional school system, consisting of Catholic and Protestant schools, again having its roots in one of the provisos of the BNA Act. There has been much ferment with regard to education in Quebec since 1961, when the government initiated a royal commission, commonly referred to as the Parent Commission, to review the organization and the financing of education in Quebec. Since that time, there has been an overall evolution towards a more unified and a more secular approach to the structure and delivery of education in Quebec (Peters 1996, 235).

One of the recommendations of this commission was implemented in 1964 when a single Ministry of Education was created, though still with two separate committees under it, the Catholic Committee and the Protestant Committee, each having limited jurisdiction over confessional matters in education alone. Schools boards were consolidated, forcing greater cooperation, and this had the effect of breaking up traditional confessional divisions. Although the dual confessional system of education remained in effect for a time, there was evidence to suggest that both Protestant and Roman Catholic schools were becoming more pluralistic and secular.[9]

In 1987, the government of Quebec introduced Bill 107, which sought to divide schooling along linguistic rather than confessional lines. The controversial nature of this bill and resultant court challenges delayed implementation. Although the legality of linguistic school boards was upheld in a Supreme Court decision in 1993, implementation was complex because of the constitutional guarantees of denominational schools. Quebec, like Newfoundland, sought amendments to the constitution, which would allow it to transform the province's confessional school system into a linguistic one by July 1998.[10]

These changes were implemented despite surveys which indicated strong parental support for confessional schools. However, some administrators and teachers, and many journalists, were very critical of confessional schools. Protesting the results of these surveys, one Montreal columnist stated, "It would be better to get religion out of the public schools entirely."[11] And once again the word "anachronistic" was used to describe a school system organized along confessional lines, this time by a Quebec educator.[12]

The last vestiges of denominational schooling in Quebec will disappear if the recommendations of the recent Proulx Task Force (1999) on the place of religion in schools in Quebec are implemented. This report recommends a radically secularized school system, drawing attention to the unfairness inherent in the traditional dualism of Quebec's schools (173). The alternative of a more pluralistic system of religious schools is specifically rejected as "a contradiction in a society which has been striving for more than 20 years to promote social cohesion based on common values and openness to diversity" (183). The report anticipated intense debate over its recommendations.

There also has been much ferment with regard to religious schooling in the province of Ontario. In 1984 the Ontario government decided to extend public funding to Catholic high schools to the end of grade 13 (Sweet 1997, 39). Sweet highlights the ways in which this decision tore various Ontario communities apart as high school students heretofore attending public schools were now transferred to Catholic schools (1997, ch. 3). The decision of the government aroused spirited controversy, and is believed to have contributed significantly towards the downfall of the Tory administration in the election that followed (Magsino 1986, 246). Further controversy has been aroused by a group of Jewish and Protestant parents, who recently launched an appeal against the Ontario government, arguing that it was discriminatory to fund Catholic schools but not independent schools. More on this later.

Thus far I have been considering examples of a close partnership between church and state with regard to educational provisions in Canada. Other examples include the provinces of Saskatchewan and Alberta, which, like Ontario, have systems of separate Catholic schools which are regarded simply as a special form of common, public schools, and which therefore receive full government funding. Some provinces – New Brunswick, Nova Scotia, Prince Edward Island, British Columbia, and Manitoba (after 1890) – have only secular, fully publicly supported schools. In actual practice, however, informal arrangements for funding Catholic schools in these provinces do exist (Wilson and Lazerson 1982, 7). Manitoba and British Columbia have begun to provide direct but partial funding to Catholic schools within the past twenty years. Also, certain schools are predominantly Catholic or Protestant, and are able to hire teachers so as to reflect the denominational character of the community (Magsino 1986, 249).

I have focused so far on religious schooling in Canada which evolved in some way from the provisions made for denominational schooling at the time of Confederation. There is, however, another quite different dimension of religious schooling in Canada that deserves separate treatment – the phenomenon of independent religious schools.[13] The controversies surrounding independent religious schools in Canada are as heated as those surrounding the denominational schools that are a result of Confederation promises.

This controversy is exacerbated by the fact that independent religious schools are growing rather rapidly, often at the expense of public school enrolment. Student enrolment in independent schools in Canada rose from 2.5 per cent of total school enrolment in 1970–1 to 4.8 per cent in 1992–3. In actual fact, the latter figure is really higher.[14] In her recent study, Sweet reports that about 260,000 students attend 1,700 independent schools that belong to the Federation of Independent Schools in Canada. Of those 1,700 schools, 1,200 are religiously based (Sweet 1997, 27). These figures are no doubt even higher, since a number of independent schools refuse to register because they are opposed to all government interference. While admitting that it is ultimately a futile exercise to find out how many Canadian children attend Christian schools, Sweet puts the figure at well over one million, which includes those that attend Catholic schools (82). A look at the growth of independent schools in a couple of provinces yields even more startling figures.[15]

This growth of independent schools has not gone unnoticed and often prompts vigorous debates about their legitimacy. Eamonn Callan has repeatedly drawn attention to the risks of religious indoctrination in denominational schools, and at one point he even wonders whether "we should eliminate denominational schooling altogether" because of these risks.[16] A one-year study on the debate over religion and educational choice in Canadian schools by Ottawa journalist Lois Sweet prompted a variety of media coverage, culminating in a widely reviewed book, *God in the Classroom* (1997).[17] Recalling her own childhood in a community that was white, English-speaking, and unabashedly Protestant, while nearby there was a French-speaking community that was unwaveringly Catholic, Sweet blames the parallel division of schooling for their learning to stereotype and fear each other (1–3). "To this day, I'm haunted by a sense of loss," Sweet reflects.[18] Various testimonials recorded in her book charge religious schools with elitism, indoctrination, being socially divisive, and fostering intolerance. Sweet herself, while deploring the neglect of religion in Canadian schooling and society at large, nevertheless is opposed to religious schools as a way of addressing this need.

Another significant component of the controversy surrounding independent religious schools has to do with the acceptability of public funding for non-public schools. Five provinces, Newfoundland, New Brunswick, Prince Edward Island, Nova Scotia, and Ontario, give no direct provincial grants to such schools for operating or capital expenditures, although certain minimal forms of direct or indirect aid are available in some cases (e.g. funds for the purchase of textbooks, exemption from property taxes on non-profit schools, income tax deductions for tuition attributable to religious instruction).[19]

Starting in 1991, an attempt was made by parents representing the Canadian Jewish Congress and the Ontario Alliance of Christian Schools to reverse the non-funding ruling in Ontario. Their argument before the Ontario courts was that the failure to fund their independent schools infringed on parental rights guaranteed under the Canadian Charter of Rights and Freedoms. They also argued that their schools should be as entitled to funding as are Roman Catholic schools. After two defeats in Ontario courts, the parents decided to take their case (known as the "Adler" case) to the Supreme Court of Canada, which ruled in 1996 that there is no constitutional obligation to fund independent schools but acknowledged that governments may do so.[20] This decision met with a good deal of consternation, especially in light of other recent court cases in Ontario which have upheld the trend towards secularization in Ontario public schools.[21] It is precisely this drive towards secularization that is prompting the growth of independent religious schools in Canada.

The remaining five provinces in Canada all provide partial funding for independent schools that meet specified curriculum and teacher certification criteria. The current level of funding for the majority of non-public schools in British Columbia, for example, stands at 50 per cent of public school operating costs (Barman 1991, 13). A private member's bill introduced in the Alberta legislature in the spring of 1997 and proposing an increase in funding led to the formation of a Private Schools Funding Task Force, mandated to review questions about funding, tuition fees, the right of private schools to select students, and accountability (Alberta Private Schools Funding Task Force 1997, 2). The government accepted the recommendation of this task force that funding for private schools be raised to 60 per cent of the basic instructional grant provided to Alberta public schools.[22]

Decisions to provide support or increase the level of such support for independent religious schools are always fraught with much controversy. For example, the private member's bill introduced in the Alberta legislature prompted the Public School Boards Association of Alberta to engage in a massive and carefully orchestrated lobbying of government MLAs and opposition members. Trustees and senior administrators were urged to write letters (two waves of letters), and were even given tips on how to write them: – "Use the phrase 'private schools' in all correspondence – as it implies exclusivity – do not use the phrase 'independent schools.'"[23] Arguments used against independent schools included the following: 1. "Public funding should correspond to public purpose, values, and goals. Private schools are private precisely because their supporters prefer private purposes, values, and goals over public purposes, values, and goals." 2. "Public funding for private schools promotes fragmentation of the community and weakens the cohesion of the community."[24] The government's decision-making regarding increased funding to independent schools was complicated by a vote taken by party members at the Progressive Conservative annual convention while the work of the task force was still going on. A surprise motion from the floor to cut all funding to private schools was passed by the membership after a fierce debate. Such a vote is not binding on the government and was obviously ignored when the decision was eventually made.[25]

One final dimension of religious schooling in Canada deserves some treatment. There has been some experimentation with having religious schools operating under the "umbrella" of public school boards (Vriend 1996). Logos Christian School, for example, was established in Calgary, Alberta in 1979, and proved both successful and controversial. In just four years it had over five hundred students at two schools and a waiting list of six hundred. Opponents of these schools feared a fragmentation of public education into a series of schools based on religious or ethnic origins. This fear was supported by the fact that two independent Jewish schools were also given alternate status under the umbrella of the public school board. The 1983 Calgary public school board elections were fought mainly on this issue with nasty accusations being exchanged on both sides. Most of the old board was not re-elected. As a result, the new public school board quickly voted to discontinue the operation of all alternate religious schools in Calgary at the end of the 1983–4 school year (Vriend 1996, 25).

But the experiment in Calgary has since been tried elsewhere in Alberta. Currently, several Christian schools operate under public school boards. For example, in 1996 the Edmonton public school board approved the application of the Logos Society to create an alternative Christian school program consisting of five Christian schools operating under the public school system (Sweet 1997, ch. 12). This move also prompted much opposition. Perhaps the most vociferous reaction came from the Alberta Teachers' Association. "The more we provide for break-off groups, the more we are encouraging people not to get along," says Bauni Mackay, president of the ATA (Sweet 1997, 243). Although Sweet herself is somewhat sympathetic with this approach – at least these schools are under the public system – in the end she is still worried about their promoting "a limited kind of one-sided learning" (244).[26]

In 1995 the Department of Education of Alberta adopted some guidelines regarding "charter schools," another experiment in allowing for choice within the public system. These guidelines are meant to promote a diversity of schools which are to remain in a semi-autonomous relationship with public school boards. The guidelines further specify that these "charter schools may not be affiliated with a religious faith or denomination ... nor are they intended to replace the services offered by private religious schools" (Vriend 1996, 25–6).[27] In 1996, however, Alberta's education minister gave approval to a proposed Almadina charter school in Calgary, providing an academically challenging program for English as a Second Language (ESL) students in grades 1–9. Although this charter school is billed as a language school, it would seem that the school is catering primarily to Arabs and Muslims. The name "Almadina" means "city of light" in Arabic. The school has come under criticism for teaching or preaching the Islamic faith, although this is denied by the officials connected with the school.[28]

Bergen concludes his study of private schools in Canada with the suggestion that "the right of choice among schooling alternatives has become an acceptable norm in Canadian society" (1989, 102). The achieving of this right has not been without conflict, and, as has been shown, there is an ongoing and perhaps even an increasing level of controversy concerning the extension of this right and the achievement of a more equitable distribution of this right in Canada. Indeed, in a more recent article reviewing the changing face of denominational education in Canada, Frank Peters draws the conclusion that "the long-standing support for a diverse, religiously pluralistic school system is disappearing" (1996, 229).

UNITED STATES

The United States is similar to Canada in that the Constitution has an important bearing on the question of religious schooling. The implications of the Constitution in the United States are much more sweeping and lead to greater uniformity in approach to education.

Of crucial significance is the First Amendment of the Constitution: "Congress shall make no law respecting an establishment of religion, or prohibiting the free exercise thereof." Historically this has been interpreted in terms of a strict separation of church and state, which has entailed that the government is barred from funding any religious schools, despite the fact that schooling in America had religious roots. Although Catholic schools have for many years lobbied for government funding, they have been unsuccessful, at least in terms of direct financial support for operational and capital expenditures. However, beginning with the Elementary and Secondary Education Act of 1965, private schools have been receiving limited funds from the federal government (Cookson 1989, 77). In most states there is some aid for incidental expenses such as transportation, textbooks, health care and lunch programs, driver education and state-required record keeping. However, even this limited form of public support for religious schools has been, and continues to be, a very controversial matter, as documented in a recent work by Doerr and Menendez, *Church Schools and Public Money: The Politics of Parochiaid* (1991).

Opposition to parochial schooling in the United States is also rooted in a deeply entrenched vision of seeing public education as playing a key role in creating national cohesion. Here again the controversy has centred around Catholic schools. Great waves of Catholic immigration in the middle of the nineteenth century created fears of a "Romanist" threat. Insensitivity, combined with outright anti-Catholic bigotry, prompted an increasing move on the part of the Catholic hierarchy to create a separate school system. At its peak year, 1965, the Catholic system enrolled 12 per cent of all American and secondary students, with thirteen thousand Catholic schools educating 5.5 million students (Bryk et al. 1993, 32). Various factors, not least of which were financial, have led to a dramatic decline in enrolment in Catholic schools – down to 5.4 per cent of the school-age population in 1990, with only 2.5 million students in nine thousand schools (Bryk et al. 1993, 33).

Cookson cites another key factor in understanding the resistance to private schools in the United States. "In the minds of most policy makers, educators, parents, and scholars, the American dream of equal opportunity began at the public-school door" (1989, 57). Early in the last century, several states even attempted to compel all children to attend common public schools, but the courts upheld the right of individuals and religious orders to found their own schools outside the public system. Cookson admits that this right seems to contradict the ideal of equal educational opportunities. This contradiction was muted by a perception that public schools were as good as if not better than private schools. Since the 1970s, however, there has been a growing loss of faith in the public school system. In one survey, the three major problems facing public schools were identified as lack of discipline, use of drugs, and poor curriculum/poor standards. Several reports in the 1980s were even declaring that the public school system was placing the "nation at risk." All this, together with a swing to the right in American politics, has prompted increasing interest in private schools in the United States.

Indeed, there has been what one writer repeatedly describes as a "flight" of children from public schools to religious schools (Goodenow 1988, 192, 208). Dwyer has recently suggested that roughly one-tenth of the fifty-two million school-aged children in the United States attend religious schools (1998, 15). Susan Rose reviews some of the statistics concerning the emergence of evangelical Christian day schools, a significant component of this flight. Various estimates suggest that such schools have been established at the rate of two per day since 1960. According to one writer, there was approximately a 630 per cent increase in Christian school enrolments between 1965 and 1984 (Rose 1988, 34–9). More recently, Dwyer observes that it is widely accepted that fundamentalist schooling is the fastest growing segment of formal education in the United States in the last twenty-five years (1998, 16). It is difficult to estimate how many such schools exist because of the fiercely independent nature of these evangelical Christian schools. However, nationally collected statistics and Christian school organizations seem to agree that, "based on the best available data, an estimate of between nine thousand and eleven thousand schools with a student population of approximately 1 million [1.5 million now] seems reasonable."[29]

This growth of evangelical Christian schools has spawned numerous criticisms and a number of critical studies. In the conclusion of a study of two such schools, Rose characterizes "their practices and beliefs" as "reactionary impulses in a time of social change" and "limiting rather than liberating" (1988, 220). Peshkin uses the concept of a "total institution" to characterize Bethany Baptist Academy, a fundamentalist Christian school located in a pseudonymous city of Hartney, Illinois (1986, ch. 10). In the final chapter Peshkin bluntly states that total institutions and absolute Truth are "anathema" to him (276). BBA represents an "organizational tyranny," a "closed universe," the "thwarting of human possibilities" (277). In a final assessment of overall costs and benefits, Peshkin rather reluctantly admits that schools such as BBA should be allowed to exist in a pluralistic democracy such as the USA, "at least until they overstep the line between safe and unsafe" (299). But he does not rule out the possibility that there might come a point when "we deem that the time has unmistakably come to fight fundamentalist Christian schools" (299).

UNITED KINGDOM

In Great Britain, religious denominational schools have been a part of the educational scene since 1870. After the Education Act of 1944, the majority of church-related schools became part of the state-maintained sector with special "voluntary" status. Such status meant that the church retained ownership of these schools, as well as some degree of control over them, while the state paid all of the recurrent costs and the bulk of new capital expenditure. At present about a third of the schools in the state-maintained sector in England and Wales have a voluntary status. In some areas such schools actually represent a majority of the local "state" schools. Most of these voluntary schools are Church of England or Roman Catholic schools. There are also a few Methodist and Jewish schools.[30]

Another significant and more recent component of religious schooling in Britain has been characterized as "the reluctant private sector" (Walford 1991b). This private sector involves a loose grouping of more than a hundred small private schools which would, in the main, like to obtain funding from the state. A significant portion of these schools belong to the "new Christian schools movement" (O'Keeffe 1992). Another component of the reluctant private sector is Muslim schools.

Since 1979, between three and eight new Christian schools have been founded each year in Britain (O'Keeffe 1992, 92). By 1992, there were nearly ninety such schools, rooted in a biblically based evangelical Christianity which at present is one of the fastest growing religious groups in Britain (Walford 1994a, 141–2). These schools have also grown very rapidly in student numbers, many beginning with a handful of students, but quickly growing to over one hundred. Indeed, many of these schools have long waiting lists of parents wanting to enrol their children.

In theory, the Education Act of 1944 allowed for the possibility of other Christian denominations and other faith groups to establish schools that could be incorporated into the state-maintained system. But in fact, until 1998, there were no Muslim or Hindu schools within the state system. Nor are any of the new Christian schools state-supported – despite the efforts of several Muslim and evangelical Christian private schools to apply for voluntary status. Their applications were invariably turned down (prior to 1998), usually by the Local Educational Authorities. In one well-publicized and controversial case, the Brent local educational authority supported the application of Islamia primary school for voluntary-aided status, but it was turned down by the Department for Education in August 1993 (Walford 1995, 2).

The reluctant private sector has been engaged in a variety of lobbying efforts, seeking to find ways to overcome the hurdles that seem to make it impossible to "opt in" to the state-maintained sector by becoming voluntary-aided or grant-maintained schools (Walford 1995). Efforts to make this easier via amendments to the Education Act or private members' bills have been hotly contested in the British Parliament and the House of Lords. Lord Dormand of Easington, for example, in one such debate argued against using taxpayers' money "to propagate religious or any other beliefs that are a matter of substantial controversy ... I believe that by their very nature religious schools are divisive ... Such schools do not contribute to social cohesion, tolerance and understanding."[31]

The recent 1993 Education Act eliminated some of the barriers that seemed to exist at the Local Educational Authority level. Decisions on new applications for grant-maintained status are now passed on directly to the Department for Education (Walford 1995, 2, 107). One of the first applications for such status under the new provisions came from Oak Hill School, a large and successful ten-year-old evangelical Christian school in Bristol, which was facing some financial difficulties. But application for grant-maintained status was refused on October of 1993, and again in 1995, after which the school shut down. One of the reasons given was that there were surplus places in existing schools in the local area from which the application was being made.[32] Since the Labour government came to power in 1997, there have been several successful applications for grant-maintained status – including one

Jewish school, two Muslim schools, and one Seventh Day Adventist school.[33] Whether future applications will succeed remains to be seen, but the controversies surrounding government funding of religious schools will make any government very cautious in approving many further applications.

And often, there is opposition to the very idea of religious schools. The influential 1985 Swann Report, for example, in advocating "education for all," not only argues against the provision of separate schools for Muslims but urges the government to reassess the long-standing partnership between church and state as expressed in the provision of voluntary schools (514, 520). More recently, Walford has suggested that "the most equitable and socially beneficial solution" to the problem of the newly emerging faith-based schools "would be to discontinue voluntary aided and grant-maintained status and encourage all schools to adapt to and encourage the faiths of its pupils" (1995, 125).

OTHER COMPONENTS OF RELIGIOUS SCHOOLING

Space will not permit a consideration of the status of religious schooling and the controversies surrounding such schools in other countries. I trust that my brief treatment of three countries has shown that controversies regarding religious schooling are widespread and often quite heated. Walford has aptly suggested that discussions about private schools tend to be polarized and often occur at the level of polemic and propaganda, leaving little room for rational analysis (1989, 1–2). Though the intent of this book is to defend religious schools, I hope to move beyond polemic and propaganda, providing a careful rational consideration of the various issues that so often come up in debates about religious schooling.

As should be evident from my treatment thus far, I will be focusing primarily on religious schools at the elementary and secondary levels. Space considerations again will not permit a detailed consideration of other contexts of religious schooling. For example, there has been a significant growth in home-schooling in all three countries being reviewed in this chapter. And most of these home-schools could be classified as religious schools. There are an estimated sixty thousand school-aged children who are being home-schooled in Canada.[34] Analysis of statewide data concerning home-schooling in the United States suggests that in recent years the number of home-schools nationwide has been growing about 15 per cent per year (Mayberry et al. 1995, 7). In 1997 it was estimated that there were approximately 1.23 million

American children being taught at home.[35] It was predicted that by the turn of the century approximately 2 per cent of the school-aged population in the United States could be children taught at home (Mayberry et al. 1995, xiii). In Britain, there are an estimated twenty thousand children being home-schooled.[36] A review of objections to children being home-schooled in religious homes will reveal many of the same objections that are levelled against religious schools and colleges.

Another component of religious schooling that could be considered is at the post-secondary level. The United States has the largest and perhaps most unusual private sector in higher education in the world, with about fifteen hundred private colleges and universities (Geiger 1986, 1). Although many of these private schools were founded with a religious affiliation, their commitment to keep pace with the academic mainstream has produced an overwhelming trend towards secularization (Geiger 1986, 183; cf. Marsden 1994; Burtchaell 1998). Geiger estimates that at present there are only about ten of the first-rate private colleges in the United States in which religious commitment plays a central and inescapable part in the educational process (183). Interestingly, the trend towards secularization in higher education seems to be driven to a significant degree by a demand for public support of private institutions, of which there has been a vast expansion in the last two decades (6, 197).

Higher education in the United Kingdom, by contrast, is predominantly public, with a slight crack opening up to private institutions with the creation of the University of Buckingham in the early 1980s (Geiger 1986, 2, 4). Geiger, however, fails to mention a fairly significant number of independent theological colleges and Bible schools in Great Britain, most of which receive little or no funding from the government.[37] Contrary to Geiger, who places Canada with the United Kingdom in giving only a peripheral role to private institutions of higher education, I would suggest that religious colleges and universities also play a significant role in Canada. A recent study of church-related higher education in Canada reveals a good number of such institutions (143 in total), displaying a rich variety of institutional forms.[38] Most of these Canadian church-related institutions of higher education receive some public support by way of a portion of operating costs, though the amount is often very small – 70 per cent of the institutions receive less than 10 per cent of their funding from government, and none receive public funds for capital purposes (Rae 1995, 32). Institutions more closely related to the university tend to receive more funding.[39]

Debates concerning funding invariably raise questions about the academic status of these institutions, and again many of the objections considered earlier in this chapter reappear also in this context. For example, a Roman Catholic college, recently established in Alberta, and having as its long-term aspiration to be affiliated with the University of Calgary, encountered opposition at its founding. In 1986/7 the humanities faculty at the University of Calgary formally expressed concern about having a Catholic college affiliate with the university, in part because this might jeopardize the "academic integrity" of the university which is "to promote free inquiry."[40] Underlying this objection is a concern about indoctrination and a lack of academic freedom, concerns which will be explored in detail in later chapters.

This completes an all too hasty overview of trends concerning religious schools and colleges in three countries where the debate surrounding such schools has been intense. I hope that this survey has put the arguments that will be considered in the remaining chapters into context. We are now in a position to begin a careful consideration of some specific objections to religious schools and colleges.

PART TWO

Problems of Social Harmony

2 The Charge of Promoting Divisiveness

I believe that by their very nature religious schools are divisive.
There can be no better illustration of that than that part of our
country called Northern Ireland … Such schools do not
contribute to social cohesion, tolerance and understanding.

Lord Dormand of Easington, during a
House of Lords debate, 1991

I begin a consideration of objections to religious schools and colleges
by looking at two frequently expressed concerns, both having to do
with social harmony – the charge that such schools promote divisiveness, and in the following chapter, the charge that such schools foster
intolerance. A 1985 report of the Commission on Private Schools in
Ontario notes that, in the 514 briefs submitted to the commission, the
social cohesion and intolerance arguments belonged to three of the
most common criticisms advanced against the funding of religious
schools (Shapiro 1985, 21, 47). Charges of divisiveness and intolerance are probably the two most frequently made charges against religious schools and colleges.[1]

Clearly there is a close relation between these two charges. Divisiveness and social fragmentation have to do with some very concrete
effects within a society. They involve consequences that can be measured, and might be thought to be more serious than fostering intolerance. But social fragmentation ultimately grows out of certain attitudes.
As we shall see in the next chapter, it is the attitude of intolerance that is
a key factor in creating social fragmentation. Though related, these two
charges are different enough to merit separate treatment.

The charge that religious schools and colleges cause division and
fragmentation within a society has had a long history. John Dewey, for
example, who in many ways is the father of North American education,
was very much concerned about the divisiveness of smaller associations
within a society. Therefore he defended the public school as a means
of providing "a wider and better balanced environment" in which

there would be an "intermingling in the school of youth of different races, differing religions and unlike customs" (1966, 21). More recently, Paul Hirst, a prominent British philosopher of education, has objected to separate schools because "such schools necessarily encourage social fragmentation in the society along religious lines" (1985, 16). Education in such schools "is likely to be ghetto-istic, concerned to preserve the tradition against other possibilities, favouring a large measure of social isolation and possibly indifference, even hostility, towards others" (7).

In this chapter and the next, I want to illustrate the charges under consideration by making reference to two government reports, one coming out of Great Britain (commonly referred to as the Swann Report, 1985) and the other from Canada (Committee 1984). A major emphasis running throughout the Swann Report is that all students need a common educational experience, given the pluralistic nature of Great Britain. Hence the title, *Education for All.* Indeed, one concern of the report is the "risk of the fragmentation of our society along ethnic lines which would seriously threaten the stability and cohesion of society as a whole" (7). After reviewing the arguments for and against separate voluntary schools for ethnic and minority groups, the Swann Committee expresses serious "misgivings about the implications and consequences of 'separate' provision of any kind" (510). The Committee even calls into question the long-standing dual system of educational provision in Great Britain involving state-maintained schools and voluntary church-related schools (520).

In a more recent discussion of a bill seeking to make it easier for independent schools to be established in Great Britain, similar sentiments were expressed by members of the House of Lords. The quotation at the head of this chapter is taken from this discussion. But Lord Dormand of Easington was not alone in his concern that such schools would be divisive and promote segregation.[2]

The Alberta Committee on Tolerance and Understanding too suggests that "we must, wherever possible, encourage shared experiences among the divers population in our schools (Committee 1984, 17). Although the present rate of growth of private schools is not considered to be cause for alarm, the Alberta report expresses worry about further increases, because "no society can function if any significant number of its people withdraw into isolation for religious, cultural or other reasons" (88, 109). Similar sentiments are expressed in many other Canadian reports and debates concerning religious schools.[3]

The same charge is also found in discussions regarding religious schools in the United States. Doerr and Menendez, for example, oppose tax support for non-public schools because this "would inevitably increase social fragmentation along religious, social class, and other lines, producing a society much less able than it is at present to cope with the country's growing problems" (1991, 133).

To understand the seeming urgency that underlies the charge of divisiveness against religiously based schools, it will be helpful to examine briefly the history of public schooling in America. A study of the history of state-maintained schooling in other Western societies would reveal a very similar emphasis.[4]

SOME HISTORICAL BACKGROUND

In his book *The Myth of the Common School,* Charles Glenn maintains that ultimately the political purpose of social cohesion was of more importance than purely educational concerns in the founding of American public schools.[5] At the heart of what he calls "the common school agenda," there was, and continues to be, "the deliberate effort to create in the entire youth of a nation common attitudes, loyalties, and values, and to do so under the central direction of the state" (Glenn 1988, 4). In part this emphasis on achieving social cohesion through public schooling grew out of the declining capacity of churches to fulfil this function. Thus, as Glenn points out, it is significant that the common school agenda arose in France, Holland, and Massachusetts shortly after the disestablishment of the official churches in each of these countries. The public school, therefore, replaced the churches as the provider of a unifying vision. According to Glenn, "The very power of the idea of the common school had much to do with its perceived role as the 'one living fountain' of meaning and inspiration, as a sort of universal church" (150).[6]

The head of this new universal church was the state. "The primary goal of the common school crusade was to form the hearts of the next generation, to ensure that they would, in the words of a leading Congregationalist journal, grow up 'with the state, of the state and for the state'" (Glenn 1988, 146). Small wonder then that the early public school supporters advocated "the defeat of private schooling as a major objective." Such schools simply did not fit in with the state objective of social cohesion which they saw as achievable only via a system of public schooling (219–22).

In an essay entitled "Public Education and Social Harmony: The Roots of an American Dream," McClellan begins to explore some of the tensions inherent in this dream of social cohesion via a system of public schooling. This dream of cohesion has driven educational policy and practice in America over the last century and a half, and has much to do with a long-standing opposition to private education, according to McClellan (1985, 41). It is the pervasiveness of this dream which leads McClellan to underscore the significance of the contemporary movement towards fragmentation in American education, and to ask why so many Americans are abandoning the dream. He even suggests that we may be standing at an important crossroads in American educational and cultural history in so far as there seems to be a strong movement towards diversity in education today, "a splintering that may represent an end to an ancient American dream that a universal public schooling could link diverse Americans to each other and create an important measure of cohesion in a society that seemed always endangered by difference and division" (33, 42). This prompts McClellan to ask the following questions. Have Americans lost faith in the possibility of a cohesive society? Or are they convinced that harmony can be brought about without the social glue of common schooling? Or has the public school failed so badly that other avenues to cohesion must now be explored (33, 42)?

This movement towards fragmentation is clearly evident in other Western societies. So are the questions that McClellan poses. The focus of this chapter is to examine critically the assumptions behind this dream of social harmony via a system of state-maintained public education. Is it true that a plurality of religiously based schools in a society leads to social fragmentation and divisiveness?

SOCIAL COHESION: HOW MUCH?

In addressing the charge that religiously based schools foster divisiveness, there is a fundamental question that needs to be addressed. How much unity do we need and want within a society? Clearly, for a society to exist, there must be some unity. But how unified does a society have to be? There is always the danger of going too far in demanding unity. Unity, carried to the extreme, entails complete assimilation and homogeneity. Aristotle, long ago, made this point in his critique of Socrates' ideal republic: "Certainly there must be some unity in a state, as in a household, but not an absolutely total unity" (*Politics*, II v). We need to heed Aristotle's warning.

John Stuart Mill, in his classic statement of liberalism, applies Aristotle's warning to education. Mill describes a state-maintained system of public education as "a mere contrivance for molding people to be exactly like one another," leading eventually to a despotism over the mind and the body (1978, 105). There is a strongly assimilative component to most, if not all, defences of state-maintained schools and opposition to educational pluralism. Yael Tamir highlights this point in a short but penetrating critical analysis of the history of public schooling in the preface to a new edition of her important study of liberal nationalism (1995a). It is the biased and oppressive nature of the melting pot strategy inherent in public education, she maintains, that is leading to an increasing awareness that there is something fundamentally wrong with many of the arguments against religious schools (xx–xxx).

Of course, liberal theorists would maintain that they are opposed to excessive uniformity and any form of totalitarianism. At the heart of pluralist liberal democratic societies, and the philosophical tradition of liberalism that undergirds them, is the attempt to find a balance between the contrasting demands of diversity and commonality. It is in the attempt to define precisely where a proper balance between universality and particularity can be found that many current debates concerning liberalism are to be located and understood.

There is clearly a liberal/pluralist agenda behind the Swann Report. The report very explicitly rejects the extreme of assimilation, "where the minority group loses all the distinctive characteristics of its identity and is ultimately absorbed and subsumed within the majority group" (Swann 1985, 4). Very early in this report the authors define and defend a concept of pluralism which involves a "balance between the shared common identity of society as a whole and the distinct identities of different ethnic groups" (5). In other words, the ideal is "diversity within unity" (7–8).

All this sounds very good, but it skirts the key question – how much unity, how much diversity? It is obviously true that "a degree of shared experience can be seen as one of the major factors in maintaining a cohesive society," but precisely what degree of shared experience is necessary (5)? Most treatments of this question suffer from this very same vagueness. Motherhood statements such as "diversity within unity" just don't help.

I would suggest that, despite the language of pluralism that runs throughout the Swann Report, the central thrust is on unity rather than diversity. The overriding ideal is understood in terms of the same education for all. And the report is very clear in rejecting a pluralism that extends to schooling (1985, 509, 514). But is this not a rather arbitrary cut-off point? If we really believe in plurality, should we not allow for a plurality of educational institutions which have such an important role to play in transmitting ethnic and religious identities? Of course, the Swann Report would argue that the function of education is not transmission but liberation (319, 321–3). But, as I have argued elsewhere, transmission is an essential component of a liberal education (Thiessen 1993, ch. 8).

Further, the kind of education advocated by the Swann Report does involve the transmission of a very specific kind of ideological commitment –

the ideology of liberalism. And here again, we find the report more committed to unity than to diversity, insisting that all children be educated only in terms of the ideology of liberalism. This point deserves further treatment, but I want to do so by refocusing on the concept of pluralism which is being advocated.

PLURALISM: WHAT KIND?

In order to understand what lies behind opposition to religiously based schools, it is important to examine the kind of pluralism being envisioned by those making the objection. We have seen that the Swann Report emphasizes diversity within unity. But what kind of pluralistic society do the authors have in mind? Commendably, the report addresses this question very early. Clearly the report is responding to the phenomenon of cultural pluralism. But in articulating the concept of pluralism being advocated, the Swann Report introduces another quite different notion of pluralism which is rooted in its ideological commitment to traditional liberalism: "It is important to emphasize here *free choice for individuals*, so that all may move and develop as they wish within the structure of a pluralist society" (6; my emphasis). "A good education must in our view give every youngster the knowledge, understanding and skills to function effectively as an individual" (319). The emphasis on individual freedom and choice should not be overlooked here. The commitment to plurality within the Swann Report is deceptive – it is fundamentally a plurality of individuals that is being advocated, not a plurality of communities or cultural/religious groups. Liberalism typically does not see cultural membership as a primary good.[7]

Indeed, the report concedes that "we are perhaps looking for the 'assimilation' of *all* groups within a redefined concept of what it means to live in British society today" (8). Here again it is important to pay close attention to the language used. Note what it is that is being assimilated. It is *groups* that are to be assimilated. This is quite in keeping with the traditional liberal emphasis on individualism which in the end destroys ethnic/cultural and religious groups.[8] While there is a plurality of sorts here, there is a strong commitment to uniformity. Marshall, after tracing this same kind of duplicity in other expressions of liberalism, argues that liberalism undercuts distinctive communities and replaces them with a uniform regime of individuals and individual choices. He concludes that liberalism is not neutral or open with respect to different ways of life (Marshall 1989, 16). In other words, the Swann Report betrays the traditional agenda of liberalism – the accommodation of differing conceptions of the good life.

Marsden uncovers a similar antipathy to a diversity of visions of the good life, values, or world-views at the heart of American society, and more particularly the American university of today. The subtitle of his work sums up the history of the university – "From Protestant Establishment to Established Nonbelief" (1994). Marsden concludes: "Pluralism as it is often conceived of today seems to be almost a code word for its opposite, a new expression of the melting-pot ideal. Persons from a wide variety of races and cultures are welcomed into the university, but only on the condition that they think more-or-less alike" (432). In a later work, Marsden points to "a deep ambiguity about the whole ideal of diversity in mainstream American culture. Is the goal 'integration' or 'diversity'? When it comes to religion in pubic life, the impulse for integration and uniformity typically overcomes diversity, despite the rhetoric to the contrary" (1997, 35). Interestingly, in a "concluding unscientific postscript" of his earlier work, Marsden argues not only for a greater acceptance of a pluralism of viewpoints within the secular university, but also for an acceptance of a plurality of institutions of higher learning (1994, 436–40).

Here it might be objected that in the last few decades serious efforts have been made to accommodate cultural pluralism within education through multicultural programs. The contemporary debate in liberal political theory is surely all about providing a more nuanced statement of liberalism which does justice to community and group identities. But many of these more nuanced versions of liberalism are still at heart strongly individualistic. Multicultural and religious education programs in our schools, while they do much to convey knowledge *about* various cultures and religious traditions, do not, and cannot, do justice to initiating students into these traditions. Indeed, as various writers have pointed out, liberalism and liberal programs in schools are much less tolerant of pluralism than they purport to be.[9] Tamir, for example, calls attention to the growing awareness of the oppressive nature of much of the liberal agenda, including its support for a state-maintained system of education, and in the end this leads Tamir to call for a radical redefinition of political institutions, especially of schools (1995a, xxv–xxvii, xvii).

The objection that religiously based schools are divisive rests on an indefensible ideal of a pluralistic society. While wanting to acknowledge pluralism, most attempts at defining the balance between unity and diversity stress unity at the expense of diversity. Further, there is often an overemphasis on the individual at the expense of religious or cultural communities. As some liberal writers are coming to realize, a healthy concept of pluralism not only does not rule out religious schools, but may even require them.[10]

LOGICAL INCOMPATIBILITY?

Here we need to face the objection that religious schools "by their very nature" are divisive (see the quotation at the head of this chapter). This objection rules out the very possibility of such schools fostering social cohesion. There are two variations of this objection.

For some critics, the very fact of separateness of these schools entails that they foster divisiveness.[11] This is an odd position, because, taken to its logical conclusion, it would have to view all separateness as divisive. This would mean that the mere existence of any particular organization, any family – indeed, any individual – would have to be viewed as contributing to divisiveness by virtue of its being separate. On this view only the complete Oneness of Eastern pantheistic monism, for example, can be seen as being non-divisive. While it is a truism that Oneness cannot be divided, this is not very helpful in dealing with real societies. This view simply flies in the face of empirical reality. Countless examples can be given where unity is achieved amidst diversity. The slogan "unity amidst diversity" is at least grounded in empirical reality! And the liberal agenda is at least realistic in acknowledging the reality of pluralism in public life and seeking somehow to achieve a minimum level of unity to encompass this plurality.

A second variant of this objection points to the exclusivity of religions such as Christianity. This issue is raised, for example, by Peshkin in the conclusion of his sociological analysis of Bethany Baptist Academy and fundamentalist supporters of religious schools like it. "As true believers, it is contradictory for them to advance a concept like pluralism. They want to thrive, but they do not want a multitude of competing doctrines to thrive. How could they if their Truth is singular?" (1986, 293). Oddly, Peshkin is forced to admit that in a comparison of BBA students with those from Hartney's public high school with regard to their commitment to pluralism, "the *overall* results were not drastically different" (292). He is also forced to admit that Bethanyites do cherish pluralism, but he maintains that this is only because the very survival of schools like BBA depends on the acceptance of the principle of pluralism in America (293). But it is dangerous to speculate about underlying motives.

Indeed, pluralism is a Christian doctrine. This is surely part of the significance of the biblical story of Babel (Genesis 11: 1–9). As David Smith has so ably shown, this is not an isolated emphasis in the Scriptures, as is sometimes assumed. "Diversity is affirmed and oppressive conformity negated, a message which is reaffirmed at highly significant junctures in the Biblical narrative" (1996, 186). Hence also the call for "mediating structures," or "intermediate communities," or "associational plurality" as a way of offering cultural protection, and as a way of mediating between the state and the individual, on the part of various Christian writers.[12]

Peshkin also seems to misunderstand the Christian concept of Truth. Surely it is possible to uphold the notion of "monolithic Truth" as an ideal and at the same to allow for many truths in the human search for absolute Truth. There is nothing logically inconsistent in believing in Truth with a capital "T" and accepting as a reality that at the temporal human level there will continue to be many truths. Yes, there is an eschatological dimension to Christian doctrine which involves a belief in an eternal perspective, a future reality, quite beyond our temporal existence, when Truth will be realized and acknowledged by all.[13] But in the here and now, we have to live with doctrinal plurality. "Disagreement about fundamental human issues is an inescapable fact of life under present conditions" (Mouw and Griffioen 1993, 106).

EMPIRICAL CONSIDERATIONS

The claim that religious schools and colleges foster divisiveness is essentially an empirical claim. And as such, one would expect to find empirical verification to back up the charge being made. It would be quite reasonable to expect, further, that claims to the effect that state-maintained common schools do foster social cohesion would also be backed by empirical evidence. But these claims are most often made without any concern for empirical backing. Sometimes critics admit the problem. For example, Cumper, after raising the question whether state-funded Muslim schools in Britain would be ethnically divisive, admits that "[t]he divisiveness charge is difficult to substantiate" (1994, 174). But he goes right on to maintain that this is a danger. Are unsubstantiated dangers really dangers?

McLaughlin too points to the fact that there is insufficient evidence to make a clear judgment on the question whether separate schools undermine cohesion within a society (1992a, 125). He further reminds us that such questions are very complex, involving a host of issues (practical, pedagogic, psychological, sociological, political, and demographic), all of which would need to be taken into account in order to come to a full assessment of the effects of religious schools (115). He therefore prefaces his treatment of the ethics of religious schools with the suggestion that "opponents of separate schools have a harder case to argue than is commonly supposed" (114). Indeed so!

In considering empirical evidence, a distinction needs to be made between two sorts of consequences – the internal effects of these schools in promoting student attitudes that are conducive to unity and societal harmony, and the external effects these schools have by virtue of their very existence. I have already referred to some empirical evidence which relates to the first type of internal consequence and which would in fact suggest that religious schools do not foster divisiveness. Peshkin, in his study of Bethany Baptist Academy, is forced to admit that BBA students were about as committed to pluralism as those from a comparative public high school (1986, 292). I want to consider the internal effects of religious schools more fully in the following chapter, which will attempt to answer the charge of intolerance.

In this chapter, I will focus on empirical evidence relating to the second of these consequences. In other words, the focus here will be on the overall consequences of a *system* of education which allows for variety of schools to exist within a society. I want to suggest that a system of educational pluralism does not foster divisiveness within a society. There are various countries such as Denmark, the Netherlands, and parts of Canada where there are a plurality of schools. Yet despite their having a system of educational pluralism, these countries are not noted for divisiveness, racism, or intolerance.[14]

The school situation in the Netherlands provides a telling example. Though religiously divided, the country has had a long history of being one of the most cohesive and tolerant societies in the world. Yet its educational system enrols three-quarters of its students in a variety of non-public schools. Sweet therefore correctly observes that an eighty-year history of funding religious schools in the Netherlands seems to point to success in the social integration of minority groups, not social division (1997, 136, cf. 127).[15] Other democracies considered harmonious and tolerant, such as Denmark and Australia, also have a significant proportion of their students in non-public schools (Van Brummelen 1990, 9). Glenn, in his comparative study of the effects of school choice in six nations, concludes: "No real evidence exists, after all, that confessional schooling has a socially divisive effect" (1989, 210).

There are several types of educational pluralism found in Canada, and again it would be difficult to maintain that these pluralistic structures have increased levels of divisiveness and intolerance in Canada. In the province of Newfoundland, the entire school system has been divided along denominational lines for centuries. Yet, I am not at all aware that there is a greater degree of divisiveness and intolerance in Newfoundland than there is in other provinces of Canada which have a more uniform system of state education. It was only when the government very recently sought to change this system that serious divisions began to emerge in this heretofore peaceful province.[16]

Then there is the constitutionally entrenched system of Catholic education which exists in many provinces of Canada. Catholic schools exist as a second major system of education alongside the public system or as an alternative within the public system of education. Yet, after over a century of this dualism in Canadian education, we find Catholics and non-Catholics coexisting in a peaceable manner. A dual system of education has not fostered divisiveness and intolerance in Canadian society, and the Alberta Report of the Committee on Tolerance and Understanding was forced to concede this point (Committee 1984, 88, 90, 92). In fact it can be argued that such structural pluralism has served to enhance the cause of unity and religious tolerance in Canada.[17]

Further, there is an important American study suggesting that separate Catholic schools are more successful than their state-maintained public school counterparts in helping minorities to assimilate into American society, in fostering human cooperation, and in promoting the common good (see Bryk et al. 1993, esp. 11, 339). The authors point out that for Catholic immigrants from Europe, ethnic schools served as important bridging institutions between two different cultures. These schools served both a preserving function and a transforming function, and ultimately facilitated the assimilation of immigrants into American life (27–8). This study confirms the results of an earlier study by Greeley and Rossi, who found no trace of a "divisive" effect of Catholic schools.[18]

Here an obvious counter-example needs to be considered. It is often maintained that the deep religious divisions in Northern Ireland are in part a reflection of a long-standing system of denominational schooling in that province. But, as Margaret Sutherland argues, in a helpful essay entitled "Religious Dichotomy and Schooling in Northern Ireland," caution is in order in interpreting this conflict (1988). From her survey of the experiments and studies in Northern Ireland, she concludes that "it is evident that the problems do not originate from within the dual system of schools" (57). Instead, she sees the problems as lying "in the interlinking of religious with cultural and political choices as well as in demands for the right to practice a chosen religion without disadvantage or discrimination" (58).

Public opinion polls during the past two decades are revealing the remarkable fact that majorities of the population, ranging from 62 per cent to 81 per cent, have been in favour of desegregating the schools. "Paradoxically, this willingness to have common schools would seem proof that the segregated schools have not produced attitudes of hostility between sectors" (52). Although the author clearly prefers common schools, she is forced to concede that it is "uncertain" whether common schools can educate students to respect other's beliefs (58).[19]

I therefore conclude that very little, if anything, can be concluded by using Northern Ireland as an example to prove that religious schools are divisive, or that common schools are essential to maintaining social cohesion. In any case, the situation there is so unusual that it would be foolish to draw any generalizations about schooling from this example.

I have already touched on a final empirical consideration that needs to be dealt with. Has the dream of social cohesion via state-maintained common schooling been fulfilled? Clearly educationalists in Western societies have viewed the common school as the common meeting ground for diverse and often contending groups, "a powerful symbol of harmony in the midst of division" (McClellan 1985, 41). But, there seems to be a growing awareness that the common schools have failed precisely in this area. Indeed, as Mark Holmes points out in the final chapter of his recent study of choice as an educational policy for pluralist democracies, "the USA, with a history of strong dependence on public-school systems, is arguably the western democracy with the most divisive social problems."[20]

A case has been made by some scholars that "Americans have attained social peace not by bringing diverse groups together, but by keeping them apart, by observing a policy of live and let live, by staying out of each other's way" (McClellan 1985, 41). This certainly is one possible interpretation of the American experience, and if true, it completely undermines the argument that social cohesion is best brought about by ensuring that all are educated within the context of common schools. As Glenn observes, the notion that the state can, and should, sponsor schools in order to mould common loyalties and values in the interests of national unity is a "myth" (1988).

And, as Wagner notes, we must not forget the "dark side" of the social cohesion argument for state-maintained public education (1995, 66). Social cohesion at what cost? Surely in a democracy we need to be sensitive to the problem of achieving social cohesion at the terrible cost of unnecessarily limiting freedom. As was argued earlier in this chapter, and as has been pointed out by various writers, if there is any connection to be made it is between public education and totalitarianism (Wagner 1995, 66).

HOW BEST TO BRING ABOUT SOCIAL COHESION

In responding to the charge that religious schools foster divisiveness, I do not want to be understood as rejecting entirely the concerns of those who uphold the ideal of social cohesion. Clearly there is a need for some unity within any society. I share the sense of urgency that pervades some recent writings as they grapple with what needs to be done in the light of the growing plurality of Western democracies. But, a final question remains. How best do we achieve harmony and the necessary degree of unity within a society in the face of growing plurality? I suggest that underlying the charge that religious schools foster divisiveness there are some problematic assumptions about how social cohesion is best achieved.

One problematic assumption is that in order to ensure eventual social cohesion, the school must itself be a reflection of society at large. Running throughout the Swann Report, for example, is an argument "for *all* pupils to share a common educational experience which prepares them for life in a truly pluralist society."[21]

The fallacy here is to assume that the conditions for the development of qualities in children that will lead to eventual social cohesion must be the same as the conditions that are necessary for the achievement of social cohesion once these children have matured. It might just be that a relatively restricted environment for children is in fact a better context than a pluralistic setting for nurturing dispositions which will foster eventual unity and harmony. I realize that this appears to be counter-intuitive. Surely some degree of exposure to plurality is essential for the growth towards tolerance and respect for others which are so essential in maintaining social cohesion.

But we must not forget the need for unity within the child's own learning environment. Children need a primary culture within which to grow (Ackerman 1980, ch. 5; McLaughlin 1984). Exposing them to plurality and a Babel of beliefs and values too soon will in fact prevent the development of abilities which are a key to later functioning in a complex and pluralistic environment. Research in the areas of developmental psychology and psychiatry by individuals like Michael Rutter, Urie Bronfenbrenner, and Reuven Feuerstein, to name only three, would seem to confirm these conclusions.[22] It is this need for a primary culture that lies behind the "paradox" identified so clearly by Esther Enkin, a Toronto Jewish mother who has chosen to send her daughter to Hebrew Day School. Enkin says she knows how important it is to teach children about living together. "And here I am, educating my child separately. But there's a paradox," she says. "The more I teach her who she is, then the better she can live with others" (Sweet 1997, 112).

There are, further, some considerations which suggest that social cohesion via government decree is in fact counter-productive. Even in a democracy, using political machinery to get things done involves having to resort to "the steam roller of majority ruling," a device which invariably produces severe and continual friction (West 1970, 76). This is the central theme of Stephen Arons's description of the culture of

American schooling in terms of "compelling belief" (1986). After a careful analysis of a variety of conflicts and court cases over the control of orthodoxy in the American public school system, Arons concludes that "nothing is more certain to fragment a community than the public coercion of private decisions" (1986, 194).

It is further of utmost importance to keep in mind that harmony and unity simply cannot be engineered but must finally come from the hearts of people within a society. This point is made well by Pierre Teilhard de Chardin: "Unification through coercion leads only to a superficial pseudo-unity ... [I]t is inwardly that we must come together, and in entire freedom" (1964, 74).

Another related error made by liberals is to assume that a community is held together by beliefs, beliefs that are shared and that can be rationally defended. But, perhaps it is not so much shared beliefs but shared hopes that play a critical role in bringing about unity within a society. This is a point that Rorty has made in his attempt to revise liberalism so as to accommodate radical pluralism more effectively. Rorty goes on to argue that the sharing of hopes creates trust. And it is trust that produces cohesion (Rorty 1991, 33, 203–10). Of course, trust generated by hope is essentially a religious notion. It involves looking to a goal that transcends the here and now. Thus Mouw and Griffioen conclude their treatment of the problem of pluralism thus: "Only by becoming aware of the 'open heaven' under which society is placed, does it become possible to promote unity without destroying plurality" (1993, 168). And, as Mouw and Griffioen document, even secular writers, when addressing the question of finding unity amidst diversity, are often driven to introduce religion as a way of achieving this goal (ch. 8). So perhaps religious schools have a unique role to play in achieving unity within a pluralistic society.

It is also a commonplace that where there is conflict between groups of individuals or nations, true unity can only be achieved if the parties stand on equal terms. I would suggest that like-mindedness among different ethnic and religious groups within a society can similarly only be brought about if these groups are given equal status in terms of educational provisions.

These are the kinds of insights that are behind the growing acceptance of the need for a "politics of recognition" (Taylor 1994; cf. Gutmann 1994). The key to promoting harmony within pluralistic democracies is to acknowledge and respect the deeply held cultural and religious differences that exist within our society. And this entails equal status for schools of differing religious traditions. I will not expand on these considerations here, since they will be pursued in more detail in the final chapters.

SOME PRACTICAL IMPLICATIONS
FOR RELIGIOUS SCHOOLS

1.   *The principle of pluralism*: Peshkin complains that he never heard a discussion, let alone an elaboration, of the concept of pluralism at Bethany Baptist Academy (1986, 293). I have already pointed to some problems inherent in Peshkin's critique of BBA on this score, e.g. that student attitudes towards pluralism were in fact very healthy at BBA. So perhaps there was more support for the concept of pluralism at BBA than Peshkin realized. However, he may still be quite justified in suggesting that more should have been done to uphold the principle of pluralism at BBA. I will concede that there is a danger that schools like BBA may not pay sufficient attention to pluralism, given their notion of truth. But this danger can be avoided. Religious schools need to teach the value of pluralism. Even with regard to confessional pluralism, students need to be taught that such doctrinal pluralism is inescapable, though, as I have argued earlier, this can still be combined with the notion of absolute truth as a heuristic goal that may only be fully realized in heaven.

2.   *Civic education*: Religious schools should develop in their students the range of qualities demanded by liberal citizenship and required for a necessary degree of unity and harmony within a pluralistic society. These include an understanding of, and a commitment to, the publicly recognized principles of justice, together with such qualities as tolerance and mutual respect, empathy, and a willingness to resolve political disputes, as well as such skills as deliberation and the ability to resolve political differences (Gutmann 1996). It should not be expected, however, that these virtues be taught in the abstract, as is so often maintained by liberals, but that resources be found within the religious tradition upheld by the school to support these civic virtues.

The above two principles are rather academic and will no doubt be seen to be inadequate to do justice to the all-important task of educating for unity amidst diversity within pluralistic societies. I have already suggested that the maintaining of this balance is more a matter of the heart than the head. Thus, a fuller treatment of the practical implications that flow from the argument of this chapter would require a consideration of how religious schools should cultivate proper attitudes such as tolerance. That will be the subject of the next chapter, and hence a fuller treatment of the practical implications of the subject of this chapter will have to wait until the conclusion of the next.

3 The Charge of Fostering Intolerance

A religious institution claiming universal validity and essential changelessness for its doctrine of salvation is necessarily intolerant.

"Intolerance," *Encyclopaedia of the Social Sciences*

Studies of Fundamentalist schools suggest that they concertedly and effectively promote intolerance of other religions and ways of life.

James Dwyer, *Religious Schools v. Children's Rights*

In December of 1982, Jim Keegstra, an Alberta high school social studies teacher, was fired for anti-Semitic teaching. He was subsequently stripped of his teacher's licence, then convicted and fined for wilfully promoting hatred against Jews. The "Keegstra affair" and the resulting "tarnishing of Alberta's image," as well as the "serious eroding of public confidence in our educational system," led the government of Alberta to establish the Committee of Tolerance and Understanding in June of 1983. Its purpose was to undertake a review of the school system and its curriculum and to make recommendations regarding ways in which greater tolerance and respect for human rights could be achieved (Committee 1984, 7–8).

Oddly, although the Keegstra affair occurred in a public or state-maintained school, as the committee hearings proceeded the focus shifted to Alberta's 124 independent or private schools, most of which were religious in orientation (Committee 1984, 104). Ron Ghitter, chairman of the committee, in an earlier speech to the Alberta School Trustees Association, pointed to what was to become a central question of the committee: "How can you encourage tolerance and understanding if our children are placed in schools which differentiate acceptability based on religious grounds?"[1] Ghitter seems to share the view of one submission to the committee by a county board of education which stated that religious schools "by their very nature" foster intolerance (Committee 1984, 108).

The committee softened its position somewhat in its final report. Still the report's overall thrust warns against the proliferation of religious schools. It holds that a strong and state-maintained system of education is a key to fostering tolerance in a pluralistic society. A fundamental principle underlying the report is that in order to enhance tolerance and understanding and respect for each individual in a diverse society, "we must, wherever possible, encourage shared experiences among the diverse population in our schools." Clearly, independent religious schools "do not adequately meet the spirit and intent" of such a principle, whereas the state-maintained public (common) schools do.[2] Hence it is argued that "wherever possible, the public education system must be strengthened and society must not permit it to become unnecessarily weakened, eroded or fragmented" (Committee 1984, 17).

The above implicit and explicit criticisms of religious schools and colleges are not at all uncommon.[3] This criticism is also found in a report published in Great Britain by the Committee of Inquiry into the Education of Children from Ethnic Minority Groups, commonly referred to as the Swann Report (1985). After reviewing the arguments for and against separate voluntary schools for other ethnic and religious groups, the committee expresses serious "misgivings about the implications and consequences of 'separate' provision of any kind."[4] The committee even calls into question the long-established dual system of educational provision in Great Britain involving both common state-maintained and voluntary church-related schools (520). Throughout the report it is argued that only if all pupils share a common educational experience will they be adequately prepared for life in a truly pluralistic society (508). Hence the title, "Education for All."

THE CONCEPT OF TOLERANCE

How then does one respond to charges suggesting that religious schools and colleges foster intolerance? It should be obvious that if one is to understand the charge, it is of utmost importance to be clear about the meaning of intolerance. I will argue that the widely held position that the existence and growth of religious schools and colleges create intolerance in a society rests on some basic misconceptions concerning the nature of intolerance. Drawing on the work of David Heyd (1996), Jay Newman (1982), and Peter Nicholson (1985), I wish to develop a more adequate notion of the concept of intolerance.[5] In fact, this is not as easy as it might seem, since tolerance is a philosophically elusive concept. This notion of tolerance has received much attention in recent years. Here I can at most provide a schematic analysis of the concept.

My focus here is on tolerance as a moral virtue of persons. I want to limit the discussion of this chapter even more, focusing primarily on the problem of religious tolerance or intolerance. The general notion of tolerance can refer to persons, beliefs, or actions. It is, as Newman points out, the element of belief that makes religious tolerance more complex than other forms of tolerance. The charge that religious schools foster intolerance often centres around a concern about differing beliefs. What do we mean when we describe religious tolerance as a virtue?

The notion of tolerance first of all presupposes deviance and disapproval. Tolerance involves an attitude towards something that is not liked, loved, respected, or approved of. Religious tolerance, therefore, presupposes that one finds the religious beliefs and practices of others objectionable.

Further, the subject of deviation and disapproval which calls for tolerance must not be considered to be trivial. Indifference must not be confused with intolerance. The person described as tolerant must care a lot about that which she is tolerating. It matters to her. This also rules out cases where one is uncertain about the objectionableness of the item implicated. Religious tolerance, therefore, only exists where one is quite sure that one strongly disapproves of the religious beliefs, attitudes, and behaviour of those being tolerated.

The way we should respond to what we disagree with or do not like brings us to another essential feature of tolerance. Newman puts it thus: "Tolerance involves tolerating, that is, accepting, enduring, bearing, putting up with; it involves acceptance in the sense of refraining from any strong reaction to the thing in question" (1982, 6). Here we must be careful not to limit our considerations to putting up with religious beliefs alone. Religious tolerance also entails that we will endure or put up with certain kinds of religious behaviour.

Some of the terms introduced by Newman are admittedly vague, though I suspect some degree of vagueness is unavoidable here. We should, however, try to spell out what it means to refrain from any strong reaction or exercise of power to suppress. Newman attempts to become more precise by defining a strong reaction as one which involves the use of force; "violence, threats, deception" (1982, 18). The notion of force, however, is still vague, but Newman seems to have three different kinds of force in mind: physical force – violence; psychological force – threats; and epistemological force – deception. Much more could be done to clarify the notion of force, but this will have to suffice.

Religious intolerance, therefore, will be understood to mean an attitude which refuses to accept, to endure, to bear, to put up with someone's holding and expressing or acting on contrary religious beliefs considered to be significantly inferior to one's own religious or irreligious beliefs. Stated in the affirmative, a religiously intolerant person reacts too strongly to another person's religious opinions and behaviour, and seeks to hurt him or her physically, psychologically, or by distorting his or her religious position.

But is Newman's two-sided response all that is required in order to describe a person as religiously tolerant? I believe there is another more positive requirement built into it. Heyd captures this requirement well when he describes tolerance as requiring "a perceptual shift: from beliefs to the subject holding them, or from actions to their agent" (1996, 11). Tolerance requires that we distinguish between beliefs and the believer, and it allows us to evaluate the opinions and beliefs of another in abstraction from the subject holding them. Toleration is therefore a subcategory of respect, which in the end will lead to restraint in how one responds to that with which one disagrees.

I believe there is even more to the positive component of tolerance, a component most often forgotten in the philosophical literature. Respect for persons must also be expressed positively in terms of reaching out to the persons one is tolerating. For example, it is not enough for me simply to bear, endure, or put up with Hindus living in my city, or even to do my best to respect them. Nor is it enough simply to refrain from forcible means to stop the spread of Hinduism, or to refrain from objecting to their building a temple. A question remains. If I otherwise ignore Hindus living in my city and refuse ever to associate with them, am I then really a tolerant person? Do we not also expect some positive attitudes such as liking or affection, and even some outward expressions of love towards Hindus? Here we must be careful not to demand too much – for example, that the tolerant person cultivate friendships with all Hindus in the city – because clearly that is often not possible. Indeed, one cannot even cultivate friendships with all those of one's own faith. But the tolerant person does give some expression of the respect that he bestows on persons with whom he is in disagreement. More on this later.

This distinction between beliefs and believers, which I have suggested is a key to defining tolerance, is also a key to resolving what is often referred to as the paradox of toleration – what is tolerated is both rejected and accepted. The believer can be accepted even though one rejects his or her beliefs. Tolerance involves a disposition to make this distinction between beliefs and believers, and then to choose to practise restraint and patience with respect to that which one opposes. Mendus raises the practical question that arises out of this seeming paradox. If you believe something to be wrong, why then tolerate it (1989, 18–19)? The answer is that you tolerate it because people are more important than beliefs. Ethics supersedes epistemology.[6]

Religious intolerance is immoral. It is beyond the scope of this chapter to defend tolerance as a virtue, though it should be noted that
there is disagreement about how this is to be done among philosophers. Here I will simply assume, following Locke's pragmatic justification, that all readers would agree that we need to be tolerant – we need
to get along despite our differences. As we have seen, tolerance ultimately rests on the principle of respect for persons and groups of persons, though the latter extension creates problems for many liberals,
as we shall see in the final chapters.

It is this underlying principle of respect for persons and for groups
of persons which also begins to define the extent and the limits of toleration, another issue on which is there is considerable debate, but
which cannot be dealt with at length here. Clearly there are limits to
tolerance. For example, choices which do not exhibit respect for persons or for groups of persons need not and should not be tolerated.
But here we are moving into the political domain, and, as Heyd correctly points out, governments cannot strictly be said to be tolerant.
"Tolerance is not only shown exclusively *to* people but also exclusively
by people" (1996, 15). The government should be, to some degree,
neutral with respect to people's beliefs, but it can and should restrain
improper behaviour that results from intolerant attitudes.

As should be apparent, I am starting from a broadly liberal point of
view where tolerance, properly defined and limited, is considered to
be a virtue and where its cultivation is considered to be an important
educational aim of schools in a liberal democratic society. The question then is whether the existence of religious schools and colleges in a
society promotes intolerance.

MISCONCEPTIONS REGARDING TOLERANCE

I want to argue that the charge that religious schools foster intolerance
is to a large extent based on misconceptions concerning the nature of
tolerance. The first misconception involves the confusion of separation
and intolerance. Implicitly or explicitly, the charge that independent or
private religious schools foster intolerance often involves the suggestion
that separation in and of itself entails intolerance. This is a conceptual
claim and as such suggests that religious schools necessarily foster intolerance. For example, in a submission to the Alberta Committee on
Tolerance and Understanding, the suggestion is made that private (religious) schools "by their very nature" are excluding and intolerant institutions (Committee 1984, 108). The Alberta Committee, in its interim
report, similarly stated that private religiously oriented schools "by their
very nature" do not adequately meet the spirit and intent of the princi-

ples of tolerance, understanding, and respect which were the very foundation of the committee report.[7]

Now there is a fundamental error here, since tolerance itself requires separation. Tolerance, as we have seen, involves an attitude towards something that is not liked, loved, respected, or approved of. In other words, there is some distancing from that which one is tolerating. Tolerance entails some degree of separateness. I can only tolerate another who is different from me.[8] It is therefore wrong to associate intolerance with separation in and of itself.

The implausibility of this conceptual identification of separateness and intolerance can be further seen by carrying such identification to its logical conclusion. If separate religious schools, by their very nature, are intolerant, then churches, clubs, yes, even homes, by their very nature, must breed intolerance. Then all individuality and all separation will be seen as an expression of intolerance. The only way to avoid intolerance is to deny distinctions, individuality, and separateness. This is simply absurd.

We see this same error expressed in the strongly assimilative or melting-pot tendencies which have characterized American education. John Dewey boldly praised "the assimilative force of the American public school."[9] It is easy to accept the ideal of tolerance after one is sure that *everyone* is assimilated into a majority mould by an effective system of state-maintained education, but that will not lead to genuine tolerance. Tolerance presupposes differences and separation. Assimilation must not be confused with tolerance. This confusion pervades the entire Alberta Report as well as the Swann Report, despite the latter's occasional explicit rejection of assimilation as a proper response to pluralism.

Jay Newman identifies another prevalent misconception concerning the nature of intolerance, a misconception which is also found in the charge that religious schools promote intolerance. It is often assumed that tolerating a religious belief is primarily a matter of refusing to make a negative judgment about the content of that belief. This cannot be so, because when a Unitarian or an atheist tolerates a Catholic's belief in, for example, the claim that God exists in three persons, there is no way that they can "accept" this belief. The Unitarian or atheist rejects this trinitarian belief. Further, he or she believes that the Catholic ought to reject it too. As we have already seen, religious tolerance is not so much concerned with the belief itself as with "someone's holding" that belief. It involves the adoption of a certain attitude towards the Catholic's "believing" in the Trinity.

This problem emerges in the Alberta Committee's expression of concern about the curriculum utilized in some private schools in Alberta as "intolerant and unacceptable" (111). More specifically, the committee objected to statements found in certain curricular units of some Christian schools which referred to other religious faiths as "false."[10]

But should the classification of another's beliefs as false be viewed as a case of intolerance? No. Religious toleration necessarily presupposes that we disagree with another person's beliefs.[11] Tolerance is required precisely because we do disagree and because we consider another person's position to be false. But, we must still respect and love the *person* who holds beliefs which we consider false. To determine whether or not those who criticize others are intolerant, we need to examine instead their attitudes and actions towards the actual *people* with whose beliefs they differ. Simply to label a belief is false is not to be intolerant.

It also needs to be stressed that Christianity, having clearly labelled certain beliefs and religious positions as false, is equally clear in advocating tolerance. Jesus, despite his very exclusive claims, exemplified tolerance, taught his disciples to be tolerant, and condemned intolerance.[12] Thus, in a classic statement on tolerance, John Locke remarks that tolerance should be "the chief distinguishing mark of the true church," i.e. the church that truly represents the teachings of Jesus.[13] This same point could be made of other religions, as Jay Newman correctly observes. "All of the principle religions of the world have preached toleration in some form" (1982, 81). Obviously the religions of the world have not always practised what they preached, but that is quite another matter.

There is one final conceptual error underlying the tendency to associate the religious commitment of religious schools with intolerance. It is often assumed that the only way to be tolerant is to adopt a relativist position with regard to truth. Indeed, historically liberalism has often associated tolerance with scepticism and relativism. This assumption is clearly found in the Alberta Report as well as in the Swann Report and is in part the basis of their opposition to independent religious schools. What is being suggested in these reports is that tolerance is necessarily linked with an epistemology which states that there is no right way, that different positions are equally positive or excellent, that there is flux in the marketplace of ideas, and thus we should avoid a blind and narrow commitment to a particular position. In other words, the only adequate foundation for religious tolerance is the acceptance of epistemological relativism. To be tolerant means to be a relativist.[14]

To show that epistemological relativism is unsound is beyond the scope of this chapter. More to the point is Newman's claim that the association of religious tolerance with relativism conflicts with the true nature of tolerance. Religious tolerance, as we have seen, presupposes disagreement, and hence a negative attitude towards the beliefs of the person one is being tolerant towards. But, epistemological relativism undercuts the very possibility of having a negative attitude towards others' differing beliefs. As such it makes the virtue of tolerance impossible. Tolerance is therefore replaced with indifference. But to be indifferent to the convictions of others is to fail to respect them as persons.

There is another way to approach this last misconception involving the association of tolerance with scepticism and relativism. In effect those making such an association are suggesting that mere tolerance is not enough. What is needed is a more positive attitude to other religions – we might call it "positive pluralism." What is required is a "positive" and complete acceptance, even a welcoming or a "celebration" of religious differences. This emphasis is invariably coupled with a supposedly more "positive" attitude concerning the epistemological status of religious belief systems where all religions are viewed as equally valid and where narrow categorizations of religions as superior/inferior, or true/false, are avoided. It is this quite different notion of "positive pluralism" which is implicit in the Swann Report and in the report of the Alberta Committee.

The basic problem with "positive pluralism" is that it fails to take religious commitment seriously. The major Western religions are exclusivistic in that each holds itself up as the true and/or best religion, as well as universalistic in that each seeks to bring all human beings over to its side. They simply cannot adopt an attitude of "positive pluralism" which vitiates such exclusivism and universalism. To foist a supposedly "positive" type of pluralism onto religions is in fact an expression of intolerance at its worst.

I would further suggest that "positive pluralism" is contradictory. While it objects to narrow categorizations of religions as superior/ inferior, or true/false, it suffers from the same sort of categorizations when it objects to exclusivistic religions or confessional approaches to religious education.[15]

This contradiction is clearly evident in a recent attack on what John Hull calls "religionism." Religionism is "tribalistic" and fosters identity based upon "rejection and exclusion. We are better than they. We are orthodox; they are infidel. We are believers; they are unbelievers. We are right; they are wrong" (Hull 1992, 70). Hull's universalist approach sounds more tolerant, but we must not be deceived by appearances. His proposed "deconstruction of the religious consciousness" is in fact the epitome of intolerance. He refuses to respect believers who feel theologically bound to make exclusive claims. He further succumbs to the very thing he condemns with regard to right/wrong thinking when he boldly maintains that religionism is wrong and he is right. He is even willing to impose his deconstructionist program on all students via a state-enforced multi-faith religious education curriculum which he sees as "the most effective antidote against religionism" (72). Indeed, Hull wants to move us beyond mere tolerance. "It is not enough for religious education to encourage a tolerant attitude towards other religions" (71). Hull's program of "beyond tolerance" unfortunately displays all too many of the attitudes underlying the holy wars he himself rightly condemns.[16]

What is needed is a proper understanding of the ideal of tolerance which combines strongly held convictions with a love for and an appreciation of people who differ. The cure for intolerance is not found in a relativistic elimination of convictions, but in a liberal education which combines teaching for commitment with the encouragement of respect for others.

I would therefore suggest that the notion of religious tolerance elucidated earlier in this chapter is in fact more positive than "positive pluralism." It does justice to religious commitment in that it respects the doctrines of exclusivism and universalism which are inherent in most religions. At the same time it acknowledges and accepts the fact that there are other religions which are similarly exclusive and universalistic in outlook. The doctrines of exclusivism and universalism do not rule out the possibility of enduring or putting up with other religious traditions.

Truth claims need to be taken seriously, not only in the area of religion, but in all areas of study. The moral challenge of religious tolerance is one of maintaining a positive attitude to the *persons* holding beliefs that we disagree with, and of defending their right to hold and propogate these beliefs even if we consider them to be false. Tolerance and commitment to a certain position can and must go hand in hand.

EMPIRICAL ARGUMENTS

Thus far, my argument has been concerned mainly with conceptual analysis and clarification. Some readers, no doubt, will have been putting up with (i.e. tolerating) this philosophical exercise, perhaps somewhat impatiently, waiting for what they consider to be truly important – concrete evidence and empirical argument. I agree that empirical considerations cannot be ignored. But we must not be too hasty. Perhaps conceptual clarification is a prerequisite to effective empirical argumentation. I would suggest that the conceptual analysis of the previous section has already considerably weakened empirical argument for associating educational pluralism with religious intolerance. Many of the arguments underlying the commonly made criticisms of religious schools and colleges rest on misconceptions concerning the nature of tolerance.

For example, if intolerance is associated with making doctrinal claims that are thought to have universal validity, as in the first quotation at the head of this chapter, then it is easy to find evidence that religious schools promote intolerance. Such schools seem to be incurably committed to making such truth claims. I have argued, however, that religious tolerance is not only compatible with, but requires the making of, truth claims which are thought to have universal validity. Thus, one kind of seemingly plausible empirical argument for the association of religious schools with intolerance is shown to be unwarranted.

The same could be said about the other misconceptions concerning the nature of intolerance. I would suggest that much of the argument in support of the charge being considered in this chapter rests on certain misconceptions concerning the nature of intolerance. Thus the clarification of this concept in the previous section has already undermined much of the empirical evidence in support of the charge made against religious schools and colleges.

That having been said, a consideration of empirical evidence is still in place. Here it is surely reasonable to expect that those making the charge that religious schools foster intolerance do so on the basis of empirical studies which back up the charge being made. But most often, one looks in vain for supporting evidence.[17] It would seem that generally the charge is based on nothing more than a hunch. This need for hard data forced the Alberta Committee on Tolerance and Understanding to adopt a much more conciliatory tone in its final report: "There is no evidence to conclude that the existence of religiously oriented schools does, in and of itself, cause intolerance in Alberta" (109). In an essay summarizing an Ontario study on the question of funding religious schools, Shapiro concedes that "no one knows just which schooling experiences will produce understanding and tolerant adult citizens." But, he goes on: "Nevertheless, in the absence of sure knowledge, it does seem plausible that tolerance and understanding will more likely arise from settings in which various groups are interacting together rather than segmented and segregated" (1986, 271). Here we have an educationalist reiterating common opinion based on nothing more than blind faith.

Interestingly, the Alberta Report makes several passing references to some evidence that shows that religious schools need not, and in fact do not, foster intolerance in a society. Twenty per cent of Alberta students attend Roman Catholic schools. Although fully funded by the Alberta government and thus often viewed as part of the public education system, these Catholic schools nonetheless form a separate system of education, whose separateness is based on religious differences. The report suggests that "it is demonstrated by the Catholic schools in this province that a religious context for education does not, in and of itself, create intolerance or narrow-mindedness" (90, 92). No hard evidence is given for this "demonstration," but it would appear that these schools have not had a noticeable effect in fostering intolerance in Alberta.

There has been some significant research done with regard to the effects of religious schools on students' attitudes to others. The most recent empirical study of Catholic schools in the United States suggests that Catholic high schools do better than public schools in promoting the basic social and political purposes that once were the inspiration of American public education and gave them the title of "common school." This includes the fostering of attitudes of compassion and tolerance (Bryk et al. 1993, 289). Other studies have come to similar conclusions.[18]

Here we need to address the seemingly obvious counter-example of Northern Ireland, where the divisiveness of denominational schools is often thought to be evident. Clearly these schools can contribute to the fostering of intolerance, given the presence of certain conditions. But these schools need not function in this narrow and destructive manner. In fact, they can have very positive aims and effects, and in some ongoing curriculum projects in Northern Ireland, these same schools have been shown to contribute to greater levels of tolerance and understanding (Greer and McElhinney 1984; 1985). Greer, in another article reviewing past and ongoing research, finds that young people most favourably disposed to religion were the most open to other religious traditions (Greer 1985, 275). Other studies support Greer's conclusions.[19] It would therefore seem that schools which cultivate religious attitudes will in fact enhance the cause of tolerance.

It further needs to be underscored that most often one also looks in vain for evidence to the effect that state-maintained public schools foster tolerance. Here too it would seem that the grandiose claims made in favour of common schools are most often based on nothing more than a hunch.[20] Indeed, intolerance can be and sometimes is fostered in such schools. Various critics of the Alberta study found it necessary to remind the committee that the specific case of fostering intolerance which prompted the study in the first place did not occur in an independent religious school but in a state-maintained school.[21] Various studies have shown that the curriculum in state-maintained common schools very often avoids any serious reference to matters of faith and religion, an omission which the Alberta Report acknowledges as contributing to intolerance, this time against religion.[22]

In considering empirical data, I would remind the reader of another dimension of the problem that was dealt with at length in the previous chapter. We need to look beyond the actual results of teaching in religious schools or public schools and examine the overall consequences of alternative *systems* of education. We need to ask what *structure* of education best promotes tolerance, a pluralistic or a more uniform and state-maintained system of education. The previous chapter focused more on the structure of education, and I argued there that a system of educational pluralism does not foster divisiveness. In fact there is evidence that such a pluralistic system of education brings about unity within a society.

A similar conclusion can also be drawn with regard to the problem of fostering intolerance. Various examples of countries that incorporate educational pluralism in varying degrees were considered in the previous chapter. Mention has already been made of the constitutionally entrenched system of Catholic education that exists in many provinces of Canada as a second major system of education alongside the public system or as an alternative within it. But this dual system of education has not fostered intolerance in Canadian society, and the Alberta Report is forced to concede this point (Committee 1984, 90, 92). Indeed, a case can be made that such structural pluralism has served to enhance the cause of religious tolerance in Canada and other countries that have experimented with educational pluralism (Netherlands, Denmark, Australia).

What conclusions can be drawn from this survey of the empirical evidence? A number of factors suggest that caution is in order when trying to make generalizations about the results of schooling. The first has to do with the difficulties inherent in providing an empirically measurable definition of tolerance. It has already been suggested that some aspects of the concept of tolerance, such as refraining from strong reactions and the illegitimate use of force, are necessarily vague and thus will resist the precise definition which is essential to empirical measurement. Secondly, we need to acknowledge the complexity of the questions at issue. There are many factors at work in moulding a child's attitudes and thus it will be difficult to isolate a cause/effect relationship between different types of schooling and the fostering of tolerance or intolerance. These difficulties contribute to a third and final problem that seems to plague research in the social sciences especially. Empirical research concerning human behaviour and attitudes is notorious for being subject to variable interpretations. My brief overview of empirical research has also been necessarily selective.

Given these problems, we must be careful not to expect too much from empirical argumentation, but I believe we can still safely draw a number of conclusions. I believe there is enough evidence to conclude that any generalizations to the effect that religious schools foster intolerance are unfounded. There is further some evidence suggesting that they in fact foster tolerance. And we must be careful not to assume that common schools in and of themselves do foster tolerance.

NURTURING TOLERANCE

How do we nurture tolerance? Here again there are several errors often made by critics of religious schools and colleges. First, as was argued in the previous chapter, it is sometimes wrongly assumed that the conditions necessary for the exercise of a certain quality of character must necessarily be the same as the conditions under which it is best developed. Thus, it must not be assumed that the nurture of tolerance of people with differing religious beliefs can only be brought about in a classroom in which there are students representing a variety of cultures and religions. We should not *a priori* rule out the possibility that the best means of *developing* tolerance in children might be precisely a narrow upbringing with relatively little exposure to people of other backgrounds and religions.

A second error is to assume that contact between children of varying religious traditions will in and of itself reduce intolerance and prejudice. This "contact hypothesis" can be easily refuted by reflecting on the history of the United States. When slavery was first introduced in the South, blacks and whites had a lot of contact with each other, but prejudice flourished. This conclusion is reinforced by a good deal of research.[23] Mere contact simply does not foster tolerance.

How then do we nurture tolerance? In the previous chapter I introduced the notion of "primary culture." It would seem that a stable and coherent primary culture is essential for children to develop a sense of identity, which is in turn a prerequisite to developing a tolerant and loving relationship with others. James Banks, in a review of existing theory and research concerning ethnic behaviour in Western societies, underlines how important it is for students to "have clarified identification with their first cultures. Understanding and relating positively to self is a requisite to understanding and relating positively to other groups and people," Banks argues.[24] This would suggest that the education of children in schools that reflect the primary cultures of the children's homes is in fact a better context in which the gradual weaning and opening-up process can occur.[25] Tolerance grows out of security and acceptance. Thus, a school that reflects students' cultural/religious heritage will be able to provide a safe and secure environment from which a child can gradually become aware of difference and can learn to accept and tolerate these differences.

This conclusion can be further supported by returning to an earlier consideration. Many studies have shown that mere contact is not enough to reduce prejudice and intolerance. Contact and interaction between students will only result in a reduction of prejudice if accompanied by such factors as mutual interdependence, equal status, informality, and social reinforcement of equality.[26] In his classic work on prejudice, Gordon Allport makes essentially the same point, emphasizing that the effect "is greatly enhanced if this contact is sanctioned by institutional supports" (1954, 281). I would suggest that a central way for a liberal society to nurture tolerance in its citizens is to allow for institutional recognition of religious differences. And educational institutions are a key expression of such recognition. Religious schools further need to be seen as having equal status to other schools. The relegating of religious schools to second-class status, as is so often the case in Western societies today, only serves to reinforce anti-religious prejudice and intolerance. Monolithic state systems of education are not only an expression of intolerance; they also provide a possible tool for fostering intolerance.[27] The cause of tolerance is best promoted in a system of educational pluralism.

SOME PRACTICAL IMPLICATIONS
FOR RELIGIOUS SCHOOLS

1. *Tolerance advocated*: Religious schools and colleges ought to be strong advocates of the virtue of tolerance. Sadly, it is necessary to state the obvious – religious institutions have not always been exemplary in this regard.[28] The history of religions is littered with examples of intolerance. The educational institutions of these religions have often served to reinforce this intolerance. It is beyond the scope of this book to document this sad tale. Such educational practices deserve to be condemned in the strongest language possible. I would further maintain that a democratic state has every right to insist that religious institutions, including religious schools, must promote tolerance.[29]

How do religious schools and colleges promote tolerance? Several practical principles emerge from the argument of this chapter.

2. *Respect for persons*: Heyd's treatment of tolerance as involving a perceptual shift provides us with an important practical principle. Religious schools need to help students to look at other people as persons without regard to the particular beliefs they hold. Disagreement with the beliefs of other persons must always be coupled with a deep

respect for the persons holding those beliefs. Catholic scholar Richard John Neuhaus reminds us that Catholic teachers used to say that "Error has no rights." The difficulty here is that errors are attached to persons and persons do have rights.[30]

Peshkin, in his critique of Bethany Baptist Academy, is not entirely happy with the notion of "loving persons despite their differences" (1986, 141–2; 289–90). But his concerns rest on a notion of tolerance as "positive pluralism," which requires full acceptance of all beliefs as equally valid – critiqued earlier in this chapter. Peshkin, however, quite rightly expresses concern about students not learning "to respect non-Christian others in their own right," particularly with regard to attitudes towards others as expressed in the evangelistic zeal of BBA (1986, 141–2). Respect for persons entails that others are valued not simply as projects for conversion. Rather all people, including those who differ from one's own religious persuasion, need to be seen as people created in God's image and therefore as having value in and of themselves.

3. *Commitment, openness, uncertainty, and humility*: Students need to be taught to be tolerant without weakening their commitment to their own cherished beliefs and preferences. I want to emphasize that religious schools must be very careful to walk a fine line between affirming their understanding of what is the truth and admitting that they may in fact be wrong. In chapter 2, I have argued that it is possible to affirm that there is absolute truth and at the same time to admit that one's understanding of that truth may be incomplete. Cognitive humility and openness can and should be combined with commitment to Truth.

What is also required to maintain this balance is to cultivate a "proper confidence" in religious beliefs (Newbigin 1995). All believing involves risk. Religious adherents cannot and should not demand absolute certainty with regard to their religious convictions. It is this need to be absolutely certain that feeds intolerance, as various writers have reminded us (Cooling 1994, 12). Religious schools must therefore help students to live with a degree of uncertainty. Confessional religious education must cultivate an attitude of continual learning even in those areas where commitment has already been made.

4. *Learning tolerance within religious schools*: Religious schools are never as monolithic in composition as liberal educationalists sometimes assume. Teachers and students differ from one another. And this provides an excellent starting point for teaching tolerance. Tolerance needs to be practised within religious schools. Indeed, as Gutmann concedes, despite her opposition to religious schools, "children often learn to respect other human beings by first learning to respect people who are close and familiar to them" (1996, 175). Clearly, the focus

must broaden eventually. Lorberbaum provides a delightful illustration of how this can be done from within the Jewish tradition.[31]

One final component of learning tolerance from within religious schools needs to be noted. Religious schools must be careful to encourage honest reflection on the history of the religious tradition represented by that school. Christian schools must therefore not gloss over the atrocities committed by the Christian church during the Crusades or the painful examples of racism in the more recent history of the church in America or South Africa.[32] Religious schools and colleges must encourage critical reflection on the past so as to ensure that the intolerance of the past will not be repeated in the future.

5.   *Learning to tolerate those outside*: While learning to be tolerant might best start from within a more closed environment, it is very important that the horizons be enlarged to include those outside. Clearly, the sense of community that is an essential element of any religious school requires a certain "turning within," and this carries with it a risk of being accompanied by a "spurning without" (Bryk et al. 1993, 289). In some cases, such narrowness is perpetrated by religious schools.[33] But this need not be the case. And I would argue that it should not be the case. The cultivation of "imaginative sympathy," and a "serious imaginative engagement" with ideas and ways of life at variance with one's own, is a legitimate and important purpose of liberal educational practice, as Callan correctly maintains (1992, 20). This also applies to religious schools. Multicultural and multi-religious education should be an essential component of all religious schools and colleges.

When dealing with differing worldviews it is imperative for teachers to treat these worldviews fairly and sensitively (Barnes 1997, 23). Teachers must be careful to avoid errors in interpretation or biased misrepresentations of other worldviews. Certainly at upper grade levels, students should be referred to original sources to get first-hand knowledge of other religions and other worldviews. Inflammatory statements and stereotyping must be scrupulously avoided.

PART THREE

Rights and Freedoms

4 The Denial of Parental Rights to Educate

What we're opposed to is public funding going into the support of children in private schools. ... [T]his Bill purports to be a Bill that looks at the rights of children, but really what it does is it transfers all kinds of rights to parents. In any kind of organized society the rights of the state have to come first. That's why you have a public education system.

Barry Pashak, during a discussion of Bill 27
in the Alberta Legislature, 1988

There have been a number of controversies over religious schools in Alberta in the last two decades, centring around another objection often raised against religious schooling, namely, that parents do not have the right to determine the kind of school their children should attend.

In response to court battles against unregistered church schools and home-schooling in the early 1980s, Alberta's government commissioned a study of private schools in the province. The resulting Woods Gordon Report, released to the public in 1985, touches on the basic conflict between the rights of parents and the rights of the state. Reference is made in the report to the agenda underlying the beginnings of universal public education: "It was felt that the state owes it to a child to provide some view of the world other than that which may be limited by the child's parents" (Woods Gordon 1984, 1).

This concern about freeing children from the confines of parental influence also surfaces with home-schooling. A Gallup poll revealed that 65 per cent of the respondents opposed the right of parents to teach their children at home (Woods Gordon 1984, 16, 56). The report recommended that private schools be allowed to operate in Alberta, though under strict control, and that home-schooling be allowed only in exceptional circumstances.

Already in the mid-1980s, the Conservative government of Alberta was pushing an agenda of more parental choice in the area of education (Wagner 1995, 36–46). Despite much controversy, the government initiated a new School Act, Bill 27, in 1988, which went farther than any other province to enshrine in legislation the principle that parents have the right to be actively involved in their children's education. In its preface, Bill 27 states: "Parents have a right and responsibility to make decisions respecting the education of their children."[1]

Surprisingly, this bill was carried forward by the government in the face of the vigorous opposition that ensued over its emphasis on parental rights. Public school supporters objected to the government "pandering" to a small "vociferous minority" who support private schools (Wagner 1995, 37). A lobby group, "Save Public Education," spent $20,000 on advertisements in eight of Alberta's daily newspapers in June 1985, demanding that the government stop funding religious schools (Wagner 1995, 38). An unsuccessful attempt was made to amend the preamble of Bill 27 so that parental rights would be "subject to the best educational interests of their children and the interests of society."[2] Another unsuccessful amendment was introduced to prevent the funding of private schools.[3] The opening quotation of this chapter is taken from this same discussion in the Alberta legislature. This provides a good illustration of the depth of opposition to private religious schools, and the underlying assumption of parental rights in the demand for such schools.

Resistance to religious schools based on a denial of parental rights has had a long history.[4] Here a puzzle arises. There seems to be widespread acceptance of the principle of parental rights in education. The Universal Declaration of Human Rights adopted by the United Nations General Assembly in 1948 offers a clear statement: "Parents have the prior right to choose the kind of education that shall be given to their children" (article 26, section 3). Parental rights have also been affirmed in various ways in the United States and Great Britain.[5] How does one explain this seeming tension between resistance to religious schools and apparent acceptance of parental rights?

I would suggest that where parental rights are acknowledged, this acceptance is often rather superficial, ill defined, and, more important, without supporting foundations.[6] There is further the well-established liberal tradition which relegates family and religion to the private sphere (McLaughlin 1984, 75). But the public/private distinction of liberalism is increasingly being recognized as problematic (Crittenden 1988, 215). These confusions are, in turn, calling into question the rights of parents with regard to education, particularly in relation to religious schools.

The central purpose of this chapter is to respond to the charge that religious schools ought not to exist because parents do not have the right to determine the religious education of their children. Clearly one cannot, in a short chapter, do justice to the complexity surrounding this question. Nor will I be able to take into account all that has been written, even recently, on this topic.[7] However, I hope to provide an outline of a response to the charge in question. I want to focus particularly on considerations and lines of argument which are often neglected.

A CLARIFICATION OF POSITION

In responding to this charge it is important to be clear about the position I am taking with regard to parental rights. I especially want to distance myself from some extreme, and in my view plainly silly, positions sometimes taken by Christians.

As an example of such an extreme position, let me refer to another controversy that had been brewing in Alberta prior to the passage of Bill 27, involving Pastor Larry Jones of the Western Baptist Church in Calgary.[8] The School Act of Alberta required that all private schools be licensed by the government, but Jones refused to license the Christian school that he began in his church in 1980.

I cannot receive a license – a license is permission by a higher authority to a lesser authority. There is no higher authority than God – by His Word [i.e., the Bible] He commanded me to teach my children just as clearly as He commanded me to preach and witness for Him. To accept a license would be a compromise of a Bible principle.[9]

This is not the place to provide a detailed critique of Jones's position from a theological point of view. Though I agree that the Christian Scriptures assign to parents unique responsibilities in relation to their children, I have difficulties with interpreting this in strict terms of line-management of authority. The situation is surely more complex, involving an intricate web of other relationships. The divine right of parenthood, understood in absolute terms, is as pernicious as the divine right of kings has proven to be historically.

Jones maintains that parents should have exclusive rights to educate their children. He does not want to concede any authority to the state – not even in terms of licensing. His lawyer's response to a government position paper calling for a partnership between parents and the state in regard to education was that "we do not have a partnership in my child. Only myself, my wife and God do" (Wagner 1995, 37). But parents sometimes err. Some parents neglect their children and others even abuse them. Some parents would, if they could, send their children to schools that would promote race hatred, for example. Surely we would say that the state has a right to intervene in these cases. Surely we would demand that the state step in to ensure that the best interests of the child are served. Once we admit that, and I believe we have to, then we are admitting that the state has some responsibility in the area of education.[10]

Jones is also guilty of describing state involvement in education in extreme terms: "The state wants control of our children, they want us to submit to Caesar (i.e. the state) in every area of our lives" (Wagner 1995, 75). While there are real dangers in acknowledging state rights in the area of education, we must be careful not to exaggerate. To say that the government has some legitimate rights with regard to education does not immediately make one an advocate of a totalitarian state. It is quite conceivable to talk of limited powers with regard to government involvement in education.[11]

Jones's approach is based on too limited a view of the alternatives. He is guilty of either/or thinking: Either the state or parents have exclusive rights. He is not alone in this. Libertarian Murray Rothbard poses the question: "Shall the parent or the state be the overseer of the child? ... There is no middle ground on this issue" (1972, 10). But there *is* a middle ground. We can say that the state and the parent each have a partial right to oversee the education of children.

I choose to disassociate myself from an extreme position that defines parental rights in the area of the education of children in exclusive terms. In contrast, I want to argue for the primacy of parental rights. This position still allows for the sharing of responsibilities for the education of children between parents, teachers, and the state. While such rights are shared, I still believe that parental rights and responsibilities are primary. (It is important to talk of both rights and responsibilities!)[12]

We can now refocus the central thrust of this chapter. Critics of religious schools often object to such schools by denying that parents have the right to choose schools that reflect the parents' religious convictions. Against this, I want to argue that parents have primary rights in the area of education. A case can then be made that religious parents should be allowed to send their children to schools that reflect their religious convictions.

CHILDREN'S RIGHTS

One way to deny the primacy of parental rights over education is to focus on children's rights. Indeed, this is perhaps the most common way in which the challenge to parental rights is expressed today. I also consider this to be the most important challenge to parental rights because other challenges include the best interests of the child as a central component.

Crittenden traces the origin of the movement for children's liberation to the 1960s, during which time various established patterns of authority, including the family, were challenged severely. This movement relied heavily on the language of rights, and in the 1970s the defence of children's rights flourished. John Holt, for example, in his 1975 publication *Escape from Childhood: The Needs and Rights of Children*, argued that children should be able to choose their own guardian and that they should have the right to control their learning. More recently, James Dwyer has taken a radical position in relation to children's rights, which he then uses as an argument against religious schools (1998).[13] Dwyer objects to "adult-centered approaches" that have dominated the discourse on educational rights, and argues instead that "the only *rights* we should recognize in the law governing child rearing are rights of children themselves" (4, 178). A central thrust of his book is to argue that "the very notion of parental rights is illegitimate" (63, 65, 104).[14]

Now I would be the first to admit that there is something very healthy about an emphasis on children's rights. Children need to be cared for and loved. They need to be treated as persons. Each child is unique. Each child needs to be helped to grow towards maturity and independence.[15] And I would even agree that these parental duties towards children can be translated into correlative rights for children. But all this is self-evident. Thanks to maternal and paternal instincts, which are natural to parents, these responsibilities are by and large carried out on behalf of their children.[16] However, there are some significant problems with the claim that children's rights should override those of their parents with regard to education. I will identify four.

One problem with children's rights theorists and activists is that all too often they have exaggerated the problem they are trying to solve. Children are seldom treated as property by parents.[17] To object to religious schools by arguing that "children are not chattels of parents," as was done in a discussion of a new school act in the legislative assembly of Alberta, and also frequently by Dwyer, is essentially just rhetoric.[18] No sincere religious parent views his or her child as a mere chattel. It is precisely because children are made in the image of God that Christian parents think it important to have their children taught about the God who created them as unique and valuable individuals. As a first step towards rational debate about parental vs. children's rights we need to be careful to avoid exaggeration, rhetoric, and polemics, which unfortunately are all too common in such discussions.

The fundamental problem with replacing parental rights with children's rights in the area of education is that this fails to take into account the unique status of children. Children are not autonomous. They need to grow towards autonomy. Contrary to Dwyer, children are not adults, and it is foolish to try to treat them as such.[19] Children do not have the resources to choose the kind of education they should get. They first need to acquire these resources. Until then, someone will necessarily have to choose for them – parents, guardians, society, or the state. If we deny this right of parents, we will not be giving it to children. That is simply not an option. It is impossible for children to exercise that right. Some adult or other will have to be making choices on behalf of children.[20]

Here let me interject my own interpretation of what sometimes underlies a preoccupation with children's rights. All too often such an emphasis is, unfortunately, an escape from parental accountability. Someone has to assume pedagogical responsibility for children, and it is an awesome responsibility. One way to escape this responsibility is to put the onus on the children themselves. Such a move is dishonest, an example of what Sartre called "bad faith." Children simply are not adults who can make important decisions regarding their education. To claim that children should be able to choose their own guardians, as some writers suggest, is just plain silliness (see Holt, quoted earlier).

Another problem with denying parental pedagogical rights in the name of children's rights is the assumption that children develop in a social and cultural vacuum. But children, starting from birth, are absorbing attitudes, values, and beliefs from their parents. Much of this is acquired simply by learning a language. Children cannot spend the first fourteen or fifteen years of their lives in "a value-neutral cocoon" (Crittenden 1988, 110). They must first be initiated into a particular belief and value system before they can grow towards autonomy. Indeed, choice is only possible after such initiation has taken place.

Finally, the affirmation of children's rights in education at the expense of the primacy of parental rights often rests on an assumption that these options are mutually exclusive. It is either one or the other. But, both can be affirmed at the same time.[21] The "best interests" of the child, an ideal so dear to child-rights advocates, is perfectly compatible with a healthy affirmation of the primacy of parental rights. Indeed, caring parents have the best interests of their children in mind.

Of course, it might still be argued that parental educational authority ought to yield to the state's authority to define what constitutes children's best interests, a position which in fact Dwyer holds, despite his claim that it is children alone who have rights in the area of education.[22] Thus we are left with two possible positions with respect to who has a right to determine the education that children receive – either parents or the state.[23]

Here it is important to note that both positions agree that young children should *not* have rights to control their own education or their own lives, because they lack the maturity to exercise such rights in ways consistent with their long-term self-interest. Both positions also assume that the best interests of the child must always be taken into account, regardless of who makes decisions on behalf of the child. "The point of disagreement concerns whose judgment regarding the child's best interests should be controlling when parents and the state disagree" (Gilles 1997, 11).

PARENTAL RIGHTS AS PRIMARY

As pointed out earlier in this chapter, the position that parents have primary rights in determining the education of children, while often assumed, is frequently stated without supporting argument. For example, the Supreme Court in the United States has generally adhered to a 1925 ruling giving parents a constitutional right to direct and control the education of their children, but the Court has never developed a theory to explain this result. I therefore wish to begin by outlining five arguments for the primacy of parental rights, drawing particularly on the writings of Crittenden (1988) and Gilles (1996; 1997).

1. *Biological argument*: From a biological perspective, the most obvious answer to the question "To whom does the child belong?" is that the child belongs to its parents. The child owes its existence to its mother and father. Procreation is generally seen as the "basic ground on which the responsibility of caring for a child can reasonably be assigned, and on which freedom from interference in the rearing of a child can be claimed."[24] While we must be careful not to regard children as merely being possessions of their parents, or simply an extension of them, the biological relationship would seem to confer special custodial rights onto parents. Even critics of the primacy of parental education rights are generally forced to concede the biological argument for such rights, at least in part.[25]

It might be argued that other adults could satisfy the needs of children as well as, and sometimes better than, their parents. I grant that there are times when other adults could serve the interests of the child better than parents. But it is surely arbitrary to prevent parents who were responsible for giving birth to a child from being the primary agents of its further development – assuming, of course, that they are willing and able to provide the care and affection needed.[26]

2. *Children's interest argument*: Parents naturally love their children and therefore have strong incentives for looking out for their best interests. True, there are some parents who do not care enough for their

children and some who even abuse them, but this is the exception rather than the rule, and might at most call for a selective departure from principle of giving parents primary educational rights.[27]

Dwyer, despite his opposition to parental rights, makes implicit appeal both to the biological argument and to the children's best interest argument when he concedes that in many aspects of children's lives we should support "a presumption of parental decision-making authority" because parents love their children and are in the best position to know what they need (1998, 81–90). Indeed, his frequent claim that parents should be seen as having the "privilege" rather than the right to make educational decisions begs the question as to why they should have this privilege in the first place.[28]

3. *Parental interests argument*: A third argument rests on the value of personal relationships. Parents generally take a special interest in their own offspring and find much satisfaction in giving them life. Further, parenting, nurturing, and educating one's children are generally tasks that parents take great delight in.[29] Even liberal writers who place more importance on children's rights or state rights are nevertheless forced to concede that parenting is of paramount importance to most individuals.[30] Given the importance that individuals place on parenting, and given liberalism's aim of enabling persons to satisfy their basic needs, it follows that parents' desire to shape the education of their children should be respected.

Here it is interesting to note that Dwyer, despite his opposition to parental rights, concedes that raising children is a large component of most parents' happiness (1998, 90). Intense desires and even the nobleness of motivation do not translate into rights, according to Dwyer (91). But surely *fundamental* interests and desires do translate into rights, as Dwyer is forced to concede (92). Our rights to life and property, for example, are in part predicated on the fact that we have a fundamental interest in these matters. And parents have a fundamental interest in raising their children. Such a fundamental interest entails that they should have the primary rights in the area of education.

4. *Primary culture argument*: My fourth argument can be seen as growing out of the previous two arguments. There is a good deal of research highlighting the importance of family as a means of satisfying children's basic needs of close personal relationships and achieving a sense of identity.[31] A stable and coherent primary culture is also necessary as a foundation from which children subsequently develop into autonomous adults. This need for stability and coherence gives parents the right to determine the character of the "primary culture" for their children, without undue interference from other individuals or agencies. Such interference would prove harmful to a child's development.

What does this need for a primary culture mean for the family? Sharing beliefs and values, influencing and educating children are essential elements of the common life of the family. They are inescapable. It is not possible for parents merely to *expose* their children to their beliefs, as Callan maintains (1985, 111). Infants aren't merely "spectators" as Callan has to assume; they are necessarily totally immersed in their parents' life, language, and culture (McLaughlin 1985, 122). To negate the parents' right to influence and educate is to destroy the family with all its benefits.

This argument can be extended even further. There is something terribly arbitrary about limiting this right of parents to influence and educate their children to the first years of their children's lives. The need for consistent influence and education continues well beyond infancy. Contrary to Ackermann, I believe this need for a stable and coherent primary culture lasts well beyond the early school years.[32] Therefore I believe the first school a child attends should reflect the parents' own beliefs and values. It follows that parents should have the right to send their children to the school of their choice.

5. *Argument from liberalism*: The primacy of parental rights can finally be defended on the basis of the generally accepted premises of liberalism.[33] A basic liberal value involves treating adults as self-governing persons entitled to choose and pursue their own "reasonable" conception of the good life, unless it rejects a basic moral or liberal-political norm on which there is a general consensus among reasonable people in a society. This principle would suggest that parents should enjoy the authority to educate their children in accord with their own conceptions of the good life, unless these conceptions are plainly unreasonable.

It can further be argued that parental educational rights should be seen as an extension of the right to free speech (Gilles 1996, 1012–33). Parents should be free to communicate their values to their children directly as well as through the speech of teachers and schools as their chosen agents. I therefore concur with Gilles that liberal statecraft should not only merely tolerate the primacy of parental rights in the area of education but should encourage and rely on it (941).

Thus far I have not introduced any distinctively religious arguments to support the primacy of parental rights. I would maintain, however, that the above arguments are quite in keeping with the arguments that evolve from the Jewish or Christian Scriptures (as well as those of other major religious traditions). Clearly the family is the natural building block of a society, according to a Jewish and a Christian social philosophy.[34] The primary authority of parents to educate is natural and part of God's creation order. Reference to God's creation order explains why this religious argument for parental rights concurs with the "secular" arguments I have reviewed above. A proper regard for nature, with or without reference to God, yields similar arguments. This is in keeping with a long-standing natural law tradition in ethics, most often expressed in Roman Catholic writings.

It needs to be underscored that by giving parents primary rights in directing the education of their children, I am not giving to parents exclusive rights. Nor am I disregarding the rights of children. I also acknowledge that when parental educational choices are plainly unreasonable, then the state (or a teacher in behalf of the state) is justified in intervening. My position is similar to that of Gilles, who gives it the label of "liberal parentalism" (1997, 9). This position is liberal, Gilles argues, "both because it sharply limits the state's role in the upbringing of children and because it limits parents' educational and custodial authority over them. Parents may not abuse or neglect their children, or deprive them of basic education; and *de jure* parental control ends when the child becomes an adult" (9).

The latter point deserves more comment. Exactly when does parental educational and custodial authority over children end? Almost everyone would agree that children are better off when caring adults make major choices for them until after adolescence. The optimal age of general or educational emancipation is ultimately an empirical question. Evidence from the social sciences suggests that adolescents lack self-control, underestimate risks, and make decisions without due regard for their long-term self-interest. Given that this pattern of unreliable decision making extends to educational choices, a good case can be made for keeping educational authority in parents' hands until after adolescence. As children mature they will and should have increasing voice and influence in decision making, but ultimate authority should still rest in the parents.[35] Here, of course, we need to take into account the fact that children mature at different rates.

STATE RIGHTS

The final challenge to the primacy of parental rights involves the claim that the state has primary rights in the area of education. This position is clearly expressed in the quotation cited at the beginning of this chapter: "In any kind of organized society, the rights of the state have to come first. That's why you have a public education system." The context of this statement is important – a discussion of a new school act in Alberta (1988), which in its preface acknowledged the educational rights of parents. The objection affirms the primary right of the state to educate. This is then used to defend state-maintained public education, with an implicit attack against private, religious schools. Opposition to religious schools is often expressed in terms of an implicit or explicit appeal to state rights in education.[36]

It should not surprise us that an appeal to the primacy of state rights should often be made within the context of opposition to religious schools. After all, there is a historical connection between the emergence of the nation-state at the end of the eighteenth century and the emergence of state-maintained public education (Tamir 1995a, xvii). Subsequently, there has been an enormous expansion of the state's role in funding and controlling schools, since the introduction of compulsory schooling in the West in the second half of the nineteenth century (Crittenden 1988, 41–3). It is therefore generally assumed that government has the power to maintain a system of public schools, and this power is comparable to the power of the government to tax, and to maintain a system of courts and a police force (Oppewal 1981, 366).

What lies behind this increasing acceptance of state authority over education? Why is it often maintained that the state, not parents, should be given primary rights when it comes to the education of its citizens? Because ultimately parents are viewed as incompetent.[37] I have alluded to the history of state schooling and the advent of compulsory attendance laws, which finally led to parents being viewed by educators as "presumptively incompetent." Hence schooling became less concerned with family aspirations and more concerned with the needs and values of society (Arons 1986, xi).

Another good example of this attitude is found in a statement made in 1914 by Archibald Murphey, the father of the public school system of North Carolina. He defended the need for children to be taught in state schools as follows: "Their parents know not how to instruct them ... The state in the warmth of her affection and solicitude for their welfare, must take charge of those children, and place them in school where their minds can be enlightened and their hearts can be trained to virtue" (1914, 53–4). The use of parental imagery in relation to the state is not uncommon.[38] Part of the focus here is on state interests, but clearly the state will have to hire teachers who have the necessary expertise (that the parents don't have) to train the children in the virtues that are essential to the state.

There are several different dimensions of parental incompetence that are alluded to in arguments for the primacy of state rights. I have already touched on one. Sometimes it is maintained that the state must have primary rights over education in order to protect children from parents who neglect or even abuse them. The position I am defending acknowledges the right of the state to intervene in the case of neglect or abuse. Giving parents primary authority over and responsibility for their own children in no way denies the secondary role of government as a backstop against parental wrongdoing (Randall 1994, ch. 5).

There is another concern implicit in the declaration of parents as incompetent in the area of education. The educational interests of parents for their children are viewed as too narrow. If we really have the children's best interest in mind, at some point they must receive an education allowing them to explore ways of life that differ from that of their parents.[39] Gutmann, for example, wants educational authority to be placed primarily in the hands of those who will maximize the future choice of children without prejudicing children towards any controversial conception of the good life (1987, 33–4). It is the state which must aid children in developing the capacity to understand and to evaluate competing conceptions of the good life, although the state will cede some educational authority to professional educators (44).

This argument fails to take into account that all caring parents have the best interests of their children in mind and want them to develop towards maturity, to become independent and even critically rational, at least to a degree. It is also an error to assume that such an opening-up process can only occur in state-maintained schools. Surely it can also occur in parent-chosen religious schools – indeed, it might be better accomplished in such schools, as I will argue in later chapters. This argument also fails to acknowledge that liberation is necessarily parasitic on nurture.

Another dimension to parental incompetence often surfaces in arguments for the primacy of state authority in the area of education. Gutmann, for example, argues that state rights must be dominant because of the importance she places on teaching the deliberative skills so necessary for a democracy (41–7).[40] In a later essay Gutmann therefore objects to religious schools and the view that the support of schools be left "at least primarily to parents and private associations" (1996, 163–5). But, as will be argued at length in chapter 13, it is quite possible for religious schools which are under parental direction to teach civic responsibilities including the deliberative skills that are essential to a democracy.

So much for the specific forms of parental incompetence. It is now time to deal with problems underlying the broader claim of parental incompetence. One problem with this broader position is the basis upon which parents are declared incompetent. Parents are being evaluated in terms of a radically liberal educational agenda. But this radical liberal educational agenda is itself problematic, as I have argued elsewhere (Thiessen 1993). Further, liberal educators, if they are true to their liberalism, should be careful not to impose their own controversial conception of the good life onto others. In order to avoid such imposition, liberal educators might just have to introduce a thinner conception of what is in the best interests of the child. Once this is done, it might just be found that parents are in fact not as incompetent as is often thought.

The argument for the primacy of state rights based on the supposed incompetence of parents is also based on an undue trust in expertise, i.e. teachers hired by the state. Some contemporary observers question whether teachers' professional training really makes a significant contribution to their capacity for effective teaching. We also need to remember that experts, including educational experts, disagree about most things. Even if we assume that all teachers enjoy working with children and value children's educational progress, a rather optimistic assumption, teachers' incentives to act in the child's best interests educationally are still weaker than those of parents (Gilles 1996, 955–6). Realism would suggest that we need to keep in mind that for many teachers teaching is just a job, and there may even be attempts to get away with as little work as possible.

State officials and teachers are all too human, fallible and morally frail. It is arrogant to claim otherwise. Even philosopher-queens are not omniscient! Sadly, a good deal of arrogance usually accompanies declarations of parental incompetence on the part of supposedly "enlightened" liberal educationalists. I would suggest that little, if anything, is gained by looking to the state as a way of overcoming parental incompetence.

Again, this is not to suggest that there is not a place for the expertise and authority of teachers. Affirming the primacy of parental authority does not entail the complete negation of teachers' authority. Here again the "either/or fallacy" keeps cropping up. It is perfectly consistent to affirm the primacy of parental rights and also to acknowledge the need for expertise. "Let parents choose teachers and the demand for expert teachers will increase" (Gilles 1996, 956). Ultimately, teacher authority is a borrowed authority. Hence the common understanding of teachers being "in loco parentis" (Hughes 1992, 83).

Further, significant additional problems are raised by giving the state or state experts primary educational rights. The fundamental problem is that any blanket appeal to expertise is perniciously despotic. We are quick to point this out in the area of politics – Plato's argument for rule by the expert entails totalitarianism. But there is a similar danger of tyranny behind an appeal to educational expertise.

The danger is multiplied if coupled with state authority in education. While I have cautioned against exaggerating the dangers inherent in state involvement in education, we must be equally careful not to underestimate the dangers inherent in such involvement. This is why Gutmann wisely rejects giving exclusive educational rights to the state, but she fails to see that similar dangers arise with her giving primary rights to the state (1987, 42). Giving to the state primary educational rights brings with it the terrible danger of the state taking on exclusive educational authority. This danger can be avoided by having multiple centres of authority to educate.

CONCLUSION

Religious schools exist because parents want their children to attend religious schools. As was noted in the introduction of this chapter, parental rights in the area of education are seldom challenged outright. Indeed, they are often assumed, and it is difficult not to do so within the context of a liberal democracy. Nonetheless, opposition to religious schools often includes implicit challenges to parental rights. For example, opposition to religious schools is frequently expressed in terms of strong support for state-maintained education, which in turn often seems to assume that state rights should override parental rights. When it comes to the controversial question of public funding of religious schools, the affirmation of the primacy of state rights often becomes quite explicit.

The central purpose of this chapter has been to defend the primacy of parental rights in the area of education. This would entail that parents do have the right to send their children to religious schools. While recognizing the primacy of parental rights, I am suggesting that there is a multiple basis for authority and rights in education and that it is wrong to locate this authority in any single institution, person, or group of persons. Here I agree entirely with Gutmann (1987, 42). Such a multiple basis for authority and rights in education is in fact a key to avoiding the dangers of exclusive authority in this area. By giving parents primary authority, I also overcome the potential problem of conflict between equal claimants to educational rights.

There is still a need to show exactly how educational authority is to be shared among parents, the state, and professional educators, while at the same time protecting the rights of the children to ensure that their best interests are maintained. It is beyond the scope of this chapter to provide a careful delineation of these rights and responsibilities.[41] It would be premature to do so, since the question of parental rights cannot be entirely separated from other questions which will be dealt with in subsequent chapters. And so I will come back to this question of division of rights and responsibilities in the final chapters. From what has already been said, however, the rough boundaries of these rights and responsibilities should be apparent.

The primacy of parental rights entails that parents should be able to send their children to schools that reflect their own ideological (secular or religious) outlook. Parents, however, must always also have the good of the child in mind. Children have the right to have the basic human goods provided.[42] The education of children should be in their long-term interest, and this includes fostering growth towards normal rational autonomy.[43] It also means that, as children mature, parents (and teachers) need to adjust their level of input in making educational decisions to the children's developing capacity for independent judgment.[44]

In broad terms, the primary function of the state is to promote justice. In relation to education this means that the state should defend by its legislation the primary right of parents to educate their children.[45] Given the pluralistic nature of a society, I believe that this entails that the state should ensure that there is a system of confessional pluralism in the school system, but a defence of the how and the why of this implication will be postponed until the final chapters.

The promotion of justice also entails that the state has a duty to protect the rights of children when these are neglected or violated by parents (Crittenden 1988, 164, 174). In extreme cases of neglect, abuse, and the teaching of distorted values such as race hatred, the state has a right to intervene (116). The state also has a right to enforce compulsory education to a certain minimal level, and to ensure that all children have equal access to a good education (194–8). A liberal state further may insist that all children be given an education that will develop the basic skills and competences necessary for normal human development and liberal citizenship.

Teachers too have certain rights and responsibilities, but always within the context of parental control of the overall direction of education. If we keep this important qualification in mind, it can then be said that decisions on issues that are specifically academic should be made by the academic community. This involves particularly such items as the formal content of the curriculum, teaching methods, and measuring student achievement (McCarthy et al. 1981, 167).

SOME PRACTICAL IMPLICATIONS FOR RELIGIOUS SCHOOLS

1.   *Larry Jones and exclusive claims*: Defenders of religious schools, and parents who send their children to religious schools, must be careful to avoid any suggestion that would give parents exclusive parental educational rights. The position of Larry Jones is philosophically and theologically unwarranted. Jones did not want to entertain any "partnership"

with regard to the education of his children (Wagner 1995, 37). But, the education of children needs to be seen in terms of a partnership between parents (as primary), professional educators, and the state, with the well-being of the child always a central concern of all those who share in this responsibility.

2.   *Government regulations*: Various writers have drawn attention to the fact that there are Christian parents who maintain that the state has no role in the area of education, and that there are Christian schools which are very reluctant to accept any government intervention.[46] I believe this position is untenable, given the argument of this chapter, which assigns to the state some quite legitimate functions with regard to education. The question of what the state should do with these extremists is difficult. I would suggest that the government of Alberta showed admirable restraint in dealing with Larry Jones. But, there does come a point, even in a liberal-democratic state, where coercive measures are required to ensure the protection of children against abusive parents and sometimes, sadly, also against abusive teachers.

3.   Boards of religious schools: If I am right about the primacy of parental rights, then it would seem that the ultimate authority in the running of religious schools should be school boards consisting primarily (but not only) of parents. Clearly, the principal and representatives from the teaching staff and students should also be on the board. It should be noted that in my analysis of shared responsibilities for education, I made no mention of the church. I believe authority for religious schools rests in religious parents, not in the church. Indeed, I would argue that churches and schools ought to be kept quite separate. More on that in a later chapter.

Unfortunately, religious schools are often tied to churches. Some evangelical schools are even located in church buildings.[47] Such close ties to churches only serve to confuse the question of authority, and ultimately violate the principle of the primacy of parental rights. This is where I am in agreement with the changes recently initiated in the Newfoundland system of denominational education. I agree with Premier Tobin when he argued the following: "There will be no constitutional rights for the churches in the new school system. What we are proposing quite simply is that the parents, not the churches have the ultimate right and responsibility to direct their children's education."[48]

4.   Teachers' rights: I have argued for shared rights and responsibilities in education. The primacy of parental rights, therefore, is quite compatible with giving teachers rights in religious schools. However, it should be noted that the very language of rights seems somewhat inappropriate when applied to this context. As various studies show, the

fact that teachers and parents share the same religious values makes for mutually supportive relationships, which simply don't lend themselves to talk about rights.[49]

However, even at religious schools there is still a need to distinguish between parental and teachers' responsibilities, which in the end can be translated into correlative rights. There is the danger, with the affirmation of the primacy of parental rights, that such rights are carried too far and thus undermine teachers' effectiveness. No doubt it is this danger which explains, in part at least, Pastor Muller's concerns about parochial attitudes on the part of parents at Bethany Baptist Academy, and his opposition to a "parent-controlled school" (Peshkin 1986, 96).[50] Parents sometimes do have parochial attitudes towards education, and there can be too much parent control in religious schools. In both cases, teachers' rights are undermined. Hence the need for delineation of responsibilities.

5.   Children's rights: Clearly, a primary concern in all religious schools should be the well-being of children. A fundamental ingredient in ensuring the best interests of students is that their education should foster growth towards "normal rational autonomy" (see Thiessen 1993, chs. 5 and 9).

Another practical implication of the argument of this chapter grows out of the recognition that children are in fact maturing over the years. An acknowledgment of their ongoing development would suggest that children should have increasing say in their own education as they mature. Peshkin draws attention to the danger of parents using coercive measures to keep their children at Bethany Baptist Academy.[51] Within religious schools, too, students should increasingly be allowed to participate in decision making about the education that they receive.

5 The Charge of Violating Academic Freedom

> To make the university a center for the propagation of any creed,
> of any system of values that divides group from group, is to destroy
> the special quality and the unique mission of the university as a
> center for the free pursuit of knowledge wherever it may lead.
>
> Robert McIver, *Academic Freedom in Our Time*

Religiously based schools and colleges are committed to a certain faith
stance. This affects not only what is taught but who does the teaching.
Instructors are often required to sign a statement of faith before they
are hired. Certain standards of behaviour, reflecting the supporting
constituencies' values, may be expected of instructors. Teaching and
research are expected to be in keeping with the faith commitment of
the institution. Failure to stay within these boundaries sometimes leads
to dismissal. Such expectations would seem to be a blatant violation of
the principle of academic freedom which is thought to undergird
healthy liberal educational institutions.

Discussions of academic freedom occur most often in relation to
post-secondary institutions. This is probably due to their orientation to
research, and the higher level of maturity of students. At primary and
secondary schools, teachers simply do not have the same degree of autonomy. Governments and school boards exercise decision-making
powers in relation to a whole range of matters: school policies, employ-
ment/dismissal, and curriculum (Magsino and Covert 1984, 250).
The issue of academic freedom is still a concern at the primary and
secondary levels of schooling, however, although the language used to
address it tends to be different – there is a preference for talking about
teacher autonomy or professionalism at the primary and secondary
school levels.[1]

Given the complexity and variety of issues involved, it will be necessary to circumscribe the discussion of this chapter. I will therefore limit
myself to a consideration of the problem of academic freedom at

religiously based post-secondary colleges and universities, focusing particularly on issues of teaching/research and employment/ dismissal. With some adaptation, the arguments presented can be extrapolated to other related issues and to other levels of education.

HISTORICAL OBSERVATIONS

The standard contemporary ideal of academic freedom has a variety of roots: the medieval concern to protect quasi-ecclesiastical universities from undue temporal interference (i.e. the state); the turn-of-the-century German ideal of *Lehrfreiheit* – the right of a professor to freedom of inquiry and teaching; the Enlightenment; the ideals of the French Revolution; and John Stuart Mill's classic defence of freedom.[2] The modern secular university grew out of a conscious attempt to free scholarly investigation from the supposed limitations that had dominated scholarship prior to the Enlightenment, particularly the "strictures" of religious tradition and authority. Academic freedom was seen as the central tenet of the modern secular university (McConnell 1993, 306).

There are a variety of concerns connected with the modern ideal of academic freedom. Of central concern is the protection of the right of faculty members to research, publish, teach, or even express themselves outside of the college or university. This freedom is generally qualified as applying to matters within faculty members' area of professional competence, subject to the professional standards of their respective disciplines and fulfilment of professional duties.[3]

The standard American ideal of academic freedom can be traced to the founding of the American Association of University Professors (AAUP) in 1915, with John Dewey as its first president. While the founding of AAUP was largely rooted in a need to protect professors who were being fired because they had defended controversial political views, dismissal on religious grounds was also an initial concern (Marsden 1993, 221). In the next few decades a widespread consensus emerged concerning academic freedom, which led to the formulation of the very influential 1940 "Statement of Principles on Academic Freedom and Tenure."[4] This statement defends freedom in teaching and research as essential to institutions of higher education and their promotion of the common good.

A precautionary "limitations clause" was included in the 1940 statement to accommodate parochial schools: "Limitations of academic freedom because of religious or other aims of the institution should be clearly stated in writing at the time of appointment" (Van Alstyne 1993, 407, b). It is important to note that this qualification is viewed as a "limitation" on the "full" academic freedom characterizing genuine institutions of higher learning. Controversy has surrounded this limitations clause. In a 1970 "Interpretive Comment" on the 1940 Statement, AAUP declared that "most church-related institutions no longer need or desire the departure from the principle of academic freedom implied in the 1940 Statement, and we do not now endorse such a departure."[5]

Marsden goes on to suggest that this more purist attitude towards academic freedom has remained a prominent stance in the AAUP and within American academia generally. If one examines reports issued by AAUP's Committee A on Academic Freedom and Tenure, investigating alleged violations of academic freedom, it becomes clear that Committee A has repudiated the limitations clause of the 1940 Statement and is assuming only the secular understanding of academic freedom.[6]

Among the more celebrated recent cases of a supposed violation of academic freedom at a religious school is Father Charles E. Curran's 1986 removal, by order of the Vatican, from the theology faculty of the Catholic University of America because of his liberal views on sexual morality, abortion, and other social issues. In a recent book that documents his own struggle, and provides a fascinating overview of the debate over academic freedom within Catholic higher education, Curran argues for *full* academic freedom at Catholic universities (1990). Here we have an example of someone within a religious educational context condemning what is occurring in Catholic higher education on the basis of the standard secular ideal of academic freedom.

Professional associations in other countries have similar concerns.[7] For example, the Canadian Society for the Study of Religion (CSSR) recently investigated a case involving a faculty member (at Saint Stephen's College, affiliated with the University of Alberta) whose contract was not renewed on grounds that appeared to have no academic basis. An *adhoc* committee of CSSR produced a report recommending that the Canadian Association of University Teachers' (CAUT) guidelines on academic freedom (very similar to the AAUP Statement) be applied to all academics teaching religion in Canadian universities, schools of theology, colleges, and seminaries, and that a distinction not be drawn between the rights of academics teaching theology in seminaries and the rights of academics teaching religion in universities. CSSR further initiated a request to have other theologically oriented societies join them in meeting with the CAUT to discuss the issue of academic freedom in theological and church-related colleges in Canada.[8]

It should be clear from this historical review that the consensus among the secular educational establishment is that such institutions simply cannot have full academic freedom because of their religious commitment, and therefore they forfeit "the moral right to proclaim themselves as authentic seats of higher learning."9

How then do educationalists in religious institutions respond to this charge? Various approaches have been taken by Roman Catholics: (1) Some defend Catholic schools by challenging the traditional statement of academic freedom; (2) Others argue for limited academic freedom; (3) Some like Curran argue that Catholic institutions of higher learning should have the same level of academic freedom as their secular counterparts; (4) Some argue that there is even greater academic freedom at Catholic schools than at their secular counterparts (Curran 1990). A similar variety of responses can be found among Protestant and evangelical academics.10

I will challenge some of the assumptions underlying the traditional concept of academic freedom. I will then propose a revised ideal of academic freedom on the basis of which it can be shown that religious colleges and universities can have the required level of academic freedom which would make them authentic seats of higher learning, just like their secular counterparts.

A PROBLEM OF DEFINITION

A basic problem with the traditional concept of "academic freedom" is its lack of clear and precise meaning. Already in its early usage in America, vagueness and inconsistencies were evident. To advocate "full freedom," while arguing for "duties correlative to rights" or "appropriate restraint" in the light of one's status as a professional and citizen, as was done in the AAUP 1940 Statement, is inconsistent (Van Alstyne 1993, 407–9). Marsden points out that the original AAUP committee recognized that academic freedom could not be unlimited, "but they argued that there should always be a presumption in its favour, with no firm lines drawn around it" (Marsden 1993, 229). The lines were indeed not firm! Hence the condoning of blatant restrictions of academic freedom in the name of the national interest prior to the First World War. AAUP even adopted a special revised statement of academic freedom, entitled "Academic Freedom in Wartime" (Marsden 1994, 309–11).

Continuing controversy about the existence of academic freedom in state-maintained colleges and universities would seem to add further weight to the claim that the concept itself is fraught with difficulties. The very titles of books are suggestive: *Illiberal Education: The Politics of Race and Sex on Campus* (D'Souza 1991); *The Closing of the American Mind* (Bloom 1987); *Zealotry and Academic Freedom* (Hamilton 1995); *Kindly Inquisitors: The New Attacks on Free Thought* (Rauch 1993); *Zero*

Tolerance: Hot Button Politics in Canada's Universities (Emberley 1996); and *The Shadow University: The Betrayal of Liberty on America's Campuses* (Kors and Silverglate 1999). Of course, these criticisms of contemporary demands for ideological conformity and "political correctness" which have encroached on academic freedom at our colleges and universities are disputed by the "radicals" (e.g. Tierney 1993). More on this later. Here my intent is only to point out that this dispute suggests a problem with the concept of academic freedom itself.

A final indication of the problematic nature of the traditional ideal of academic freedom is that many religiously based schools do maintain academic freedom as an operative principle within their institutions.[11] Obviously, these claims, and statements of academic freedom within these schools, will not satisfy many academics who see themselves as religiously uncommitted. I draw attention to these controversies to highlight the fact that the question of the existence of academic freedom at religiously based colleges and universities is not as clear-cut as many assume.

Underlying the debate concerning the presence or absence of academic freedom at either religious or secular schools is a problematic definition of academic freedom. As Marsden concludes, after providing a brief history of this ideal, "it is a concept fraught with deep ambiguities" (1993, 231).[12] More attention needs to be paid to defining what we mean by academic freedom. In the next sections, I will examine and critique the traditional understanding of academic freedom, thereby preparing the groundwork for a revised and more philosophically defensible principle.

PROBLEMS WITH THE TRADITIONAL IDEAL OF ACADEMIC FREEDOM

1. *Freedom*: At the heart of current conceptions of academic freedom is an assumption of absolute individual intellectual freedom in research and teaching.[13] I have already made reference to the tension inherent in the AAUP's early attempts to define the level of freedom possible in academic freedom. The 1940 Statement as a whole breathes a "spirit of untrammelled inquiry," as one early Catholic critic put it.[14] Thus we are reminded in the 1940 Statement that the teacher is entitled to "full freedom" in research and in the publication of the results (Van Alstyne 1993, 407). It is further significant that, although the Statement seems to acknowledge the right of religious educational institutions to impose religious requirements on teaching employees, such requirements are seen as "limitations" of academic freedom. The assumption is that "full" academic freedom would have no such restric-

tions. The failure to endorse this limitation clause in the AAUP 1970 "Interpretive Comment" on the 1940 Statement would again suggest that the ideal is seen as having full academic freedom.

Current conceptions of academic freedom are rooted in a concept of freedom which has its origins in the Enlightenment. One important legacy of the Enlightenment that remains to this day is the belief in free inquiry, inquiry that is freed from the constraints of tradition and authority, particularly as found in religion.

[handwritten margin note: religion discourages inquiry → lack of freedom]

The notion of absolute freedom is a myth. Freedom, whether individual, social, or political, is necessarily limited. Freedom is always freedom in context. Freedom is only possible in the context of what restricts freedom. Hence notions of "full" freedom in research and teaching are by their very nature problematic.

This conclusion is reinforced in Haworth's attempt to counter the romantic notions of autonomy that still abound, which he then replaces with a more coherent, comprehensive, and realistic account of "normal autonomy" (1986). Haworth further stresses the institutional context within which autonomy must express itself. While institutional structures do have a face of constraint, he argues that they also have a face of opportunity (ch. 6).

Polanyi has underscored the institutional context of scientific research, often put forward as the paradigm of free inquiry. For example, students must submit to those who have mastered the science. Scholars get grants which are distributed according to certain criteria and whose proposals are refereed by other colleagues. Publication of the findings of scientists is subject to all kinds of controls, and if scientists depart too far from established opinion, they may not be successful in getting their work published (Polanyi 1964, ch. 2). So even in science the spirit of inquiry is not utterly unfettered. Hence, typical statements of academic freedom are forced to acknowledge the constraints imposed on academics by academic disciplines themselves. Academic freedom brings with it correlative duties.[15]

Teaching similarly is subject to a host of constraints. Teachers first need to be educated and certified. They teach in schools which are subject to any number of guidelines and pressures, both formal and informal, coming from a variety of sources – administration, government, and local sentiments. Any teacher who ignores these does so at his or her peril. Most often these guidelines are simply assumed, and hence teachers may not even be aware of them. The fact that most teachers are not aware of these constraints does not mean that they don't exist.

It is because there is and can be no such thing as unlimited academic freedom that one invariably finds contradictions in descriptions and definitions of liberal notions of academic freedom. Further limitations of freedom will be identified in the sections that follow. My point here is a general one, so eloquently summed up by Caston – statements of absolute academic freedom, whether applied to the individual academic or to the university as a whole, "are ideals which cannot be, never have been, and arguably should never be, totally realised" (1989, 307).

2. *Epistemology*: Underlying the traditional concept of academic freedom is also an epistemology which can only be called "naïve" given the more recent developments in this field. At the heart of the contemporary ideal of academic freedom is a spirit of free inquiry which has always been thought to be best exemplified in science. Marsden has clearly shown that the original formation of the AAUP and its position concerning academic freedom assumed an ideal of free and objective scientific inquiry which would rid us of the parochial past, together with the passion, prejudice, and partisanship associated with tradition.[16]

But developments in the philosophy of science, the sociology of knowledge, and feminist epistemology, to name but a few, show that the search for truth is always guided by assumptions and preconceptions which function as constraints on freedom of inquiry.[17] The Enlightenment quest for absolute objectivity is inherently futile. It is a quest for a "view from nowhere," as Thomas Nagel has aptly described it (1986). A view from nowhere is impossible because all rational activity is "inescapably historically and socially context-bound" (MacIntyre 1988, 4). The idea of a universal and neutral rationality is now recognized to be itself an expression of a particular narrative, an Enlightenment narrative.

It would be a mistake to view the assumptions and preconceptions that any rational person begins with as functioning only as constraints on freedom of inquiry. While functioning as limitations in one sense, they must also be seen as preconditions of rationality. In other words, they make possible the search for truth.

Advocates of the traditional ideal of academic freedom further err in their epistemology by assuming that a commitment to certain religious presuppositions precludes an honest and open search for the truth. Open-mindedness is not the same as empty-mindedness (Hare 1979, 53). Indeed, there are no empty minds. Locke's *tabula rasa* is a myth.

The prevailing ideal of academic freedom rests on an epistemology which is now generally recognized to be fundamentally flawed. It is surprising that the 1940 formulation of academic freedom by AAUP, and others similar to it, still persist. They are in desperate need of updating.[18] The distrust of any limitations on academic freedom fails to recognize that a researcher or teacher inherits a standpoint, a point of view, from which he or she pursues and expounds the truth.

What is needed is a new ideal of academic freedom which recognizes that we are all situated in a particular time and a particular place; that the best scholarship is honest in admitting the limitations imposed by its prior commitments. Good scholarship will, of course, go on to defend the possibilities opened up by starting with these prior commitments.

The epistemology being appealed to as a basis for a revised ideal of academic freedom is not without its pitfalls. But we must not let these dangers lead us to hang on to an ideal of academic freedom whose epistemological foundations have crumbled.

3. *Individualism*: Another fundamental problem with contemporary definitions of academic freedom involves their extreme individualism. In the AAUP 1940 Statement, for example, it is the individual teacher or the individual researcher who is to be given academic freedom and tenure.

Although the individual is important, we are by nature also social beings, and our search for truth always occurs within the context of a community. The teacher or researcher is simply not "a socially disembodied being" who can or should be given *full* freedom in research and teaching (MacIntyre 1988, 4). Even scientific scholarship, often seen as the paradigm of free and individual inquiry, typically occurs within the context of a community. Moreover, there is also an institutional context of this scientific research.

One other dimension of institutional limitations on academic freedom needs to be underscored. Educational institutions need financial support and there is always some sort of supporting constituency, whether society at large or smaller religious societies. Such support will always be contingent on these institutions serving the interests of the supporting constituency. Hence, the reference, in the AAUP 1940 Statement of Academic Freedom, to the "common good" (Van Alstyne 1993, 407). What is not sufficiently acknowledged is the extent to which such a reference to the common good might limit academic freedom (Marsden 1993, 230). Tierney has therefore quite correctly pointed out that academic freedom has never existed in a political vacuum (1993, 144).

This political dimension of academic freedom is dealt with in Conrad Russell's recent and insightful treatment of the clash between the British government and the universities during the debate over the Education Reform Bill of 1988 (Russell 1993). Russell argues that there has always been a tension between state support of the university and the freedom of the university. The protection of academic freedom really depends on government, and governments will only provide this protection if they see it to be in their own interests (22).

No university has a natural right to exist, Russell points out (47). Hence governments do not have to support universities. Of course, I believe it would be tragic for a society not to do so, but we as academics need to recognize our dependence on society, and respond honestly and humbly to societal concerns. This obviously imposes limits on our academic freedom. To talk of "full academic freedom" is simply idealistic sky-gazing.

Obviously, there is a danger that society might stifle the freedom of the academic too much. What is needed therefore is a careful definition of proper balance between the interests of the society or state and the interests of the academic. Russell attempts this in his own work, but it is beyond the scope of this chapter to evaluate his proposed balance (ch. 3). My point here is to uncover another way in which the traditional ideal of academic freedom is problematic in being too individualistic, thereby failing to do justice to the limitations arising from the social and political context within which an academic must work.

THE POSTMODERNIST CHALLENGE

There is clearly a postmodernist ring to my criticisms of the traditional ideal of academic freedom. For postmodernists, the idea of an ahistorical, non-contingent, rational self is a myth. Therefore complete objectivity is impossible. Knowledge and truth are to some degree relative to place, society, culture, historical epoch, and conceptual framework. Truth needs to be seen as located within the context of discourse communities (Weinstein 1995, 378). Scholarship, too, is necessarily situated within a present and a particular. A defensible notion of academic freedom needs to recognize this.

Postmodernism, at its core, is a reaction to the Enlightenment (Carr 1995, 78). At the core of the Enlightenment, which set the agenda of modernity, was a desire to search for truth apart from tradition and authority. The oral, particular, local, and timely were all viewed with suspicion (Toulmin 1990, 30–5). This same emphasis is very much in evidence in early formulations of the traditional Western ideal of academic freedom. Marsden highlights the fact that behind the formation of professional societies such as AAUP in 1915 was a desire "to define and control a national culture at the expense of local cultures." They "were creating loyalties and self-definitions based on the scientific standards of national organizations, and thus undermining loyalty to particular institutions and their traditions" (Marsden 1993, 227; 1994, 306). This same spirit created a suspicion of religious educational institutions. Hence the "limitations clause" of AAUP's first statement on academic freedom. Suspicions about religious colleges and universities remain to this day.[19]

At the heart of postmodernism is the attempt to recapture pre-Enlightenment respect for tradition and that which is bound to a particular time and place. My critique of the assumptions underlying the modern ideal of academic freedom clearly rests on a postmodernist rejection of the agenda begun during the Enlightenment.

Here a fundamental problem arises. If, with the postmodernists, I stress the context-bound nature of rationality, am I not opening the door to epistemological relativism? Does not my position also suggest that knowledge is a social and political construction which privileges some and silences others. And does not this demand a radical reinterpretation of academic freedom in terms of protecting the rights of the silent and the marginalized, which will then enable them to gain a voice? Such a reinterpretation along the lines of critical theory has been recently attempted by William Tierney (1993).[20]

The problem with such a radical politicization of the notion of academic freedom is that the search for truth is replaced with a battle for survival. Tierney is quite explicit in calling for a replacement of a "consensual model" of knowledge and academic freedom with a "conflict model in which we assume that competing interests will always exist" (148). Such a conflict model of truth is frightening. I would suggest that we have yet to reap the full consequences of the increasing acceptance of this model in our universities. Here I can only refer to conservative critics of the academy who have, over the last decade, issued warnings about the radical orientation that currently resides in our college and university campuses.[21] A most eloquent plea to counter the latest wave of ideological zealotry from the "fundamentalism of the radical academic left" is made in a recent book by Hamilton (1995).

TRUTH

There is a further theoretical problem with Tierney's radical postmodernist reinterpretation of academic freedom – it does away with the notion of truth and the search for a common truth. Tierney is very open about rejecting the conservative ideal of the academy that relies on "a singular notion of truth" towards which we are striving (1993, 144, 147, 158).

The problem here is that without the notion of truth, or the ideal of searching for truth, we have undermined the very heart of education and research. Indeed, what postmodernists like Tierney fail to realize is that without the notion of truth, they have in fact undermined their own critique of the academy. Why listen to the radicals if they are merely one voice among many other relative voices? Postmodernists further invariably contradict themselves. They seem unable to avoid talking about postmodernism as better than modernism. Better in terms of what? Such evaluation points in the direction of an ideal of objective and universal truth.

Here I am in agreement with a basic idea inherent in the traditional notion of academic freedom – the search for truth is important, and we need to protect the search for and the exposition of claims to truth from arbitrary limitations. While I have stressed the limitations inherent in our search for truth and our need to be honest about these limitations, I in no way want to do away with the notion that human beings must, and invariably do, attempt to transcend these limitations in their search for universal truth. Without balancing the emphasis on limitations with an equal emphasis on the need to try to transcend these limitations, we end up with epistemological relativism and the radical politicization of the academy which we see on our campuses today. What I am proposing therefore is a reconciliation of the insights of modernism and postmodernism concerning epistemology and human nature, avoiding the extremes in either position. I will have more to say on this in chapter 12.

This will lead to a balanced view of academic freedom in which it is acknowledged that while teachers and researchers are unavoidably rooted within a tradition, they will invariably also be seeking to transcend their limitations in an ongoing search for truth. While the notion of pure objectivity is an illusion, the notion of "a view from nowhere" must be kept as a heuristic principle in order to encourage an open-minded search for truth. What is needed, therefore is an ideal of "normal academic freedom."[22]

ACADEMIC FREEDOM
IN RELIGIOUS SCHOOLS

We are now in a position to answer the charge that the ideal of academic freedom is violated in religiously based colleges and universities; that such schools are inferior because they can only have a limited degree of academic freedom. This charge rests on a muddled, unrealistic, and philosophically indefensible concept of academic freedom. Once this concept is updated so as to acknowledge the inescapable limitations of freedom that accompany teaching and research *in any context*, the religious commitment of these schools does not of necessity entail the absence of academic freedom.

The "limitations clause" in the AAUP 1940 Statement of Academic Freedom unfairly singles out religious institutions as having only limited academic freedom. *All institutions have limited academic freedom.*

A more honest approach to academic freedom would be to see the limitations clause as applying to *all* institutions. Both those defined as serving the public, and those serving religious communities should openly state the actual bounds of their academic freedom.[23] Here I cannot help but suggest that if the limitations clause were to be seen as also applying to state-maintained colleges and universities, and if they were required to openly declare the boundaries of academic freedom that in fact exist, it would lead to a good deal of embarrassment about what the boundaries to research and teaching are, and how many such boundaries there are.[24]

At the same time it should be stressed that all schools, religious as well as secular, can and should be engaged in an open and honest search for the truth. This openness, however, should be coupled with an equally open admission of the limiting context within which this search for truth is being conducted. Much more needs to be done by way of defining a proper balance between such limitations and freedom.

What this revised ideal of academic freedom entails is that religiously based schools should be seen as having equal status with secular educational institutions. As Marsden puts it, "colleges and universities that represent alternate viewpoints, based on traditional Christian and other religious commitments, should be fully recognized as equally legitimate with those who have claimed universality on the basis of the alleged authority of value-free science" (Marsden 1993, 233).

This is not to say that there are not violations of academic freedom at religious schools, just as there are at "secular" schools. My primary concern here is to argue that academic freedom is possible at religious schools and that the religious commitment that pervades such an institution does not in and of itself negate the possibility of academic freedom.

Here it might be argued that religious institutions have some *unique* limitations to academic freedom which are not present at "secular" universities and colleges. At religious colleges and universities, appeal is made, for example, to revelation or to certain creeds which are viewed as authoritative.[25]

It is important, here, to note that although "secular" schools tend to look with suspicion at divine revelation as a starting point for the discovery of truth, they cannot help but adopt some other presuppositional framework of their own as authoritative in their own search for the truth. It is impossible to escape choosing some model for truth-seeking before one engages in the search for truth. "Secular" universities and colleges tend to prefer the scientific model, but there are others. As McConnell points out, it would be contrary to the anti-dogmatic principles on which the case for academic freedom rests to adopt a single model of truth-seeking.[26]

Further, a distinction needs to be made between first accepting revelation or a creed as authoritative, and its subsequent influence on the religious person's thinking. The initial decision to accept revelation or a creed as authoritative can surely be based on an open and rational assessment of the person considering the same. Further, as with any commitment to a particular conceptual framework, there is a degree of tenacity that is assumed and even required if this conceptual framework is to do its work in enabling a person to be rational.[27] But even here, there is nothing to stop one from reassessing one's initial commitment to revelation or a creed from time to time. Intellectual integrity demands such periodic reassessment.

Those who do not share these religious presuppositions will have their own reasons for rejecting them. But what they must not reject out of hand is the possibility that for Christians, for example, revelation or the confessional creed from which they start is seen "as an academic asset, not a liability. For we see light in God's light" (Hardy 1995, 16). Considerations such as this lead Hardy to suggest the following as a helpful definition of a church-related college: "an elective association of scholars working in a tradition of inquiry according to constraints it accepts and believes will assist it in tracking the truth about the world" (16).

TOWARDS EDUCATIONAL PLURALISM

It might still be argued that there is a greater degree of academic freedom at a secular university because it allows for a plurality of viewpoints and is neutral with regard to which initial commitments its teachers and researchers use as their basis for the search for truth.[28]

The difference between religious and secular colleges or universities is not as great or as significant as is generally assumed, however. McConnell points out that it is not unusual for some university departments to have a disproportionate concentration of faculty representing a particular school of thought within a discipline (1993, 319n48). There is, further, an obvious prejudice against attempts to introduce religious interpretations of truth within academic disciplines in most university classrooms (315). There would also seem to be an insistence on only one model of truth-seeking at our secular colleges and universities. There was a clear bias towards a scientific model of truth-seeking in the earlier AAUP formulations of the principles of academic freedom. Indeed, the overall alleged neutrality of universities is being seriously challenged in our day from a variety of standpoints – critical theory, neo-Marxism, and feminism (see Tierney 1993).

Moreover, although there may be some plurality at secular universities, it is primarily a plurality of individuals. If truth is found within epistemic communities, as I maintain along with postmodernists, then perhaps a healthier kind of pluralism could be found in a plurality of educational institutions, where each is committed to finding truth based on its particular standpoint. Individuals by themselves are in a position of weakness in terms of challenging established opinion. Within a system of educational pluralism, if each institution allowed the results of individual inquiry to be critiqued by those within the institution, as well as by those in other institutions, starting from very different presuppositions, I believe this would enhance the larger human quest for truth more effectively than our present arrangements of monolithic state-supported systems of education.[29]

Of course such an arrangement presupposes a level of tolerance and respect for other educational institutions and other understandings of reality. These virtues are not precluded by healthy religious commitments. For those who like to extol these virtues from a liberal point of view, I would suggest that they themselves need to display greater levels of tolerance and respect towards religious educational institutions. As McConnell has reminded us, it is surely important that the principle of academic freedom, which was born of opposition to dogmatism, should not itself become dogmatic and authoritarian (1993, 314).

SOME PRACTICAL IMPLICATIONS FOR RELIGIOUS SCHOOLS

1. *Parameters of academic freedom*: Religious colleges and universities should be quite open about the religious parameters within which their research and teaching take place. Contrary to Curran, there can be no such a thing as full freedom at a religious institution, or at any other institution for that matter.[30] There are limitations to academic freedom at all educational institutions, so there is nothing to be embarrassed about regarding specific limitations that exist at religious schools and colleges. Indeed, I prefer to talk about "parameters" rather than "limitations" of academic freedom, because the religious assumptions that define a religious college or university are not limitations but academic assets – they enhance, and even make possible, the search for truth.

It is, however, possible for the creedal requirements of religious schools to be ill conceived, thereby impeding the pursuit of the academic mission of a religious school (Hardy 1995, 9). For example, the creedal net can be, and sometimes is, defined too specifically, excluding those who could make a genuine contribution to the mission of a religious school.[31] Or, the creedal net can be, and sometimes is, too wide, admitting those who are in fact hostile to the religious tradition which defines the identity of the school.[32]

I would suggest that for Christian schools the creedal boundaries need to be defined in several tiers: the core beliefs of all Christians; the core beliefs of the particular denomination supporting the school, if the school has a specific supporting constituency; the peripheral beliefs where questions and doubts are allowed; and perhaps even an area of beliefs which are entirely up for grabs. Once defined, these boundaries should not be allowed to shift, except by mutual consent of all involved, since one important purpose of such boundaries is to serve as a protection for faculty.

Unfortunately, many religious colleges and universities have lost their identity precisely because of their acceptance of the secular notion of full academic freedom (see Marsden 1994). Curran concedes that this has occurred in many of America's most prestigious colleges and universities which began as Protestant institutions (1990, 79). Strangely, he feels that somehow Catholic institutions will be immune to this danger. In fact, there is abundant evidence that Catholic universities too have lost their distinctive Catholic identity because of their acceptance of a wrong-headed notion of full academic freedom.[33]

2.   *Freedom*: While admitting that there are religious parameters to academic freedom at religious colleges and universities, it must be emphasized, at the same time, that there should be freedom to explore truth within these parameters. Marsden provides us with a useful description of academic freedom that maintains a proper balance between "limitations" and freedom. "To enhance the creativity of a community, academics should be as free as possible within the framework of their other higher commitments to explore and communicate even unpopular and unconventional ideas. A presumption of freedom within defined limits is an immensely valuable way of defining academic life" (Marsden 1994, 434). Unfortunately, such freedom does not exist at some religious colleges and universities.[34]

A healthy religious college or university will also encourage periodic and ongoing reflection even on the fundamentals that define the parameters of freedom at that institution. A healthy living tradition will allow for this, as philosophers as diverse as John Stuart Mill and Alistair MacIntyre have argued.[35] Healthy religious institutions should therefore have mechanisms in place for periodic reflection upon their operating assumptions (Hardy 1995, 17). There is, however, also a need for continuity and a clear institutional identity. Here again there is a need for balance, a balance between these two emphases, though we should be careful not to expect a precise definition of a proper balance.

3.   *Hiring*: Religious schools should be able to hire teachers and scholars who share the school's overall faith commitment. It should be noted that religious schools are not entirely unique in being discrimina-

tory in hiring. If academic freedom is necessarily limited, then certain kinds of discrimination in hiring must exist at all educational institutions.[36] Clearly, there may be a difference in the criteria used in hiring at secular and religiously based colleges and universities. Religious schools will include religious criteria in hiring. It should not be objected that "non-academic" factors are being allowed to influence the hiring process at religious schools (Horner 1992, 38). Religious commitment cannot simply be dismissed as a non-academic factor, given the epistemological position that has been outlined in this chapter.

If you deny the right of a religious school to hire people who share the confessional stance of the school, you are in effect denying the right of this school to exist. Epistemic communities require schools that are an expression of their epistemic commitments, and the right to hire is a key to the identity of a school reflecting such an epistemic community. To deny the right to hire is in effect to deny the right of an epistemic community to exist, and this is surely the height of intolerance (McConnell 1993).

4.   *Criteria in hiring*: It is further important for religious schools to spell out clearly their faith commitment when hiring faculty (Horner 1992, 40). This is of course a restatement of the "limitations clause" of the AAUP 1940 Statement of Academic Freedom, and I am essentially not in disagreement with this clause.

My only concern is with seeing this practice as an unusual and unnecessary limitation of academic freedom characteristic only of religious schools. As I have already argued, all schools, including secular schools, need to define the bounds of their academic freedom. If these boundaries are clearly spelled out in hiring, then a faculty member who accepts a position at this institution voluntarily accepts these boundaries of academic freedom. They count as self-limitations and therefore cannot be seen as infringing on his or her autonomy.[37]

5.   Dismissals or resignations: At any educational institution, there is always a tension between institutional and individual commitments and freedoms. This problem is not always faced in discussions of academic freedom (McConnell 1993, 305). Here it is important to keep in mind that if the boundaries of academic freedom were clearly defined when a faculty member was appointed, the faculty member, when accepting the position, will have voluntarily agreed to the confessional stance of the school. I would therefore suggest that when a teacher or a professor can no longer submit to the faith statement of the school, he or she has a professional obligation to resign. This would get around the awkwardness of institutions having to dismiss an individual because of incompatible confessional stances. For any teacher at a religious college or university, there are professional

obligations, one of which is to work within the boundaries of academic freedom which have been defined by the institution at which one is teaching, and the other is to resign when one can no longer do so. This introduces limitations based on nothing more than professional requirements.

CONCLUSION

Clearly, these practical guidelines about academic freedom at religious educational institutions are not as precise as some might wish. Indeed, though one aim of this chapter has been to clarify some of the vagueness and ambiguity surrounding the concept of academic freedom, it should be apparent that vagueness still persists. While I have argued that limitations to academic freedom are inescapable, and that there must be a balance between limitations and freedom, this balance has not been precisely defined. I don't believe that it ever can be defined with mathematical precision.

In religious schools with a healthy academic atmosphere, there will always be a degree of tension between the individual faculty member and the institution. There simply are no perfect fits, given that both the institution and the individuals in it are invariably in a state of flux and hopefully also growth. Hence, what is perhaps most essential is that a spirit of generosity, respect, trust, and charity pervade a religious educational institution. No abstract statement of academic freedom can be a substitute for these virtues (Ericson 1991, 190).

The above practical guidelines have focused on religiously committed educational institutions. Lest this focus lead to a misunderstanding, I want to reiterate a point made earlier, namely, that all schools have limited freedom, and therefore similar guidelines should also be in place for "secular" colleges and universities. Sadly, there is an arrogance that tends to pervade the "secular" establishment, and a peculiar blindness to the biases that exist within it.[38] I would suggest as one piece of evidence of this blindness the failure to revise, or even to consider revising, the ideal of academic freedom in the light of the radical shifts in our thinking about epistemology and freedom that have occurred and are now generally accepted within academia.

The foundations of the traditional ideal of academic freedom have crumbled, but the secular edifice still stands – though just barely. When it does come tumbling down, I hope that religious schools will be recognized as equal partners with secular schools in being "authentic seats of higher learning."

PART FOUR

Economic Concerns

6 Funding of Religious Schools and the Separation of Church and State

Public funding should correspond to public purpose, values, and goals. Private schools are private precisely because their supporters prefer private purposes, values, and goals over public purposes, values, and goals.

Jim Rivait, Government Affairs Coordinator,
Alberta School Boards Association, 29 April 1997

Economic considerations often come to the fore in arguments concerning religiously based schools and colleges. In this chapter and the next, I will focus on four of the central economic-related objections to religious schools or their being funded by the state: separation of church and state, the public-private distinction, the charge of elitism, and the problem of limited funds. Some of the arguments in the other chapters of this book implicitly introduce economic considerations.

CHURCH-STATE OBJECTION

I begin with the appeal to the principle of the separation of church and state (hereinafter referred to as the SCS principle) as a way of objecting to providing public aid for religious schools. This is probably the most commonly used argument against such aid. It would seem to be one of the strongest arguments because it involves a matter of principle.

The SCS principle has perhaps been invoked most frequently in the United States because of the First Amendment, which begins with the Establishment Clause ("Congress shall make no law respecting an establishment of religion"), immediately followed by the Free Exercise Clause ("or prohibiting the free exercise thereof"). This has been well documented in a study by Doerr and Menendez, entitled *Church Schools and Public Money: The Politics of Parochiaid* (1991).[1] "Parochiaid" refers to any form of direct or indirect public aid for parochial and other non-public elementary and secondary schools. This term, coined by Michigan journalists in the late 1960s, has become a household word (11).

Doerr and Menendez make their case against parochiaid by appealing to a strict interpretation of the First Amendment. They remind us that Jefferson, in 1802, declared that these words build a "wall of separation between church and state" (15). They refer repeatedly to the Supreme Court statement made in *Everson v. Board of Education* in 1947, in which the establishment of religion clause was interpreted as prohibiting any form of parochiaid. Again Jefferson's wall of separation is referred to: "That wall must be kept high and impregnable. We could not approve the slightest breach" (16, 112–3, 127). In a survey of parochiaid referenda held in America over the past-quarter century, Doerr and Menendez conclude there has been an overwhelming support for the principle of separation as it applies to the financing of education (ch. 5). In a review of court decisions, they quote Justice William J. Brennan, "the grand old man of church-state separation," who sums up the separationist argument in a 1985 Supreme Court ruling in *Grand Rapids School District v. Ball*:

Providing for the education of schoolchildren is surely a praiseworthy purpose. But our cases have consistently recognized that even such a praiseworthy, secular purpose cannot validate government aid to parochial schools when the aid has the effect of promoting a single religion or religion generally or when the aid unduly entangles the government in matters religious. (Doerr and Menendez 1991, 120)

Unfortunately, the language used by Doerr and Menendez is often strident. Negative motivations are frequently attributed to the proponents of government aid to religious schools.[2] Their book clearly documents the controversy and summarizes the SCS argument against government funding of religious schools. Since the writing of their book, the controversy appears to be heating up even more. Cases involving parental-choice programs allowing parents to use a state-supported voucher to send their children to religious schools have been making their way through state and federal judiciaries (Viteritti 1996, 115). Here again, opponents keep raising the argument that such aid violates the constitutional standards for the separation of church and state. Although reference to the constitution is inescapable when dealing with the SCS principle in the American context, my primary concern will be with the principle itself rather than with the constitutional expression of the principle.

Canada, unlike the USA, was not founded on the SCS principle. As pointed out in the first chapter, the British North America Act gave legal protection to the rights of denominational schools. Protestants in Quebec, and Roman Catholics in Ontario, were guaranteed the right

to public funding of their schools. Various provinces have further extended partial aid to other independent religious schools. It should
therefore not come as a surprise that objections to providing aid to religious schooling based on the SCS principle do not occur as often in
Canada. But debates concerning the separation of church and state
nevertheless did surface with the emergence of the common school in
the mid-nineteenth century (Sweet 1997, ch. 2; Wilson 1970, 195).
Even now, implicit, and sometimes even explicit, appeals to the SCS
principle are made in expressing opposition to the funding of religious schools. The quotation at the head of this chapter illustrates an
implicit appeal to the SCS principle made by the Alberta School
Boards Association, 29 April 1997, in response to private member's
Bill 209, calling for more funding for private schools in Alberta.[3]

It is curious that implicit appeals to the SCS principle also occur in
Great Britain with its long tradition of an established church. In a
House of Lords debate concerning an amendment to the Education
Act seeking to extend government funding to independent religious
schools, frequent reference is made to the need for a separation of
public state interests and private religious interests. "I do not believe it
is the proper role of the state to propagate religious or any other beliefs that are a matter of substantial controversy. That is not, I believe, a
proper use of taxpayers' money." Another lord was more specific when
he expressed his opposition to allowing "the Islamic faith to be taught
with the aid of the public purse."[4]

HISTORY OF SCS

How then does one respond to the appeal to the SCS principle as a way
of opposing the funding of religious schools and colleges? Considerable debate exists concerning the originally intended meaning of the
SCS principle in the drafting of the United States Constitution.[5] However, numerous constitutional scholars agree that it is fairly obvious that
the intent was *not* a strict wall of separation, as is maintained by opponents to public aid to religious schools such as Doerr and Menendez.[6]
Further, we must not forget that Jefferson, often cited as the exemplar
of secular government, quite likely shared the general view that government support for religion was not in itself an evil.[7]

Constitutional expert Stephen Carter reminds us that the original
intent of the religion clauses was to protect the church from the state,
not the state from the church (1993, 115). What Jefferson really
wanted to prevent was the state's exercising coercive authority over religions, especially over those dissenting from established churches
(117). The concern of the religion clauses was that no *single* religion

should be established in the United States, lest the church-state con-flicts of Europe be transferred to the New World.[8] The fundamental objective of the SCS principle was to secure religious liberty, which Jefferson called "the most inalienable and sacred of all human rights" (106–7).

Further, it is very important to keep in mind that in colonial Amer-ica, as in other Western countries, the first initiatives for education came from the church. Contemporary educationalists too often over-look this indebtedness to the church. Both Catholics and Protestants were very active in founding college-seminaries, primary, and second-ary schools in colonial America (Bryk et al. 1993, 17–23; Nord 1995). All schools were parochial schools. The idea that churches were estab-lishing a separate educational system distinct from the "public" one would have seemed foreign at the time. No such system existed in the Western world. The distinction between public and private schools re-mained unclear throughout much of the nineteenth century (Bryk et al. 1993 23). Until 1825, Catholic schools in New York City received public aid (23). Even as a distinct "public" school system began to emerge after 1830, Catholic schools continued to receive support in various states (23).

This brief review of American education serves to reinforce the ar-gument that separation of church and state was not seen originally as precluding state support for religious schools. Even the "public" school system, though trying to be non-sectarian, was nevertheless es-sentially Protestant in orientation. Hence state support for these schools entailed support for Protestant education (Glenn 1988; Nord 1995). So both before and immediately after the emergence of com-pulsory state education, schools were religious, and it was not thought to be a violation of the SCS principle to support education with a reli-gious orientation.

It is beyond the scope of this chapter to trace the emergence of a very different and strict interpretation of the SCS principle. My point here is simply to underscore that even in the USA, the Establishment Clause was not always interpreted in such a way as to prohibit state sup-port of religious schools. We must therefore be careful not to be mis-led by modern revisionists of American history and their blinkered arguments for a strict interpretation of the SCS principle.

Indeed, as Viteritti clearly shows, since 1980 the Court has shifted away from the strict separationist interpretation of the Establishment Clause, moving towards a more generous reading of the free exercise provision. While still interpreting the Establishment Clause in a way that inhibits the direct flow of public funds to parochial schools, the Court has given approval to indirect aid (1996, 141). In fact, a set of guidelines has been developed to help policymakers at the federal, state, and local levels to determine when aid is acceptable. Viteritti goes on to argue that even direct aid is permissible under the Establishment Clause of the United States Constitution, given a proper understanding of the SCS principle (116, 192).

STRICT INTERPRETATION OF SCS

It is now time to move beyond historical and constitutional considerations to a more general evaluation of the SCS principle itself. Keep in mind that the principle is frequently invoked as an argument against public aid for religious schools, even in countries where the constitution does not have an Establishment Clause like the USA.[9]

I would argue that a complete separation of church and state is impossible. As long as church and state exist in one society, there will invariably be some degree of interrelation between them.[10] The very principle of freedom of conscience and religion is a kind of support for religion. When the state builds a road that runs by a church, it is supporting that church. To adopt a radical separationist interpretation of the SCS principle, and to assume that it means "to completely separate church and state," is absurd because it is impossible (Doerr and Menendez 1991, 14). Doerr and Menendez are forced to acknowledge this when they accept, as one implication of the principle of religious freedom, that religious schools should be allowed to operate, though without financial support (138). In doing so they are in fact allowing for an indirect kind of government support for religious schools. Elsewhere, they explicitly allow for "peripheral forms of tax aid" (127).

A careful review of what in fact occurs in the USA and other Western countries reveals an array of interrelations and even support of the church by the state. Examples include the use of oaths taken on the Bible in courts of law, assignment of chaplains to legislative bodies, recognition of religious ceremonies of marriage as legally binding, and recognition of clergy as persons who can attest to declarations on some civil documents. All of these involve some supportive connections between church and state (Miller 1986, 284).

I would suggest that the separation of church and state can never be absolute but is always a matter of degree. To talk about this in all-or-nothing terms, as is done by Doerr and Menendez in their passionate opposition to parochiaid, is fundamentally misguided. The more appropriate question is whether state support for religious schools falls under an acceptable *degree* of separation of church and state. Doerr and Menendez, in their review of court cases regarding parochiaid, are forced to introduce the language of degrees. They refer to various court opinions which talk of an "intolerable degree of entanglement," or they distinguish between "mere excessive entanglement" and the "merger of church and state" (1991, 117). This would seem to allow for the possibility of some entanglement – a much more realistic position, I would suggest. But such a position undercuts the separationist argument against any form of tax aid to religious schools, though of course there is still the worry that such aid "unduly entangles the government in matters religious (120).

Complete separation of church and state is impossible. It is also undesirable. A strict interpretation of the SCS principle entails that the deepest beliefs of millions of Americans (or Canadians) are somehow rendered suspect in terms of having any implications for political life (Carter 1993, 113). Various writers have underscored the seeming hostility to, or at least indifference towards, people of faith and the churches to which they belong, given a strictly secular understanding of the state and a strict interpretation of the SCS principle.[11] Indeed, the resulting jurisprudence has promoted a freedom from religion rather than a freedom of religion (Viteritti 1996, 140). One of the fundamental purposes of the SCS principle – freedom of religion – is therefore undermined. Without intermediate institutions such as churches to challenge what is done by governments, there is the terrible danger of tyranny, as Tocqueville reminded us some 150 years ago (Carter 1993, 123). A strict separation of church and state further fails to do justice to the ability of religion to contribute to the development of civic virtues that are essential to the healthy functioning of a democratic state. There is abundant empirical evidence to support this connection.[12] The state needs the church.

DEGREES OF ENTANGLEMENT

I would suggest that it is the impossibility and the undesirability of completely separating church and state that lie behind the gradual move of the courts in the USA towards a more accepting attitude of state support for religious schools. Once it is acknowledged that a strict interpretation of the SCS principle is impossible or undesirable, then one is forced to talk about degrees of entanglement.

Once one allows a degree of entanglement between church and state, a difficulty emerges: namely, defining exactly what constitutes an acceptable degree. In 1971, the Supreme Court in the U.S.A. introduced a three-part "Lemon test," which forbids any government action that: (1) has no secular purpose; (2) has a "primary effect" of advancing religion; and (3) fosters "excessive entanglement with religion" (Viteritti 1996, 133). But the Lemon test has proved well-nigh impossible to apply. Justice Rehnquist argued in 1985 that the Lemon test "has no basis in the history of the amendment it seeks to interpret, is difficult to apply, and yields unprincipled results."[13]

Doerr and Menendez grudgingly allow for at least "peripheral forms of tax aid to religious institutions," when they appeal to some elements of this Lemon test to justify their position (1991, 127). For example, they maintain that certain kinds of state aid may be made available to parochial schools, e.g. bus transportation, textbook loans, and services for the educational health and welfare of the student, "so long as it is manifestly clear that the performance of these services is absolutely secular" (121).

The distinction between services that are "absolutely secular" and those that are sacred is not as neat and tidy as assumed by Doerr and Menendez and the Lemon test. For one thing, even as the Court found, the secular and the religious missions of parochial schools are "inextricably intertwined" (Viteritti 1996, 189). Cannot religious education and even religious nurture encourage intellectual growth, and even develop critical abilities, which are generally accepted as legitimate "secular" objectives of education? Against this possibility Doerr and Menendez devote an entire chapter showing the pervasiveness of religious aims in church schools (1991, ch. 2). Their objective is to show that such schools are not sufficiently committed to "secular" academic objectives to merit tax support. This argument only holds if you assume that religious objectives are incompatible with academic objectives. This is to commit the either-or fallacy. Surely it is possible to achieve academic aims via religious means. If this is so, then perhaps government aid should be extended to the religious component of church schools: they fulfil the "secular" objectives for which state support is no problem. Indeed, studies show that religious schools do fulfil the same secular objectives as state-maintained schools, and do so even better than these schools (Bryk et al. 1993).

PUBLIC/PRIVATE

The sacred/secular dichotomy inherent in the above argument as well as in the Lemon test is closely related to another dichotomy which deserves separate treatment. The public/private dichotomy can be seen as another expression of the SCS principle which is at the heart of objections to offering tax aid to religious schools.

The quotation at the head of this chapter gives concrete expression to this public/private dichotomy. This quotation is from a letter of the Alberta School Boards Association expressing opposition to a call for more funding for private (religious) schools in Alberta. The letter repeatedly tries to tie public funding to public purposes, values, and goals, and then highlights the private nature of religious schools whose supporters prefer private purposes and values.[14] When the Alberta government decided to increase funding to religious schools a year later, the same association fired off a strong letter making the point once again: "Private schools are just what the name implies – private, and no further public money should be advanced to support them."[15] The sentiments expressed in these statements are widely shared. Opposition to the funding of religious schools is often expressed in language that draws on the public/private dichotomy because the use of this language makes it seem contradictory to use "public money for private education."[16]

The distinction between the public and the private domain has been at the heart of the philosophy of liberalism since the seventeenth and eighteenth centuries. From the beginning it has also been a problematic distinction. J.S. Mill gave us the classic formulation of this distinction, but even he ran into problems with it.[17] Today there is much ferment in the philosophy of liberalism. Much of the debate centres around this same public-private distinction. There is difficulty in defining the so-called "public values." And "private values" invariably turn out to be very public in their effects. If the distinction between public and private values is problematic, then so is the argument that private schools should not be publicly funded.

Contrary to the letters from the Alberta School Boards Association, I would suggest that religious schools do not just support private purposes, values, and goals over public purposes, values, and goals. Indeed, I would argue that religious schools do a lot of public good, and therefore deserve public support. For example, many (if not most) religious schools teach their students to be honest, kind, tolerant, and loving.[18] They encourage children to be hard-working, to participate in the community, and to support their government. The teaching of these values contributes to the public good. Indeed, one recent study has shown that religious high schools do better than public high schools in promoting the basic social and political purposes that were once the inspiration of American public education and gave these schools the title of "common school" (Bryk et al. 1993). Religious schools that serve the common good as well as if not better than public schools therefore surely deserve public funding.

Finally, religious people are part of the public. They are ordinary citizens who pay taxes and who deserve the same rights as those who don't claim to be religious. The "public" in a democracy includes everyone – atheists and Christians, male and female, those of French background and those of English background. In a democracy, all members of the public should be treated equally, and it is unfair to relegate the deepest convictions of one segment of the public to the private domain (Carter 1993, 115). So-called "public knowledge" is inextricably intertwined with what is often thought to belong to the private domain. All knowledge rests on faith, as I will argue in a later chapter. If, therefore, some of the public citizens want to have their children educated in accordance with public knowledge that is grounded in their deepest convictions, their desires should not be dismissed on the grounds that they belong to the private domain.

I conclude that objections to funding religious schools based on the commonly made public/private distinction are unsound. Religious schools are as committed to the common good, to public values, and to public knowledge as are public schools. Nothing stops a liberal democracy from having religious schools authorized by a public authority, held accountable by the public, and financed by the public, to introduce a few other dimensions often associated with the notion of a public school.[19]

A REVISED SCS PRINCIPLE

There are problems with a strict interpretation of the SCS principle. There can be no absolute separation of church and state. Nor is such separation desirable. However, it is not my intention to challenge the SCS principle in its entirety. There is still something very important and beneficial about the SCS principle that needs to be retained. I still support some of the basic ideas that have always been inherent in the SCS principle – protection of religious freedom, protection of minority religions from religious and secular establishments, ensuring that all religions are treated fairly, protection of religion from unnecessary state intrusion and control, and ensuring that religions are independent centres of power – independent moral voices that can act as intermediaries between the citizen and the state.[20]

According to Viteritti, the high wall of separation between church and state began to fall in 1980 (1996, 135). He goes on to show that although the Rehnquist Court has not always demonstrated a consistent First Amendment philosophy, it has gradually moved towards a clearer set of guidelines for interpreting the First Amendment, guidelines that have produced a more liberal approach to government aid to religious schools. Viteritti summarizes these guidelines in terms of three basic points:

(1) that aid is given to an individual parent or child rather than to an institution; (2) that any benefit accrued by an institution is the result of individual choices made by the parent or student; and (3) that aid is appropriated on a

religiously neutral basis to those who attend public schools as well as those who attend private and parochial schools. (1996, 142)

Following these principles consistently would ultimately suggest that "tuition assistance provided to parents who choose to send their children to schools with religious affiliations is permissible under the United States Constitution" (116).

Here again I want to move beyond constitutional and contextual considerations to a focus on philosophical argument. I will focus on the basic ideas behind a reinterpreted SCS principle in order to see what they entail with regard to the funding of religious schools.

DISESTABLISHMENT IMPLICATIONS

One of the very legitimate concerns behind the SCS principle is the prohibition of state coercion with regard to religious belief (Carter 1993, 189). Nor should state power ever be used to establish one particular religion. Sadly, the history of Christianity is replete with violations of these key implications of the SCS principle – the Holy Roman Empire, Cromwell's England, and Calvin's Geneva. More sadly still, remnants of such constantinianism persist today, what with the established Church of England, Muslim fundamentalism supported by the state in Arab countries, and the agenda of the "religious Right" in Great Britain and North America.

The disestablishment implications of the SCS principle, when applied to the area of education, would suggest that it is wrong to use a state-maintained public school system to impose one religion on students. I therefore agree with the banning of school prayers in public school classrooms. Carter is surely right in maintaining that it is impossible to design a non-coercive approach to school prayer (1993, 188).

I also disagree with current legislation in Great Britain which requires that all maintained schools should provide religious education and a daily act of collective worship – the latter to be "wholly or mainly of a broadly Christian character."[21] The state should never impose a particular kind of religious worship on its citizens, particularly in the case of children. Sadly, constantinianism is still with us, and is often advocated by evangelical Christians.[22]

By the same token, it is wrong for the government to enforce non-religious orthodoxy on its people. There are many people today who have come to realize that public schooling in North America has become essentially secular, if not anti-religious.[23] This leads Stephen Arons to describe the culture of American schooling in terms of *Compelling Belief* (1986). Such compulsion has generated endless battles over the control of orthodoxy in our schools. Schooling cannot be value-free, according to Arons (205). The solution, according to part 4 of Arons's study, is the application of the SCS principle, properly understood, which would in turn require a reconstruction of our school system.

Such a reconstruction would be based upon the individual's right to be free of government coercion where the formation of beliefs and conscience are at stake. Wherever beliefs, worldviews, values, or ideologies are at stake, the Constitution must be read to impose the same government neutrality as is brought into play with regard to religion. (Arons 1986, 212)

This can only be accomplished if we break away from the present majoritarian control of schooling, and facilitate genuine school choice for all families, unless compelling justifications exist. And this would further entail full public financial support of religious schools.[24]

IMPLICATIONS OF FAIRNESS

I have argued that strict government neutrality with regard to religion is impossible. There will necessarily be some degree of entanglement between church and state. Therefore, a proper interpretation of the SCS principle requires that the state be strictly impartial with regard to the support of the various religions. I would further maintain that the state should also be impartial with respect to religious and secular ideologies. This principle of fair treatment is, of course, central to all Western democratic societies.

Therefore, in allocating aid directly or indirectly to religious educational institutions, it is important that such aid be distributed equally. All religious institutions must be treated the same (Viteritti 1996, 190). It is further important that such aid be appropriated on a religiously neutral basis to those who attend public schools as well as those who attend private or parochial schools (142, 190).[25] A consistent application of the SCS principle would require equal funding for state-maintained public schools and religious schools.

What is rather alarming is that this principle of fairness is so often blatantly disregarded when it comes to arguments concerning government support for religiously based schools. We have seen, for example, that in Canada Roman Catholic schools get full government funding in several of the provinces. Yet, despite the reaffirmation of the principle of fairness in the 1982 Charter of Rights and Freedoms, large discrepancies continue to exist in the support given to independent religious schools compared to the support given to Roman Catholic schools. Surely the principle of fairness entails that all religious schools should be given equal financial support.[26]

The same discriminatory practice also exists in Great Britain, where about a third of the state-maintained schools are Church of England or Roman Catholic schools which have voluntary status and hence get full government funding. Yet, this status is being denied to independent religious schools who have been aptly described by Walford (1991b) as the "reluctant private sector" since they would like to "opt in" to the state-maintained sector but are prevented from doing so by discriminatory legislation and practice.[27] Walford admits there is "considerable power" in the argument for equal funding for *all* schools (1991b, 130).

One way to get around this fair treatment implication of the SCS principle would of course be to eliminate government funding for all religious schools.[28] This is behind a frequently recurring suggestion in Great Britain that the present dual system of education is in need of a thorough reevaluation.[29] It is no doubt also part of the rationale behind a strict interpretation of the separation of church and state in the USA. What better way to ensure non-preferential treatment than consistently to give no support to any religious schools?

Three problems arise here. First, it can be argued that discrimination still occurs, because, while many parents are quite content to send their children to state-maintained secular schools, many religious parents are not, and hence they are being treated differentially. For example, these parents are penalized through double educational expenditures. Magsino is surely right in stressing that equality or justice "imposes a prima facie obligation on government to support private-school parents no less than it does their public-school counterparts" and that "the burden of proof falls on an institution or person practicing differential treatment of others to prove that the practice can be justified" (1986, 245, 256–7). Yes, the principle of fairness can be overridden, but only in the face of stronger considerations. Whether there are any compelling reasons for such differential treatment is in fact the question that is being considered in the other chapters of this book.

The second problem with the seemingly non-discriminatory policy of providing no financial support for all religious schools is that another kind of discrimination still remains: this arrangement seems to favour the rich. Democratic governments, in keeping with the principles of freedom, generally do allow private and religious schools to operate, though without funding. But now the poor are discriminated against because many of them simply cannot afford the extra costs involved in sending children to a religious school. This problem should be of particular concern to those who uphold some form of egalitarianism, which will be the focus of the next chapter. Here I merely want to note that this arrangement seems to provide cover for what is underneath a kind of religious differentiation. It strikes me as odd that differentiation on the basis of wealth is so readily accepted as a cover-up for religious discrimination.

The final problem with trying to overcome preferential treatment of some religious schools by providing no support for all religious schools is that this position again assumes that it is possible to withdraw all support of the state for religion. Again there is the assumption of a complete separation of church and state, which I believe to be impossible.

CHURCH/STATE/PARENTS

There is one final point that needs to be made with regard to the funding of religious schools and the SCS principle. Here I return to the traditional understanding of the SCS principle and bring to the fore an important assumption that is being made when this principle is used to object to funding for religious schools. Problems of church/state separation with regard to education only arise if it is assumed that education is the responsibility of the state or of the church. If either of these assumptions is rejected the problems really disappear. I have argued that parents have the primary responsibility for educating their children. If religious schools are under the jurisdiction of parents, and not churches, then the state could fund these schools without violating the SCS principle.

This is a central point in Viteritti's defence of the constitutionality of public funding of religious schools. Viteritti maintains that more emphasis needs to be placed on the free exercise rights of individuals in interpreting the First Amendment (1996, 178, 187). Based on the child benefit theory, financial aid for education can be given to the parent or the child rather than the institution, thus circumventing the idea that the state is giving direct aid to a religious institution.[30] Thus, Viteritti can argue that providing tuition assistance to parents who choose to send their children to schools with religious affiliations is permissible under the United States Constitution (116). It is also permissible given the acceptance of the SCS principle.

It could further be argued that the state shouldn't be involved in providing education at all, in which case, again, problems with regard to the separation of church and state would not emerge. Even if it is granted that the state has some responsibilities in the area of education, this still does not necessarily create problems with regard to the SCS principle, if religious schools are under the control of parents.

One important function of the state with regard to education is to protect the rights of parents to bring up their children within the religious (or irreligious) commitments that the parents themselves hold. I believe the state today needs to be especially careful about the power of individuals (or groups of individuals) to determine the values that are taught to other people's children. A government-determined orthodoxy, whether religious or secular, conveyed by a state-maintained system of common schools, is surely a violation of the very religious freedom that the SCS principle was meant to protect.

I would further add that a key to defining a proper balance between the intermingling and the separation of church and state is to keep separate the notions of state *financial support* for education, and state *provision* of education. As will be suggested in the following chapter, an argument can be made for state support of education in order to ensure equality of opportunity. This does not at all entail that the state must be involved in the actual provision of education, or in determining the organizational structure of education (Shapiro 1986, 267, 274). Schools could be managed by societies of like-minded parents, but supported by the state. A voucher system is another way to separate the financial support and the provision of education, though it is quite beyond the scope of this book to defend a voucher system. Here I am mainly concerned to defend the idea of a plurality of schools, religious and secular, all of which could legitimately be funded by the state.

SOME PRACTICAL IMPLICATIONS FOR RELIGIOUS SCHOOLS

1.   *Government support of religious schools*: In this chapter I have argued that even if we accept the SCS principle with proper qualifications, there is nothing wrong with the state providing full funding for religious schools, as long as this support is distributed equally to all schools, religious or secular. Of course, such financial support will invariably have some strings attached. As already noted in chapter 4, many religious schools are very concerned about government regulations. Barman reports that some non-funded independent schools were deeply opposed to a new School Act which offered partial funding of such schools in return for mandatory registration, because they were afraid of government intervention (1991, 24). This attitude is not at all unusual.[31] But it is unfortunate and misguided. The state has a legitimate interest in the education of its citizens. Religious schools therefore should accept a certain degree of state supervision and control.

2.   *Funding and compromise*: Once one accepts the inescapability of some degree of state supervision and control as a result of financial

support, a problem emerges. How does one define an acceptable level of such supervision and control? I will have more to say about this in subsequent chapters. Here I merely wish to focus on one danger.

There have been several studies on the effects of government funding on religious schools. In a British Columbia study, Barman maintains that increased funding for religious schools and the increased accountability to the public that runs parallel to such funding not only affects but even "tempers" the philosophical and religious underpinnings of such schools. Indeed, she suggests that "[t]he didactic function of most such schools now differs little from that of their public counterparts" (1991, 26). Wagner, in her study of "God's Schools" in America, similarly maintains that these schools "are fraught with compromise with the American popular culture that surrounds them. The Christian alternative school is not as alternative as it could be" (Wagner 1990, 5; cf. Rose 1988, ch. 10). I would add that such schools are often not as alternative as they *should* be.

If there is one significant and unique contribution that religious schools and colleges can make to the state and to society at large, it is to serve as a counter-cultural force and to provide responsible critique of the destructive values that often dominate our societies and state-maintained schools.[32] They can serve as a much-needed conscience to societies that are often facing a moral void. Sandel has recently described America as "in search of a public philosophy," as needing a substantive moral discourse that is adequate to sustaining democratic life (1996). Perhaps religious schools and colleges are the unique solution to this search and this need. Of course, *how* this is done within such schools is quite another matter. Here I will only remind the reader that constantinian attitudes must be scrupulously avoided.

The danger inherent in religious schools and colleges accepting public funding is that such schools will no longer have the courage to fulfil the unique functions described in the previous paragraph. In accepting public funding, or in seeking more public funding, there is a tendency to move towards increasing secularization.[33] I am not convinced that this slide towards secularization is inescapable, but religious schools need to be careful that they do not betray their religious identity for a mess of secular pottage. And governments need to make sure that the regulations and requirements they impose on religious schools and colleges are not such as to undermine the unique religious identity of the institutions.[34]

3. Religious schools and religious freedom: Religious schools ought to be supportive of religious freedom for all. Unfortunately, this is not always so. In this chapter I have already referred to the controversy over a private member's bill introduced in the Alberta legislature in 1997,

attempting to increase the level of funding to private schools in Alberta. The government responded by setting up a Private Schools Funding Task Force with a mandate to provide Albertans with the opportunity to express their views on how private schools should be funded. Among those making presentations to the Task Force during the public hearings was the Medicine Hat Catholic Board of Education.[35]

Strangely, this document vigorously opposed additional funding for other religious schools – indeed, this was the position of other Catholic schools and boards in Alberta. Much was made of the "private" nature of other religious schools. Catholic schools by contrast were described as "a publicly funded separate school system." It was also emphasized that because of their private nature, these other religious schools only serve "some" students. The fact that Catholic schools serve primarily Catholic students was somehow forgotten. The obvious inconsistencies of this position, together with the appeal to question-begging definitions, represent a failure in logic. Even more tragic, though, is that this position also represents a failure in faith. Surely a school board representing the Catholic faith should be supportive of equal rights for other religious schools. Surely, a Catholic school board should not take refuge in the constitutional protection they have at the present time. Constitutions can, after all, change, as should be apparent from recent developments in the Canadian educational scene.[36] Religious schools should surely act on ethical and religious principles, and therefore should support equal freedom for all religious groups.

Thankfully, there are also positive examples of Christians supporting equal religious freedom for all. Sweet, in describing the Dutch model of educational pluralism where over 80 per cent of all schools are publicly funded religious schools, also describes how the extent of Dutch tolerance has been put to the test in the light of a recent influx of a significant number of Hindu and Muslim immigrants to the Netherlands (1997, 128–9). The demand by these new immigrants for their own schools sparked a brand new debate. Arie Oostlander, a member of the Christian Democratic party, a party that was actually founded over the issue of free Christian education, argues thus: "It's because we know how important religion is to us that we have a responsibility to create similar opportunities for others" (Sweet 1997, 130). I would suggest that some Canadian (and some British)[37] Christians have much to learn from the Dutch Christian Democratic party.

7 The Charge of Elitism and Other Economic Objections

> Parental choice has become a powerful ideological force which has been used, in part, to conceal the New Right's political objective for a more inequitable and hierarchical educational system.
>
> Geoffrey Walford, *Educational Politics: Pressure Groups and Faith-based Schools*

"Slay this dragon for public schools!" This startling call to arms appeared in the lead editorial of the *Toronto Star* (4 February 1989). Exactly what dragon was threatening to devour public education? The possibility of "private" school funding (i.e. extending financial aid to independent religious schools). The editorial went on to cite two arguments often raised against "private" school funding. First, because of underfunding, this was the wrong time to "take more money from the public schools." Second, "if parents want a special religious or luxury-packaged education, they should expect to pay for it."[1]

In chapter 1, reference was made to a private member's bill introduced in the Alberta legislature in the spring of 1997, proposing increased funding for independent religious schools. The government responded by setting up a Private Schools Funding Task Force, mandated to review questions about funding, among other issues. Two concerns about increasing funding to independent religious schools surfaced again and again in submissions from the public and separate school boards in Alberta.[2] First a financial one; it is silly to use taxpayers' dollars to create another educational bureaucracy which would only duplicate the services of an already trimmed public education system – "it will cost more for everyone."[3] The second involved the elitism of independent religious schools. Interestingly, representatives from Catholic schools (which in Alberta are publicly funded) objected to the religious exclusivism of independent religious schools. "Private schools serve *some* Albertans. There will always be the elite who prefer to opt out of the public education system."[4]

In the last chapter I began to deal with some economic considerations that were linked to the issue of the separation of church and
state. I have begun this chapter with illustrations of some additional
objections that call for a response: the charge of elitism, and the claim
that we simply cannot afford a two-tiered, or even a multi-tiered, educational system. Sometimes these concerns are raised to object to the
funding or the increased funding of such schools. Sometimes they surface as a way of objecting to the very existence of religious schools
(Miller 1982).

THE EGALITARIAN IDEAL

The ideal of equality lies at the heart of the vision for public education
or common schooling. In chapter 2, I examined how social cohesion
was at the root of the American dream of a universal system of public
education. But equality was seen as a key ingredient of social cohesion.
"The strict equality of the classroom, educators argued, would temper
the arrogance of the rich, give hope to the poor, and wear away the
sense of distance that always threatened to develop into an 'animosity
of orders'" (McClellan 1985, 39). E.G. West, in his classic study of the
political economy of state education in Great Britain, says this: "In everyday discussion on education, the phrase 'equality of opportunity'
crops up probably more often than any other" (1970, 50).

This same egalitarian ideal is also often used as an argument against
private or religious schools and their being publicly funded. Walford
concludes his study of pressure-group politics of faith-based schools in
England with a warning about "the deleterious effects that increased
diversity may have on equity and justice for all children."[5] Non-public
schools tend to be academically selective, tend to enrol children of
families with higher average incomes, are not required to serve handi-
capped students, and have a racial imbalance, Doerr and Menendez
argue, and therefore parochiaid (public financial aid for parochial
schools) is wrong (1991, 134, 146–7).

While a detailed evaluation of the egalitarian ideal is obviously far
beyond the scope of this chapter, some problems should at least be
noted. There are difficulties, first of all, with regard to the meaning of
"equality" (West 1970, ch. 5). Equivocation abounds in discussions
about equality in education. Does "equality" mean equality of opportunity or equality of achievement or outcomes? Even the term "equality
of opportunity" is not without problems.

Amy Gutmann identifies three different interpretations of the ideal
of equal educational opportunity (1987, 128). (a) Maximization: In its
most liberal interpretation, the principle of equal educational oppor-

tunity requires that the state devote as many resources to schooling as necessary in order to maximize the life chances of all its future citizens. (b) Equalization: A more common interpretation requires that the state distribute educational resources so that the life chances of the least advantaged child are raised as far as possible towards those of the most advantaged. (c) Meritocracy: Probably the most common interpretation of equal educational opportunity requires the state to distribute educational resources in proportion to children's natural ability and willingness to learn.

My intent in outlining Gutmann's helpful analysis is to highlight the difficulties in defining what "equality of educational opportunity" means. There is simply a lot of confusion concerning what is meant by "equality" in discussions about education. This same ambiguity also colours charges of elitism often made against religiously based schools. It is therefore difficult to understand and respond to these charges.

Not only is the definition of equality elusive, the desirability of the egalitarian ideal is by no means obvious. Indeed, as Pojman (1991), Narveson (1993), and John White (1994) have reminded us, arguments for egalitarianism are rare. For the most part, egalitarians seem content simply to affirm the ideal – they don't think it needs argument.[6] In a review of "arguments" often implicitly made, Pojman, Narveson, and White find all of them wanting.[7]

Perhaps the most influential argument involves the moral arbitrariness of desert. Rawls, for example, has argued that the differences between us that are due to our basic endowments from Nature, and also those that are due to our being born into "happy family and social circumstances," are "arbitrary from a moral perspective." Why? Because the causes of these social inequalities are beyond our control and therefore we cannot be thought to *deserve* them.[8]

We see here the basis for the persistence and the passion behind egalitarian defences made for a state-maintained system of education. The purpose of state education is to overcome the arbitrariness of children's natural assets. As a sociologist once put it, "It is the business of education to eliminate the influence of parents on the life-chances of the young."[9] This kind of thinking also lies behind the concerns for any inequalities that might be introduced by allowing for independent religious schools.

Surely there is something terribly arbitrary about this admittedly historic mission of the state-maintained system of education. Surely there comes a point where we need to accept what we are born with, both the limitations and the advantages that are the outcome of a "natural (or divine) lottery" (Rawls 1971, 74). Intellectually talented children surely deserve more education than those who are disadvantaged, even if the former cannot take credit for their greater talents. Thus there would seem to be some truth to the meritocracy interpretation of the ideal of equal educational opportunity which does give some weight to inequality.[10]

Further, defenders of equality, including Rawls, are forced to concede that some inequality might be justified if it benefits the worst off in a society.[11] In fact, a thoroughgoing radical egalitarianism very quickly becomes absurd, as it destroys all difference and all variety, resulting in the impoverishment of society as a whole (Gutmann 1987, 133). To fully equalize educational opportunity would also entail a violation of an important liberal ideal of family autonomy.[12] It would further be very difficult, if not impossible, for a government to enforce full equality (West 1970, 60–1). Hence Nagel's pessimism concerning an egalitarian society, despite his strong sympathies for it: "[A] strongly egalitarian society populated by reasonably normal people is difficult to imagine and in any case psychologically and politically out of reach" (1991, 128).

Despite these problems, there is still something to be said for the ideal of equality.[13] I want to affirm a moderate form of egalitarianism, very much along the lines of Gutmann's democratic interpretation of equal educational opportunity, which involves a blend of equalization and meritocracy. Surely there should be a minimal level of educational opportunity that should be equally distributed to all children so that they can participate effectively in the democratic process. But, as various writers have shown, even this goal is not so much driven by the desire for an equal society as it is based on the desire to help others to flourish.[14] Beyond this minimum threshold, however, educational opportunity may be, and I would argue should be, distributed according to merit (Gutmann 1987, 134, 136–9).

I therefore conclude that the charge of elitism against religious schools is not as serious a charge as is commonly assumed. Radical egalitarianism is indefensible and impractical. And in so far as the existence of independent religious schools does preserve some degree of inequality within society, I believe we need to accept this as normal and good.

I would further argue that Walford's oft-expressed concern that pleas for more parental choice are ideologically driven, and that they "conceal the New Right's political objective for a more inequitable and hierarchical educational system," is somewhat misplaced (1995, 111). I, for one, am defending parental choice while at the same time conceding a good deal of truth to the ideal of equal educational opportunity for all children. Clearly I am allowing for some inequality, but, as I have argued, the radical egalitarianism that Walford assumes is impractical and indefensible. There is also an *ad hominem* element in

Walford's charge. Conspiracy theories deserve to be treated with a good deal of suspicion.

ECONOMIC ELITISM

We have already seen that religious schools are frequently described as being elitist or symbols of privilege. Doerr and Menendez maintain that independent religious schools enrol children of families with average income levels considerably higher than those of public school students (1991, 134). An Alberta public school teacher recently waxed poetic in responding to a proposal to increase funding for religious schools in this province. He argued that this would result in "a system which would lead to the fragmentation of a society into enclaves of privilege in a wasteland of the dispossessed."[15]

Certainly there are some schools in the non-public sector of schooling in Canada, Great Britain, and the USA that cater to the wealthy and are very obviously elitist. These schools are not necessarily religiously based. They are not the focus of this study. The schools being defended here are independent schools whose separateness centres primarily on their being religious.

With regard to independent religious schools in Canada, it is by and large a serious error to classify them as elitist in terms of wealth. It is true that families who send their children to these schools need to pay fees, but for many of the families this entails considerable sacrifice. Their willingness to do so is a measure of their commitment to religious education, and not a measure of their wealth. One Alberta study pointed out that 70 per cent of the families that send children to private schools in Alberta have incomes below the national average (Wagner 1995, 42). It should also be noted that the school fees charged are generally not exorbitant, and substantially lower than the per capita cost of state-maintained education. It is also important to keep in mind that at many religious schools, special funds are available to enable poorer families to send their children to these schools. In some such schools the fees charged are based on family income, which in effect means that the families with somewhat higher incomes are subsidizing the poorer.[16] The same can be said for independent religious schools in Great Britain and Catholic schools in America.[17]

Empirical evidence therefore overwhelmingly suggests that the charge of elitism against religious schools is unwarranted. Thus it is odd to find someone like Walford, who frequently warns against the dangers of such schools becoming elitist, admitting that "Christian schools are not themselves elitist" (1994a, 149). In fact, he concedes that some of these schools serve children from the most deserving segments of our society. Elsewhere he admits that the Netherlands provides an example of a country where the funding of religious schools has not led to elitism (1989, 220–1). Why then this continuing warning, when the evidence seems to point in the opposite direction? One can only conclude that there must be some ideological blinders at work in Walford's thinking. Yet he is very concerned about the ideological forces that supposedly conceal the New Right's political objective in their support for parental choice. Is this perhaps a case of finding a mote in another's eye when there is a beam in your own?

The fact remains, however, that the tuition fees of independent religious schools will prohibit some parents from sending their children to them. Hence the underrepresentation of families with incomes under $10,000 in American Catholic schools (Bryk et al. 1993, 71). Bursaries and ability-to-pay schemes can only go so far in eliminating financial difficulties. Thus it would seem that some degree of elitism remains. This problem, however, could be overcome if independent religious schools were supported in the same way as schools in the state-maintained sector. It seems a little unfair to charge these schools with a degree of elitism when there is an unwillingness to provide them with the resources that are available to state-maintained schools. It is also unfair, for the same reason, to criticize religious schools for not providing services for students with special needs, the handicapped and visually impaired (Doerr and Menendez 1991, 134). Given the resources that state-maintained schools have, religious schools could also accommodate all these needs.

There is a further point of contrast that needs to be noted. The charge of elitism against religious schools is often made against the backdrop that state-maintained schools are much better at fostering the ideal of equality. In response it needs to be pointed out that schools in the state-maintained sector are not as "equal" as is generally assumed (Holmes 1992, 38–9, 125). In any city there are obvious differences between schools located in the less prosperous neighbourhoods and those in the wealthier suburbs (Holmes 1998, 271). Fundraising is a feature that exists in virtually all state-maintained schools, and the differences between rich and poor neighbourhoods will again result in differences in funds raised and hence in the kind of provisions that can be offered in schools. Jonathan Kozol has graphically portrayed these differences in American state-maintained schools in his book *Savage Inequalities* (1991). He is not alone in expressing shame about how little is done to ensure equality of opportunity in state-maintained schools.[18]

The point being made in the previous paragraph is simply a factual claim. Since inequities occur in the state-maintained system, one is tempted to respond to the charge of elitism against independent religious schools by saying "You do it too. What is all the fuss about?" But this would be to commit the *tu quoque* fallacy. My purpose in describing the inequities that exist in public schools is rather to raise questions about the possibility of creating a completely egalitarian system of education, or of promoting equality via a state system of education. Perhaps there are limits on how much equality we can achieve. The evidence of the previous paragraph would then substantiate the argument of a previous section against the possibility of radical egalitarianism. The practical difficulties inherent in creating a fully egalitarian system of education might just arise because of the theoretical difficulties inherent in the egalitarian ideal itself.

Since the purpose of this study is not to deal with state education, but with a defence of independent religious schools against a variety of charges, I do not wish to pursue the point being made about state-maintained schools in the last few paragraphs. However, a final comparative point needs to be made. Perhaps independent religious schools might be better able to achieve the historical goal of equality of opportunity than a state-maintained system of education. An important recent study by Bryk and associates confirms the results of past studies showing that Catholic schools are in fact significantly better than public schools at serving the needs of the disadvantaged. "In the typical Catholic school, the biggest advantages accrue to the most disadvantaged students ... In fact, a student of the lowest social class in a disadvantaged Catholic high school is outperforming the majority of students in a comparable public school" (Bryk et al. 1993, 266). These data, together with evidence suggesting that the typical Catholic school is more internally diverse with regard to race and income than the typical public school (73), confirm a generalization made by Holmes that choice of schools based on religion may in fact be the best way to overcome the divisiveness that results from socio-economic distinctions within a society (1992, 73; 1998, 236).

We must also not forget the historical data which West refers to when he quotes another writer who points out that "there is probably no period in English history at which a greater number of poor men have risen to distinction" than the end of the eighteenth and the early part of the nineteenth century when a system of national education was deficient or rather non-existent (1970, 69).

ACADEMIC ELITISM

There is another form of elitism that worries opponents of independent religious schools. It is sometimes maintained that these schools are academically selective (Doerr and Menendez 1991, 134). Gutmann highlights the connection between academic elitism and the economic elitism of the previous section when she worries that "private schools will siphon off the most affluent and the academically best students, leaving public schools with a student body that is disproportionately poor, economically and academically" (1987, 116).

Shapiro highlights the way in which academic elitism can, in the end, undermine the goal of equal educational opportunity. Shapiro admits that state-maintained schools have not always served the disadvantaged or fostered equality of educational opportunity (1986, 272). He even allows for the possibility that religiously based schools might accomplish these tasks better. Yet, he objects to the funding of religious schools, and he does so by introducing some other considerations that relate to a kind of academic elitism. If public funding were extended to these schools, it might result in a large transfer of either the higher-achieving or the more affluent students from the public to the private schools, thus leaving public schools as "schools of second choice," which can no longer offer equal educational opportunity (272).

In response to such concerns, we need to be reminded of the problems inherent in the ideal of equal educational opportunity. Earlier in this chapter, I agreed with Gutmann that there is some truth to the "meritocracy" interpretation of the ideal of equal educational opportunity. There is something very unfair about depriving the academically better students of an education that will challenge them and help them to reach their full potential. Better students deserve a better education. That is why one finds enriched programs within the state-maintained system of education, which prides itself on providing equal educational opportunity. It is therefore unfair to point to academic elitism in religious schools, and to view this as a bad thing, when in fact it occurs and indeed *should* occur in all schools.

But, do religious schools serve primarily the academic elite? I have already referred to empirical studies which suggest that this is not the case. Bryk and associates have verified earlier studies, all of which have clearly shown that Catholic schools in America are more internally diverse with regard to race and income than the typical public school (1993, 73). Gutmann challenges the empirical assumptions underlying the above concerns thus: "Far from siphoning off only the best and the brightest, private schools admit students with almost as broad a range of abilities as public schools. Private schools are more segregated than public ones by religion, but not by class, race, or academic talent" (1987, 117).

Bryk does concede that there is some selectivity in the students who attend Catholic schools in the USA, in that some students transfer from Catholic elementary schools to public high schools, and this is for two reasons: financial and academic. The higher tuition fees at secondary schools force some children from less affluent parents to transfer. There is also evidence that the lower-achieving students in Catholic primary schools transfer to public high schools where the academic orientation is less demanding and where there is greater opportunity to enrol in business and vocational courses (Bryk et al. 1993, 186).

But even the little selectivity that does exist would be eliminated if equal funding were extended to religious schools. With a thoroughgoing structural pluralism within our educational system, there would eventually be a general redistribution of students, and it can be safely assumed that all schools would have the usual blend of academically superior, average, and academically weak students (West 1970, xlii–xlvii).

ELITISM OF COMMITMENT

There is one final expression of concern about elitism which focuses instead on parents. It is sometimes maintained that religious schools, because they demand special commitment on the part of parents, result in "a self-selected population." Often these parents are deeply concerned about education, and have the commitment and the ability to work towards improvements in education. Parents in such schools are "precisely the ones who are vital to the support of a strong public school system."[19] The growth of independent religious schools is therefore seen as depriving the public school of the needed support and commitment of parents who are especially concerned about education. As a result, public schools become weaker, "schools of second choice," and "a wasteland of the dispossessed."

Walford highlights the egalitarian concerns that underlie this argument. He too is concerned about the harm done to state schools because of the presence of private religious schools which result in the removal, from the state sector, of those parents who are most likely to ensure that high standards of provision and teaching are maintained. "The education provided in state schools may thus deteriorate with the exit of those parents with the greatest concern or financial resources" (Walford 1994a, 149). Walford goes on to argue that it is the duty of the state to ensure that the less privileged or powerful are not harmed by the actions of the more privileged or powerful.

Here again we need to be very careful with the radical egalitarian agenda that is driving Walford's and other critics' concerns. Earlier in this chapter I argued that many egalitarians concede that some differences in privilege and power can be allowed as long as everyone in society benefits. Walford therefore has to prove that there is indeed more harm than good in allowing committed parents to devote their resources and energy to schools of their choice.

Another problem with this argument is that it assumes that if there were no independent religious schools, parents who would be sending their children to these schools would instead direct their commitment and energies to the public school system. There are several considerations that make this assumption problematic. One of the problems in public schooling in Western countries is the sheer size of school districts and schools. This results in an increasing sense of alienation between parents and school bureaucracies (Holmes 1998, 203, 233). It is precisely because parents feel they have little or no input in the public school system that they are looking to independent religious schools. Here they are more directly in control of the education of their children.

Given the predominantly religious nature of the concerns of parents wanting to send their children to independent schools, it is further doubtful that the public schools could, in fact, respond to their primary concerns. Religious parents who would like to provide input to public schools are frustrated because of a basic incompatibility of values. Hence the increasing trend to send their children to independent religious schools.

It should finally be noted that this drain of parental energy and commitment from the state-maintained school system could be avoided if all independent religious schools were somehow incorporated into the public school system. The same would apply to the distribution of students. If our monolithic state-maintained system of education were replaced with a genuine structural pluralism, all schools would have the usual distribution of rich and poor, gifted and not so gifted, committed and not so committed, given proper regulation by the state. Indeed, there is evidence to suggest that with a significant decentralization and pluralization of education, the commitment of parents could be enhanced, and thus all would benefit.[20] Small is indeed beautiful!

LIMITED FUNDS

There is another very common and seemingly straightforward economic argument against public funding of independent schools – funds are limited. One writer goes so far as to suggest that it is time to forget about philosophical arguments and become practical – to support a public as well as a private school system from a limited, and often diminishing, pool of funds is ultimately going to hurt the education of *all* students.[21]

It is easy to be misled by this argument because of its disarming simplicity. But its fundamental flaw is quite easy to expose. Given society's commitment to cover the costs of educating all children, an additional commitment to fund independent religious schools will in the long run not add to the costs – it will merely involve a redistribution of the funds that are available for education (West 1970, xlii). There are only so many students to be educated. Government funding of independent religious schools will no doubt result in a transfer of some students from state-maintained schools to these schools, but over time the education costs of state-maintained schools should diminish in proportion to the loss of students experienced, and hence there should be no increase of overall costs.

In effect, the public failure to support independent religious schools, either partially or completely, really involves a saving in educational expenditure. This leads Bryk and associates teasingly to remind the American public that they might want to be concerned about the continued survival of Catholic schools. If all these schools were to collapse there would be a significant upsurge of pressure on the public purse as more than six hundred thousand students currently enrolled in 1,300 Catholic high schools entered the public sector (1993, 340).

Here it might be argued that a thoroughgoing structural pluralism in education will result in a greater number of smaller schools which will then make it impossible to take advantage of economies of scale (Doerr and Menendez 1991, 130). This argument was prominent in the recent dismantling of the unique denominational system of education in Newfoundland which was described in chapter 1. Interestingly, the final report of the 1992 Royal Commission admitted that it was not fair to make comparisons between denominational and non-denominational systems of education when known efficiencies could be introduced into the existing denominational system.[22] Very different figures therefore emerged with regard to the savings that might accrue with restructuring, revealing that there is a good deal of subjectivity involved in any comparative costing of differing systems of education.[23]

This subjectivity, no doubt, lies behind the high degree of public scepticism concerning expert advice on saving money by creating mega-structures in education and elsewhere. Holmes points to the strangeness of the argument for mega-structures when used by Western capitalists who, in most other areas, consider public monopoly to be inefficient (1992, 39). Holmes goes on to identify some countries which have a pluralistic system of education and yet have not run into any major financial problems. Australia, for example, has more than one-quarter of its students in publicly supported independent schools, and yet Australia spends considerably less on its schools than do some other countries in the West, such as Canada.[24]

Even if a pluralistic system of education did cost more than a state-maintained monolithic system, it could still be argued that the benefits outweigh the extra costs. Here we need to keep in mind that cost-effectiveness is not the only criterion that should be used in evaluating a system of education, or an economic system, for that matter. For example, quality of education surely should rank even higher than cost-effectiveness when assessing differing systems of education (Holmes 1992, 35).

Walford describes a "Human-Scale Education Movement" in England which has three main initiatives for action and support: minischools, small schools, and flexischooling, the latter approach involving the combining of school-based learning with home-based or community-based education.[25] Much of the disenchantment with state-maintained systems of education has to do with the sheer size of inflexible bureaucratic structures, and the resulting alienation felt by both students and parents. Thus, Ravitch and Viteritti point to a "decrepit," "industrial-era factory model of schooling," leading to "the highhandedness and uniformity of the hierarchical bureaucratic system," which they see as coming to an end in the growing demand for reform in American education (1997, 1–3). A pluralistic educational system of small schools might very well be worth the modest extra costs.

There is one final dimension of the limited-funding argument that deserves to be addressed. Some writers argue that, given the great variety of religions and Christian denominations, the attempt to accommodate them all, either as alternative schools within a public system or in a radically pluralistic system of education, will lead to an uncontrollable and harmful segmentation of the public school system.[26] In fact, support for religious schools might very well still leave the public school system as the major school system of most Western democracies.[27]

The assumption that there will be an unlimited demand for a variety of religious schools also fails to acknowledge the possibility of government-imposed controls on the proliferation of such schools. Surely it is possible for a government to develop certain guidelines concerning the proliferation of schools which would take into account such very legitimate considerations as financial constraints. These sorts of controls seem to have been operative in Newfoundland, where, until recently, the entire system of public education was divided along denominational lines. Smaller denominational groups cooperated to form "Integrated School Districts" representing the following denominations and nearly 60 per cent of the population: Anglican, Moravian, Presbyterian, Salvation Army, and the United Church of Canada. Catholic and

Pentecostal Committees governed the other two major kinds of schools in the province.[28] The one obvious problem with the pluralistic system in Newfoundland was that it did not do justice to the "non-Christian" public. I would suggest that if a secular school system had been allowed to develop alongside the religious school systems, this would have led, eventually, to a majoritarian secular system of education along the lines that have been proposed by Holmes (1992). Such an adjustment would have made the radical structural revisions that have just been introduced in Newfoundland unnecessary (although I would concur with the need to separate religious schools from churches).

CONCLUSION

The main purpose of this chapter has been to answer various objections often raised against independent religious schools that relate in some way to economics. Some of my arguments have entertained the idea of full funding for religious schools. It is not my aim in this chapter, however, to argue for full funding of religious schools. The central objective has rather been a defensive one. I have tried to show that the arguments against public funding of religious schools are not as strong as is generally assumed. To argue further that there should be full funding for such schools is beyond the scope of this chapter. Indeed, such an argument is premature, since there are other factors that might come into play and there are other arguments against religious schools that still need to be answered.

I will concede, however, that some of the arguments of this chapter seem to point in the direction of full government support for all schools. Exactly how the resulting system of educational pluralism should be organized and financed is quite another matter. One possibility would be to have religious schools operating under the umbrella of what is now thought of as the state-maintained system of education.[29] There are other possibilities.

I conclude by cautioning against one possible misinterpretation of the central argument of this chapter. It might seem that my argument is in keeping with the many calling for the privatization of schooling based on a market model.[30] Expanding the educational market, it is thought, will set up a healthy competition and thereby improve our public schools. Here I want to stress that the privatization agenda is not at all part of my own agenda. Indeed, I confess that I have grave problems with the assumptions of an *extreme* free-market ideology, particularly when applied to education. Here I concur with Bryk and associates, who point out that it is difficult to envision how unleashing selfishness can become a compelling force for human caring (1993,

311). I further believe that the state has some interests in education, as has been argued in the previous chapter, and therefore radical free-market metaphors are simply inappropriate. For me, as for many advocates of choice, the most pressing considerations are not economic and market-driven but moral and religious (Nord 1995, 354).

SOME PRACTICAL IMPLICATIONS FOR RELIGIOUS SCHOOLS

1. Equality and meritocracy: Independent religious schools should be structured in such a way as to express the moderate egalitarianism that I have defended in this chapter. A minimal level of educational opportunity should be equally distributed to all children in all schools within liberal democracies, including religious schools. Beyond this minimum threshold, educational opportunity should be distributed according to merit.

I would therefore suggest that advocates of religious schools should be alert to the dangers inherent in the market policies that are now shaping educational reform in Britain and North America. Brown (1994) has highlighted what he sees as a recent shift in thinking about educational opportunity, from an ideology of meritocracy, which supports a system of education where all must be given an equal opportunity of gaining access to jobs concomitant with their abilities, to "parentocracy," which involves a major program of privatization under the slogans of "choice," "freedom," "standards," and "excellence," and which is supported by market policies. This represents a shift towards "a system whereby the education a child receives must conform to the *wealth* and *wishes* of parents rather than the *abilities* and *efforts* of pupils" (51). In putting this shift into a sociological context, Brown maintains that, given hard economic times, the middle classes have decided that educational success has become too important to be left to the chance outcome of a formally open competition. Hence, they seek a form of "social closure" which ensures that their children will be guaranteed success despite their academic abilities (62).

Brown's analysis is weak for reasons already dealt with earlier in this chapter.[31] But it serves as a healthy warning about the danger that supporters of religious schools can run into. An emphasis on parental rights must not be used to cloak arguments for the protection of privilege. While there is nothing wrong with parents caring especially for their own children, this care must be balanced by a healthy level of concern for everyone's children. Particularity must be balanced with universality. Partiality must be balanced with equality, and this balance is possible, contrary to Nagel (1991).[32]

2.   Government regulations regarding equality: I would further argue that the state has a role to play in ensuring that the moderate egalitarianism that I have defended in this chapter is upheld in a society. The state can therefore insist that all children have access to a minimal level of education that is essential to "normal development."[33] However, it must careful not to insist on equality of outcomes – this would be unfair to gifted children, who deserve more by way of education so they can reach their full potential. Government regulations must therefore strike a balance between the equalization and meritocracy interpretations of the equal educational opportunity ideal considered earlier, and religious schools should submit to such regulations.

In response to religious schools which object to any government regulations, I want to draw on the advice given by Robert Tielman, who, though a humanist, defends the system of educational pluralism in the Netherlands, and who also recognizes a state responsibility to create the conditions under which both religious and humanist institutions can exist and thrive (Sweet 1997, 128). Tielman goes on to challenge the North American assumption that "the more laws you have, the less freedom you have." "We don't believe that. Because we live below sea level, we're aware of how much work it takes to survive. Our country exists because of incredible planning and regulation. This is the paradox of culture: you need a lot of legislation to guarantee freedom" (Sweet 1997, 128–9). Many supporters of religious schools need to learn this lesson. Creating equal opportunities for the education of all children might just require some legislation.

3.   Concern for the underprivileged: Religious schools should be characterized by special concern for the poor and the underprivileged. Jews and Christians in particular should be sensitive to this principle, given their view of God, who, because he has the same loving concern for each person he created, cares especially for the weak, the disadvantaged, and the oppressed.[34]

Sadly, God's concern for the weak and the poor is not always reflected among Christians today.[35] These same attitudes are sometimes evident in Christian schools where children from poor homes feel alienated and where parking lots include a good number of expensive cars. Schools that fail to reflect a biblical concern for the poor have forfeited their right to be called genuinely Christian schools.

But, as has already been argued earlier in this chapter, the charge of elitism against most religious schools is unwarranted, and most religious schools simply do not reflect the elitism that does exist in some private schools that obviously cater only to the very wealthy. As has already been pointed out, there are many religious schools in Britain, and Catholic schools in the United States, that have an enviable record in serving the underprivileged. This is as it should be.

4. Cooperation: Earlier in this chapter, reference was made to the problem of the great variety of religions and Christian denominations. Educational systems simply cannot incorporate all the religious difference that exists in most Western societies. There is therefore a need for religious groups to cooperate in the area of providing education for their children. Among Christian denominations, there is surely more agreement than disagreement concerning the basic doctrines of Christianity that shape the curriculum of a Christian school. I would suggest that the differences in doctrine occur most often at the more peripheral level. Therefore there should be no need for each denomination to demand its own school. I would suggest that even Catholics and Protestants have more in common with regard to educational philosophy than is commonly realized. Where there are differences, it should be easy to accommodate these within the context of a common Christian school by way of special classes that allow for education with regard to denominational differences. The Integrated School System of Newfoundland, referred to earlier, serves as a positive example. Active cooperation among religious groups with regard to education would go a long way in overcoming some of the monetary concerns of the critics of religious schooling.

PART FIVE

Problems of Narrowness in Religious Education

8 The Charge of Indoctrination

> As a total institution BBA [Bethany Baptist Academy] logically
> indoctrinates its students, refusing to treat issues to which
> doctrine applies as matters for discussion.
>
> Alan Peshkin, *God's Choice: The Total World of a*
> *Fundamentalist Christian School*

Barrow and Woods, in their popular introductory text in the philosophy of education, introduce the topic of indoctrination with an imaginative description of a Catholic school as a paradigm case of indoctrination (1988, 70). Susan Rose concludes her study of evangelical schooling in America with the comment that many of the practices in these schools are "limiting rather than liberating" (1988, 220). More recently still, James Dwyer, in a blistering attack against religious parents and religious schools and the traditionalist religious communities that they represent, charges that they strive "to repress the minds of children so that they are incapable of rejecting the community's beliefs or pursuing a life outside the community as adults" (1998, 168).

This chapter will provide only a very brief summary of a reply to the charge of indoctrination against religious schools and colleges. I have already answered this charge in a book entitled *Teaching for Commitment: Liberal Education, Indoctrination and Christian Nurture* (Thiessen 1993).[1] In what follows, readers will be referred to relevant parts of this book, should they want a more detailed discussion of the arguments being reviewed.

THE MEANING OF INDOCTRINATION

Much has been written about indoctrination by educational philosophers over the past forty years. Most of this writing has been within the analytic tradition, which places much importance on defining concepts.[2] Philosophers within this tradition attempt to find the necessary

and sufficient conditions that govern the use of the term "indoctrination." Four criteria have frequently been thought to be essential to defining "indoctrination."

Content (see Thiessen 1993, ch. 3): One of the central features most
often associated with indoctrination has to do with its content. Spiecker
(1991) and Kazepides (1989, 1994) both consider doctrines to be central to defining indoctrination. Doctrines are generally thought to be
found primarily in such areas as religion, politics, and perhaps also morality. Hence this comment by Kazepides: "The paradigm cases of indoctrination are to be found in religious communities and institutions"
(1994, 398). It is further generally assumed that science contains no
doctrines and hence indoctrination is thought to be impossible in science (Kazepides 1994, 397; Barrow and Woods, 1988, 76).

Methods (see Thiessen 1993, ch. 4): The content criterion of indoctrination is often closely associated with the methods criterion.
Peshkin, for example, in his critique of Bethany Baptist Academy, links
doctrine with methods when he argues that BBA indoctrinates its students, "refusing to treat issues to which doctrine applies as matters for
discussion" (1986, 284). Kazepides similarly links doctrines with questionable teaching methods: "The indoctrinator, because he is inculcat-
ing doctrines, must resort to some educationally questionable methods
such as failing to provide relevant evidence and argument or misapply-
ing them, misusing his authority, etc." (1994, 400). Generally it would
seem that indoctrination is associated with the use of non-rational
teaching methods (Spiecker 1991, 17).

Intention (see Thiessen 1993, ch. 5): Others have tried to define indoctrination in terms of certain intentions. Spiecker identifies "*content*
(doctrines) and *intention* (to still the development of a critical attitude
with regard to certain beliefs)" as the central conditions of "indoctrination."[3] More generally, indoctrination is frequently described in
terms of the intentional inculcation of unshakeable beliefs.[4]

Consequences (Thiessen 1993, ch. 6): The intention criterion is
closely connected to the final criterion often thought to be essential
in defining indoctrination – namely, consequences. Such consequences are frequently described in terms of "a closed mind." For example, indoctrination, for Hare, "involves coming to hold beliefs in a
closed-minded fashion" (1985, 21). Often the ideal of open-
mindedness is associated with the ability to criticize one's beliefs;
hence the frequent reference to "critical openness."[5] Indoctrination
therefore is thought to involve the failure to produce minds that are
open and critical.

Philosophers continue to disagree on which criterion, or which
combination of criteria, serves to define adequately the concept of in-

doctrination. As one philosopher has picturesquely described the situation, "various combinations of these standard ingredients still emerge from philosophers' kitchens with astonishing regularity, but nobody has yet apparently managed to digest anyone else's concoction."[6] It is not possible here to review the decisive objections that can be and have been raised against each of these criteria proposed as essential to indoctrination, except to note that philosophical debate concerning the right definition of indoctrination seems to get bogged down in a round robin of proposing definitions and searching for exceptions, "the usefulness of which is in inverse proportion to its truth" (Young 1988, 53).

Here I merely want to suggest that the failure of philosophers to agree on a correct analysis of the concept of indoctrination might indicate that the concept is vague, confused, and perhaps void of cognitive meaning. Thus I find it strange that despite all this disagreement, people go on making the charge of indoctrination against religious schools as though the meaning of the term were perfectly clear to them.[7] On the contrary, I would suggest that we are by no means clear what is really meant when the charge of indoctrination is made.

Here it might be objected that a concept can have meaning even though philosophers (and lay-people) are unable to define it.[8] Surely, we can use the word "indoctrination" correctly and yet be unable to give a satisfactory conceptual analysis of its meaning. Contrary to Nielsen, however, there is also disagreement about identifying paradigm or "clear, unequivocal cases" of indoctrination. For example, this chapter began with the citing of Catholic schools as a paradigm of indoctrination. Yet various writers, including Catholics, non-Catholics, and even some secularists, disagree.[9] Further, parents of religious persuasion frequently express concern about the secular humanistic philosophy that pervades the curriculum of the public school, and the point is often made that children are being indoctrinated into secular humanism.[10] Defenders of the public school consider the charge unfounded; the schools, they claim, are committed to objectivity and rational thought. Thus, charges and counter-charges abound. There is significant disagreement and debate about how and when it is appropriate to apply the word "indoctrination" to situations. I would therefore suggest that the inability of philosophers to define or to cite uncontentious paradigm cases of indoctrination is a reflection of more basic problems in the ordinary usage of the term.

This then leads to the first reply to the charge of religious indoctrination: if the concept of indoctrination is unclear, then the charge of indoctrination against religious schools is also unclear. Until a more adequate concept of indoctrination is forthcoming, there is a problem in understanding the charge and, thus, really no charge to answer. Of course, a word void of cognitive meaning can still have emotive meaning. I suggest that those making the charge of religious indoctrination against religious schools are, in fact, giving expression to their feelings of disapproval. Rational defence against such expressions of emotion is futile and unnecessary.

SOME UNDERLYING PROBLEMS WITH PAST DEFINITIONS

The first answer to the charge of indoctrination might suggest that little more can and should be said on the topic. After all, if the notion of indoctrination is unclear, should we not, to be consistent, stop talking about it? However, I believe that more can and should be said, but to do so we need to move beyond "the sterility" of conceptual analysis, and try to take, instead, "a contextualist approach" to understanding indoctrination.[11] In other words, we need to acknowledge that the way we use words is shaped, at least to some extent, by historical and social realities. "Meaning is not there to be found; it is created in social situations" (Nieman 1989, 55). Therefore we need to move on to consider the assumptions implicit in the way in which we have come to use a concept such as indoctrination.

I would further suggest that the continuing philosophical disagreement concerning the correct analysis of the concept of indoctrination reflects some deeper problems concerning the assumptions that underlie the charge of indoctrination together with the ideal of liberal education out of which this charge emerges. I therefore want to consider some of the key problems associated with the traditional understanding of indoctrination.

One of the central problems of past treatments of indoctrination is that they tend to focus on the shaping of beliefs, where beliefs are construed in strictly propositional ways. This leads philosophers to view indoctrination as essentially an epistemological issue, and hence the focus on non-rationality as an essential feature of indoctrination. I would suggest that we need to shift our focus from beliefs to the believer, from propositions to persons. This will of course introduce a host of subjective considerations, but these simply cannot be ignored when we consider indoctrination. We need to worry also, when talking about indoctrination, about the formation or reformation of personality in all its dimensions – coercive mind-control, high-pressure salesmanship, the programming and deprogramming of religious cults, the hidden curriculum of schools, advertising, and the influence of the media.[12]

Second, there is a problem with the epistemology that underlies most discussions about indoctrination. There seems to be general agreement that indoctrination has to do with the rational justification of individual beliefs. Concern about rationality comes up in each of the four criteria traditionally associated with indoctrination. What is missing in these accounts of rationality "is just about every issue that has occupied epistemological debate for the last several decades" (Page 1980, 37). There is a general failure to take into account important discussions in the philosophy of science, the sociology of knowledge, and Marxist and feminist critiques of liberal definitions of knowledge. Past accounts of indoctrination are generally based on a foundationalist approach to epistemology which assumes that knowledge must be grounded on "basic facts" which we can know with complete certainty and approach with complete objectivity. Foundationalism also assumes that there is a "basic methodology" which allows us to draw conclusions in a formal manner and which will again yield complete certainty. Both of these assumptions are seen as problematic by many philosophers today (see Wolterstorff 1984). Foundationalism assumes that epistemology can be conceived of as essentially distinct from psychological and sociological conditions under which beliefs develop, an assumption which again is being challenged by many today. More will be said about these epistemological assumptions in chapter 12.

The third problem that comes to the fore in past discussions of indoctrination is that they fail to address adequately the question of what is involved in educating young children. There are classic statements which acknowledge that education is a transaction between the generations of human beings in which newcomers to the scene (i.e. children) are *initiated* into the human inheritance of sentiments, beliefs, imaginings, understandings, and activities.[13] But such an initiation is essentially a non-rational and non-critical process. Children learn by imitation and identification. Initiation is a kind of apprenticeship into the human condition.

It is precisely here where past understandings of indoctrination founder, because if, as we have seen, indoctrination is understood primarily in terms of non-rational teaching and learning, then indoctrination would seem to be inescapable. This leads some writers to admit that some indoctrination is inevitable and good. But this tends to confuse the issue because indoctrination is generally understood to be a pejorative term.[14] If, as is the case in the traditional understanding of the concept, indoctrination is thought to involve non-rational teaching and learning, and if indoctrination is immoral, then it is inconsistent to allow for some indoctrination via non-rational methods when dealing with children. Yet, it seems we must do so, given past definitions of "indoctrination."

Some writers respond to this argument by making a sharp distinction between initiation and education. Kazepides, for example, admits that education has its prerequisite foundation, but "the acquisition of this foundation is the result of primary socialization – not the result of education" (1989, 389). But this is to win an argument by arbitrary definition.[15] Initiation must be seen as an essential component of education, as has been recognized by various writers.

A fourth problem with past discussions of indoctrination is that they give to children a status in relation to personal autonomy which they cannot have. Children are simply not autonomous and it is an error to suggest that we should treat them as such. For example, Sweet, very early in her book, which rejects religious schools as a way of addressing what she sees as the pervasive neglect of religion in the public school classroom, clearly identifies her assumptions about the nature of a good education: "a quality education is one that respects children's ability to think for themselves, to draw conclusions for themselves, and to make choices and decisions for themselves within a context and understanding of a liberal democracy."[16] Indoctrination involves the refusal to allow children to think and choose for themselves, according to Sweet (1997, 159).

But this position fails to take into account the fact that education cannot start with children thinking and choosing for themselves. The very young child is incapable of doing so, and Sweet is forced to admit that it is "patently absurd" to suggest that six-year-old children should be asked what kind of education they want (1997, 176). The ability to think and choose needs to be nurtured.

The fourth problem with past discussions of indoctrination is that they are based on an idealized notion of personal autonomy which is indefensible. Growth towards autonomy always occurs within a certain context. We are necessarily shaped in part by our past and by our environment, and therefore we can only achieve limited autonomy. Also, human beings cannot achieve complete independence, perfect rationality, total objectivity, or complete openness. They cannot subject everything they believe to critical evaluation. Yet the charge of indoctrination often rests on the assumption that finite human beings can achieve this ideal of rational autonomy. What is needed is a more realistic ideal of *normal* rational autonomy, to use a term introduced by Haworth (1986).

Finally, past treatments of indoctrination rest on an ideal of liberal education which is really an abstraction. "You need institutions. How else can you make ideas real?" says a young journalist who is seeking revenge on a boss who has fired him, in a play entitled *Pravda* (Brenton and Hare, 1985). Ideas do need institutions and are inevitably transmitted via institutions. Our thinking as human beings is necessarily shaped by institutions, as has been so ably demonstrated in Mary Douglas's book *How Institutions Think* (1986). Thus any attempt to ignore the institutional context of liberal education is fundamentally inadequate and incomplete. But, this is what is done in most discussions of the violations of the principles of liberal education, including that of indoctrination. Hence the general tendency to ignore the problem of indoctrination in state-maintained public schools.[17] And yet it is often the institutional context of religion that is pounced on when making the charge of indoctrination – see for example the Peshkin quotation at the head of this chapter.[18]

Given these problems inherent in past discussions of indoctrination, I would suggest that the charge of indoctrination, as applied against religious schools, is much weaker than generally assumed. Those making the charge should be much more cautious in making it. If one were to work out all the implications of the above-mentioned problems, it could be shown that there is no necessary connection between religious nurture in religious schools and indoctrination, and that the alleged probable connections are considerably weaker than they are often thought to be.

RECONSTRUCTION OF THE IDEAL OF LIBERAL EDUCATION

We must be careful, however, not to dismiss completely the charge of indoctrination. What is needed is a more adequate and contextualized concept of indoctrination. To achieve this, I would suggest that we first need to reconstruct the ideal of liberal education that typically underlies charges of indoctrination. Here it should be noted that I am not rejecting the traditional ideal of liberal education in its entirety. I am merely attempting a reconstruction.

1.   *Metaphysics*: There was a time when Christian nurture was not only compatible with liberal education, but viewed as an essential ingredient. The ideal of liberal education has undergone a process of secularization, and it is for this reason that initiation into a specific religious tradition is viewed with suspicion today. There are, however, some problems with the dogmatic empiricism that often underlies the scientific ideal and the secularist frame of mind. I would therefore suggest that there is a need to return to the older ideal of liberal education based on a more open-minded metaphysics (cf. Plunkett 1990).

2.   *Human nature*: The whole Western liberal and rational tradition has tended to focus on the human being as a learner, as mind. But a person is more than a rational animal. There is a need for a more holistic view of human nature which recognizes that our rational nature is intimately bound up with the emotional, physical, moral, and spiritual dimensions of our being (Plunkett 1990, 72). Thus we will not be able to define indoctrination in purely epistemological terms. Related

to the above is the need to recognize human existence as "necessarily situated in a contingent, historical, cultural and social context" (Allen 1982, 205). We are not atomistic selves or dislocated strangers, but we are always attached to others – social beings (Sandel 1982). We are also finite and dependent on others. All this will entail some revisions of the traditional liberal ideal of rational autonomy. At most, human beings should strive for *normal* rational autonomy. Education must also aim for the development of normal rational autonomy which does justice to the finiteness, contingency, and dependency of human nature.

3.   *Epistemology*: I have already discussed the foundationalist epistemology that underlies past discussions of indoctrination and liberal education. A theory of liberal education needs to be based on an epistemology that recognizes that all observation is theory-laden, and that theorizing is an incredibly complex process, involving the justification of whole belief systems, rather than individual claims. Theorizing also depends on a host of ingredients such as concepts, observations, presuppositions, past theorizing, and present public agreement. We cannot divorce epistemology from certain personal, social, historical, and material factors, as the foundationalists tend to do. Education too must do justice to these subjectivities. I will have more to say about a revised epistemology in chapter 12.

4.   *Initiation/liberation*: Charles Bailey has captured the heart of the traditional ideal of liberal education when he describes it as an education which liberalizes a person and moves him or her "beyond the present and the particular" (1984).[19] But Bailey, along with many other philosophers of education, fails to address adequately the question how we get into the present and the particular in the first place. It should be obvious that children must first of all be initiated into a particular home, a particular language, a particular culture, a particular set of beliefs, before they can begin to expand their horizons beyond the present and the particular. Liberal education, as traditionally understood, is therefore necessarily parasitic on something else, namely initiation into a present and a particular. The traditional ideal of liberal education is an abstraction from a larger whole. My reconstruction of the ideal of liberal education will therefore be more holistic in focus.

I propose that liberal education be reconstructed so as to include both initiation and liberation (see Thiessen 1987; 1989). My proposal is in keeping with the central thrust of Kimball's historical analysis of the idea of liberal education and his call for restoring a balance between the ancient oratorical ideal of liberal education, with its emphasis on passing traditions on to the uninitiated, and the post-Enlightenment, liberal-free ideal of liberal education, with its emphasis on freedom and critical reason (1986). In my reconstruction,

liberal education will be seen more in terms of a process of development, where due regard is given to the initiation phase of education.
Particularity will be valued in and of itself, and initiation into a particular religion will not be viewed with suspicion simply because of its alleged narrowness. It will be especially important to adjust the
"liberating" phase of education to the psychological needs of the
child. As various writers have argued, children need a stable and coherent "primary culture," and this is a precondition of their subsequent growth towards rational autonomy.[20] To expose them to "an
endless and changing Babel of talk and behaviour" too soon will hurt
them and prevent further development (Ackerman 1980, 141). As
they mature, the need for stability and coherence lessens. Thus the liberating phase of liberal education can be introduced gradually.

This more holistic and developmental concept of liberal education
will lead to a rather different definition of "indoctrination." I would
suggest that the core idea of indoctrination be thought of in terms of
the curtailment of a person's growth towards normal rational autonomy.[21] Several things should be noted about this definition. The focus here is not
on propositions, but on persons, whole persons, whose growth towards
normal rational autonomy can be curtailed in any number of ways.
The developmental nature of my definition of indoctrination should
also be noted. Indoctrination will mean different things at different
stages of a person's development. It is especially important to note that
initiation into the present and the particular is a necessary phase of a
person's growth towards rational autonomy and therefore the charge
of indoctrination is not applicable to this stage of development. It
should finally be noted that indoctrination is understood as frustrating
the growth towards *normal* rational autonomy, not complete independence, or perfect rationality. There are limits to the growth of any human being, since we are all finite and situated within a contingent
present and particular.

CONCLUSION

Given this reconstructed ideal of liberal education and the resulting revised definition of indoctrination, it should be apparent that religious
schools and colleges do not of necessity indoctrinate. The probability of
indoctrination is also considerably weaker than is often assumed by the
critics of such schools. This is not at all to suggest that indoctrination
does not sometimes occur in religious schools and colleges.[22] I am only
suggesting that the charge is weaker than is often assumed.

On the other hand, there are many religious schools where growth
towards rational autonomy is nurtured and where serious grappling

with the fundamentals of the faith is allowed and encouraged.[23] What is curious is that the critics of religious schools are often forced to admit as much. Rose, for example, despite her opposition to Christian schools, is forced to concede that Covenant, an independent charismatic school in upstate New York, encourages student autonomy and initiative, class discussions, the acquisition of analytical skills on the part of students, and the teaching of critical thinking skills (1988, 93, 98, 220). Indeed, Covenant leaders worry that our public schools do not do enough by way of teaching critical thinking skills (220).

Similarly, Sweet, although she objects to religious schools which "unabashedly exist to indoctrinate children in the dogma of their particular faiths," is forced to admit that graduates from religious schools whom she interviewed have become confident, critical, and open citizens who actively contribute to society at large (1997, ch. 8). She also expresses surprise at the critical capacity of students now attending religious schools (94, 165).[24]

Peshkin, finally, despite his condemnation of Bethany Baptist Academy as a total institution, concedes that BBA "neither desires nor has automatons for students" (1986, 220). He goes on to describe the "intellectual independence of students" at BBA (249–50, cf. 216, 253). Perhaps Peshkin is simply working with a wrong definition of indoctrination.[25]

In the interest of brevity, this chapter does not conclude with the usual section concerning practical implications for religious schools. The final chapter of my earlier book includes an extensive treatment of "Some Practical Suggestions" (Thiessen 1993, ch. 9). I would also refer the reader to the practical implications of the next chapter on censorship, as well as in chapter 11, dealing with fanaticism, since the implications that grow out of these charges are very similar to those that grow out of the charge of indoctrination.

9 The Charge of Censorship

> And, most important, education should be governed by standards
> of excellence, not orthodoxy. ... Those who would restrict
> teachers' lesson plans and students' reading lists are doing
> something even worse than denying young people information;
> they are preventing them from learning to think for themselves. A
> growing mind must be encouraged, not shackled.
>
> Mark West, *Trust Your Children: Voices against
> Censorship in Children's Literature*

Another charge often made against religious schools and colleges is
that they practise censorship. This is a central concern of Alan
Peshkin's, in his careful sociological study of Bethany Baptist Academy,
an American fundamentalist K-12 school. "Bethany fosters no Jeffersonian marketplace of contending ideas; none is intended," Peshkin
complains (1986, 190). BBA's librarian "shamelessly censors" (296).

It would seem rather foolhardy to defend Christian schools such as
Bethany Baptist Academy against this charge, because it is obvious that
such schools do make "a conscious, planned effort to control ... the instructional and library materials available" in accordance with "the dictates of one, uncontested, overarching belief system" (Peshkin 1986,
284–5). A fundamental axiom of liberal democracies is that censorship is wrong, always wrong.[1]

This makes me hesitate in attempting to defend religious schools
against the charge of censorship, but I shall do so, inspired in part by a
courageously written book by Sue Jansen (1988). This book, Jansen
says, "goes against the grain of much conventional wisdom" with regard to the issue of censorship. But Jansen dares to challenge the prevailing assumption that "there is very little left to be said about
censorship" (3). There is indeed more to be said!

DEFINITION AND ORIGINS

Contemporary opposition to censorship is rooted in a certain ideal of
intellectual freedom. For a statement of the reigning paradigm of

intellectual freedom we can do no better than to go to the "Introduction" of the *Intellectual Freedom Manual* of the American Library Association (1989).[2] Here "intellectual freedom" is described as:

the right of any person to hold any belief whatever on any subject and to express such beliefs or ideas in whatever way the person believes appropriate ...
the right of unrestricted access to all information and ideas regardless of the
medium of communication used. (American Library Association 1989, ix)

The common understanding of censorship in its broadest meaning is
that it involves any activity which would inhibit intellectual freedom as
just defined. This ideal of intellectual freedom has its roots in the eighteenth century when the heroes of the Enlightenment did away with
(or thought they did away with) church and state censorship. According to "enlightened" historians, the great achievement of "The Age of
Reason" was to free reason, especially from religious superstition and
tyranny. Or, as Sue Jansen puts it, the Enlightenment was thought to
have "severed the knot that had always bound knowledge to power"
(1988, 4). Here we have another useful way of conceiving of the notion of censorship – control over the power to define and distribute
knowledge (Jansen 1988, 7–8). The Enlightenment was thought to
have eliminated such abuse of power.

I will be so bold as to suggest that the prevailing ideal of intellectual
freedom that we have inherited from the Enlightenment simply will
not stand up under careful philosophical scrutiny. Hence, the concept
of censorship based on this ideal of intellectual freedom is also problematic.[3] In the sections that immediately follow, I will examine the
problems inherent in the standard contemporary ideal of intellectual
freedom and the notion of censorship that grows out of this ideal.

INCONSISTENCIES

There are a number of inconsistencies that emerge when one examines down-to-earth librarianship, inconsistencies which would suggest
that the ideal of intellectual freedom, supposedly being adhered to, is
problematic. There is first of all a tension between the moral idealism
inherent in the assumed statement of intellectual freedom and the way
in which this ideal is carried out in practice in libraries. John Swan,
himself a librarian at a secular college, describes the Library Bill of
Rights as "a purist document," "a document that is radically divorced
from the actual practice of librarianship." Indeed, "theory-versus-
practice ironies abound" in the practice of librarianship, according to
Swan, and are all too easy to call forth (1979, 2043). In practice all

librarians select and reject books, define limits and priorities in acquisition, take into account the wants and needs of the readership, and
practise self-censorship by adjusting acquisitions to the sensitivities of
their readership. Swan concludes by boldly admitting that all librarians
are censors.[4]

Here it might be argued that to point out that librarians don't practise what they preach is not a legitimate criticism of the ideal itself.
This inconsistency might simply point to a failure on the part of librarians. The ideal of intellectual freedom might still be a good one.
I would maintain, however, that it is impossible for them to practise
what they preach, because of the problematic nature of what they
preach. This more serious problem will require more argument. At
this point, I am only suggesting that the discrepancy between theory
and practice might indicate that there is something wrong with theory.

Will Manley, also a public librarian, points to this more serious problem when he notes that there is "a tremendous gap" between what
many practising librarians *think* about intellectual freedom and what
they *say* they think (1986a, 41). This is a more serious problem because
here we are dealing with a theoretical inconsistency. Publicly, librarians
make "self-righteous," "pompous," and "extreme" statements about intellectual freedom, but this is a "distortion of how many of us who are
practicing in the field and facing the public everyday really feel about
the subject," Manley argues (40). In practice, most public librarians are
very cognizant of the fact that they will of necessity betray the purist interpretation of intellectual freedom upon which librarianship is based.

Manley goes on to bemoan the fact "that as a profession we can't
even talk about the problem" (41). He recalls a librarians' conference
where a speaker who called for a more realistic and restrictive concept
of intellectual freedom was almost booed off the stage by a hostile au-
dience of not so tolerant librarians. How ironic, that the defenders of
intellectual freedom are themselves so intolerant! Surely a consideration of the limits of intellectual freedom deserves a more open-
minded response.

SELECTION VS. CENSORSHIP

Here we need to deal with another objection that might be raised
against my suggestion that all librarians practise censorship. While it
must be admitted that the librarian evaluates and then selects materials that are to be included in a library, this process must be distinguished from censorship, it might be argued. Much has been written
about this distinction, and it is generally accepted that censorship
differs fundamentally from selection.[5] Asheim, in a paper that has

become a landmark in the professional literature, argues that there is a difference in motivation – the selector's motivation is positive while the censor's is negative.

> To the selector the important thing is to find reasons to keep a book ... For the censor, on the other hand, the important thing is to find reasons to reject the book ... Selection, then, begins with a presumption in favour of liberty of thought; censorship, with a presumption in favour of thought control. (Asheim 1954, 95; 1953, 67)

Clearly there is something to be said for beginning with a presumption in favour of liberty of thought, and my criticisms of this distinction are in no way intended to undermine such a starting point. But a presumption in favour of liberty of thought cannot be as neatly separated from a presumption in favour of thought control as Asheim suggests. While it must be admitted that there is a difference as to *when* library selection and censorship occur, this difference is incidental, and sidetracks us from the central issue that needs to be faced. What is commonly labelled "censorship" typically occurs *after* a library selection has been made, because that is the only point at which the library user, who might have some concerns about library holdings, has any input. If the library user/censor had input during selection, matters of concern could be raised *before* the selection occurs, and it might be discovered that the issues raised by the library user/censor are in fact the very same issues that entered the mind of any professional librarian when the selection was first made. Many examples could be provided, of librarians who have in fact rejected materials for a library on the basis of perceived user response.[6] That is what any good librarian does and should do. Librarianship is, in the end, a matter of matching books with user interests and possible responses, as even those who still want to retain the distinction between selection and censorship are forced to admit (Schrader 1995, 115; cf. 14). In fact, except for questions as to *who* does each, and *when* each is done, there is no essential distinction to be made between selection and censorship.

There is a deeper commonality between library selection and censorship that needs to be brought to light, leading us to the heart of the argument of this chapter. Censorship and selection both involve an exercise of power and control. I agree with Jansen that the term "censorship" should be used to refer to any expression of "power-knowledge."[7] Library selection involves a *hidden* exercise of power, power that it is very easy to ignore or even deny because it is simply part of established consciousness. But it is censorship, nonetheless, and the influence is the more insidious because it is unrecognized.

Stephen Arons argues in a similar vein in his fascinating study of the battle over orthodoxy in American schooling (1986). He argues that "the process by which any books or curriculums are selected – even by liberals – is also censorship. Whoever wins a battle for control over orthodoxy in schools is, by definition, a censor" (26). Arons maintains that "[t]he censors do nothing fundamentally different from what is done by the 'selectors' of books or designers of curriculum" (27). The same applies to libraries and librarians. The distinction between selection and censorship, whether it is applied to textbooks, curriculum, or library holdings, "is a classic case of a distinction without a difference" (70).[8]

THE INESCAPABILITY OF CENSORSHIP

My arguments thus far have entailed that censorship is in fact inescapable. The inconsistencies inherent in defences of freedom of expression point to such an inescapability. Awareness of what is involved in the selection of textbooks or materials for any library again suggests that censorship, in the broad sense of ideologically grounded control, is in fact very much present. Other arguments come to mind. For example, the fact of limited resources and space which finally affect library holdings leads to the same conclusion. Somebody has to be charged with the responsibility of selecting materials within these limitations. Such limitations will of necessity again involve a form of censorship.

With Sue Jansen, I want to argue that "censorship is an enduring feature of all human communities" (Jansen 1988, 8, 181). Jansen is very much aware of the fact that she is going against the grain of much conventional wisdom. This raises the question why conventional wisdom concerning censorship has been so badly misled. What is the underlying error? I would suggest that the failure of liberal advocates of freedom of expression to acknowledge the inescapability of censorship rests on a purist definition of knowledge having its origins in the Enlightenment. Jansen argues that the program of the Liberal Enlightenment was based upon inadequate understandings of the sociological and psychological basis of human perception and knowledge (Jansen 1988, 8). Studies in communications, anthropology, the sociology of knowledge, economics, and post-critical theory, all in different ways, support the conclusion "that time, place, kin, class, and ego leave their imprint on ideas … that power and knowledge are bound together in an inextricable knot."[9] These insights are of course in keeping with postmodernism and its challenge of the Enlightenment program. What is needed is that these postmodern insights also be applied to the ideal of intellectual freedom. When this is done, we will then have to acknowledge that censorship is inescapable.

Jansen goes on to document the history of censorship, showing how censorship has in fact always been present, not only in socialist societies but also in capitalist ones (1988, chs. 3–7). Chomsky, in a very similar manner, argues that although in liberal democracies we like to think that we have freedom of expression and a free marketplace of ideas, this is really an illusion, as it is in fact a very carefully "guided market system."[10] He singles out the educated classes in particular as instruments of propaganda (Chomsky 1992, 109; cf. Ellul 1969, 6). Of course the factual claims about the presence of propaganda and censorship in all societies can be overridden by high-minded idealism which argues that this ought not to be the case. I have argued, however, that complete freedom of thought is impossible.

Here I need to caution against one possible misinterpretation of my argument. It is not at all my intent (nor that of Jansen or Chomsky) to reject entirely the ideal of freedom of thought or to advocate censorship. What I am arguing for instead is that we need to face up to the fact that *some degree* of censorship is inescapable. The task that remains is to distinguish between acceptable and unacceptable levels of censorship.

ABSOLUTE FREEDOM

Another fundamental problem with the Enlightenment ideal of intellectual freedom which has given rise to contemporary concerns about censorship is that this ideal rests on a notion of absolute freedom. The alleged great achievement of the Enlightenment was to free reason and the search for truth from any encumbrances, external or internal. Hence, the concern about possible external constraints in the form of interference from the state or the church. Hence also the emerging ideal of absolute objectivity – reason entirely free of presuppositions and other subjective influences.

This ideal surfaces in the statement of the intellectual Freedom Manual of the American Library Association when it talks about "the right of unrestricted access to all information and ideas." "Unrestricted access" is an absolutist term, and it would seem that many librarians take a "purist" approach to this ideal, interpreting it as allowing no limits on intellectual freedom (Berry 1978).

There can be no such a thing as absolute freedom, intellectual or otherwise. Freedom occurs within a particular context which sets limits on it. There has never been, never will be, and never can be such a thing as unrestricted access to all information and ideas. Human beings are after all very human, and therefore always face limitations of ability, time, and money, to name but a few of the limits that circumscribe our intellectual freedom.

Even if absolute freedom were possible, it is not desirable. Robin Barrow focuses on the desirability of absolute intellectual freedom when he argues that "censorship is never acceptable," and that "any kind of censorship in schools is morally repugnant" (1991, 94). He draws on Mill's defence of liberty, "noting in particular his point that it is a question of all or nothing here" (94). Barrow is bold in his conclusion: "freedom of expression should be absolute" (101).

Barrow, however, fails to make freedom of expression an absolute. Like all other purists on the subject of intellectual freedom, he tries to ignore contextual considerations, but in the end he contradicts himself. Barrow wants curricular and textbook decisions in schools to be based solely on educational criteria (96). But if there is anything we should have learned from postmodernism, it is that we need to bury the notion of a neutral ideal of education. Barrow himself is unable to define these educational criteria without introducing political and ideological considerations. In doing so he is in fact defending a kind of censorship – freedom of expression is subject to certain political and ideological values.

It should further be noted that Mill, whom Barrow appeals to in defence of his position, did not treat intellectual liberty as an "all or nothing" affair. Although Mill's position is not without ambiguities, Mill does not advocate unrestricted freedom of speech, and his defence of freedom clearly implies a teleology: freedom is required because it serves an intellectual and moral purpose (Canavan 1984, ch. 5). No society could continue to exist if *any* method of expressing ideas was allowed. All kinds of restrictions are in place in every society, so as to maintain a level of social order. For example, freedom of speech is restricted so as to prevent injury to others in the form of hate literature, fraudulent advertising, unfair trials, and unjust accusations against a neighbour (Canavan 1984, 11).

Hence, the frequent contradictions that appear among those who supposedly advocate absolute intellectual freedom.[11] Supporters of liberalism are gradually recognizing that intellectual freedom has its limits (Manley 1986b, 43). For example, even anti-censors become censorious about books that reinforce sexist or racist stereotypes (Nodelman 1992, 121).

The error here is the same as that which occurs so frequently in discussions of free enterprise. It is not surprising that the notion of "a free marketplace of ideas" is appealed to in the conventional view of intellectual freedom.[12] The problem here is that complete freedom is not possible or desirable, either in the economic marketplace or in the marketplace of ideas. Marketplaces are always carefully circumscribed so as not to lead to anarchy (Chomsky 1988b, 7; 1988a, xii). This is not to deny some validity to the idea of a marketplace of ideas, but here I am only underscoring the limits of freedom within any marketplace.

EDUCATION AND CHILDREN

Concerns about censorship, especially within the educational context, also rest on some underlying problematic assumptions concerning the nature of education and the nature of children. Some of these educational assumptions have already been alluded to in earlier chapters, but they deserve mention here because they relate to the issue of censorship.

1. *Socialization vs. Education*: Those opposed to any form of censorship within a school context assume a particular notion of liberal education. They further assume that this reigning paradigm of liberal education can be sharply distinguished from socialization. Barrow, for example, admits that his opposition to all censorship rests on the possibility of making a sharp distinction between education and socialization (1991, 99). But all education, including a liberal education, includes a component of socialization (Thiessen 1993). Thought would not be possible if it were not for the social structuring of the mind (Jansen 1988, 184). The current struggles over censorship in public schools in America are really over who has the right to determine the orthodoxy into which children will be socialized (Arons 1986). There would be no struggle if there were not a significant socialization component to education. Once this is acknowledged, of course, then we will be more ready also to acknowledge that establishment control of curriculum, textbooks, and library holdings in public schools is really a form of censorship which simply cannot be erased by honorific phrases of freedom of expression by liberal opponents of censorship (Arons 1986, 25).

2. *Autonomy*: Those defending intellectual freedom are very often opposed to censorship at all levels. Teachers defend "The Students' Right to Read," and writers of children's books appeal to the rights of children to choose what they wish to read.[13] A fundamental assumption here is that children should be treated as though they are autonomous. This assumption is at the very least problematic. Children are very dependent creatures, although the wish of every caring parent or teacher is that his or her children or students will grow towards increasing independence. Even here we need to remember that the goal can never be *complete* independence. Human beings are fundamentally social beings who are always interdependent. Unfortunately, this developmental understanding of children is frequently forgotten in talk about children's rights in the area of intellectual freedom.[14]

Another error that is often made is to assume that the conditions for the exercise of autonomy are the same as the conditions for the development of autonomy. There is considerable evidence to suggest that a narrow and non-permissive upbringing is essential to nurturing autonomy (Thiessen 1993, 140–3). By extrapolation, censoring what children read might just be essential to nurturing their development towards autonomy.

A proper understanding of the importance of nurture as a necessary foundation for development towards autonomy calls into question an assumption illustrated in the quotation at the beginning of this chapter. It is frequently stated that by denying children information we are preventing them from learning to think for themselves (Nodelman 1992, 128–32). But what if a temporary "shackling" is essential to a growing mind? Children can only learn to think for themselves if they have first been given a framework from which to think. Critical thinking can only develop if a child has first been given something to be critical about.

Curiously, the defenders of children's rights in the area of reading often admit that they themselves censor what their own children read.[15] One such writer admits that when it comes to children's books, "we are all censors" (Nodelman 1992, 121). Indeed, perhaps we should be! Censorship may not only be inescapable but also desirable.

This is not at all to say that there should not be a gradual lessening of censorship as children mature. An appreciation of the gradual psychological and cognitive development of children will entail that there should be a parallel gradual lessening of constraints.

3. *Moral Concerns*: One of the most frequent motives behind calls for the censoring of books for children (also within religious schools) has to do with the moral content of these books.[16] It is here that advocates of intellectual freedom become most vociferous in denouncing would-be censors. It is silly to protect children from reading materials that include the vile and the ugly and the shocking, because the world in which they live is itself vile and ugly and shocking, it is argued. Ignorance is thought to be harmful. Knowledge about evil is the key to protecting children from evil. Others go so far as to maintain that moral criteria should never be used in evaluating children's literature.[17]

The arguments here often border on the absurd. One can only conclude that there are ideological assumptions at work which blind the liberal-minded to the obvious. Children's moral characters *are* shaped by what they read and see. Children need to be inspired by positive models. This wisdom is as old as Plato and Aristotle. Of course the causal connection between good reading and good character is difficult to establish. We must be careful not to engage in naïve question-begging, as is done, for example, by Nodelman: "I've never met any-body, not one single person, who admits to having personally learned to be evil or violent from the evil or violence they encountered in the books they read as children" (Nodelman 1992, 123). How scientific! In the next breath, Nodelman admits that children might well be influenced by evil or shallow or silly books and TV shows without proper adult supervision (131). Yes, indeed! An intuitive grasp of the truth is sometimes stronger than the pseudo-scientific rationalizations of ideological biases. There is no need for scientific proof of the obvious. At least with regard to young children, it should be obvious that they can suffer serious and often irreparable harm if they are exposed too early to hate and violence and moral degradation in real life or in the life of their minds.

Anti-moralists are also curiously inconsistent. While denying that children can be corrupted by bad literature, they are often the first to admit that good literature plays a significant role in intellectual and moral development. Hence the concern that children's literature avoids all sexual stereotypes (Nodelman 1992, 121). Here, a little bit of censorship would seem to in place. Yes indeed! There does come a point where even anti-moralists are forced to admit that there are some universal moral principles that ought to be held up as ideals and reinforced in a variety of creative ways, especially for children.

4.   *Who censors?* In answering this question we find that opposition to censorship, when expressed in terms of a plea for children's rights, is sometimes quite explicit in undermining parental rights. For example, the *School Library Journal* carried an article suggesting that the Library Bill of Rights should rid itself of this craven concession to the "rather despotic rights we have customarily accorded parents."[18] While I have no intention of defending "despotic" rights, parental rights, properly qualified, can and have already been defended. Even the most ardent supporters of intellectual freedom for children will often concede that parents have the right to censor what their children read and see.[19]

5.   *Truth*: There is a final educational and epistemological assumption underlying the prevailing liberal concept of intellectual freedom, namely uncertainty about the existence of standards of truth, goodness, or beauty, on which a limitation of freedom of expression could be based (Canavan 1984, 145). Canavan suggests that the liberal temptation is an even deeper one: "to lapse into radical scepticism and moral relativism in order to leave the individual free to set his course by whatever standards he chooses" (145). But there are standards of beauty, goodness, and truth, as even the most liberal relativist is forced to admit. More on this in chapter 12.

Here it is most important to distinguish, as does Canavan, between truth as a transcendent ideal towards which we are striving, and the human grasp of truth. It is precisely because human beings are finite and fallible, because they always have an incomplete grasp of the truth, that we need freedom in exploring and expressing ideas. This is the point that J.S. Mill expressed so well. The memory of the church unjustifiably censoring Galileo should forever stand as a reminder of the dangers of authoritarian responses to the genuine search for truth (Johnson 1990, 63).

This danger, however, is only recognizable if we are searching for truth. As Canavan so ably documents, the classic defences of liberty of thought, including that of Mill, all assume that there is such a thing as truth. Unfortunately, the ideal of intellectual freedom has now evolved "into a doctrine that grants the right of free expression to everyone, whether or not they are engaged in the pursuit of truth" (Johnson 1990, 63). The "marketplace of ideas" is the operative model and is seen as having intrinsic value apart from any reference to a search for truth.[20]

It is not possible, or even desirable, to expose students to the entire range of the marketplace of ideas. Without truth as a limiting goal of all expression of thought, the ideal of intellectual freedom becomes vacuous. Once radical scepticism and moral relativism set in, anything goes, but for what purpose? Without the ideal of truth, contemporary liberals have in fact undermined any rational basis for attaching importance to intellectual freedom (Canavan 1984, 145). We must not forget the contradictions that are inherent in the contemporary ideal of intellectual freedom – there is no truth except the truth of liberalism; and there are no values, except the value of intellectual freedom.

RESPONSE TO THE CHARGE

We are now in a position to respond to the central thrust of a charge often made against religious schools, namely, that they of necessity practise shameful censorship. How do I respond to Peshkin's strong condemnation of Bethany Baptist Academy, "BBA's librarian shamelessly censors; academy educators unapologetically denounce particular movies, books, and songs" (1986, 296)? Yes, there can be no denying that BBA practises censorship, given the generally assumed definition of censorship. But, as I have argued, there is a problem with the way in which censorship is generally understood. The very notion of censorship assumed in making the charge is incoherent, and hence the charge is emptied of its force.

My basic response to this charge is that it rests on a problematic ideal of intellectual freedom and a problematic concept of censorship.

I have argued that intellectual freedom cannot be absolute, and that a degree of censorship is inescapable. Therefore, the presence of censorship does not in itself give us reason to condemn BBA or other religious schools and colleges. The traditional ideal of intellectual freedom is not even applicable to secular and public institutions which allegedly adhere to liberal principles. Surely it is somewhat hypocritical to judge and criticize librarians of religious institutions on the basis of an ideal that isn't even put into practice (and cannot be put into practice) in so-called liberal institutions.

Yes, textbooks are carefully selected and library holdings are carefully monitored at religious schools, as Peshkin correctly notes. Such selection and monitoring do involve censorship, if by censorship we mean anything that stifles unrestricted access to books. But I have argued that selection of textbooks and monitoring of library acquisitions are an inescapable ingredient in any school or public library. Therefore it is unfair to criticize BBA for being selective and for restricting access to literary and artistic works, when selectivity is in fact inescapable.

Here some might argue that the principles of selection at religious schools such as BBA are not based on educational criteria. Education "should be governed by standards of excellence, not orthodoxy," as is maintained in the quotation at the head of this chapter. Here we must be careful not to assume that the textbook preferences of teachers in religious schools are not themselves based on sound educational principles. Christian educators, for example, do appeal to educational criteria when selecting textbooks and acquisitions for libraries.[21] Critics should be careful to avoid question-begging in making the charge. What might be at issue in debates about censorship is some underlying differences about what is educationally worthwhile (Strike 1985, 245).

Peshkin's rationale for the charge that Bethany Baptist Academy is guilty of shameful censorship is clear – BBA does not offer, nor does it intend to offer, a Jeffersonian marketplace of contending ideas (1986, 190). It is not possible for any school to offer to its students the entire range of ideas from which they can then freely choose. And Peshkin is forced to acknowledge that there is clearly a degree of "intellectual independence" at BBA, and that different viewpoints are in fact debated at times (249–10, 253, 156). Perhaps Peshkin would have found an even greater variety of perspectives at BBA if he had looked for them.

All this should not be taken to imply that there might not be an unacceptable level of censorship at BBA and other religious institutions. It is not my intention to engage in a blanket defence of all religious schools. My primary concern is to respond to the charge that religious schools by their very nature must practise an unacceptable level of censorship. Of course, the distinction between acceptable and non-acceptable levels of censorship needs to be clarified, and I will deal with this problem later in this chapter. My purpose at this stage is simply to respond to the broad generalizations that are often made against religious schools with regard to censorship. My primary response to such charges is that they are based on a problematic concept of censorship. We must therefore attempt a reconstruction of this concept.

A RECONSTRUCTED IDEAL OF INTELLECTUAL FREEDOM

It is not possible, in the space of a short chapter, to provide a detailed analysis of an alternative ideal of intellectual freedom which overcomes the weaknesses that I have identified in the prevailing contemporary ideal. Such a reconstruction would also be premature. It would require an examination of the philosophical foundations of this ideal. This will in fact be touched on in chapter 12, where I will point to a reformulation of liberalism as the broader answer to the charges against religious schools and colleges that are being considered in this book. However, it is important to provide at least the broad outlines of a reconstructed ideal of intellectual freedom in order to clarify the distinction that I have made between inescapable censorship and censoring that should be condemned. I also want to pave the way for the practical suggestions to librarians with which this chapter will conclude. My sketch of a reconstruction will again draw from some of the suggestions that Sue Jansen makes in part 2 of her important book on censorship (1988).[22]

My critique of the current popular ideal of intellectual freedom would suggest that a reconstructed ideal must include at least the following ingredients. It must affirm the importance of a degree of intellectual freedom for individuals. Here I can only refer to Mill's defence of liberty of thought as partial justification. A reconstructed ideal of intellectual freedom must be realistic, being able, for example, to account for the actual practice of librarianship, and it must do justice to the fact that such freedom is always limited to some degree. A revised ideal of intellectual freedom must be seen as growing out of a particular context, a community which has certain values and for whom knowledge is defined within certain parameters. It must acknowledge the inescapability of a degree of censorship, which then brings with it the need to distinguish between acceptable and non-acceptable degrees of censorship.

It should be clear that in proposing these qualifications to the Enlightenment ideal of intellectual freedom, I am drawing on the insights of postmodernism. This is essentially the project of Jansen, though it seems to me that Jansen becomes too enamoured with post-modernism and its reaction to the Enlightenment. An emphasis on the subjective dimensions of knowledge brings with it the danger of relativism, and Jansen at times seems to succumb to the spectre of rela-tivism.[23] We still need to retain some aspects of the Enlightenment de-sire to transcend these limitations in our search for universal truth. We need to retain the core concerns inherent in the Enlightenment ideal of freedom of thought. Balance is needed between the emphasis of the Enlightenment and the insights of postmodernism.

Such a balance, when applied to the issue of intellectual freedom, entails that we must, while acknowledging the limits of such freedom, at the same time stress the importance of a degree of intellectual free-dom. Knowledge cannot be divorced entirely from passion, power, and the institutional arrangements that are an expression of power, as Jansen correctly maintains. But Jansen is quick to point out that power can be abused in securing knowledge. We can, and must, try to escape the abuses that invariably accompany power-knowledge. We therefore need to distinguish between a normal degree of association of knowl-edge and power, and an excessive use of power to support knowledge. It is only arbitrary and excessive censorship that must be condemned.

This is where Jansen, drawing on Habermas, has some very helpful things to say, though I believe her account is incomplete. According to Jansen, we need to expose the hypocrisy behind any claims to have achieved complete intellectual freedom (1988, 190, 203). This entails, in particular, that we must expose the lie of liberal societies since the Enlightenment, namely their claim to have abolished censorship. Enlightenment liberalism didn't eliminate censorship; censorship merely took on a form where it was hidden.[24] We need to expose what is hidden, and there needs to be a freedom to engage in such exposure.

Another way to ensure that we avoid excessive censorship is to en-able people to become aware of the inescapable level of censorship that does exist. This means that censorship must be "inventoried, cal-culated, compared and tabulated," a task that Jansen herself under-takes in several chapters (203). We particularly need to become aware of the power of the mass media and bring to the fore the ideologies built into consciousness industries, including mass education (212–3, 155–6).

Jansen also underscores the importance of attaining some kind of balance of power in the consciousness industry. We need to achieve "reflexive power talk" (8–10, 202–17). We need to empower critical discourse. People need to reclaim their voices. We need a pedagogy of the oppressed. We need to remove the epistemological privileges that experts and intellectuals routinely invoke (9). Alternate interpretations of reality must be provided so that people become aware of interpretations reinforced by the establishment. In all this Jansen stresses that she is not trying to eliminate all domination, but make it visible and legible (217).

There is one final suggestion I would add to those made by Jansen – we need a system of educational pluralism in order to achieve reflexive power talk. Although Jansen does touch on mass education as one expression of power-knowledge (155–7), she fails to address the need for an alternative approach to structuring education as a key to overcoming excessive and arbitrary censorship. Schools play a key part in shaping human consciousness and defining knowledge.[25] If we want to provide for alternative interpretations of reality, which will have the power to challenge established opinion, we will have to allow for alternate schools which initiate children into these alternative interpretations of reality.

Our primary concern should be with institutional censorship – the censorship inherent in a state system of education, large corporations, and the media – the censorship which is largely hidden. The best way to overcome institutional censorship is to ensure a plurality of these institutions. In other words, we need a system of educational pluralism, a point which Mill himself strongly affirmed (1978, 105). I will have more to say on this in the final chapter. Of course, we also need to worry about excessive censorship within each particular institution. More on that shortly.

ANOTHER RESPONSE TO THE CHARGE

My broad outline of a reconstruction of the ideal of intellectual freedom should serve to provide an additional answer to the frequently made charge of censorship against religious schools and colleges. Yes, the libraries of religious schools practise censorship, as do the libraries of all schools, even that of a prestigious school like Cornell University.[26] Censorship, understood in the broad sense of control over the definition and distribution of knowledge, is inescapable. The fact that the library of a religious school will by its very nature be stronger in its collection of books that reinforce the religious position of that school does not in and of itself entail that the school should be charged with censorship, where "censorship" is understood as a pejorative term.

To make this negative charge, it would have to be shown that excessive censorship is present at a religious school. One would have to ask whether no attempt has been made to balance the biased book selection in the library with books representing other points of view. It is impossible to define in a precise manner exactly what that balance is. But the charge of censorship, understood in the negative sense, can only be made if insufficient attention has been paid to representing other worldviews and also critiques of the worldview advocated by the school in question.[27]

Interestingly, Paul Cors, in an essay found in the *Intellectual Freedom Manual* of the American Library Association, provides a very realistic account of the level of intellectual freedom that should be found in religious schools.

> While it must be conceded that the library in a college operated by a religious organization, for example, may have to function within doctrinal limits imposed by that organization, the library still has an obligation to provide the most diversified collection possible within those limits. (Cors 1989, 130–1)

Unfortunately, this realistic and balanced account of intellectual freedom is the exception rather than the rule in this *Manual.*

Finally, we must not forget that religious schools, and the censorship that is practised in religious schools, are essential to combatting the much more widespread and dangerous form of hidden censorship that permeates a society as a whole and is imposed by those with power.

SOME PRACTICAL IMPLICATIONS FOR RELIGIOUS SCHOOLS

A full treatment of the implications of intellectual freedom and censorship for religious schools would have to cover an array of contexts – for example, textbook selection, classroom discussions, hiring policies, and library holdings. This chapter has focused primarily on libraries, which is the context within which the topic of censorship typically arises. I will limit my discussion in this final section to libraries as well.

1. *Censorship balanced with freedom*: The first practical implication can be dealt with briefly because it has already been outlined in the previous section. Religious schools, if they take their religious orientation at all seriously, will practise censorship.[28] Bias will clearly be evident in the policies governing the selection of books for their libraries. A Christian college library collection, for example, will have a higher proportion of materials written from a Christian perspective than a library that serves a comparable secular institution (Johnson 1986, 68). Contrary to Peshkin, there is nothing "shameful" about this. It is simply another case of the kind of specialization that takes place in most libraries serving the public interest.

However, it is important that libraries in religious schools do not carry this kind of censorship to an extreme. Bias needs to be balanced with a degree of openness. All libraries need to strive for a degree of intellectual freedom. Thus libraries in religious schools should also include books representing other points of view and even critiques of the religious tradition represented in the school.[29] This balance cannot be defined with mathematical precision. We need to be realistic in our expectations. To demand, for example, that there should be an equal number of books that articulate and critique the religious tradition of the school is to be unrealistic and too precise.

2. *Developmental approach to censorship*: Another reason why it is impossible to define in a precise manner a proper balance in the library holdings of a religious school is that this balance will vary depending on the maturity of students being served. The higher the level of education, the greater the diversity that can be expected within libraries associated with religious educational institutions.

3. *Selection policy*: A religious school should have a clearly articulated policy on the selection of library materials. It is further important for religious schools to be very open about the limitations to intellectual freedom that exist in the library. I would agree entirely with Cors that a religious institution "has an obligation to inform both its patrons and employees of exactly what those limits are" (1989, 130–1). My only concern with Cors is that he fails to see that this principle of defining limitations applies to all libraries, secular as well as religious. These limitations should be clearly defined in faculty handbooks, student handbooks, and library policy manuals. However, here again I would caution against expecting precisely written policies. Instead, policies should be defined in terms of broad principles.

4. *The librarian as a professional*: The librarian plays a key role in defining the policies that govern any library. After all, he or she is the expert, though we must be careful not to allow the appeal to expertise to preclude input from other stakeholders of the library. Once these policies are in place, it is important to continue to treat the librarian of any school as a professional. The librarian of a religious school or college must be given the authority to make judgments about the selection and retention of library materials within the defined parameters. Such judgments will of necessity be in part subjective, even though there are objective institutional values and policies which form the basis for making judgments. Different librarians might make differing judgments using the same criteria. This is no different from doctors disagreeing about the diagnosis of a particular case, even though there are objective criteria which are the basis for making their diagnosis.[30]

5. *Complaints policy*: It is imperative that all libraries, not only those at religious schools, have a policy in place that allows patrons to raise concerns about the books and materials that are included in a library

collection.[31] Here especially, open and honest dialogue needs to be fostered by librarians and administrators. Policies need to be carefully explained and defended. Dialogue needs to be encouraged as an expression of what Jansen refers to as "reflexive power-talk." It is important to democratize dialogue, not appealing to expertise as a way of stifling criticisms. The person making the complaint will often not have had an opportunity to influence selection policies, and so this is the only means by which he or she can begin to exercise such influence. Complaints should therefore also be seen as providing opportunities for reviewing the selection policies in place, and if necessary, even revising them.

In all this, it is of course very important for librarians and administrators to defend a degree of intellectual freedom that is so essential in any educational institution. The librarian, while engaged in censoring, must at the same time also be opposed to censoring (Swan 1979, 2042). Attempts will therefore be made to help the complainant to understand what education is all about, and why the development of critical openness and hence the need for more than "established opinion" in library collections is essential to the educative process.

PART SIX

Theology and Education

The Possibility of Christian
Curriculum and Scholarship

> In particular, there has now emerged in our society a concept of
> education which makes the whole idea of Christian education a
> kind of nonsense. From this point of view, the idea that there is a
> characteristically or distinctively Christian form of education
> seems just as much a mistake as the idea that there is a distinctively
> Christian form of mathematics, of engineering, or of farming.
>
> Paul Hirst, "Christian Education:
> A Contradiction in Terms?"

The above quotation contains another frequently raised objection
against religious education as it occurs in Christian or church-related
schools, colleges, and universities. The very idea of a distinctively
Christian education or a distinctively Christian approach to mathematics
or chemistry is viewed as impossible. Hence the title of George
Marsden's response to this objection: *The Outrageous Idea of Christian
Scholarship* (1997). A closely related concern has to do with the undesirability of introducing personal religious perspectives into a classroom. Science, not faith, should carry the day in the modern school,
college, or university, some scholars feel.[1] James Dwyer goes so far as to
suggest that American states should extend their current regulations
governing religious schools so as to deal with the "harmful practice" of
"teaching secular subjects from a religious perspective" (1998, 179).

In the fall of 1977 a group of conservative Mennonites in central
Alberta removed their children from the local public school and
placed them in a school of their own, even though the Alberta Department of Education had rejected their earlier application for private
school status.[2] This led to the prosecution of the parents, who were
charged with contravening the compulsory attendance regulations of
the School Act. Two issues were central to the case. The Mennonites
maintained that public schools are not religiously neutral because of
the liberal progressive philosophy prevailing in them. Secondly, the
Mennonites were concerned that their children be educated in accordance with their own religious beliefs. This gave rise to a central argument of Mr Pidruchney, who entered the case as an *amicus curiae*, or

friend of the court: "The threads of their religious beliefs are tied to education and the exercise of religious freedom in relation thereto."[3] To separate religious education from secular education, as was necessary if they sent their children to the public school, was offensive to the Mennonites. They wanted their own school, where the entire curriculum would reflect their own faith.[4]

This case again raises the critical questions that will be addressed in this chapter: Is a religiously neutral curriculum possible? Is there such a thing as a distinctively Christian curriculum? If we answer "yes" to the first question and "no" to the second, then of course it can be argued that religious parents should be content to send their children to state-maintained public schools. The religious component of education can then be treated as an add-on, to be dealt with at home or in the church. There simply is no need for religious schools.

I am limiting myself to a discussion of the possibility of a Christian curriculum or Christian scholarship, in part because that is the context out of which the objections I am considering arise. It is also necessary to become more focused here, since theological considerations must be entertained. It needs to be stressed that these same issues arise within other religious traditions.[5] My argument can be easily extrapolated, but that is beyond the purpose of this chapter.

HIRST AND AUTONOMOUS FORMS OF KNOWLEDGE

To come to a better understanding of what underlies the objection against the idea of a Christian curriculum, it will be helpful to look more carefully at the now-classic curriculum theory of Paul Hirst, an influential Cambridge philosopher of education.[6] The quotation at the head of this chapter has its source in the early writings of Hirst. At the heart of Hirst's objection to the idea of a Christian curriculum is a thesis concerning the autonomy of the forms of knowledge. This thesis grows out of his attempt to analyse the rationale behind the traditional division of knowledge into subjects, disciplines, or areas of research.

Hirst argues that there is a definite structure to knowledge which provides the basis for the subject divisions that have become common in school curricula. He identifies several "forms of knowledge," each of which is distinguishable in terms of certain central concepts that are peculiar to that form, a distinctive logical structure, and unique criteria with which to test statements made against experience (1974a, 44). Hirst usually treats religion as a form of knowledge, although at times he expresses doubts about this.[7] It will be assumed here that religion is a form of knowledge, although I do not believe that the problem under consideration hinges on that question.

For the question being considered here, the important feature of Hirst's curriculum theory is his claim that "the logical structure of knowledge is one of distinct, unique, irreducible forms" (1974a, 137). Hirst variously describes each form of knowledge as "logically distinct, autonomous, independent, unique, fundamental" (1974a, 84). It is for this reason that the idea of a Christian curriculum is impossible. He argues, for example, that "intelligent Christians have come to recognize that justifiable scientific claims are autonomous and do not, and logically cannot, rest on religious beliefs" (1976, 155). If science and the other forms of knowledge are completely autonomous, then it follows that it is not possible to integrate religion and the other forms of knowledge, and thus the idea of a unique Christian perspective in science, history, and mathematics is indeed contradictory.

The basic problem with this argument is that the forms of knowledge are not completely autonomous, and Hirst himself is forced to admit this. While stressing that each form is ultimately unique and irreducible, Hirst points out that this does not mean that the forms of knowledge are "totally independent of each other" (1974a, 89). Indeed, he repeatedly insists that the forms are interrelated.[8] This explains why "one discipline often makes extensive use of the achievements of another."[9]

Hirst even expresses sympathy with the notion of an "overall hierarchical pattern" of logical relations between the forms (1974a, 91). Thus, it might be that "logical and mathematical knowledge is seen as presupposed by knowledge in the physical sciences which in its turn is presupposed by knowledge of persons. The sequence might be continued to give an order of, say, moral, religious, artistic, and philosophical knowledge."[10] So now we even have an ordered set of interrelations between the forms of knowledge.

There is an obvious problem in Hirst's analysis. He has not resolved the tension that exists in his claims that the forms of knowledge are at one and the same time autonomous and interdependent. If the forms of knowledge are interdependent, then religion can be seen as in some way interrelated to the other forms of knowledge. It follows that the idea of a Christian curriculum is not nonsense on Hirst's own grounds.

EPISTEMOLOGY OF NEUTRALITY

Hirst's analysis rests on a very specific approach to epistemology, an approach which we have inherited from the Enlightenment. At the heart of Enlightenment epistemology and the scientific approach which grew out of the Enlightenment are the notions of objectivity and a universal kind of rationality. But epistemology and the philosophy of science have undergone a revolution since the ground-breaking work of Thomas Kuhn. It is now generally acknowledged that observation is theory-laden and that rationality is inescapably rooted in a host of subjective factors. All seeing and all thinking take place from a particular place and in a certain time. This is at the core of postmodernism.

Indeed, Hirst in his most recent writings has expressed some dissatisfaction with the idea of a universal, secular rationality which underlies his earlier analysis of the structure of knowledge (1993). Thus it would seem that Hirst has come to acknowledge the new epistemology, which recognizes that thinking in all the forms of knowledge is necessarily shaped by ideological commitments such as are found in religion. All this lends credence to the idea of a uniquely Christian curriculum.

I return to the Mennonite case referred to earlier. "The threads of their religious beliefs are tied to education and the exercise of religious freedom in relation thereto," their lawyer argued. The Mennonites could not accept the idea that religious education could be separated from secular education as is maintained in the public school. They wanted a school where the entire curriculum reflected their religious faith. There is nothing incoherent about such a demand.

INCONSISTENCY

What is curious is that the educational implications of the new epistemology are frequently acknowledged in academia, though, for some reason, they are not extended to include the idea of a distinctively Christian scholarship.[11] As Marsden is at pains to point out, in mainstream academia there are now various Marxist, feminist, gay, postmodern, African-American, conservative, or liberal schools of thought (1997, 5–6, 52, 64, 72). The very existence of each of these schools of thought is premised on the assumption that such factors as the identities and social location of human beings have intellectual significance. Scholarship is in part shaped by who we are.

Surely consistency would demand that there should also be room in academia for explicitly Christian points of view. Thus, Michael McConnell, professor of law at the University of Chicago, draws attention to the existence of courses in feminist jurisprudence at most major secular law schools, though he is not aware of any such course in Christian (or other religious) jurisprudence. It would seem that in mainstream academia, "any hint of a religious approach to the subject matter would be deemed academically inappropriate," suggests McConnell (1993, 315).

Why this inconsistency? McConnell dares to suggest that there is an anti-religious bias in modern academic culture (1993, 315). This does not mean that most modern academics oppose the private practice of religion. What they oppose and what they consider "outrageous" is the suggestion that religion might make a difference in academia itself, according to Marsden (1997, 7). As long as religious scholars compartmentalize their faith and their academic pursuits, everything is all right. This anti-religious bias has led to widespread "self-censorship" on the part of academics who are religiously committed, according to Marsden (1997, 13, 51–2).

I recently encountered this demand for compartmentalization in a blind assessment report of an application for a research grant. A strong anti-religious bias pervaded the entire evaluative report. Let me quote just one example:

Could Dr. Thiessen overcome his own personal religious convictions and concentrate on developing philosophical arguments that could compel and stand against any critical inquiry simply because they represent philosophical thinking at its best regardless of one's religious affection or affiliation.

This is an outrageously biased request that is rooted in a dogmatic secular mind-set which is unable to appreciate anything that smacks of a religious orientation in scholarship. It is precisely this kind of prejudice that I am seeking to counter in my work generally, and more specifically in this chapter.

HOW DOES FAITH INFORM SCHOLARSHIP?

It is one thing to defend the idea of a Christian curriculum. It is quite another task to explain precisely how starting from a Christian perspective will lead to a distinctively Christian curriculum. Here it is not enough to talk vaguely about "faith-informed scholarship," or about a Christian perspective "influencing" a curriculum.[12] We need to try and define the connection more carefully. Here we also need to be aware of the danger of begging the question in the very way in which we describe the problem. Some writers have argued that faith and learning should not be seen as two separate entities needing to be connected (Zylstra 1997). But even if faith and learning might better be seen as a seamless whole, it is still possible to treat each as an abstraction from the whole, and hence we must try to become more precise in understanding how these abstractions are related to each other.

I would suggest that it is the difficulty surrounding the problem of defining this relation more precisely that has led to scepticism concerning the very possibility of a Christian curriculum.[13] We therefore need to focus on this additional question. Even if we allow for the possibility of integrating religion and the other forms of knowledge, are there not difficulties in actually describing this relation and then translating this into the curriculum? What difference can religion make to such claims as $2 + 3 = 5$ or $E = mc^2$?

This question has been the focus of an ongoing and lively debate among evangelical scholars. In what follows, my indebtedness to this debate, as well as to what has come to be known as Reformed epistemology, will be apparent.[14] I want to consider three ways in which the relationship between faith and learning can be described.

It could be argued first of all that religion is *logically* interconnected with the other forms of knowledge. Here religious presuppositions are related to the rest of knowledge in the same way in which the axioms of a system are related to the system. Conclusions reached in science, history, and mathematics then follow with logical necessity from these religious axioms. For the Christian, these religious axioms are presumably taken from the Bible. This would, at times, seem to be the position of Reformed thinkers such as Abraham Kuyper, Cornelius Van Til, and Herman Dooyeweerd.[15]

The basic problem with this approach is the difficulty of showing exactly how conclusions in science, history, or mathematics can be logically deduced from religious presuppositions. George Mavrodes illustrates the problem when he reports that he had occasion to study one of the writers of the Reformed tradition with a group of Christian professors, many of whom had international reputations for their research achievements. He reports that they couldn't think of "plausible examples of (say) mathematical conjectures or chemical theories which we might reject because of our Christian commitment, nor of new research experiments in astronomy which that commitment might suggest."[16] Another fundamental difficulty with this view of the relation between religion and the other forms of knowledge is that it would seem to make all discussions between thinkers who differ in their religious points of departure impossible.

Christian scholars who object to this position, however, run into problems of their own. The basic problem is that those making these objections invariably contradict themselves. Smith, for example, argues that Christian presuppositions simply "do not lead by a single chain of linear deduction to an invariant set of educational contents or practices." However, he is forced to concede that the Bible debars, permits, commends, and even requires certain subject content in the curriculum (1995, 16, 24). Surely there are some implications for curriculum and scholarship that do follow logically from Christian pre-suppositions. For example, the doctrine of creation logically entails that the naturalistic assumptions underlying macro-evolutionary the-ory are wrong. The biblical doctrine concerning the dignity and free-dom of human beings logically entails that determinism is false.

I would agree with contemporary Reformed philosopher Roy Clouser, however, who objects to the "encyclopedic assumption" of fundamentalists who expect "the guidance of Scripture to take the form of offering infallible information about virtually every subject matter" (1991, 94). The connection between Christian presupposi-tions and curricular content is often a good deal more complex than strict logical deduction. Here we must be careful, though, not to con-clude that just because it is often difficult, if not impossible, to show the logical interrelation between Christian presuppositions and the forms of knowledge, there is no relation whatever.

I would suggest that Hirst's difficulty, for example, in seeing how reli-gion can be related to the other forms of knowledge is due to his think-ing only in terms of "logical interrelations" or a "logical hierarchy." Interestingly, in another context Hirst himself entertains the possibility of a non-logical relation when he defends the relevance of philosophi-cal belief to educational theory and practice. Here he calls for a "much looser" type of connection.[17] But, if a looser non-logical relation is ap-propriate and possible here, then why cannot the same type of relation exist between religion and the other forms of knowledge?

Hirst's call for a looser type of connection between philosophical be-liefs and educational theory points us to the second way in which the re-lation between religion and the forms of knowledge can be explained. Indeed, Hirst comes very close to expressing the position of Reformed epistemology, at least when stated in a more nuanced fashion. Clouser provides us with a helpful analysis of the notion of a presupposition and this looser connection between religious presuppositions and curricu-lum content (1991, 101–7). Presuppositions stand in a certain relation to another belief – they serve as an informational requirement for hold-ing the other belief. Presuppositions need not be consciously held for them to exercise their influence on other beliefs that one holds. Even when unconsciously assumed, they still direct or regulate the way one thinks. Religious core-beliefs, he argues, act as presuppositions to the making of *theories* in philosophy and the sciences.[18]

Clouser refers to the Bible as the source of these presuppositions for the Christian. But he reminds us that the Bible is first and foremost a book of religion (Clouser 1991, 98). Therefore it would be an error to read the Bible as a science textbook, though what is said in the Bible clearly impinges on matters of science. Instead, the Christian sees the Bible as providing the basic religious presuppositions which serve as a guide to thinking in all disciplines.

A third useful way to understand this relation is to introduce the notion of a worldview, which is increasingly becoming part of normal discourse given the new epistemology that was described earlier in this chapter. A worldview (derived from the German word *Weltanschauung*) is like a set of sunglasses which colour everything that we see. Smith, for example, suggests that "worldviews are primarily lenses with which we look at the world" (1995, 21).

Walsh and Middleton therefore describe the Christian worldview as a "transforming vision," which makes us look at the world in a different way from, say, a naturalistic framework (1984).[19] Other worldviews make us see the world differently once again. For example, Schumacher has given us a classic statement on the difference between a Buddhist over against the standard Western capitalist perspective on economics (1973, ch. 4).

Walsh and Middleton stress that worldviews are not to be confused with philosophical systems of thought. But in the end, it would seem that talk about worldviews as *perceptual* frameworks invariably leads to talk about *conceptual* frameworks. They refer, for example, to Kuhn's notion of a paradigm as capturing part of the meaning of a worldview (Walsh and Middleton 1984, 169–70). But a paradigm functions as the scientist's conceptual framework, though, as Kuhn points out, one certainly cannot deduce consequences logically from a paradigm in order to verify or refute it. Paradigms, like worldviews, do finally shape the way we think and reason.

BELIEF SYSTEMS

Harvard philosopher Willard Van Quine provides some useful descriptions and analogies of the structure of knowledge that serve to integrate all three of the above interpretations of the relation between faith and learning. His illustrations also explain why it is that some disciplines seem to be less affected by religious presuppositions than others. Quine suggests that we need to look at what we believe in terms of a system of interlocking beliefs which we use in trying to explain experience. "The beliefs face the tribunal of observation not singly but in a body," he maintains (Quine and Ullian 1978, 22). This is most important for our discussion because our tendency is to look at beliefs one at a time, in isolation from their supporting context. This tendency makes it difficult to acknowledge the possibility of religion influencing curriculum.

Quine reinforces this point with the use of several analogies in an oft-reprinted essay entitled "Two Dogmas of Empiricism."

The totality of our so-called knowledge or beliefs ... is a man-made fabric which impinges on experience only along the edges. Or, to change the figure, total science is like a field of force whose boundary conditions are experience. (Quine 1961, 42)

Quine highlights the unity of our belief systems. They are a "totality" or a "field of force." He goes on to stress that the total field is "so undetermined by its boundary condition, experience, that there is much latitude of choice" in making adjustments to our beliefs in our attempts to account for experience (1961, 42). Even our central beliefs can be revised, although our "natural tendency" is not to do so. Quine is also suggesting here that there are varying degrees of importance in the beliefs of a belief system. Beliefs in the interior of the field are more central and basic than empirical statements at the periphery. Thus, the entire system of beliefs is loosely interconnected, each influencing the other, though not in ways that can be logically defined.

The following diagram is inspired by Quine's analysis of a belief system, taking some liberties in interpreting the levels of beliefs and their varying degrees of importance (see figure 1).[20] What I am trying to illustrate in this diagram is that presuppositions (or worldview perspectives) lead to philosophical theories, which in turn lead to scientific theories, which in turn finally lead to the making of specific claims. All beliefs, however far removed from the centre of one's belief system, are influenced by one's presuppositions to some degree. The influence of presuppositions can be compared to the diminishing ripples caused by a stone cast into a pond. The influence of one's presuppositions is very evident in the philosophical theories one adopts, but less so with regard to specific claims about the colour of one's shoe, $2 + 2 = 4$, or the chemical composition of salt.[21] But even in mathematics and chemistry, different interpretations are evident, as any book on the philosophy of mathematics or the history of science will show.[22]

Building on Quine's description of belief systems and the above diagram, I would suggest that there are some basic Christian doctrines that are at the centre of a Christian's belief system. These doctrines include the existence of God, creation, the fall of man, and the possibility of redemption. These basic religious doctrines are the foundation of the Christian's entire belief system.[23] Though Christians often cannot define precisely how these basic beliefs do affect other specific beliefs, they influence them nonetheless, mainly via the philosophical and scientific theories that they inspire. Clearly important beliefs

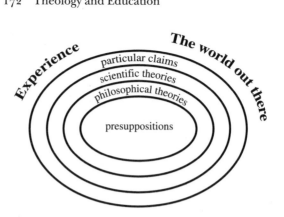

Figure 1
Belief Systems

closer to the core of a Christian belief system, e.g. theories about human nature, will be more significantly shaped by these presuppositions. Indeed, some beliefs can be logically deduced from these presuppositions. A uniquely Christian curriculum or scholarship is therefore not only possible but very feasible.

PROBLEMS OF INCOMMENSURABILITY, RELATIVISM

It is time to face some objections to my defence of the possibility of a distinctively Christian curriculum. My defence assumes that all thinking is shaped by presuppositions and worldviews, and also, to some extent at least, by the context of the thinker. But if all thinking rests on presuppositions and worldviews, which vary from person to person or from cultural group to cultural group, don't we finally end up with a situation in which we can no longer communicate with each other? In philosophical terms, don't we end up with incommensurable discourse frames? And does this not also raise the spectre of epistemological relativism? These are surely among the most fundamental problems that emerge from my appeal to postmodernist themes in order to support the idea of a Christian curriculum.

Postmodernists, of course, not only admit all this but accept the ensuing incommensurability and radical relativism as a good thing. For example, Walter Anderson, in a book with the colourful title *Reality Isn't What It Used to Be: Theatrical Politics, Ready-to-Wear Religion, Global Myths, Primitive Chic, and Other Wonders of the Postmodern World* (1990), boldly defends constructivism. We create our view of reality, he argues, and there is not one single symbolic world, not even as an ideal towards which we can strive.

But Anderson, like all postmodernists who carry their ideas to an extreme, contradicts himself. In the last chapters he tells us of the need to adjust to the global village we are living in. "All the World's a Stage," he entitles the second to last chapter, which suggests that we are not quite as isolated as he thinks. The final chapter is entitled "The Emergent Fiction." Clearly Anderson is describing his own postmodern worldview as the one that is emerging and that is gaining a world-wide consensus. He talks about some fictions as "better" than others – but better in relation to what? Better presupposes a best! So, Anderson, like all the other relativists I know, contradicts himself.

I do not believe that the acceptance of presuppositionalism and the possibility of a uniquely Christian curriculum entails this kind of radical constructivism with its attendant problems of incommensurability and relativism. While our beliefs are to some extent human constructions, this is not to say that they are *just* that (Clarke and Gaede 1987, 82). Somehow, we need to retain some elements of the universal language of Enlightenment-inspired modernism. We must be careful not to overreact, however, and reject entirely the insights of constructivism. We must acknowledge, with Toulmin, that the problem with the agenda of modernity is that it overreached itself (1990, 175). I believe the same problem exists with regard to postmodern thought. We must beware of going to extremes and seek instead a reconciliation between the epistemological insights of modernism and postmodernism (Toulmin 1990, 175).

Here let me suggest four ways in which I am denying a radical kind of incommensurability and relativism, despite my acknowledgment of ideological and religious presuppositions underlying all our thinking. The first way concerns the starting point of all thinking and belief systems. All individuals or groups of individuals have to live in the real world. Our beliefs serve a very pragmatic function of trying to help us cope with the real world. Although we may to some extent be locked into our particular discourse frames, these discourse frames must still try to make sense of the common world that we all live in. Thus, at a common-sense level, communication is possible, a point stressed by common-sense philosophers such as Thomas Reid.[24]

Secondly, there is a common goal to all reasoning and believing. We are seeking the truth. Indeed, human beings seem to be passionate about advancing human understanding. Radical constructivists like Anderson invariably defend their position as better than other positions. The fact that we disagree and argue with each other is an implicit acknowledgment that there is truth, and that it is worth arguing about. William James captures this regulative function of absolute truth well when he describes the absolutely true as "that ideal vanishing point towards which we imagine that all our temporary truths will someday converge" (1968, 170). It is important to stress that the truths that we hold are indeed temporary – we must always admit that we might be wrong, as fallibilists have reminded us. Christians too need to affirm with Paul that we only know in part, that we only have an incomplete grasp of the truth (1 Corinthians 13: 9, 12). Both James and Paul locate the full knowledge of truth as a future hope.

However, we must be careful not to assume that knowledge and truth are only possible in the future. We must somehow do justice to the fact that, despite our differing presuppositional frameworks, we can and do come to agreement about quite a few matters, and this agreement might surely be at least a sign that we are coming closer to the truth.[25] This leads to my third response to the problem of incommensurability and relativism – there is considerable overlap between competing interpretations of reality. This point deserves expansion and will therefore be treated later in a separate section.

The final level of common ground between adherents of differing presuppositional frameworks occurs at a meta-epistemological level, and is rather abstract. Most evaluation of beliefs occurs within a belief system. Reasoning and justification only make sense given the presuppositions of that belief system. It is, however, possible also to talk about evaluation at another level, the evaluation of belief systems as a whole. Such evaluation is much more complex than ordinary evaluation, but it is still possible, though only a few do this in a disciplined way.

Here again, Kuhn is instructive. Kuhn, with his emphasis on paradigms, is often thought to be a relativist. But he still maintains that there are objective criteria in theory choice that are acknowledged by other writers.[26] He mentions empirical accuracy, consistency, breadth, simplicity, aesthetic elegance, fruitfulness. Kuhn stresses that there are subjective aspects to the application of these criteria, but the process of paradigm evaluation is not completely adrift in a sea of subjectivism. Evaluating whole belief systems is very complex, so that it is difficult to get agreement about which belief system is the best. But it is still possible, and hence relativism can be avoided.

COMMON GROUND

In the previous section I alluded to the possibility of overlap between competing worldviews or presuppositional frameworks. This point is very important but easily misunderstood, and therefore deserves some expansion. The idea of overlapping consensus is also very important for contemporary liberalism, and since I will be referring to various liberal writers at length in the final two chapters, and since these writers too often misinterpret the notion of overlap, it will be helpful here to prepare some groundwork for this later discussion.

What I am countering with my emphasis on some common ground between differing presuppositional frameworks is the position of radical postmodernists as well as some Christians who seem to maintain that a Christian belief system is completely incompatible with other belief systems, thus making communication with others impossible.[27] But clearly people with differing presuppositional frameworks do communicate with each other, and so this position is ultimately sheer nonsense. Indeed, postmodernists and Christians who take this extreme position invariably contradict themselves by conceding that some communication is indeed possible.[28]

Is there not a problem here in wanting to say that Christians think in a distinctive way, and yet are able to communicate with people of differing belief systems? In response, I would maintain that it is possible to affirm at one and the same time that one's belief system is unique, and that it shares truths with other belief systems. "That worldviews overlap does not mean that they cannot be distinguished," argues Smith (1995, 21n47). Marsden introduces a helpful illustration. "One would hardly argue that because virtually any question or scholarly agenda that might be proposed by a Marxist could be posed by a non-Marxist that therefore a distinctive Marxism was not shaping the scholarship" (Marsden 1997, 69). Surely the same can be said about Christian scholarship.

Here another picture might be useful (see figure 2).[29] Imagine a series of ellipses, each representing a different worldview, but all overlapping to some degree. Each ellipse is unique, and yet there is some common ground. This diagram is meant to illustrate the fact that we invariably find that there is a partial convergence of differing worldviews. Cooling suggests that it is this "overlapping of belief systems that produces secular knowledge, creating a sort of neutral middle ground" (Cooling 1994, 116). Here we must be careful not to misinterpret Cooling, as he clearly rejects the idea of a neutral rationality or knowledge (ch. 6). The common ground represented by the area of overlap of these circles will be interpreted and justified in very different ways in each particular belief system. So there is both uniqueness and commonness in what we believe.

Why is there such an overlap? We live in the same world. Regardless of our worldviews, we have a common source of data, which imposes constraints on the extent to which we can interpret reality. Human nature is roughly the same. We are trying to understand the same reality.

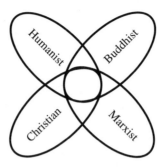

Figure 2
Overlapping Ellipses

We are striving for the same truth. Here the reader will note that these points were all considered in the previous section as an answer to the problem of incommensurability and relativism.

This position can also be defended from within the Christian tradition. It is captured theologically in the Calvinist doctrine of common grace and the Catholic doctrine of natural law. What both of these doctrines maintain is that all human beings have access to some of God's truth by virtue of being created by God and living in the world that God created. Then there is what theologians refer to as "general revelation" – God's revelation in nature (Romans 1: 20; Psalm 19: 1–4). This general revelation is accessible to all people, regardless of their worldviews.[30]

DISAGREEMENT

There is another objection that needs to be dealt with briefly. Christians don't agree when it comes to working out the curricular and scholarly implications of their religious presuppositions. This is in fact another argument that Hirst uses to draw the conclusion that "a distinctive Biblical or Christian view of education simply is not discoverable" (1974b, 79). But, this same argument could be used against Hirst and others who profess to base their view of education on objective rational principles. Disagreement abounds among so-called rationalists as well, and yet Hirst would surely not advocate the abandonment of these rational principles or suggest that we simply give up the entire enterprise of developing a rationally coherent philosophy of education.

The fact that people disagree doesn't mean that they ought to disagree. Maybe all Christians *should* agree on the nature of a Christian approach to psychology. But given the finiteness of the human mind, including that of Christians, disagreement persists. In fact, the task of working from general presuppositions to specific application to curriculum is a very complex one, and hence we should expect disagreement. Not only might there be misinterpretations of the Christian Scriptures, but there might also be misinterpretations of "general revelation," i.e. the data from experience. Christians may also be mistakenly allowing their thinking to be shaped by influences that run counter to their Christian presuppositions.

Disagreement among Christians is therefore a sign of academic health – academic debates can lead to new insights. Marsden correctly warns against speaking of any one approach as *the* Christian view on any subject (1997, 70). To title a work *The Christian Philosophy of Education Explained* is simply presumptuous (Perks 1992). At the same time, we should not conclude from the diffuseness of Christian approaches to various disciplines that there is no possibility of developing a Christian approach to the various disciplines.[31]

SOME PRACTICAL IMPLICATIONS FOR RELIGIOUS SCHOOLS

1. *Commitment to a Christian curriculum*: If the argument of this chapter is sound then it follows that Christian schools should teach all subjects from a distinctively Christian perspective. Unfortunately, there is a good deal of evidence to suggest that this is often not the case in Christian schools and colleges in Canada, the United States of America, and the United Kingdom. Here I can only provide a sample of the evidence.

In a report of the Catholic Committee overseeing Catholic schools in the province of Quebec, it was found that in most schools there was "silence surrounding the religious question," and many of the people surveyed admitted "that they hesitate to say they are Catholic or to qualify their school as Catholic" (1989, 13, 26). The report itself, while still wanting to retain the commitment of Catholic schools to the Christian faith, is ambiguous when it seems to go out of its way to stress that the Catholic school is "a humanistic school" which "does not differ from others," and that "its educational goal is its only mission."[32] No doubt this ambiguity is a result of these schools being "public" schools, open to all students of any or no faith. But, then why bother with an identifiable and separate Catholic system of education? It is this question which no doubt lies behind the recommendation of the recent Proulx Task Force, to eliminate the last vestiges of denominational schooling in Quebec (1999).

Allen Fisher, in a study of sixty-nine colleges affiliated with the Presbyterian Church in the United States, found that a comparison of course offerings of these colleges with that of other colleges with no religious affiliation revealed that, with few exceptions, there was no apparent difference in what was being taught.[33]

In a 1985 study of Anglican colleges in the United Kingdom, it was found that 27 per cent of the staff had no Christian affiliation. Further, very few of the staff "consider that Christianity should be an important element in influencing the curriculum." The suggestion that Christian insights should appear on the curriculum ranked low in a list of objectives which were put to staff. While there may be other considerations involved here, it would surely be fair to suggest that in part the issue is one of a lack of commitment to Christian distinctives in education.[34]

Of course these results in both Catholic and Protestant schools and colleges are simply an expression of the more general process of the secularization of education in Western societies.[35] Sadly, this process of secularization of religious schools often occurs because of the desire to get public funding (Marsden 1994, 438). I want to dare to suggest that a Christian school or college that does not teach from a distinctively Christian perspective forfeits its right to exist. Any course at a Christian school or college that does not exhibit the influence of Christian presuppositions similarly forfeits its right to exist.

Thankfully, there are many positive examples of Christian schools and colleges which have resisted the trend towards secularization. Marsden also provides many examples of first-rate scholarship which reflects discernible and substantial Christian perspectives.

2. *Compartmentalization*: In assessing the distinctively Christian character of Christian schools and colleges, we must not be fooled by the presence of theology departments and regular times of worship for students. Such schools and colleges may in fact be well along the road to complete secularization. By limiting the study of religion to courses in the theology department, they are in effect sending the message that religion is irrelevant to the rest of thought and life in the public sphere. Such schools and colleges would seem to have accepted the liberal line of relegating religion to the private sphere. As such they are replicating what has been and is being done in our public schools and colleges – religion is tamed by keeping it in a tight compartment where it cannot interfere with what is really important.

Zylstra identifies another type of compartmentalization when he objects to the very language so often used to describe the idea of Christian scholarship (1997). For example, he objects to George Marsden's tendency to think of the problem in terms of relating faith *to* scholarship, or in terms of integrating faith *and* learning.[36] In order to avoid this kind of religious/academic schizophrenia, faith needs to be seen as providing the necessary foundation for all learning and scholarship. A better term would be "faith-based learning" (Zylstra 1997, 4). Or we could borrow a slogan from the medieval philosophers, *fides quaerens intellectum* ("faith seeking understanding"). This slogan, which has been identified as the hallmark of Augustinian thought, is also the guiding spirit behind Reformed philosophers and others who have refused to limit theology to the strictly religious sphere, and have instead sought to explore all of creation in the light of the biblical faith.

It is this deeper understanding of the idea of a Christian curriculum or Christian scholarship that I have tried to explore and defend in this chapter, and which I would hold out as the ideal for Christian schools and colleges. The biblical motto should always be that of making every thought captive to Jesus Christ (2 Corinthians 10:5).

Evelyn Kelly, the principal of a Catholic school in Ottawa, provides a clear and positive example of what should be occurring in Catholic schools. Interestingly, attendance at Mass is not mandatory in her school. For Kelly, "the most important feature of Catholic education is the fact that religion isn't compartmentalized, but is present in such a way that it can permeate every facet of a student's life and studies" (Sweet 1997, 100).

The dangers of compartmentalization do not, however, mean that there is no place for times of worship or the study of the Bible and theology at Christian schools and colleges. I am only arguing here that these by themselves do not make a school or college Christian. I would further suggest that there is a need for a unique kind of study of the Bible or theology at Christian colleges and universities, what might be labelled "worldviewish theology." I would suggest that every Christian college should have a course devoted to this study. There are some excellent resources for a course such as this.[37]

3.   Superficial integration: Christian schools and colleges must also avoid what can only be described as superficial attempts at developing a Christian curriculum. For example, a lesson in history does not become genuinely Christian because it begins with a short prayer. Teaching arithmetic does not become Christian simply because you have students adding up angels instead of apples in order to learn that $2 + 2 = 4$. Nor should we think that the slapping of a few Bible verses onto the end of a research paper makes that endeavour genuinely Christian.[38]

4.   Other scholarship: In a pluralistic world, Christian scholarship and a Christian approach to curriculum exist alongside Marxist, feminist, Muslim, and secular scholarship and curricular proposals. The curriculum of Christian schools and colleges should not be characterized by a narrow restriction to the Christian perspective alone. There should be increasing exposure to other worldviews as students mature. Especially in high school and at the college level, students in Christian schools should study how the curriculum would be shaped differently by other religious traditions.

At the same time, the pluralism within the Christian community should be recognized. There are schools of thought within the Christian academic world just as there are in the secular academic world. Christians should avoid speaking of any one approach as *the* Christian view on any subject. Any attempts at working out a Christian curriculum or doing Christian scholarship should be offered tentatively and should be open to correction. This calls for critical thinking and constant re-evaluation of suggested offerings of Christian thinking in various disciplines and research programs.

And how do Christians relate to others adhering to different world-views and belief systems? There needs to be dialogue in which each remains true to his or her own presuppositions, and seeks to understand the presuppositions of the other. The Christian can approach the other with a genuine attitude of wanting to learn from the other. Truth in other belief systems needs to be affirmed.[39] Such affirmation can further serve to invigorate the Christian's own understanding of truth.

11 The Danger of Fundamentalist Fanaticism

> Fanaticism and intolerance are central characteristics of
> fundamentalism and Thiessen should have dwelt longer on the
> question how in an orthodox Christian upbringing the risk of the
> development of a fundamentalist mentality can be prevented.
>
> Ben Spiecker, "Review Article:
> Commitment to Liberal Education"

> [T]he true believer [is] the man of fanatical faith who is ready to
> sacrifice his life for a holy cause ... It [fanaticism] was a Judaic-
> Christian invention.
>
> Eric Hoffer, *The True Believer*

We are afraid of religious fanaticism, and quite rightly so. Fanaticism is
often associated with the cults. The tragic mass suicide of the Heaven's
Gate cult was very much in the news when I first began working on this
chapter. Thirty-nine men and women in a California mansion method-
ically killed themselves in the belief that it was time to take leave of
their "vehicles" or "containers" (i.e. bodies) in order to rendezvous
with a spaceship they believed was trailing the Hale-Bopp comet. Their
beliefs were an odd mixture – part Christian, part Asian mystic, part
Gnostic, part New Age, mixed with a good dose of science fiction and a
love for Star Wars and X-Files. And of course, there was the inevitable
guru, Marshall Herf Applewhite, age sixty-six, who had founded the
group in 1975, first known as "Guinea Pig," then "Human Individual
Metamorphosis," and finally "Heaven's Gate," until their demise (or
transformation to a higher form of existence) in March of 1997. This
sad event occured just eighteen years after the cultism of the 1970s ar-
rived at its dark crescendo in Jonestown, Guyana, where more than
nine hundred members of Jim Jones's People's Temple died at his order, most by suicide.[1]

Fanaticism is not limited to the cults. The distinction between cults
and "genuine" religions is rather subjective, and it must surely be admitted that cultic faith or fanaticism is also possible in the traditional
religions. Josephus, though a loyal, believing Jew, referred to the
Jewish Zealots of his time as dangerous fanatics.[2] Some modern equiv-
alents are easy to identify – militant Islamic fundamentalists and

Christian anti-abortion crusaders who even go so far as to destroy abortion clinics and kill abortionists.

One does not have to look far to uncover expressions of suspicion about commitment and teaching for commitment in educational writings. My book entitled *Teaching for Commitment* (1993) was an attempt to defend such teaching with respect to Christian nurture; to show that teaching for Christian commitment can be reconciled with a reconstructed ideal of liberal education. Ben Spiecker, in a major review article of my book, agrees with a suggestion that I make in the conclusion of the book: that many people will object to my defence of educational pluralism by pointing to the danger of such schools serving as breeding grounds for fanaticism and intolerance (Spiecker 1996, 288).[3] He goes on to ask the following question as raising the major challenge to my thesis: "Is it possible to teach for Christian commitment without promoting a fundamentalist mentality" (1996, 290)? Many others would join Spiecker in suggesting that one of the major problems with religious schools is that they frequently, if not invariably, foster religious fanaticism.

John Hull, for example, has made a distinction between "religionism" and genuine religion. "Religionism describes an adherence to a particular religion which involves the identity of the adherent so as to support tribalistic or nationalistic solidarity ... Religion is in principle universal in its outlook but religionism is committed to the partial" (1992, 70). Here again, we see religious commitment described in a negative light. Only uncommitted multi-faith religious education will be able to combat the tribalism inherent in commitments to particular religious traditions, according to Hull (72);[4] religious schools are by their very nature sectarian, and their approach is to nurture students into a tribalistic religious commitment, rather than to provide a liberal religious education. In other words, religious schools cannot avoid teaching for religious fanaticism.[5]

There can be no denying that religious schools teach for commitment. Christian schools, for example, will teach their students to heed Jesus' challenge to believers to love the Lord your God, with all your heart, soul, strength, and mind (Matthew 22:37). Jesus is here recalling the Hebrew Shema, which, after one statement of it in the Old Testament, is immediately followed by a call to "impress" this and other commandments on your children. "Talk about them when you sit at home, and when you walk along the road, when you lie down and when you get up."[6] This is obviously a call to teach for commitment. But surely such teaching runs the risk of also promoting religious fanaticism.

The call to commitment and to teaching for commitment grows out of some basic tenets of Christian theology. While the same could no doubt be said about other religious traditions, I will again limit myself in the main to the Christian tradition. My argument can, I believe, be easily extrapolated to other religious traditions.

THE POSSIBILITY OF HEALTHY
RELIGIOUS COMMITMENT

How then does one respond to the charge that any form of teaching that both begins with and aims at religious commitment runs the serious and perhaps inevitable risk of promoting religious fanaticism? In order to answer this charge we will first need to look at commitment and religious commitment more generally. A major part of this chapter will attempt to remove some of the conceptual confusions that often surround the notions of religious commitment and fanaticism. Here we need to dispense with one problem that might stand in the way of any possibility of an answer to this charge. Many critics of religion maintain that religious commitment is dangerous per se, and that there simply cannot be any such thing as a healthy religious commitment. Jay Newman, in his study of fanaticism and hypocrisy, quotes a writer as saying, "[P]eople tend to view committed others suspiciously." He adds, "And what is perhaps most disturbing of all is the spreading inclination to perceive the properly committed person as a dangerous fanatic" (Newman 1986, 119).

Clearly if every true believer is viewed as fanatical, then of course there really is no point in proceeding any further. The argument is won by definition, and there is nothing more that can be said. In this case orthodox Christianity is by definition fanatical, and teaching for commitment will therefore also result in fanaticism by definition. This is no doubt the position of many sceptics, though I do not think that Spiecker wants to frame the challenge in this way. He admits, for example, that a system of educational pluralism with schools teaching for commitment would not *necessarily* imply the fostering of such perversions as fanaticism and intolerance (1996, 288). Not all writers are as careful as Spiecker (e.g. Hull). Hence I draw attention to the danger of ruling out, by arbitrary definition, the very possibility of a healthy religious commitment and teaching for healthy religious commitment.

HEALTHY COMMITMENT AND
ITS PERVERSIONS

In order to proceed with the argument of this chapter, it will therefore be necessary, first of all, to see if it is possible to distinguish between healthy religious commitment and religious fanaticism. Jay Newman attempts this in his important study of fanaticism and hypocrisy (1986). He first examines commitment generally.

Commitment, in the modern sense, is pledging or binding oneself to behave in a way that grows out of one's acceptance of a worldview, Newman maintains (1986, 11–12). Drawing on Newman, who in turn is influenced by the German philosopher of culture Wilhelm Dilthey, I want to isolate four defining features of a person's commitment to a worldview: (a) belief: acceptance of certain broad convictions (presuppositions) about the nature of life and the world;[7] (b) emotion: emotional habits and tendencies based on these beliefs; (c) value: a system of value-judgments, purposes, and preferences; (d) behaviour: the beliefs, attitudes, and values are acted on in daily life, all of which serve to give life unity and meaning.[8]

Newman goes on to define a proper or healthy commitment in terms of an Aristotelian mean between the vice of excess (fanaticism) and the vice of defect (hypocrisy) (18). I believe Newman's vice of defect would be better labelled "undercommitment," a term which he himself uses at one point (84–90). Undercommitment involves a deficiency in belief, a kind of "underbelieving"; emotional restraint or sluggishness; "undervaluing"; and finally, "weakness of will," or indifferent behaviour – after all, it doesn't matter what you do (1986, 91, 98, 100, 104, 30). Undercommitment is the vice that pervades Western societies, according to many social commentators. In a famous passage of his *Grammar of Assent*, Cardinal Newman describes liberal Englishmen as professing to believe, but their religion is not real and their assent to religious beliefs does not affect their conduct.[9]

At the opposite extreme is the fanatic, who is characterized first of all by "overbelieving," or the believing of something too strongly. Here one believes with more certitude and conviction than evidence warrants, or one becomes preoccupied with a certain idea at the expense of other equally important ideas (Newman 1986, 42–8). The fanatic is, secondly, one who is too angry, too zealous, or too excited about his or her commitment (48–51). Thirdly, fanatics attach too much importance to their causes or to certain of their values at the expense of other values they hold or ought to hold (52). For example, the chess fanatic allows his or her love for chess to overshadow other loves that he or she should have (53). Finally, fanaticism is characterized by compulsive, over-zealous behaviour. Sometimes bigotry, credulity, intolerance, and superstition are associated with fanaticism, but Newman sees these qualities as different from fanaticism and only contingently related (34–6).[10]

Newman acknowledges that religious fanaticism is the paradigm of fanaticism because religious faith has historically been the main example of commitment to a worldview (68). He also admits that the distinction between healthy commitment and its perversions is somewhat subjective (69–74). If, for example, one is very anti-religious, there is a tendency to see any form of religious commitment as fanatical – a tendency that is common today. Attacks on religion can themselves be excessive, and thus anti-religious writers like Voltaire, Feuerbach, Nietzsche, and Marx are at least as fanatical as most of the religionists that they condemn (69). (Here is another response to the problem of arbitrary definition considered earlier!) The context we live in also plays a part in ascribing the label of fanaticism. Thus, too, new or strange beliefs, practices, and values are seen as excessive to outsiders (68). For example, the *OED* notes that the label "fanatic" was applied in the latter half of the seventeenth century to Nonconformists as a hostile epithet (38).

While acknowledging a degree of subjectivity, Newman tries to avoid a radical ethical relativist position concerning judgments about fanaticism (1986, 73). The ascription of fanaticism is no more subjective than that of other vices such as prodigality or excessive fearlessness. There is an impressive cross-cultural consensus concerning what constitutes a clear paradigm of these vices (74). We can achieve a degree of objectivity in making such ascriptions. Thus, for example, Josephus, himself a Jew, is able to condemn the small, militant, anti-Roman band of fellow Jews, the Zealots, whose very name prompts the label of fanaticism, though he can empathize with their commitment (69–71). Like all vices, fanaticism admits of degrees, and this too makes ascription difficult, but not impossible (79).

It needs to be underscored that fanaticism is a vice, not just a disease (Newman 1986, 25). Religious fanaticism (when properly defined) is wrong, and deserves universal condemnation. Therefore teaching for fanaticism is also wrong and must be condemned. The question that remains is whether it is possible to teach for religious commitment without teaching for fanaticism. But first we need to deal with another word often associated with fanaticism: fundamentalism.

FUNDAMENTALISM AND FANATICISM

As has already been noted, Ben Spiecker raises the problem being addressed in this chapter by introducing the term "fundamentalism." "Is it possible to teach for Christian commitment without promoting a fundamentalist mentality" (1996, 290)? It should be noted that for Spiecker, fanaticism is a central characteristic of religious fundamentalism (288). He is not alone in making this association (cf. Newman 1986, 144). The term "fundamentalism" obviously carries very pejorative overtones for many people.

Emotionally laden terms, however, call for special caution. We must beware of arbitrary definitions. Unfortunately, Spiecker fails to distinguish clearly between orthodox or evangelical Christianity and fundamentalism, saying only that "they share some necessary conditions" (1996, 289). He also fails to distinguish between Christian fundamentalism as a historical movement within Protestant Christianity and the problem of religious fundamentalism generally, which tends to be associated with fanaticism. It is very misleading to associate *all* Christian fundamentalism with fanaticism. It is only the narrow, closed-minded, radical, militant, and political fringe of Christian fundamentalism that deserves the pejorative label.[11] This also applies to other expressions of religious fundamentalism, for example, Islamic fundamentalism.[12] Clearly there is some overlap between fundamentalism and fanaticism, and so Spiecker's concerns deserve some attention.

One feature that Spiecker associates with Christian fundamentalists is that adherents must "stick" to the fundamentals – believers must adhere to the traditional central truths of the faith; for example, the substitute passion of Christ, the virgin birth, the resurrection of Christ (1996, 289). Spiecker is obviously worried that sticking to these fundamentals leads to a "fundamentalist mentality," understood in a pejorative sense (289). Spiecker is not alone in having these concerns.[13]

I would argue that believing in certain fundamental doctrines cannot in itself be considered suspect or be seen as the source of the pejorative overtones inherent in the term "fundamentalism." Every school of thought, even in the sciences, can be defined in terms of certain fundamentals (e.g. quantum theory, behaviourism). The critical question is *how* one *sticks* to these fundamentals. Even liberalism has some fundamental tenets! I would dare to suggest that there are liberal fundamentalists who do not hold on to the fundamentals of liberalism in a rational open-minded manner.

I believe it is possible for fundamentalist Christians to "stick" to the fundamentals of Christianity in a rational, open-minded manner, humbly acknowledging that they may be wrong, and respecting those who differ. It might be desirable to reserve the term "fundamentalism" for an unthinking and closed-minded approach to religion, although I'm not sure that even this is entirely fair. In any case, orthodox and evangelical Christians share with Christian fundamentalism the acceptance of the basic doctrines of the Christian faith, but they would distance themselves from unthinking, narrow-minded, and intolerant attitudes often associated with fundamentalism.

Part of Spiecker's concern with Christian fundamentalism (and orthodox or evangelical Christianity) would seem to be that he simply disagrees with some of the fundamentals. For example, Spiecker sees some doctrines of Christianity, such as the doctrine of sin, as giving rise to "feelings of irrational fear, guilt and despair" (1996, 7). But what makes guilt irrational? And who defines what is irrational? The question raised by MacIntyre in the title of his book *Whose Justice? Which Rationality?* is most appropriate here (1988). Clearly, for orthodox Christians, feeling guilty before a God who will someday hold them accountable for their actions is not at all irrational.

One may disagree with this, but liberals, according to Rawls, must accept the "burdens of judgement," allowing that reasonable persons may affirm differing reasonable doctrines (1993, 12–13). Macedo even acknowledges the possibility of "reasonable fundamentalists," though his concern is more with a willingness to engage in dialogue in the political realm despite the fact that fundamentalists might disagree with others about their ultimate ideals (1995a, 476, 477).

Another aspect of Spiecker's (and others') concerns about fundamentalism has to do with the source of these fundamentals. Obviously revelation plays a key role in defining the fundamentals of Christianity. An appeal to divine revelation should not in itself be seen as a ground for holding fundamentalism (and orthodox Christianity) suspect. Rational and critical approaches to revelation are quite in keeping with an evangelical version of Christianity with which I identify.[14]

A final concern of Spiecker's is with the making of exclusive truth claims. The fundamentalist claims that "there is only one salvation," and this undermines the need for "broad sympathies" and leads to fanatical intolerance (1996, 289, 290). These concerns are also behind Hull's identification of teaching for commitment with tribalism. Having already dealt with the problems of intolerance, I want to challenge the idea that making exclusive truth claims invariably leads to fanaticism.

I would argue that any truth claims are by their very nature exclusive.[15] Spiecker himself makes an exclusive claim when he condemns fundamentalists – they are wrong and he is right. His Wittgensteinian interpretation of religious language is again a very particular exclusivist position, which leads him to reject an orthodox interpretation of Christianity as mistaken. A liberal theological position might sound more tolerant, but we must not be misled by appearances. A refusal to allow orthodoxy to define itself displays a profound lack of respect and tolerance which is unfortunately all too common among liberal theologians, as well as among those who defend liberalism generally.

Let me sum up this discussion of the content of orthodox Christian commitment. Clearly orthodox Christian commitment involves the acceptance of certain credal content which is viewed with a good deal of suspicion by sceptics and adherents to some other religious traditions, including that of liberal Christianity. However, just because we disagree

with the beliefs of a religiously committed person does not give us sufficient grounds to declare them irrational. After all, people who are otherwise quite rational do adhere to these beliefs. It is arbitrary to call
someone a fanatic just because we find their beliefs to be irrational.

Newman therefore quite properly hesitates in making the content
criterion central to distinguishing between healthy and fanatical commitment. Our concern should instead be focused more on the "mode
of commitment" than on the "credal content" of the worldview to
which someone is committed (Newman 1986, 9–10, 21, 40–1). Worldviews are by their very nature all-encompassing and hence difficult to
prove in a strict rational manner. At best, they can be defended on the
basis of a "soft rationalism" (Abraham 1985, ch. 9). Hence Newman is
careful to demand of healthy commitment only that the worldviews be
"reasonably plausible."[16]

CHRISTIANITY AND HEALTHY
RELIGIOUS COMMITMENT

I now want to return to the four distinguishing features of healthy
commitment outlined earlier and ask whether Christian commitment
of an orthodox variety can satisfy them.

(a)   *Belief component*: In part I have already touched on the belief
component of Christian commitment in the previous section dealing
with fundamentalism. But there are a few more aspects of the belief
component of commitment that deserve to be highlighted. Christian
commitment is often associated with a freezing of attitudes and beliefs,
hence with fanaticism. Barrow and Woods, for example, castigate
Catholic teachers for deliberately attempting to inculcate in their pupils an "unshakable commitment" to the truth of Catholicism (1988,
70). This criticism rests on a misunderstanding of the nature of commitment and of orthodox Catholic belief.

It is simply mistaken to assume that religious commitment necessarily entails closed-mindedness. It is possible to combine strong convictions with critical openness, as even John Stuart Mill recognized in his
classic defence of freedom of thought.[17] Open-mindedness is not
empty-mindedness, as Hare reminds us (1979, 53). Nor is commitment, and the believing component of commitment, an all-or-nothing
affair, as is so often assumed by the critics. A dispositional approach to
believing now seems to be the favoured approach among philosophers.[18] Although we might opt for a certain belief as a preferred belief, confidence in this belief comes in degrees.

A dispositional analysis of believing is well illustrated in Jesus' sympathetic response to a father requesting that he heal his epileptic son.

"I do believe; help my unbelief," the father pleads (Mark 9:24). This honest portrayal of believing is repeated elsewhere in the New Testament, where appeals to commitment stand happily alongside appeals to critical openness, as Hull has argued (1984, 190–5, 207–224). Indeed, critical openness is essential, given the fallibility of human nature, and given that the Christian only has a partial grasp of truth, as Paul reminds us in his letters to the Corinthian churches.[19] Moreover, there is evidence to suggest that devout Christians are more open-minded and tolerant than the average citizen.[20]

I therefore conclude that it is quite possible for an orthodox Christian to avoid the sin of "overbelieving" which Newman identifies as one ingredient of fanaticism (Newman 1986, 43–5).

(b) *Emotive component*: Agreeing with Newman, I have also described the fanatic as one who is too angry, too zealous, or too excited. Here a problem arises. Just how do we measure being too zealous or too excited about one's commitment? Newman suggests that such excesses in emotion should be measured either in relation to conventional behaviour or in terms of undesirable consequences for the agent or society (1986, 48–51). Is conventional behaviour a proper measuring stick? Not so, if, as I will argue later, Western societies are to a large extent suffering from the other extreme in regard to commitment – undercommitment. So we are left with measuring excessive emotion in terms of undesirable consequences for the agent or society. The problem here is that it is very difficult to measure the effects of commitment on an individual person or on society as a whole. We must therefore be careful not to expect more precision than the subject matter allows, as Aristotle warned us long ago.

Religious devotion can be very sincere and yet not suffer from excessive emotion leading to undesirable consequences for the devotee or for society at large. There are studies which seem to show that sincere religious devotion leads to happiness and well-being, and that society as a whole seems to be better off if the majority of the people take their religion seriously.[21]

For the devout Christian, Jesus is the model for life. Even sceptics would agree that it is difficult to describe Jesus as a fanatic in terms of expressing excessive emotion. True, there was a single-mindedness to his religious expression, and this finally led him to the cross (more on that later), but most people would agree that there was balance in Jesus' emotional life. For example, with regard to anger, Jesus must surely be described as hitting Aristotle's golden mean – being angry at the right time and the right place and to the right degree and in the right way.[22] Jesus was justifiably angry at hypocrisy and self-righteousness (e.g. Matthew 23), but he could also be very gentle and forgiving (John

8:1–11). Overall, Jesus' life was characterized by emotional balance, which benefited not only himself but also society at large. Since Christians are to be followers of Christ, it is therefore surely unfair to describe the orthodox Christian as necessarily fanatical in terms of emotional imbalance.

(c)   *Value Component*: Newman has described fanatics as attaching too much importance to their causes or to certain of their values at the expense of other values they hold or ought to hold (1986, 52). I have already conceded that the language which the Bible uses to describe the commitment of believers is very strong – love God with your whole being. Here we need to remember that there is a sequel to this "first and greatest commandment." It is to "love your neighbour as yourself. All the Law and the Prophets hang on these two commandments" (Matthew 22:39). The principle of loving God is balanced with the principle of loving one's neighbour. Spiritual devotion is balanced with caring for those on earth. This kind of balance runs throughout the Christian Scriptures.[23] It is true that all values are somehow subsumed under the ultimate value of loving God, but these other values are not entirely rejected.[24] Rather, they become an expression of, and are inspired by, the believer's love to God. Love to God gives a unity to all other values, which is precisely what healthy commitment is supposed to do, according to Newman. So here again, one finds that the expression of Christian commitment does not entail a fanatical distortion of proper valuing.

(d)   *Behavioural component*: Although Newman prefers a dispositional analysis of fanaticism, he would not be entirely averse to my adding a behavioural component to a complete description of the meaning of fanaticism. Ultimately dispositions are expressed in actions, though we must be careful not to be too rigid in this association. For example, religious martyrs might seem to be fanatical, but Newman is surely right in suggesting that, on balance, many heroic martyrs who fight for a just cause must be regarded as having "a positive, constructive, and hence *virtuous* mode of commitment" (Newman 1986, 77). Their behaviour may be based on careful, rational, and critical assessment of what they feel needs to be done to promote their cause, and hence it would be wrong to view them as fanatics. The key, again, is balance. In healthy religious commitment, emotions, values, and behaviour must all display a balance. There are countless examples of devout Christians, even Christian martyrs, whose lives overall are characterized by such balance – St Francis, Mother Theresa, Martin Luther King, early Anabaptist leaders like Conrad Grebel and Felix Manz, and Dietrich Bonhoeffer, to name but a few.

From a theological perspective, we need to be reminded that in the New Testament, Paul specifically warns against the danger of religious commitment leading to dangerous fanaticism. This can occur if commitment isn't accompanied by reflection. "For I can testify about them that they are zealous for God, but their zeal is not based on knowledge" (Romans 10:2). The imperative for orthodox Christians is to express a healthy and sensible commitment to God, which avoids the excesses of overcommitment and undercommitment.

The central purpose of the last few sections of this chapter has been to argue that healthy religious commitment is possible for orthodox and evangelical Christians, and therefore that teaching for commitment need not lead to fanaticism. All too often fears about breeding fanaticism are based on a failure to distinguish this evil from normal conviction and commitment. The former is a perversion of healthy commitment. It is true that teaching for commitment can lead to such a perversion, but it need not. We must not let the fear of perversion make us miss out on the benefits of healthy commitment. Love has its perversions too, but we do not let this stop us from praising the virtues of love.

NEED FOR HEALTHY COMMITMENT

Thus far my focus has been on defending the possibility of a healthy Christian commitment that is not fanatical. We need to move on to the educational implications of this analysis. Before I do this I want to briefly defend the desirability of commitment and more specifically religious commitment.

Jay Newman begins his study of fanaticism and hypocrisy with a bold statement that healthy commitment is necessary for human existence. For the individual, healthy commitment is "a *sine qua non* of happiness, self-realization and peace of mind," according to Newman (1986, 9). I have already referred to studies that bear out this conclusion with regard to Christian commitment. Healthy commitments are also a key to fostering the well-being of a society.[25] "A civilized society," according to Newman, "is dominated by people who have a healthy and socially constructive commitment to some reasonably plausible and morally efficacious world view. A society in which such people gradually lose influence drifts towards a condition of barbarity" (1986, 9). Indeed, as is being increasingly argued by both serious social critics and casual observers of the contemporary scene, we are facing a crisis of commitment in Western societies.

Robert Bellah and associates critique the cancerous individualism of American life, the failure to see the individual in relation to a larger whole, a community and a tradition (Bellah, et al. 1985). In the final chapter they quote from John Donne, who in 1611 at the very beginning of the modern era gave poetic and prophetic expression of the consequences of this cancerous individualism and lack of commitment: "Tis all in peeces, all cohaerence gone; All just supply, and all Relation; Prince, Subject, Father Sonne, are things forgot" (276). Allan Bloom too, in his *The Closing of the American Mind,* which he calls a "meditation on the state of our souls," talks of crises: "an intellectual crisis," "the crisis of liberal education," and "the crisis of our civilization" (1987, 346). At bottom, the concern of both of these popular and oft-reviewed books is a crisis of commitment.

Thus far in this chapter I have focused on the vice of overcommitment, namely, fanaticism. If the social critics I have just referred to are right, then perhaps what we should be more worried about today is the opposite vice of undercommitment. Galston describes the problem in this way: "The greatest threat to children in modern liberal societies is not that they will believe in something too deeply, but that they will believe in nothing very deeply at all. Even to achieve the kind of free self-reflection that many liberals prize, it is better to begin by believing something" (Galston 1991, 255). Lewis Smedes describes today's problem more bluntly: "Hell is a forever without commitment" (1988, 153).

Here we have another explanation for the tendencies today to view any sort of commitment with suspicion and to associate commitment with fanaticism. As has already been mentioned, there is some subjectivity in identifying the vice of fanaticism. When one starts from within a context where undercommitment is the norm, then any degree of commitment will be interpreted as already being a case of overcommitment. Undercommitted persons are simply not in the best position to recognize the vice of overcommitment.

ORIGINS OF SUSPICION ABOUT
TEACHING FOR COMMITMENT

So far in this chapter I have tried to combat the tendency to link religious commitment with fanaticism. But the widespread failure to distinguish healthy commitment from its perversion of overcommitment prompts the question why this failure has come about in the first place. What are some of the underlying causes of contemporary suspicion about conviction and commitment? Has this suspicion always existed? If not, when did it arise? Here I will only very briefly sketch an answer to these questions. I will provide a more detailed analysis in the next chapter in the context of addressing the larger question of the historical context of opposition to religious schools and colleges.

The Enlightenment figures significantly in explaining the origin of suspicion about commitment and teaching for commitment. It was the Enlightenment that gave rise to the more recent ideal of liberal education – what Kimball calls the "liberal-free ideal" of liberal education (1986, 115). Liberal education now came to be associated with liberation – freeing children from their parochial backgrounds and from narrow prejudice.

Special importance is given, in the liberal-free ideal of liberal education, to the value of tolerance. Kimball points out that this was "a new virtue," appearing at the turn of the eighteenth century. Previously, the notion of tolerance had implied weakness or cowardice, that is, a lack of commitment to one's professed beliefs. But now, certainty was viewed as "the mother of intolerance" (121). Liberal education therefore involves subjecting our inherited systems of belief to doubt, starting with a clean slate, searching for truth apart from tradition and authority. Here we see the beginnings of scepticism about commitment inherent in the liberal-free ideal of liberal education.

Stephen Toulmin, in his study of the origins of modernity, puts Kimball's analysis into an even broader historical context (1990). Modernity arose in the seventeenth century as a response to a specific historical challenge – religious strife (1990, 70). It was within the context of turmoil and crisis in Europe that intellectuals rejected the religious authority and tradition which were blamed for the problems of society. The religious/political impasse also prompted the intellectual leaders of the time to adopt some of the key values that have come to define modern liberalism. In order to overcome conflicts that arise because of religious differences and differing conceptions about the good life, modern liberalism assumes an agnosticism about the good life, relegates religion to the private domain, and emphasizes the importance of not imposing one's values and one's way of life on anyone else. Hence neutrality is frequently seen as a defining characteristic of liberalism (e.g. Goodin and Reeve 1989). Again, commitment comes to be seen as a negative thing in modern liberalism.

Several issues need to be raised in response to this brief historical excursus. First, we need to question the motivation behind the adoption of the explicit agenda of modernity and the modern liberal-free ideal of liberal education. Somehow, it was religious commitment, authority, and tradition that were blamed for the problems in seventeenth-century Europe. Causal analysis is very risky, especially when one is dealing with broad social and political phenomena. Was it really religious commitment that was the cause, or was it a corruption of religious commitment? Was it religious authority and tradition that were the culprits, or was it the abuse of authority and the stagnation of tradition? Might the ultimate cause be something much deeper, having to do with the depravity of human nature, for example? Once we entertain questions such as these, we are of course led to the conclusion that modernity was perhaps a mistake. What was needed was not the elimination of religious commitment, but the restoration of healthy religious commitment.

Indeed, it can be argued that modernity/liberalism was wrong not only in its causal analysis but also in the solution that it offered. A case can be made that modernity/liberalism is in fact responsible for the contemporary crisis of commitment – anomie, aimlessness, the almost promiscuous picking up and dropping of values and aspirations.[26] This vice of undercommitment often leads to the opposite vice of over-commitment. Indeed, Bellah and associates go so far as to suggest that modernity/liberalism is in fact responsible for the ideological fanaticism that became so rampant in the twentieth century (1985, 277). And this problem continues into the present century.

By the same reasoning we are led to entertain the idea that the emergence of the liberal-free ideal of liberal education during the Enlightenment was perhaps a mistake. What was needed was not the elimination of teaching for religious commitment, but the restoration of teaching for *healthy* religious commitment.

Further, what this excursion into the history of ideas shows is that opposition to commitment and conviction rests on some very particular commitments of its own – a commitment to the ideology of modernism/liberalism. Today, it is increasingly acknowledged that ideological commitment is in fact inescapable. There is "no innocent tradition," including that of modernity, Tracy argues (1990, 5–6). All seeing and all thinking take place from a particular place and in a certain time. The notion of ideological neutrality is a gigantic piece of bad faith.

The historical analyses of Kimball and Toulmin further show that the ideology and the values underlying suspicions about conviction and commitment are not universally shared in that there was a time when quite another ideology and quite another paradigm of liberal education were broadly accepted. Indeed, there are many today who object strongly to the values inherent in the liberal-free ideal of liberal education, in liberalism, and underlying "the hidden agenda of modernity," to use the subtitle of Toulmin's book.[27] Some go so far as to suggest that modernity and liberalism are dead.

It will be argued in the next chapter that we must be careful not to go too far in reacting to the ideological commitments of the past. We must acknowledge, with Toulmin, that the problem with the agenda of modernity is that it overreached itself (1990, 175). I believe the same problem exists with postmodern and post-liberal thought. We must beware of going to extremes and seek instead a reconciliation between the ideologies of modernism and postmodernism (Toulmin 1990, 175).

TEACHING FOR COMMITMENT
WITHOUT FANATICISM

Such a reconciliation between modern and postmodern values will entail a rethinking of our attitudes towards commitment and teaching for commitment. One of the basic problems with the liberal-free ideal of liberal education which emerged during the Enlightenment has to do with its attitude towards tradition and authority. Bailey, for example, describes liberal education in terms of liberation from the limitations of the present and the particular (1984, 20). The word "limitations" is important. A commitment to the present and the particular is viewed as a limitation, a restriction, and an impediment from which one must be liberated.

Bailey's basic error is that he fails to address adequately the question of how we acquire that from which we need to be liberated. It should be obvious that children grow up in a particular home and will of necessity be initiated into a particular set of beliefs. Only later can they begin to expand their horizons beyond the present and the particular. Critical thinking is only possible if you first have something to be critical about. Doubt can only come after belief. The liberating function of a liberal education is necessarily dependent on children first being initiated into a present and a particular. Or, to use a metaphor of Brenda Watson's, nurture is the necessary "cradle" of liberal education (1987, 9).

Watson, among others, also stresses the psychological need of children to be initiated into a "primary culture" as a way of achieving identity and self-esteem and as a basis for further development towards autonomy (1987, 58–9). Indeed, the need for the security of being grounded in the present and the particular and of having this reinforced by "plausibility structures" persists throughout a person's life, according to Peter Berger (1969, 16, 22).

What this entails is that teaching for commitment is essential for one's mental health. It also needs to be seen as an essential ingredient in liberal education. Hirst, among others, is therefore wrong in making a sharp distinction between two different concepts of education, and describing the primitive and traditionalist notion of education in pejorative terms (1985). Nor can this kind of education, which clearly involves teaching for commitment, be distinguished from the supposedly more sophisticated ideal of liberal education. Instead of talking about two different concepts of education, I prefer to talk about different phases of liberal education (see Thiessen 1993, ch. 8). What is needed is a new paradigm of liberal education which recognizes that initiation into a present and particular commitment is an essential first

phase of liberal education. Indeed, to some degree, it is an ongoing ingredient of liberal education.

Hull is therefore also wrong in describing the confessional approach to religious education such as occurs in religious schools as
tribalistic, thereby implicitly suggesting that it leads to fanaticism
(1992, 70). His criticism rests on an ideological assumption that is itself problematic, as I have already shown. There is nothing inherently
wrong with initiating a child into a particular religious commitment
within a home or a religious school. Indeed, initiation into some kind
of worldview is inescapable.

This would further suggest that neutrality is impossible in teaching.
It is interesting to see how often liberal education is today associated
with neutrality.[28] There are a host of practical and theoretical problems with the ideal of neutral teaching. For example, neutrality on the
part of the teacher is a betrayal of the teacher's own personhood. We
are all people who are situated within a present and a particular, and
to deny this entails a level of hypocrisy. I would suggest that honesty
about our own commitments is the highest level of objectivity that we
can achieve in our teaching. The commitments of teachers are furthermore a valuable resource in the classroom, as Hulmes has reminded us
(1979). They allow students to observe how mature individuals grapple with commitments that are not shared by everyone.[29]

Once we acknowledge the impossibility of neutrality in teaching and
the need to teach for commitment, we are forced to address the additional question of the institutional context in which such teaching can
occur. State-maintained common schools, colleges, and universities
would seem to be ill suited to teaching for commitment, given the pluralistic nature of our societies. There simply are too many commitments represented in the typical classroom of the common school.
There is the further problem of a monolithic state-maintained system
of education being very much open to the charge of institutional indoctrination. A pluralistic system of education is best able to achieve
the needed balance between teaching for specific commitments and
also teaching for commitment to the common liberal values that are
essential for the coexistence of a variety of peoples with various commitments in pluralistic liberal democracies.

SOME PRACTICAL IMPLICATIONS FOR
RELIGIOUS SCHOOLS

In each of the chapters in which I have answered a specific charge
against religious schools and colleges, I have concluded with a treat-

ment of some practical implications for these institutions. My problem in doing so in this chapter is that there is very little that is left to be said. If the practical guidelines considered in the previous chapters are followed, then I believe religious schools will in fact teach for commitment without teaching for fanaticism. Let me summarize briefly.

A fundamental practical principle is that teaching for commitment must be balanced with teaching for openness. Students therefore need to be encouraged to reflect critically on the committed perspective into which they have been nurtured. There will also be an opening up of horizons where students are exposed to other belief systems. They will be encouraged to affirm that which is positive in other religious traditions, and they will be taught to respect the people who are committed to these other religious traditions.

Students will also be encouraged to develop a deepening understanding of the rational underpinnings of the religious tradition into which they have been nurtured. An attempt will be made to cultivate a balance between reason and emotion, between the spiritual and the mundane, between the divine and the human, and between the religious and the secular. The aim is to help students grow towards normal rational autonomy.

Having said all this, I want at the same time to emphasize the legitimacy of boldly teaching for religious commitment in religious schools and colleges. Healthy commitment is necessary, both for individual happiness and for the stability of society as a whole. If educators want to achieve these ends, they will have to teach for commitment. Sadly, we have become embarrassed about teaching for commitment. Evidence for this is found in the tendency of religious schools and colleges to lose their religious identity.

Who is it that really suffers? We need to listen again to the words of a shepherd-prophet written some three thousand years ago: "The days are coming, declares the Sovereign Lord, when I will send a famine through the land – not a famine of food or a thirst for water, but a famine of hearing the words of the Lord. Men will stagger from sea to sea, and wander from north to east, searching for the word of the Lord, but they will not find it. In that day the lovely young women and strong young men will faint because of thirst" (Amos 8: 11–13).

I believe we are facing that kind of famine today, and one important contributing cause of it is the way in which we tend to approach education. Liberal education is understood primarily as an ongoing, neutral, and never-ending search for something. We can't even say it is a search for truth, because liberal educators are often nervous about truth – it sounds so definite and final.[30] Christian educators must be careful not to assume that they are immune to this kind of thinking. Unfortunately, they are shaped more than they realize by their culture. The result: there is a famine in the land.

Interestingly, there are many secular writers who, while they would no doubt object to the overtly religious language of Amos, nevertheless acknowledge that we are facing a crisis of commitment in our day. Echoing Amos, Newman has argued that "it is a matter of brute, cold fact that commitment – like food, clothing and shelter – is one of those things that, given their nature, human beings cannot do without" (1986, 128). Drawing on Kierkegaard, Newman describes the profound existential need for commitment on the part of human beings, a need to "get clear about what I must do," "to find the idea for which I am willing to live and die" (131).

If this is so, then the solution is to dare to restore teaching for commitment to its proper role in education. However, such teaching needs to be done in such a way as to cultivate the "normal" liberal virtues that have been assumed throughout this book. Education in religious schools and colleges, then, will not lead to fanaticism.

PART SEVEN

Conclusion

12 Liberal Values:
The Underlying Problem and
a Proposed Revision

> If our country is called Illyria, then at least in our public life, we
> must sometimes place justice to our Illyrian fellow-country-
> persons before our community loyalty as Greek Orthodox,
> Catholics, Jews, Muslims, or whatever … In its possessive sense, we
> "belong" to no group. We are our own men and women with our
> own lives to live.
>
> Colin Wringe, "Educational Rights in
Multicultural Democracies"

In the previous chapters of this book we have looked at a variety of specific objections frequently raised against religious schools and colleges.
It is now time to take a broader perspective. Is there anything that
unites all these objections? Are there perhaps some common underlying themes? Are they rooted in some particular theoretical framework? And, are there perhaps some uniting principles that underlie
my specific *responses* to each of the objections that have been considered? The purpose of this chapter is to take a broader perspective on
both the charges and my responses to these charges.

This chapter will of necessity be somewhat tentative and sketchy.
Clearly the uncovering of the basic assumptions underlying the predominant approach to theorizing about schooling in Western societies
over the past few centuries deserves a book in its own right. My intent
is merely to *point* the way to a more general understanding of the widespread and strong opposition to religious schools. As well, I want to
point the way to a philosophical foundation which will lead to a more
sympathetic understanding of religiously based schools and colleges in
pluralistic liberal democracies.

ROOTS OF OPPOSITION:
LIBERALISM/MODERNISM

As a first step to moving from the specific to the general, it will be helpful to identify some values that keep coming to the fore in the standard

charges made against religious schools and colleges, values that have surfaced again and again in the previous chapters. To show in detail how these values are at the root of the charges made would be to belabour the obvious, and so I will identify them with little comment.

Autonomy is surely one of the central values that permeates opposition to religious schools and colleges. Autonomy is itself a complex value, including such ingredients as freedom, individuality, independence, and the ability to reflect critically on the choices one makes. Closely related but deserving separate mention is the importance placed on individual rationality and critical thought.

Another central value that comes to the fore repeatedly has to do with fostering unity and social harmony within the nation-state. That which we share in common with other human beings (universality) is viewed as more important than that which makes us unique (particularity). The rights of the individual student are more important than those of the family or the community. Tolerance is a virtue. Fanaticism is a vice. Elitism is also viewed negatively as contributing to disunity. Equality is seen as a virtue.

The notion of neutrality also surfaces repeatedly, though in differing ways. A religiously neutral state (or a neutral state-supported system of education) is seen as a way of promoting common identity and social harmony. The curriculum in schools too is seen as religiously neutral – it must be defined in terms of "public" knowledge.

Finally, education is seen as playing a key role in fostering growth towards rational autonomy, and thereby leading to the emancipation of the individual – freeing the individual from the bonds of the present and the particular (i.e. narrow upbringings), and in the end, leading to the emancipation of society – a democratic social order.

I want to suggest that these values can be loosely identified as belonging to "liberalism." There are some writers who see such a label as problematic, since liberalism has so many meanings that one cannot really talk of it as an intellectual tradition or a political theory or movement (Kimball 1986, 255). Despite the rich historical diversity behind liberalism as a movement, and the manifold varieties of liberalism, it is surely still possible to see this diversity in terms of variations on a small set of distinctive themes.

Gray, in a recent account of liberalism, identifies four central features of the liberal tradition:

[I]t is *individualist*, in that it asserts the moral primacy of the person against any collectivity; *egalitarian*, in that it confers on all human beings the same basic moral status; *universalist*, affirming the moral unity of the species; and *meliorist*, in that it asserts the open-ended improvability, by the use of critical reason, of human life. (1995, 86)

Of these four, Gray suggests that the last two are most centrally constitutive of a liberal political outlook, and are definitive of liberalism as a political philosophy.[1]

While there is also some dispute concerning the origins of liberalism, there is widespread agreement that modern liberalism, as a political movement, as an intellectual tradition, and as an identifiable strand in thought and practice, is no older than the seventeenth century (Gray 1995, xi). Marshall, drawing on various writers, traces the roots of liberalism to the following developments in the early modern era:

(a) the appearance of independent men (or families) due to urbanization and the growth of the market economy, leading to a stress on autonomy and freedom; (b) the attempt to found the state on a non-religious basis due to the problem of the religious wars of the sixteenth and seventeenth centuries; and (c) the growth of Enlightenment philosophies leading to anti-dogmatism and a belief in the autonomy of reason from belief. (1997, 46–7)

More broadly, the origins of liberalism can be traced to the beginnings of what is commonly referred to as "modernity." For Gray, liberalism is the political theory of modernity (1995, ix). Indeed, discussions of modernity invariably reveal the same values as those I have identified as key to defining liberalism.

Toulmin (1990), in his definitive study of the origins of modernity, addresses the interesting question of why these values have come to shape the modern worldview. For Toulmin the values of modernity arose as "a timely response to a specific historical challenge – the political, social and theological chaos embodied in the Thirty Years' War" (70). Within this context of turmoil and crisis in Europe, intellectuals rejected religious authority and tradition, which were blamed for the problems of society. Descartes's methodology of doubt was seen as a key to evaluating critically our inherited systems of belief, thus enabling us to try to start with a clean slate and to search for truth apart from tradition and authority. The oral, particular, local, and timely were all viewed with suspicion, according to Toulmin (30–5). It was within this context that intellectuals searched for a solid foundation upon which to base society so it could become a "cosmopolis," a society which was as rationally ordered as the Newtonian view of nature (67–9). The central values of this solid foundation were written instead of oral, universal instead of particular, general instead of local, timeless instead of timely.

LIBERALISM/MODERNISM AND EDUCATION

The values of liberalism and modernity also find their expression in the widespread acceptance of state-maintained schooling and the ideal of liberal education that these schools are committed to. Kimball has argued specifically for a connection between liberalism and what he identifies as a modern "liberal-free" ideal of liberal education (1986, 255–9). There is first of all the obvious linkage in the language used – talk about "liberation," "liberalism," and "freeing" occurs frequently in both. Kimball also points to the historical parallels as providing justification for the linkage. Both emerge during the Enlightenment. Thinkers associated with the formation of liberalism defended the liberal-free ideal of liberal education. The rise of science was an important factor in the rise of both. There is finally an obvious parallel between the basic liberal values that define liberalism and that underlie liberal educational theory and the modern/contemporary ideal of liberal education.

I have already touched on the origins of the modern and contemporary ideal of liberal education in the previous chapter, and have provided a more detailed account of these origins elsewhere (Thiessen 1993, ch. 2). It will be helpful to contrast the modern ideal of liberal education which emerged during the Enlightenment with an older ideal of liberal education. Kimball suggests that historically there have been two central ideas of liberal education. The first is an oratorical conception of liberal education which became dominant in Roman times, taking a critical stance against speculation and the endless pursuit of truth (1986, 33, 35, 206). What was stressed, instead, was the need to pass on traditions to the uninitiated. This ideal was adapted to Christian aims during the Middle Ages and persisted in Renaissance humanism and the Reformation, according to Kimball (ch. 4).

The second conception of liberal education has its roots in Socrates, with his uncompromising, never-ending search for truth. With the rise of science and the dawning of the Enlightenment in the seventeenth and eighteenth centuries, there emerged what Kimball calls the "liberal-free ideal" of liberal education. Kimball highlights a number of characteristics of this ideal (1986, 119–22, 228). The foremost emphasis is on freedom, especially freedom from tradition and authority. There is also an emphasis on individualism, rationality, critical scepticism, tolerance, and egalitarianism.

Kimball goes on to suggest that what has happened to liberal education in the nineteenth and twentieth centuries is a series of "accommodations" to these earlier ideals, though tensions between the two ideals persist. It would seem that the liberal-free ideal of liberal education is by far the predominant ideal in modern and contemporary educational thought and practice.[2] Clearly the central values of this modern liberal-free ideal of liberal education are the same as the values of liberalism, both having their origins in the Enlightenment.

One final educational expression of liberalism needs to be highlighted. Those who hold liberal values tend to favour state-maintained common schools. Again there are historical parallels. Yael Tamir points out that the emergence of the nation-state at the end of the eighteenth century also marked the emergence of public education whose main goal was to galvanize all citizens into one homogenized nation (1995a, xvii). As already noted in chapter 2, at the heart of "the common school agenda" there was "the deliberate effort to create in the entire youth of a nation common attitudes, loyalties, and values, and to do so under central direction by the state" (Glenn 1988, 4). Today, common schools are still held up as the ideal because here we can have "Education for All" (Swann 1985). This emphasis on the same education for all students embodies, of course, such liberal values as equality and universality. Common schools also would seem to be ideally suited to fostering social harmony and tolerance.

Another feature of common schools deserves separate mention: the ideal of neutrality thought to be embodied in them. I have already alluded to the ideal of neutrality often associated with liberalism. A central aim of modern liberalism is to overcome conflicts that arise because of religious differences and differing conceptions about the good life. Modern liberalism therefore assumes an agnosticism about the good life, relegates religion to the private domain, and emphasizes the importance of not imposing one's values and one's way of life on anyone else. Hence a frequent reference to neutrality as a defining characteristic of liberalism.[3]

This same neutrality is also associated with state-maintained common schools, which are thought to embody the ideal of liberal education. Clearly liberal education, and common schools committed to it, are not neutral in a straightforward sense. They are committed to fostering such values as autonomy, rationality, and a range of determinate ethical and political positions. There is still a certain kind of neutrality that is advocated – a neutrality with respect to substantive judgments about matters that are controversial, such as religious questions. This has both negative and positive implications for common schools committed to providing a liberal education. "On the negative side, the school must avoid insisting upon, or otherwise transmitting, a definitive view on the disputed questions. On the positive side, it must promote the pupils' understanding of the issues and their capacity for personal reflective judgement in relation to them" (McLaughlin 1992b, 108–9).

With regard to religious matters, therefore, the modern ideal of liberal education and common schools committed to it typically emphasize that children must not have their substantive religious commitment determined in any way. Instead, they should be given a broad introduction to the religious domain and be exposed to a variety of religious beliefs in an unbiased way, enabling them to make their own informed judgment. All this is of course far removed from seeing religious education as religious nurture or as initiation into a particular religious tradition, such as would take place in religious schools. Here we begin to see how liberal values, as traditionally understood, entail opposition to religious schools.

I conclude my survey of how liberal values underlie opposition to religious schools and colleges by referring to the theme of liberation which is at the heart of traditional liberalism and contemporary approaches to schooling and education. A fundamental assumption of liberalism/modernism is identified by Peter Berger when he challenges the widely accepted "unexamined prejudice" that modernization "is necessarily a process from lower to higher forms of social life" (1974, 199). According to this assumption, human beings are slowly evolving out of a primal, primitive, pre-rational past in which they were defined by their ethnic, cultural, and religious heritage, and moving towards ever-larger forms of associations, from families to tribes to city-states to nations.

Coleman and Hoffer (1987) show how this assumption is related to the statist orientation towards common schooling which has dominated Western societies. This orientation

sees schools as society's instrument for releasing a child from the blinders imposed by accident of birth into this family or that family. Schools have been designed to open broad horizons to the child, transcending the limitations of the parents, and have taken children from disparate cultural backgrounds into the mainstream of American culture.[4]

A liberal education, it is thought, can facilitate this emancipation from the narrowness of particular backgrounds because liberal education liberates. It moves a person beyond "the present and the particular," to employ a phrase that Bailey uses in the title of his book, which attempts to analyse the character of liberal education (1984). "A general liberal education is characterized most centrally by its liberating aspect indicated by the word 'liberal' ... What it liberates the person from is the limitations of the present and the particular" (20).

Given these views about liberal education and schooling based on the evolutionary assumptions inherent in the Enlightenment, the contemporary widespread opposition to religious schools should come as no surprise. Religious schools are thought to belong to the primitive and pre-rational past. Religious schools can only serve to reinforce particularities, when what is really needed is liberation. Hence Paul Hirst associates the Christian nurture or catechesis which occurs in Christian schools with a "ghetto mentality." Such "education" is opposed to rationality and autonomy, and must be viewed as "inadequate," committed to goals that can only be described as "improper, even sub-human."[5] Another contemporary writer suggests that "it is only those who belong to a sect, not a church, who want their own Christian schools to provide nurture *instead of* education" (Hull 1984, 40). What is needed, according to Hull, is a liberal multi-faith religious education in common schools which educate for all. Only such education will be able to combat the "tribalism" inherent in particular religious commitments (1992, 70).

POST-LIBERALISM/POSTMODERNISM/ COMMUNITARIANISM

In the previous two sections I have tried to show how the charges against religious schools and colleges are more broadly rooted in the values of liberalism or modernism, each having its roots in the Enlightenment. An appreciation of this source of the charges leads in turn to a broader response to the charges that we have been considering in the previous chapters. If the foundation of these charges is in any way problematic, then these charges are themselves made problematic.

Liberalism/modernism is indeed in trouble today. Some go so far as to suggest that the intellectual scaffolding of modernity is systematically being dismantled (Toulmin 1990, ch. 4). Others maintain that liberalism is crumbling and in disarray, and that we are entering a post-modern and post-liberal era. John Gray, for example, in the conclusion to his study of liberalism, argues that "the Enlightenment project which informed and sustained liberalism is now a dead letter ... The intellectual foundations of the Enlightenment project have fallen away" (1995, 85). He therefore gives the subtitle "postliberalism" to his conclusion, which begins with this rather dire note: "As the political theory of modernity, liberalism is ill-equipped to address the dilemmas of the postmodern age" (85).[6]

Indeed, it would seem that liberalism is also faltering *practically* – it does not seem able to solve the problems that originally prompted its formulation. It is this practical inability of liberalism to resolve the problems of religious and ethnic strife that is no doubt causing many to call into question the theoretical foundations of liberalism and modernism. Nationalistic feelings seem to be on the rise, and this is coupled with a growing awareness on the part of national minorities within pluralistic societies that the liberal ideal of a neutral public sphere really embodies a dangerous and oppressive illusion.[7] The titles of recent books speak to the conflicts we are facing: *Culture Wars: The Struggle to Define America* (Hunter 1991); *The New Cold War? Religious Nationalism Confronts the Secular State* (Juergensmeyer 1993).

According to the latest work of distinguished political scientist Samuel Huntington (1996), history may well be entering a momentous and dangerous phase as we face the coming "clash of civilizations," a clash involving antagonisms based on collective cultural and religious identities that will dwarf the controversies of the past. Huntington too points to the danger of Western imposition of supposedly universal liberal values on all other civilizations: "What is universalism to the West is imperialism to the rest" (184). Only if the United States forgoes its pretensions as the vanguard of universalism can it hope to avoid catastrophe, according to Huntington (ch. 12).

Education too is in turmoil, and again the liberal ideas that are at the heart of contemporary education and schooling seem unable to resolve the tensions that exist. Arons has aptly described the "war" over orthodoxy in the public schools of America, going so far as to suggest that this war is the modern equivalent of the wars over state religions fought in the seventeenth and eighteenth centuries (1986, 20–21).

It is not my intent, in this chapter, to provide a detailed critique of liberalism/modernism. Indeed, this has, in effect, already been done in the previous chapters within the context of responding to various charges that are often made against religious schools and colleges. The approach to be taken here is to look more generally at the problems of liberalism/modernism, and to do so by looking briefly at what have been proposed as alternatives to liberalism and modernism – i.e. post-liberalism and postmodernism.

While there have always been those who have been critical of liberal values inherent in liberalism and the theory of liberal education, there would seem to be renewed criticisms of these theories today. There are, for example, the communitarian critics of liberalism.[8] Then there are of course critiques from a conservative perspective.[9] Still others criticize from the perspective of philosophical hermeneutics, critical theory, philosophical historiography, or what is sometimes simply referred to as postmodernism.[10]

Postmodernism is not easy to define, and there are some who doubt that it can be defined. Here again, there are family resemblances in the now numerous postmodernisms. Whatever else it means, "postmodernism" is intended to announce that "modernity" – the "age of

209 Liberal Values: The Underlying Problem

reason" to which the Enlightenment gave birth – has now given way to a "postmodern condition" which produced irreversible changes to the way in which we think and live. What more than anything else characterizes the postmodern world is "a common rhetoric of rebellion against the Enlightenment narrative" (Carr 1995, 78).

Stated positively, postmodernism is an attempt to recapture the pre-Enlightenment respect for tradition and that which is bound to a particular time and place. At the heart of postmodernism is an emphasis on particularity and "the celebration of diversity." Postmodernism is therefore sometimes identified with an appreciation of multiculturalism, and in the educational context, this leads to an emphasis on multicultural education.

For postmodernists, the idea of an ahistorical, non-contingent, rational self is a myth, and therefore complete objectivity is impossible. Knowledge and truth are to some degree relative to place, society, culture, historical epoch, and conceptual framework. Truth needs to be seen as located within the context of discourse communities.[11] Finally, there is an emphasis on emancipation and empowerment in postmodernism. There is concern about the injustices resulting from the dominance of the Enlightenment narrative (Weinstein 1995). More generally there is concern about oppression caused by dominant cultures. Therefore, the emphasis is on empowering the disenfranchised. Education is seen as providing the key to emancipation. This postmodern emphasis on emancipation is, interestingly, similar to the emphasis on liberation in the Enlightenment ideal of liberal education, though the agenda has clearly changed.

It should be evident to the reader that my defence of religious schools and colleges is very much in keeping with these postmodernist themes. The postmodernist emphasis on particularity and the celebration of diversity certainly would lend support to a system of educational pluralism, while Enlightenment universalism prompted the development of state-maintained public schools committed to a liberal education. Indeed, the debate between those defending state-maintained common schools and those defending educational pluralism is, in part at least, an expression of the debate between modernism and postmodernism.[12]

But we must be careful here. To settle the matter by opting for postmodernism would be too easy. Perhaps the death announcement of modernism and liberalism is premature. Perhaps there are also problems with post-liberalism and postmodernism. Indeed, there are some fundamental problems! An emphasis on particularity can lead to isolationism and even hostility between the particular identities. To stress the psychological and social embeddedness of knowledge and truth leads to radical relativism. The emphasis on emancipation and empowerment tends to transform our educational institutions into battlefields.

Again it is quite beyond the scope of this chapter to provide a detailed critique of postmodernism or communitarianism. Instead, my aim has been to set the stage for a reconciliation of the polarities that exist and are in danger of hardening. It should be evident that my general criticisms of postmodernism really draw on liberal or modernist themes. So we seem to have come full circle. In critiquing liberalism via post-modernist themes we have in fact been forced to return to liberalism. I want to underscore once again that there is much in liberalism and modernism with which I am in agreement. Given the deeply felt differences inherent in a pluralistic society, we need to find some common ground. There is an urgent need to cultivate tolerance and respect for those who differ from us. We need to keep searching for the truth with open (but not empty) minds. Thus I am unable to divorce myself entirely from the values of Enlightenment liberalism and modernism. Is there perhaps a middle way?

RECONCILIATION

I want to suggest that one of the problems underlying current debates between liberalism and communitarianism, or between modernism and postmodernism, is that they fall prey to what Amy Gutmann has called "the tyranny of dualisms" (1985, 316–18). One does not have to choose to adopt *either* liberal *or* communitarian values exclusively, because liberal values can be reconstructed so as to accommodate the important insights of the communitarian critics. One does not have to choose between modernism and postmodernism because modernism can be reconstructed to accommodate the important insights of postmodernism. Surely it is possible to recognize not only discontinuities but also continuities between modernism and postmodernism. If so, it is perhaps better to see modernity not as having come to an end, but rather as entering a new phase. Applying this to education, Carr suggests that "the real challenge of postmodernism is to reconceptualise the relationship between education and democracy in a way which acknowledges – rather than simply repudiates – the postmodernist critique of Enlightenment philosophical thought" (Carr 1995, 79).

What is needed is a genuine reconciliation between modernism and postmodernism, and between liberalism and communitarianism.[13] In what follows, I want to begin this task, highlighting a few central themes in which such a reconciliation is especially needed, thereby providing a foundation for a reconceptualization of the "problem" of religious schools and colleges to be considered in the next chapter.

UNIVERSALISM AND/OR PARTICULARISM

Perhaps the broadest way in which to describe this reconciliation is in terms of a reconciliation between universalism and particularism. Universalist values are those which are associated with our universal identity by virtue of our being human beings – as individuals we have certain features that are common to all humankind. Particularist values are those that make us unique – they belong to the individual by virtue of his or her gender, race, ethnicity, or religious commitment (Singh 1995, 21). There is a communal dimension to particularist values. They arise out of our being part of an identifiable group (gender, race), our growing up in a family, our social attachments, our belonging to a cultural community, and our membership in associative communities (Tamir 1995a, 10).

What we have inherited from the Enlightenment is an emphasis on universalism. Particular attachments which are bound to local places and specific times were all viewed with suspicion during the Enlightenment. This suspicion persists in the contemporary embarrassment over family affiliations, religious allegiances, and cultural attachments.[14] There are also educational expressions of this embarrassment, such as in early American thinking. Jefferson's picture of humanity was one of a homogeneous, universal species of rational individuals, and so he downplayed other loyalties such as families or ethnic groups. The aim of education, according to Jefferson, was to nurture universal peoplehood.[15]

Postmodernism, on the other hand, stresses the particular. Communitarians argue that the notion of a common identity is an abstraction. Much of our identity is given. We are defined by our family affiliations, our racial identity, and our cultural attachments, even though these are not chosen.

I would argue that while liberalism/modernism suffers from an overemphasis on universalism, postmodernism/communitarianism suffers from an overemphasis on particularism and the "celebration of diversity." What is needed is an *equal* emphasis on our universal and our particular identities. Universalism without particularism leads to a society where we treat each other as strangers (Sandel 1982, 183). Particularism without universalism leads to isolationist tribalism. We need a balance.

I further believe we need to start with particularity in order to achieve that balance. Our particular identity always precedes our uni-

versal identity. Edmund Burke was right in saying that all true universalism is grounded in loyalty to one's own little platoon.[16]

UNIVERSAL AND/OR
PARTICULARIST REASON

At the heart of the Enlightenment was the notion of an objective universal reason which is capable of grasping truth that should be the
same for all. This approach to reason is of course closely related to the
universalist conception of human nature dealt with in the previous section. Rationalism is based on an abstract reason which is impersonal,
formal, ahistorical, and disembodied. Science is seen as epitomizing
this ideal of reason.

This understanding of universal reason has been shown to be problematic. Since the ground-breaking work of Thomas Kuhn and the publication of his *The Structure of Scientific Revolutions* (1970), the
philosophy of science has generally acknowledged that observation is
theory-laden and that the doctrine of "immaculate perception" which
underlies the traditional conception of science is fundamentally flawed
(Leahy 1990, 140). It is also generally acknowledged that the scientist
(as well as any other thinker) brings a host of convictions, commitments, assumptions, and values to his or her task. The Enlightenment
quest for absolute objectivity is inherently futile – a futile quest for a
"view from nowhere," as Thomas Nagel has described it (1986).

Other developments in epistemology point in the same direction.
The new sociology of knowledge has highlighted the extent to which
knowledge is defined by social conditions of human existence (Young
1971). There are Marxist and neo-Marxist critiques of liberal definitions of knowledge (Apple 1990, 1993). Communitarians have
stressed the tradition-bound nature of thinking (MacIntyre 1988).
Feminist epistemology has made us more sensitive to the fact that
there may be gender biases in our definitions of knowledge (Garry and
Pearsall 1989). Then there are Christian philosophers suggesting that
all knowledge rests on religious presuppositions (Clouser 1991; Middleton and Walsh 1995).

While I do not agree with all aspects of these arguments, and while
I think that some of the claims suffer from exaggeration, the cumulative
argument is strong. Rationality, knowledge, and the justification of our
beliefs are, to some degree, shaped by historical, social, and even psychological conditions. Today, we can no longer glibly dismiss the question raised in the title of Alistair MacIntyre's influential book, *Whose
Justice? Which Rationality?* (1988). The idea of a universal and neutral rationality is now recognized to be itself an expression of a particular

narrative, an Enlightenment narrative, that has gone out of fashion. There is "no innocent tradition," including that of modernity.[17]

Emphasis on the particularity of human reason is not without its own pitfalls, however. It does away with the notion of truth and the search for a common truth. What postmodernists reacting to the Enlightenment fail to realize is that, without the notion of truth, they have in fact undermined their own critique of the Enlightenment.[18] Why listen to postmodernists if they are merely one voice among many other relative voices? Postmodernists further invariably contradict themselves. They seem unable to avoid talking about their postmodern viewpoint as better than that of old-fashioned modernism. Better in terms of what? It seems difficult not to talk about objective and universal truth in some sense.[19]

It is here that I see the need to arrive at a more thorough reconciliation of the epistemological insights of modernism and postmodernism. Yes, there are limitations inherent in our search for truth and we need to be honest about these limitations. However, I in no way want to do away with the notion that human beings must, and invariably do, attempt to transcend these limitations in their search for universal truth. Without balancing the emphasis on limitations with an equal emphasis on the need to try to transcend these limitations, we end up with epistemological relativism. While the human search for truth may be relative, we still need a notion of Truth with a capital "T" (see figure 3: Ladder of Truth).

Here it might be helpful to return to Nagel.[20] Although we cannot get a view from nowhere, according to Nagel, there is within each of us an impulse to transcend our particular personal point of view. This occurs because we recognize that it *is* merely a point of view, a perspective, and not simply an account of the way things really are. "The recognition that this is so," he writes, "creates pressure on the imagination to recast our picture of the world so that it is no longer the view from here" (1986, 70). In other words, each of us is aware of the possibility that our particular perspective might be wrong, and so we aspire to "the view from nowhere," to a view uncontaminated by any perspectival factors.[21]

This aspiration which drove the Enlightenment is admirable, but what we cannot do is transcend our particularity in any absolute manner, and it is here that we need to listen to what the postmodernists have to say. For Nagel, this quest for self-transcendence is bound up with a realist account of human knowledge, that is, an account in which "the universe and most of what goes on in it are completely independent of our thoughts" (92). Without this approach of "critical realism" (i.e. a critical search for truth about objective reality) we remain stuck in the quagmire of relativism or scepticism.

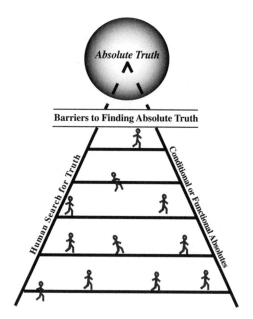

Figure 3
Ladder of Truth

FREEDOM AND/OR LIMITING CONTEXTS

Freedom is a core value of Enlightenment liberalism. There are several components to freedom that could be considered. I wish to focus on two central ideas: freedom as non-restriction of options, and freedom as connected with the autonomous person (Gray 1995, 58). Closely related to these two central ideas are the specific liberal freedoms, such as freedom of speech and expression, association and movement, and occupation and life-style. These "basic liberties" (Rawls's term) can best be seen as framing the necessary conditions for autonomous agency.

One problem with the liberal conception of freedom is that it often seems to take on the connotation of absolute freedom, with the self characterized in terms reminiscent of Sartre – a self-defining and self-determining nothingness. But there can be no such thing as absolute freedom, and the notion of a self as fully autonomous is absurd. Real human beings always find themselves in limiting contexts. The notion of an ahistorical, unencumbered, disengaged self is a myth (Sandel 1996, 11–13). Communitarians have taught us that we cannot ever be fully independent. We are in fact always to some extent interdependent, and the individual self is defined in part by relationships to the community (Sandel 1982, 179–83).

The communitarian conception of the self, however, is in danger of overstressing the contingency and the historical embeddedness of the self. In the end, the self becomes completely determined, locked into the tradition into which one was born.[22] If it is entirely futile to try to escape from the finitude of one's time and place, then, of course, there is nothing more to be said, and we must be content to remain locked into the confines into which we are born.

What is needed here again is a balanced view of human nature which affirms the value of individual autonomy while recognizing the limits of autonomy. With Haworth (1986), I would argue for a more realistic ideal of autonomy, and have elsewhere defended the notion of "normal autonomy" which seeks a middle ground between independence and dependence, individuality and community (Thiessen 1993, ch. 5). Yael Tamir, one of the very few contemporary liberals who achieves such a balance, develops the notion of the "contextual individual," which combines individuality and sociability as "two equally genuine and important" features of human nature (1995a, 33). "[N]o individual can be context-free," Tamir argues, but "all can be free within a context" (14).

Tamir's statement can also be applied to the practical dimension of freedom as absence of restraint. Here again we need to acknowledge that complete freedom is impossible and dangerous. Robert Bork has recently highlighted the dangers inherent in complete freedom within a society in his analysis of modern liberalism's contribution to the decline of America (*Slouching towards Gomorrah*, 1997). His central argument is that liberalism's constant tendency to view with suspicion any constraints on personal liberty as imposed by religion, morality, law, family, and the community has moved America to a point where decent social existence becomes virtually impossible. Balance is needed between affirming the value of freedom and insisting on the importance of responsibility and the inescapable limitations to freedom. Restraint isn't all bad. "Liberty is not license but is 'ordered liberty' – liberty in response to moral truth" (Neuhaus 1997, 51).

Of course, this raises the difficult question of the source of moral truth. This in turn raises the epistemological questions dealt with in the previous section. Although we cannot know moral truth with certainty, we must strive to know it as best we can, and then allow our understanding of it to circumscribe the freedom that we also value.

Sandel describes the weakness of liberalism in terms of its detaching freedom from moral truth and communal identities in this way: "By insisting that we are bound only by ends and roles we choose for ourselves, it [liberalism] denies that we can ever be claimed by ends we have not chosen – ends given by nature or God, for example, or by our

identities as members of families, peoples, cultures, or traditions"
(1996, 322). Freedom needs to be balanced by submission to ends we
have not chosen.

INDIVIDUALISM AND/OR
COMMUNITARIANISM

There is one final and very important area of reconciliation that needs
to be considered. I want to argue for a genuinely equal balance between
the traditional liberal and democratic emphasis on the individual and
the more recent postmodernist and communitarian emphasis on cultural communities. By a cultural community I mean "a community of
people who believe they share an identity and a sense of belonging and
loyalty as a result of holding in common, and valuing the distinctiveness
of, at least one (and normally several) of the following characteristics:
language, religion, ethnicity, history and tradition."[23] This notion of a
cultural community must be distinguished from that of a political community, which, at least in its liberal democratic version, is a community
of individuals (citizens) who are given equal rights and fundamental liberties irrespective of their particular identities.

Here a very significant problem emerges within liberalism. Traditional liberalism does not consider cultural membership to be a *primary* good.[24] The quotation at the head of this chapter illustrates this
position. In an imaginary liberal country, the universal demands of justice must be placed before our community loyalty as Greek Orthodox,
Catholics, Jews, Muslims, or whatever. "In its possessive sense, we 'belong' to no group" (Wringe 1995, 290). Traditional liberalism does attribute some value to cultural membership, however. Indeed,
liberalism is often seen as protecting the value of cultural membership,
but only by virtue of the value placed on it by individuals. Liberalism,
at least in its more traditional form, is committed to allowing individuals to pursue their preferences, desires, and interests regardless of the
way in which these were formed (Tamir 1995b, 168). In other words, if
individuals see cultural membership as a good then it should be seen
as having value, though only as a private good, and only as a secondary
good which is dependent on individual choice (Tomasi 1995, 603).[25]

I want to go much further than to treat cultural membership only as
a private, secondary good which is dependent on individual choice.
I want a genuine reconciliation between the values of modernism and
postmodernism. I want to equalize "respect for individuals" and "respect for groups" (cf. Tomasi 1995, 583).

Here we must beware of the danger of overreaction. I concur with
Halstead when he says that while cultural membership has been un-

dervalued in classical liberalism, the danger is that the pendulum may swing too far in the other direction (1995, 271). The communitarian emphasis on the social self sometimes succumbs to this danger. Too much of an emphasis on the social self is a violation of individual integrity. Too much of an emphasis on national, cultural, or religious identity may lead to the adoption of closed versions of culture or community, and to a refusal to engage with the difficult problems that arise from having to live with difference. Communities also are not as clearly defined, separate, or unchanging as is often assumed, and individuals most often are a part of several communities (Wringe 1995, 290). Thus we seem to be driven back to the individual as one who finally has to sort out what community membership means. Indeed, without the corrective of the individualism inherent in liberalism, communitarianism is suspect, both philosophically and practically. Again we seem to be driven to a middle position with regard to the dichotomy between the individual and the community.

THE POLITICS OF RECOGNITION

My review of some areas of needed reconciliation would be incomplete without an acknowledgment that there is indeed a lot of ferment in contemporary liberal thought, precisely over attempts to accommodate pluralism and the postmodern critiques of the Enlightenment liberalism.[26] Much of this debate has centred around what has been called "the politics of recognition," the seminal essay here being Taylor's 1994 essay by this title.[27] It is quite beyond the scope of this chapter to provide a careful evaluation of this literature, except to suggest that most of these attempts fail to achieve a genuine and balanced reconciliation between the polarities under discussion.[28] Of all contemporary liberals, I believe Tamir comes closest to achieving the balance that I am arguing for.[29] Interestingly, Tamir is one of few liberal writers to defend religious schools (1995a, Preface).

BACK TO EDUCATION

The argument of this chapter has been rather abstract, and the reader may have felt that I have strayed from the field of education. The abstractness is due to a major objective of this chapter – I was looking for some values, principles, worldviews that were at the root of the various objections against religious schools that have been considered in the previous chapters of this book. I have argued that these objections have their origins in the Enlightenment and what has subsequently been labelled modernism. Liberalism too is very much a modernist philosophy.

Postmodernism is at its core a reaction to the Enlightenment, and while I sympathize with its critique of Enlightenment thinking, I believe that it is just as much guilty of extremism as is modernism. I have therefore proposed a reconciliation between modernism and postmodernism, between individualism and communitarianism, between unity and diversity. Much of this chapter has dealt with defining and defending this middle way.

We are now in a position to work out the educational implications of this reconciliation. Among contemporary liberal writers, Amy Gutmann has been at the forefront of the debate concerning the possibility of the reconciliation I have been describing, especially as it applies to education. From the beginning Gutmann has been very clear in her desire to discover politics "that combines community with a commitment to basic liberal values" (1985, 320). More recently she has said again that her aim is to achieve "a genuinely principled combination" of "transcendent universalism" and "separatist particularism" (1996, 156, 162, 165). Despite her laudable aim of reconciling the polarities dealt with in this chapter, Gutmann remains opposed to religious schools.

I believe that Gutmann still fails to achieve a genuine balance between universalism and particularism, or more generally between the values of modernism and postmodernism. The following chapter will provide a careful justification of my critique of Gutmann's attempt to achieve this balance with regard to education. This will then lead to my concluding argument – a genuine and balanced reconciliation between modernism and postmodernism seems to point in the direction of a system of educational pluralism.

13 Towards Educational Pluralism

Public education is the premier public institution for the
preservation of democracy.
> Jerome Hanus and Peter Cookson, *Choosing Schools:*
> *Vouchers and American Education*

Restructuring school systems is the single most important policy
issue facing western education.
> Mark Holmes, *Educational Policy*
> *for the Pluralist Democracy*

The major thrust of this book has been a defensive one – answering
various objections raised against religious schools and colleges. In the
previous chapter I began laying the groundwork for an offensive strategy. Postmodernism and communitarianism, with their emphasis on
particularity and the respecting of plurality, would seem to lead naturally to a positive argument for religious schools and colleges. Such
schools can surely better accommodate the multicultural and multi-
faith nature of our society. But, as I argued in the previous chapter,
postmodernism and communitarianism are themselves not immune to
criticism. I am therefore distancing myself from this approach to defending religious schools.[1] My positive defence of religious schools
and colleges takes a more sophisticated and difficult route.

I have proposed, instead, a reconciliation of modernism and postmodernism, a blending of the values of liberalism and communitarianism. What is needed is a balance between a recognition of particular
values inherent in the great variety of cultures and traditions that make
up our Western societies today and an emphasis on cultivating the universal virtues that are normative because of our common human nature. Only such a reconciliation will help us to overcome the social and
religious controversies and conflicts that seem to be surfacing in our
societies with renewed intensity, given the growing loss of cultural cohesion and common values, and given the growing multicultural nature of most Western societies today.

What does this proposal for a reconciliation between modernism
and postmodernism, or between liberalism and communitarianism,

entail for the structure of education? That is the central question to be addressed in this chapter. While there has been a growing body of recent literature on this question, I do not believe that these discussions have as yet faced the full educational implications of the reconciliation under consideration.[2] I want to argue that a genuine reconciliation between modernism and postmodernism, or between liberalism and communitarianism, entails a pluralistic educational system. Here it needs to be pointed out that there may well be other considerations that come into play in a final resolution of the implications of the argument of this book with regard to the structure of education (for example, practical, political, financial, and demographic considerations). My discussion is limited to working out the educational implications of the previous chapter. Hence the somewhat tentative title of this chapter: Towards Educational Pluralism.

STATE-MAINTAINED COMMON SCHOOLS

Most of the recent discussions in educational philosophy about achieving a proper balance between universal, unifying values and the recognition of difference in pluralistic societies assume a context of state-maintained common schools. Discussions concerning the meaning of citizenship and the requirements of civic education in multicultural societies are a variant on this theme. In both discussions most writers maintain that an appropriate reconciliation between universalism and particularism can *only* be achieved within the context of state-maintained common schools. Alternatively, some maintain that a balance can *best* be achieved within this context. In either case, it is most commonly maintained that a happy blend between the universality inherent in modernism/liberalism and the particularity inherent in postmodernism and communitarianism either cannot be achieved in religious schools, or is very difficult to achieve within this context. I dare to question established opinion. First some concrete examples of prevailing opinion.

The opening chapter of the Swann Report of Great Britain is entitled "The Nature of Society," and very quickly calls on all religious and ethnic groups "to participate fully in shaping the society as a whole within a framework of commonly accepted values" (1985, 5). At the heart of this report is the ideal of a society which is "both socially cohesive and culturally diverse," containing "diversity within unity" (6, 8). The educational implications are already apparent in the title of the report, "Education for All." They are also summarized in a concluding statement: "Throughout this report we have argued for *all* students to share a common educational experience which prepares them for life in a truly pluralist society" (508). The assumption is that such an education occurs in common state-supported schools. The report argues further that "the best and perhaps the only way" to achieve the ideal of "diversity within unity" is via an educational system of common schools (509). What about religious schools? "Throughout the report we stress our misgivings about the implications and consequences of 'separate' provision of any kind, explicitly catering to ethnic minority pupils" (510).

Amy Gutmann, a distinguished American political theorist, has been trying to overcome "the tyranny of dualism" that she finds implicit in communitarian critiques of liberalism (1985, 316–18). Gutmann's project is, I believe, an attempt to give *equal* emphasis to the universality of traditional liberalism and the particularity inherent in the politics of recognition. In a recent essay, Gutmann has also struggled with the educational implications of a political theory which achieves such a combination (1996). For Gutmann, the answer is found in a "democratic education" which involves "a genuinely principled integration of universalist and particularist values" (156, 170). This combination is best achieved within publicly supported schools, according to Gutmann, though she suggests more needs to be done by way of respecting religious differences within these schools (165–9). Public schooling can foster the self-esteem and identification of individual students with their particular cultures, according to Gutmann. Such schools can also promote tolerance, mutual respect, and the skills of deliberative democracy which are so essential to getting along in a multicultural society (160–1, 165).

On the surface, it would seem that state-maintained common schools inspired by liberal principles are ideally suited to providing an education that integrates particularist and universalist values. A common school that brings together students from various religious and cultural traditions becomes a microcosm of the larger pluralistic society. Here students will naturally get to know each other, to understand their varying cultural and religious backgrounds. They should become more tolerant and respectful of each other as they are "forced" to talk to each other, practising some of the skills necessary to living in a multicultural society. Common schools can also provide a common education, preparing students to live harmoniously in one society. It is hard to disagree with what seems to be so obvious a way to achieve the blend being defended in these final chapters.

I believe there are a number of serious problems with the ability of common schools to achieve a genuine and equal balance between universalism and particularism. Other problems with state-maintained common schools could be considered.[3] I am limiting myself to the problems relating to the balance in question. Before addressing these problems, I will outline an alternative pluralistic structure for schooling which I consider to be a better way of achieving the required balance between universalism and particularism that I see as essential to a healthy pluralistic liberal democracy.

A MODEL OF EDUCATIONAL PLURALISM

The model of educational pluralism that I am defending in this final chapter grows out of a more general ideal of a pluralistic liberal democracy, which in turn grows out of the reconciliation between universalism and particularism (and its variants) defended in the previous chapter. I can only elucidate a few key elements of this more general notion.

What I am proposing is a radical rethinking of the nature of liberal democracies.[4] What is needed is an acknowledgment of the growing pluralism of Western societies, namely, a growth in the variety of cultures and traditions, or what Tamir refers to as "cultural communities" (Tamir 1995a, 68).[5] Contrary to traditional liberal forecasts, there also seems to be increasing importance placed on parochial identities based on ethnic and religious allegiances (Juergensmeyer 1993, 1–2). What is further needed is a greater awareness of the seriousness of the problem of deep differences concerning values and conceptions of the good life between differing cultures and traditions.[6] Somehow we need to see this pluralism and these deep differences not as a problem to be overcome but as a positive resource to be used to build consensus and reinforce political civility.[7] My revised model of pluralistic liberal democracies contains elements of what have been termed "pragmatic liberalism," "consociational democracy," "chartered pluralism," and "liberal nationalism."[8] Some writers prefer to describe this ideal in terms of structural and confessional pluralism.[9]

A central feature of my ideal of a pluralistic liberal democracy is a balance between individual and group rights. The driving force of the majoritarianism of traditional liberal democracies "is to homogenize the public side of society by ignoring group rights and recognizing only the rights of individuals" (McCarthy et al. 1982, 112). I have argued, on the contrary, that we need to give equal recognition to our communal identities. Tamir quite correctly calls for a balance between the notions of personal autonomy and communal belonging, viewing these concepts as complementary rather than conflicting. She proceeds by "suggesting that no individual can be context-free, but that all can be free within context" (1995a, 14).

We must further acknowledge what Mouw and Griffioen label "associational pluralism" (1993, 16). Within any society there are, and should be, a diversity of associations, like families, clubs, corporations, unions, churches, and schools. Some writers use the term "structural pluralism" to characterize these various modes of association. Others refer to "intermediate institutions," each of which should be given relative autonomy, its own rightful area of jurisdiction (Berger and Neuhaus 1977). Each should allow the other to perform its role, and see itself as partner with the other. Each will be given equal protection under the law and will be treated with equity and justice.

A genuine pluralism must also do justice to the fact that we live in a world in which there is "confessional pluralism" – a wide variety of worldviews and conceptions of the good life – the traditional problem that liberalism has tried to address. The concept of pluralism I am advocating allows the differing communities to express their values institutionally, via establishing their own schools, churches, and cultural and communal centres. Structural pluralism must therefore also be infused with confessional pluralism. Fundamental to my vision of a pluralistic society is the freedom for individuals and communities to express their particular faith in each of the intermediate institutions that are part of the social order.

The aim of politics is to give the space to live out our deepest differences, not only at the individual level, as has been stressed by traditional liberalism, but also at the communal level. Freedom to live in accordance with our deepest convictions, both individually and communally, is an essential ingredient of the kind of liberal democracy I am proposing. Freedom of religion (i.e. freedom to live in accordance with our deepest convictions) is not only a precious, fundamental, and inalienable human right, it is also a key to living together despite our deeply held differences. Here it is most important not to restrict religious freedom to church life – a social structure that is generally seen as separate from the state in Western countries (Skillen 1994, 84). Because religion expresses itself through all of society, religious freedom must be extended to the structural pluralism of all the intermediate institutions within a society.

What does this revised ideal of pluralistic liberal democracies entail for education? Different cultural and religious communities should be allowed to have their own schools. While I am arguing for a plurality of schools, each of which is committed to teaching its particular set of values, I want to argue that all schools also need to be committed to teaching the universal and civic values that are essential to living at peace within a pluralist society. I want to stress the need to maintain an *even* balance between an emphasis on particularist education and an emphasis on universalist education. The particularist component of education, involving the initiation of students into a particular culture or religion, should not crowd out the universalist component of education, involving the cultivation of universal values and the development of critical and deliberative skills. Nor should the reverse happen, as is all too often the case in state-maintained common schools.

In chapter 4 I argued that parents have a right not only to nurture their children into a particular culture or religious (or secular) tradition, but also to choose schools for their children that reflect their own commitments. Here I want to caution against a possible misinterpretation. While I reject a monolithic state-maintained system of education, it is not at all my intent to reject entirely the role of the state in education. What a liberal democratic state cannot do is use a state-maintained system of education to prescribe for all students a single and debatable conception of the good life.[10] However, the state has a legitimate role to play in ensuring that all schools provide for a minimal level of requirements for normal human development, including development towards "normal" rational autonomy, as defined in earlier chapters. The state also has a legitimate role to play in ensuring that all students get a common civic education. Schooling within pluralistic liberal democracies must include the cultivation of those shared values and skills that are essential to maintaining a democracy. We must be careful, though, not to insist on too thick a version of these common state-imposed values. With Tamir, I agree that the thinness of liberal discourse is "its major virtue."[11]

Here I am in agreement with Gutmann on the importance of schooling in educating future citizens, except that she mistakenly thinks that this requires "public schools" (1996, 165). I am arguing for a plurality of schools, each of which is required by the state to teach a minimalist set of common values and skills that are essential to healthy democracies. One other confusion in Gutmann should be noted. She tends to equate universal with common civic values. This confusion, which is prevalent among liberal theorists, rests on the assumption that Western liberal values are universal values. Citizenship is presented as "an embodiment of abstract humanity, of those human qualities that unite all human beings" (Tamir 1995a, xxiii). While we do talk about a "world citizen," most often citizenship is related to a particular nation-state. I agree that there may be a thin version of liberal values that are indeed universal, but we must at least entertain the possibility that some Western liberal values are merely an expression of a particular culture, be that American or British or Canadian. In other words, we must entertain the possibility of there being a Western bias underlying much of the traditional liberal-democratic political discourse. We therefore need to distinguish between universal and civic values.

It should further be noted that I am quite deliberately distancing myself from any position which gives the church a stake in the schooling of children, as was argued in chapter 6. The church can clearly have an influence on schooling via the parents, but this influence should always be indirect. I am also distancing myself from any established church tradition, official or unofficial, which assumes that state-maintained schooling should be Christian (or Muslim, etc.).

I am arguing for a plurality of schools, reflecting the plurality of cultural and religious commitments in a society. Clearly there are additional considerations that must be taken into account in determining the degree of educational plurality that can be accommodated within a society. For example, there may be financial constraints. Such constraints may necessitate cooperation between like-minded religious and cultural traditions in setting up schools. Wherever feasible, parents should be able to send their children to a school that reflects their own values and religious (or non-religious) commitments. Here we must allow for differing approaches depending on context. The level of educational pluralism should reflect the level of plurality of cultures and faiths within a society. Obviously, in a society in which there is a majority culture or religion, most schools will reflect this majority position.[12] This also entails that in a largely secular culture, most schools would be secular.

These are the broad parameters of my model of educational pluralism. I do not want to get into the question of financing such a system of schooling, except to say that it should be fair. All schools, provided only that they uphold the values thought to be essential to a liberal democracy, should be given equal funding. There are several approaches to dealing with the funding question – complete state financing and administration of a pluralistic school system, a voucher system, or a blend between these two approaches. I tend to favour the latter, but I leave it to other writers to settle this matter. My main concern is to defend the principle of educational pluralism, and even here, my argument is limited to a consideration of the implications of maintaining a balance between particularity and universality.

Sadly, there are only a few concrete examples of such educational pluralism in Western democracies. The system of education in the Netherlands is probably the best known.[13] Not only are there few examples of a genuine and just system of educational pluralism, there is also widespread opposition to such a model. Strangely, this opposition persists even among liberal writers who are struggling to achieve the balance between particularity and universality which I defined and defended in the previous chapter. I have already referred to Amy Gutmann's defence of state-maintained common schools as the best way to achieve such a balance. Gutmann further argues specifically against religious schools (1996, 163–5). Separate schools will certainly do justice to the particular values of the supporting communities, but Gutmann worries "that separatist schooling is not designed to promote the civic values" (164). Indeed, although Gutmann is not entirely clear in defining her position, it sometimes appears that she views separate schooling as simply incompatible with the promotion of a common civic education.[14]

Other writers who are similarly concerned to revise traditional liberalism so as to accommodate the politics of recognition, like Gutmann, still seem to be opposed to a system of educational pluralism as the best answer to achieving a balance between particularism and universalism.[15] Even Yael Tamir, who probably provides the clearest exposition and defence of this balance in relation to a liberal form of nationalism, and who clearly identifies the problems inherent in a state-maintained system of education, nevertheless still gives only grudging affirmation of religious schools.[16]

I quite agree that state-maintained common schools based on liberal principles can maintain a certain kind of balance between universality and particularity. With this approach, individual students from a variety of cultural/religious traditions can rub shoulders with each other within the same classroom and can also be taught the same universal and civic values. I want to argue, however, that this approach leads to an unequal balance between universality and particularity. I am not sure that a better balance can in fact be achieved within a system of public schools. Sadly, there is a peculiar blindness among supporters of state-maintained public schooling to the possibility of achieving a genuine balance between universalism and particularism in another way. Surely another possibility is to have a plurality of schools, each school reflecting differing cultural/religious values, while at the same time requiring each school to teach the same universal and civic values that are thought to be essential for a multicultural society and a democracy.

THE POSSIBILITY OF UNIVERSAL
EDUCATION IN PARTICULARIST SCHOOLS

Before I consider the question whether a pluralistic educational system with particularist schools might do a better job than common schools in achieving a balance, we need to face the prior question whether it is even possible for particularist schools to provide universal and civic education, and to accommodate liberal/democratic values. As already noted, Gutmann sometimes seems to suggest that separatist schooling is not (and cannot be) designed to promote universal and civic values. Other writers similarly suggest a fundamental incompatibility between particularist schooling and the promotion of liberal/democratic values. For example, Peshkin maintains that schools like Bethany Baptist Academy cannot advocate pluralism and the universal or civic virtues surrounding pluralism because of their doctrine of exclusive truth. "As true believers, it is contradictory for them to advance a concept like pluralism" (1986, 293).[17]

It is of course possible to win this argument by arbitrary definition. Here particularism is simply seen as precluding universalism. Any form of separateness is thought to preclude any concession to inclusiveness. To win an argument by arbitrary definition is a hollow victory, however. Gutmann, though I don't think she wants to win the argument simply by definition, succumbs to this approach with her tendency to polarize extreme positions – separat*ist* particularism (e.g. Afrocentrism; cf. "unregulated particularism"), that "educates by exclusion," and transcendent universalism, unmodified by multiculturalism (1996, 157–60, 161, 165). There simply is no reason why separate religious schools cannot incorporate a common civic curriculum and a broadening universalizing education. That is why Gutmann does at times admit this as a possibility. It is only "some" fundamentalist Christian academies that are separatist in the extreme (158).

Peshkin's worries are also unwarranted. As I have already argued in earlier chapters, the doctrine of absolute truth does not preclude an attitude of humility on the part of Christians. Indeed, given the fallibility of human beings, Christian doctrine acknowledges partial understandings of truth and insists on respect for differing viewpoints. There are even theological grounds for affirming plurality.[18] It is possible for religious schools to accommodate pluralism and to have as their aim the cultivation of the virtues of tolerance and respect, virtues typically associated with pluralism.

Claims to exclusive truth also do not preclude the possibility of having some truth in common with others. Rawls's notion of an "overlapping consensus" has its Christian adherents.[19] The possibility of shared convictions and beliefs is quite in keeping with long-standing Christian beliefs such as the Roman Catholic doctrine of natural law or natural reason, and the Protestant doctrine of common grace. I would further suggest that these shared doctrines include the liberal/democratic favourites: justice, religious freedom, tolerance, criticism, equality, and a commitment to deliberation.[20] Thus orthodox Christians can be liberals, and Christian schools can be committed to cultivating liberal values.

In saying this, I do not deny that there are some religious adherents and cultural/religious traditions which are simply illiberal and for whom such a compromise is impossible. But I don't think that this problem is nearly as pervasive as it is often made out to be. As was argued in chapter 11, the problem of religious fanaticism has been grossly exaggerated. This problem of exaggeration rests on a more basic problem, namely that of defining what is liberal or illiberal. There is in fact considerable dispute within contemporary liberalism about proper definitions of these terms.[21] Comprehensive liberals condemn any society that does not foster personal autonomy, while those advocating political liberalism maintain that we should not be so demanding, and still others maintain there is very little difference between the two positions (cf. Callan 1997, ch. 2). Some consider the Amish to be illiberal, while others are willing to concede, though perhaps grudgingly, that maybe they aren't all that bad after all (cf. Macedo 1995a, 488). Then there is the problem of using the troublesome issues of differences over sexual norms, the status of women, and abortion to define what is liberal or illiberal.[22] I would suggest that many of these controversial issues are better relegated to the realm of "reasonable moral disagreements," or "reasonable pluralism," to use terms that Gutmann and Rawls themselves use.[23] In other words, these are issues over which equally reasonable people differ, and it is wrong to classify those who differ from us as illiberal on the basis of these issues.

My central concern here has been to defend the possibility of religious schools teaching liberal/democratic values, alongside the particularist values that will be taught at such schools. Given that it is possible for religious schools to maintain the balance between particularism and universalism, there still remains a question of how probable it is. At the same time, I want to address a comparative question. Would a system of educational pluralism be better or worse than a system of state-maintained common schools at fostering this delicate balance between universalism and particularism which I defended as an ideal in the previous chapter?

A COMPARISON OF PROBABILITIES

While Gutmann's position is not entirely clear, she can be interpreted as suggesting that it is merely very improbable that religious schools will teach universal values. It is only "some" schools that accommodate universal values by including civic education (1996, 158, 164). Gutmann further argues that public schools are the "primary institution by which a democratic society educates future citizens," and the reason why some culturally segregated schools are attractive to some people is that such schools "neglect teaching some of the public values that are central to democratic education" (165). Clearly Gutmann favours public schools as the best means to achieve a balance between particularity and universality, and she is not alone in holding this position.[24]

But nowhere does Gutmann offer any empirical evidence to support this claim. Indeed, there is empirical research which suggests that religious schools are better able to maintain an educational balance between particular and universal values than are state-maintained public schools. In a recent book entitled *Catholic Schools and the Common Good* (1993), Anthony Bryk and associates, based on a ten-year in-depth field study of seven Catholic high schools in America, confirm earlier studies (e.g. Greeley and Rossi 1966) suggesting that Catholic high schools do better than public high schools in promoting, among other things, the basic social and political purposes that once were the inspiration of American public education and gave public schools the title of "common schools" (cf. Greene 1998).

Of special interest here are two of the four foundational characteristics that are identified as explaining the effectiveness of Catholic high schools: their communal organization and their inspirational ideology. Though these characteristics are not easily captured "in statistical analyses or summarized with numbers," it would be a serious mistake to ignore the way in which Catholic ideology shapes these schools (Bryk et al. 1993, 304). This ideology provides a unifying vision for all involved, inspires trust, inspires teachers to see their work as a calling, and imparts Christian values, particularly the values of caring for persons.

The authors go on to suggest that some of the principles that make for the success of the Catholic school could not really provide a basis for educational reform in the public school system. This is because the public school simply cannot become a "voluntary community," a notion which is suggested as capturing the essence of the Catholic school (312). There is also a basic incompatibility between the vision underlying the Catholic school and the vision underlying public schooling "that is increasingly dominated by market metaphors, radical individualism, and a sense of purpose organized around competition and the pursuit of individual economic rewards" (11). In the end, it is the ideology underlying public schools that would have to change, and that seems unlikely, if not impossible. So it is the particularity of the Catholic school that accounts for its success, not only in terms of creating a community, but also in terms of fostering the universal and civic values associated with the common good.

There is further evidence to suggest that state-maintained common schools throughout the Western world are experiencing considerable strain, and much of it has to do precisely with the failure to achieve the required balance between a transcendent universalism and a separatist particularism. Gutmann herself gives an example – the controversy surrounding the 1989 case of three Muslim adolescent girls who were forbidden to attend class because they refused to remove their chadors in class, a violation of a French law which prohibits the wearing of religious symbols in government-run classrooms (1996, 162–3). A nearly identical case occurred in England in 1990, among many other controversies in the history of multicultural education in England in the last twenty years (Halstead 1992). Arons describes some of the growing number of censorship wars in American public schools and concludes that these and other conflicts are due to "a government school system that seems to be bent upon cannibalizing subcultures."[25] In Canada the Islamic Schools Federation of Ontario sued the Ottawa Board of Education for not giving equal recognition to Islamic holy days in the schedule of school holidays (Sweet 1997, 199–203). These and many other controversies that could be cited point to the seeming inability of the common school to accommodate the particularist pole of the balance between universality and particularity (cf. Spinner-Halev 2000, 116–17).

Why is it that state-maintained common schools are experiencing difficulties in balancing particularity and universality? And why do religious schools seem to be better at maintaining this balance? In the next few sections I want to look at the underlying reasons behind the empirical evidence.

EDUCATION INTO PARTICULARITY

The first set of issues I would like to deal with concerns the need for education into particularity. I want to argue that there is a problem with the way in which the plurality of particularities is accommodated in the common school. While it is true that public schools bring together students from differing cultural/religious backgrounds, it is important to note that they are brought together as *individuals,* not as groups. Gutmann repeatedly stresses that "the self-esteem that is compatible with mutual respect among citizens must be earned by individual students ... rather than acquired by means of group identification" (1996, 161, 159). She expresses a common prejudice of traditional liberalism in refusing to give intrinsic value to cultural or religious groups – cultural groups do not have a "right to survival as such," she argues (170).

We see here why liberalism tends to favour the common school – it is an expression of the individualism that is at the heart of the traditional liberal agenda. As such, the common school is a betrayal of the compromise between individualism and community that was defended in the previous chapter and that is being assumed here. The particularity that I am defending is that of a community, not an individual. To do justice to particularity, schools must somehow accommodate the plurality of communities, and this the state-maintained common school is ill equipped to do by virtue of its very structure. I have provided some examples of problem areas in this regard in the previous section. It is only if we introduce plurality into the structure of schooling that we will be able to do justice to the plurality of communities.

The individualism of liberalism which permeates the common school has many consequences. The individual student from a minority group within a society feels isolated from the cultural or religious tradition which normally defines personal identity. This leads further to feelings of vulnerability. Healthy development requires a "primary culture" within which children find security.

Here it might be objected that children surely need to be exposed to other cultures and other beliefs at some point in their development. Is it not the case that individuals are never as isolated as is assumed by communitarians? Group identities and primary cultures are never totally homogenous. Indeed, individuals themselves are shaped by a variety of cultural influences.[26]

I quite agree with all this, but there is a psychological question that needs to be addressed here. At what point in time is it best to expose children to a Babel of values and cultures? As has already been argued in earlier chapters, most developmental psychologists would agree that exposure of children to greater plurality should occur gradually. Otherwise, such exposure will be too threatening to the child. We must also be careful that such exposure does not lead to a premature loss of identity. The common school simply cannot accommodate a gradualist approach to this broadening of children's horizons. Feinberg gives an example of two Japanese children who found themselves "linguistically paralyzed" during the first few weeks in a first-grade classroom in an American school.[27] Public schools are simply ill adapted to accommodate the psychological needs related to particularist identities.

I want to underscore that I am arguing for a balance between particularist education and universalist education. Here another question arises. Where do we start? Do we start with the particular or with the universal? Nature really dictates the proper order. We are born into a particular home with a particular culture and a particular religious tradition, and we acquire a particular language. Universality can only grow out of the particular, and this is best accomplished if it is done gradually and slowly within the context of schools that reflect particular identities.[28]

MULTICULTURAL/MULTI-FAITH PROGRAMS AND INITIATION

There is one element of the state-maintained common school often thought to accommodate the particularist dimension of education. Gutmann (1996), for example, sees the multicultural and multi-faith programs of the common school as addressing the particularist pole of the balance between universalist and particularist education that she is advocating, as I am. Clearly the common school seems to be well suited to helping students come to understand and even to appreciate other cultural and religious traditions. The common school can even help a particular student learn more *about* his or her own cultural/religious tradition. That is very different, however, from being educated *into* a cultural/religious tradition. Genuine particularistic education involves *initiation* into a particular culture or religion. It involves Christian or Muslim *nurture*, not just teaching about Christian or Muslim values.[29]

Common schools typically shy away from this dimension of education.[30] Indeed, it cannot be accommodated, given the paradigm of liberal education that dominates the common school, a paradigm which prefers to talk about *liberation from* the present and the particular rather than *initiation into* the present and the particular (Bailey 1984). Initiation into a particular religious tradition is further generally associated with indoctrination, a taboo in common schools committed to a liberal education. Such initiation into a particular way of life also violates the principle of liberal neutrality which is thought to undergird state-maintained common schools.[31] If the common school gave up the ideal of neutrality, there is still the very practical difficulty of trying to accommodate all of the cultural/religious traditions in a typical school. There are simply too many particularities to be accommodated.[32]

Gutmann too rejects initiation into a present and particular as part of the function of public schools (1996, 170).[33] Throughout her writings, her only concession to particularity is to talk about multicultural education that is taught to *all* students (159). This does not do justice to the particularist education that different cultural or religious groups want, and that the politics of recognition requires. For religious adherents, multi-faith programs cannot help but trivialize religious commitments. Instead of treating them as serious life-consuming commitments, "rival creeds are cast together in a common educational environment, and religious scruples and practices are celebrated as so many charming ornaments of ethnicity" (Callan 2000, 57).

A system of educational pluralism, on the other hand, where different schools reflect the different cultural and religious traditions within a society, will be able to initiate students into particular traditions. Why do we need schools to initiate students into a particular culture or tradition? Can't this be done in the home, as many liberals argue (cf. Gutmann 1996, 164)? We need schools to initiate students into particular values just as we need schools to initiate students into universal and civic values. It is simply a matter of balance! Oakeshott has given us a classic statement on the important of schooling. The idea of "school," according to Oakeshott, involves "the deliberate initiation of the newcomer into a human inheritance of sentiments, beliefs, imaginings, understandings and activities" (1972, 23). Clearly particular cultural/religious traditions will have a unique understanding of the human inheritance they want to pass on to their children. By extrapolation, particularist schools are needed to initiate/socialize newcomers *systematically* into particular cultural/religious inheritances.

Of course, these schools should also have multicultural and multifaith programs in order to do justice to the universalist pole of the balance we are seeking. This can and should be done alongside particularist education.

INCONSISTENCIES

Here we need to note a curious inconsistency on the part of liberal educators. They accept initiation in certain areas, but not in others. In a classic statement concerning liberal education, R.S. Peters (1965) maintains that teachers don't want students just to learn *about* physics; they want them to get inside the form of knowledge, to care about the valuable things involved – to become a physicist or a mathematician. In the area of religion, however, liberal educationalists object to students being initiated into a particular religion. Of course this difference is thought to be justified because it is assumed that physics has a different epistemological status from religion. However, in the previous chapter I have argued that more recent developments in epistemology call into question these supposed differences. Hence we should be as willing to initiate students into a particular religion as we are to initiate them into physics or history.

This same inconsistency comes to the fore again when we consider the need for civic education, or education into the universal values of liberal democracies. "Public schools," Gutmann argues, "are the primary institution by which a democratic society educates future citizens, preparing them to share in responsible self government" (1996, 165). In other words, public schools facilitate *initiation* into the democratic way of life. Here it is important to see democracy as having "a substantive character" – it isn't just a neutral procedure, but "a way of life," a point which is now thankfully generally admitted by liberals (Walzer 1995, 187). Gutmann too concedes that democratic education is not neutral, and yet she calls for the "cultivation" of democratic virtues in public schools (1996, 168, 176).

But, if public schools initiate into the democratic way of life, should they not also facilitate the initiation of a student into the particular way of life that defines his or her own identity? But they cannot, or will not, and should not do this, as I have already argued. Hence also the tendency to pass off the responsibility to initiate children into particular ways of life to "parents and private associations," as Gutmann does (1996, 164). But this is a cop-out. We need schools for particularist education just as we need schools for universalist education. State-maintained common schools cannot do justice to particularist education. What is needed is a different kind of school which can do justice to both elements. What is needed is a system of educational pluralism.

OVEREMPHASIS ON UNIVERSALIST EDUCATION

Again, let me remind the reader that the basic question at issue here is whether the common school can achieve what Gutmann calls a "genuinely principled combination," or a fair balance, between universalist and particularist values (1996, 156). I have argued, however, that Gutmann has not at all done justice to particularist values because she has confused "cross-cultural education" with particularistic "communal education." She simply fails to include initiation into particular traditions as part of her supposed balance.

It is further important to note that multicultural or multi-faith education really belongs to the universalist pole of the balance that Gutmann, and other liberal educationalists, are trying to achieve. Indeed, a careful reading of Gutmann will reveal that whenever she talks of the multicultural dimension of education, the language changes to that of "respecting cultural differences" (1996, 156). Cultivating "respect" for other identities doesn't really belong to the particularist strand of education at all. It belongs instead to the civic stratum of education, i.e. it is part of the traditional liberal agenda, and therefore Gutmann really fails to delineate an education for common schools which does justice to both universal or civic values and particularist values.[34] Both parts of her principled combination in fact belong to the civic strand of education.

This imbalance is very frequent in discussions about the importance of multicultural education in common schools. The predominant emphasis in publicly supported schools tends to be on educational aims that have to do with the general public interest. Gutmann is open about this – "precedence" should be given to the teaching of democratic principles, and "a major reason for mandating and publicly subsidizing schooling for all children" is to teach them the liberal/democratic values of mutual respect, liberty, opportunity, and deliberation. This is the "primary purpose" of public education.[35] I have no quarrel with this objective. But let's not pretend that it does justice to the particularistic strand of education.

Our common schools simply do not achieve the balance that I am arguing for, a balance between universalism and particularism in education. Indeed, they cannot. The only way in which such a balance can be achieved is if we start with schools committed to particularist education, and have them include universalist education as part of their program.

CIVIC EDUCATION

So far my primary concern has been with the failure of the common school to do justice to communal values. I now want to argue that there are also problems with the ability of the common school to cultivate universal and civic values. Teaching liberal/democratic values in common schools would seem to presuppose a kind of epistemological neutrality. What is required in the classroom of the common school, according to Rawls and Macedo, is that students and teachers "bracket" their ultimate commitments when liberal/democratic values are being discussed, limiting themselves to a "public reasonableness."[36] Gutmann too seems to appeal to such a neutral public reasonableness when she assumes that we will all recognize these values as "reasonable" (1996, 169).

Macedo admits that some people will find the strictures of liberal public reason "burdensome" (1995a, 478). The much more serious problem with Rawls's, Macedo's, and Gutmann's liberal public reason is that it does not exist. As I have argued in the previous chapter, the notion of a public reason rests on an epistemology which is now generally acknowledged to be problematic. There is no neutral or objective public reason. All thinking is rooted in a particular worldview and rests on particular presuppositions. This does not preclude the possibility of people from differing frameworks coming to agreement on some common civic principles. It might be possible to reach an "overlapping consensus," but such agreement should be sought within the context of a dialogue which allows each participant to be true to his or her own particular theoretical commitments.

State-maintained common schools are ill suited to letting students speak their own languages with regard to the common civic curriculum which seeks to inculcate liberal/democratic values. Civic education based only on public reasonableness requires a kind of intellectual schizophrenia of all students.[37] It forces students to leave behind their most cherished beliefs when it comes to public discussions. It is a betrayal of particularity. So once again, common schools fail to achieve the required balance between universality and particularity.

This is not at all to say that an education in "universal" liberal democratic values is not important. I appreciate the pragmatic need to come to agreement on these values, and I agree that our schools have an important role to play in teaching students both the importance of these values and the skills required to achieve consensus about them. But the *justification* of these values is also important for educational purposes, and here we cannot simply appeal to a neutral public reason that all students supposedly possess. There is an incompleteness to any civic education that seeks to cultivate liberal/democratic values without their particular justifications. Common schools cannot deal adequately with this component of civic education. What is needed are schools that not only teach the civic virtues, but also teach the justification of these virtues within the context of a particular comprehensive supporting worldview.

Only this will overcome Carter's quite legitimate complaint against liberalism, which he says requires religious believers to "split their public and private selves," treating their religion as a hobby – discrete, unimportant, and confined to the weekend.[38] Civic values need to be integrated with religious values for the religious believer. Indeed, the new epistemology would suggest that civic values cannot be understood apart from some kind of comprehensive theoretical framework. Particularist schools are a logical extension of the insights of the new epistemology.

It further needs to be underscored that civic virtues can be best cultivated within the context of a particular community which reinforces these values, both theoretically and practically. Thus again schools which are an expression of a particular culture or religion will be more successful in reinforcing liberal/democratic values than common schools. There is a growing realization in the field of ethics that what is needed today is character formation, not just a theoretical discussion of abstract moral principles, such as tends to be encouraged by liberalism. In Sandel's words, liberalism's "vision of political discourse is too sparse to contain the moral energies of democratic life" (1996, 323). Virtue ethics maintains "that moral character and identity can be forged *only* within a specific community and through a clear set of practices, shared covenants, and symbolic meanings held jointly by a committed group of individuals."[39] Such character formation is again best developed within the context of particularist schools.

Here we need to consider one possible objection to my argument that religious schools will do better than common schools even in the area of civic education. This objection is best examined in the context of the emphasis in contemporary political theory on "deliberative democracy."[40] As was already noted in the previous chapter, Gutmann argues that schools should be concerned not only to cultivate an appreciation of cultural diversity but also to teach students "how to engage together in respectful discussions in which they strive to understand, appreciate, and if possible, resolve political disagreements that are partly rooted in cultural differences" (1996, 160). Educational institutions "can serve as models for deliberation, by encouraging rigorous, honest, open, and intense intellectual discussions, both inside and outside the classroom" (Gutmann 1994, 23). But separatist schooling is simply not designed to foster this sort of deliberation, according to Gutmann (1996, 174). The isolating of students into separate schools leads to a kind of "voluntary apartheid" which makes it impossible for students to develop deliberative skills (cf. Halstead 1995).

Callan carries the argument further by drawing on the familiar Aristotelian thesis that virtues, like skills, are acquired through their exercise, and therefore the skills of deliberative democracy are best developed within a common school where children of diverse backgrounds "can join together to create a morally grounded consensus on how to live together" (1995, 263). Callan is also concerned that religious schools will not allow for a sufficiently "inclusive" or "open-ended" deliberation (2000, 64).

I believe these concerns represent the strongest objection that can be raised against the position that I am defending in this chapter. The concerns of Gutmann and Callan are not a decisive objection to religious schools, however, since they rest on a number of problematic assumptions. For one, we need to keep in mind that particular cultural/religious traditions are never quite as homogeneous as is sometimes assumed, a point that is conceded by Gutmann (1993, 182–8). Thus differences will need to be discussed. Deliberative skills can be developed even in schools that centre on one cultural or religious tradition.

Cultural and religious traditions are also invariably in flux, and the writings of a tradition are, at their best, "work-in-progress, work struggling to integrate – to weave together – the multiple and diverse strands that compose us" (Rorty 1995, 221). Hence, as students are asked to read the works of their own tradition, they can become "active interpreters rather than passive consumers" of their religious tradition, placing themselves in the position of "working/author/agents" (222). Thus deliberative skills can be learned within particular traditions.

Clearly, what I have in mind are living cultural/religious traditions, which are evolving and growing – an ideal that is advocated by authors as diverse as J.S. Mill and Alasdair MacIntyre.[41] This pattern of evolution and growth should also be exemplified in the schools that represent these traditions.

Another fundamental problem with this objection to religious schools is its failure to take into account my earlier argument concerning human development. Deliberative skills are best developed within the context of a secure and stable environment. If children are transplanted into an environment where their parents' cherished beliefs are subjected to criticism by others in the classroom, this can in fact lead to discontent and restlessness and can hinder rather than help growth in deliberative skills (Halstead 1986, 27). Deliberative skills need to develop gradually and slowly and can best do so from within particular cultural and religious traditions.[42] In my ideal of a separate school, I would want growing exposure to other cultures and religious traditions. Multicultural and multi-faith education would be an essential component in all schools, as I have already suggested. Thus, with a gradual broadening of horizons, there will at the same time be increasing opportunity to cultivate deliberative skills.

To his credit, Callan does attempt to take into account the developmental dimensions of cultivating deliberative skills (1995, 266–7). He even concedes that separate schooling of a limited duration "may be regarded as one way of creating the developmental antecedents of the mature liberal virtues" (267). He also admits that separate schools can create "imaginary interlocutors" as a way of cultivating deliberative skills (263). I would add further that there is nothing stopping a separate school from arranging for genuine dialogue by inviting representatives from other religious traditions into the classroom, particularly at the upper levels of schooling.

This does not satisfy Callan. He wants to bring together children from widely different backgrounds so that they will be forced to converse with one another. Practice makes perfect! Here we must be careful not to demand more of children than they are ready to cope with in terms of dialogue with diverse voices. In the end Callan simply doesn't do justice to the developmental dimensions of the problem. Yes, deliberative skills need to be developed in such a way as to include an increasingly diverse representation of values held by the participants, but again, we must be careful not to impose an adult agenda onto small children.[43]

I therefore question Callan's claim that the need for a common education for the citizens of a liberal democracy, together with the need to cultivate reasonableness, creates "a presumptive case for common schooling" (1995, 268). I also disagree with Gutmann's claim that religious schools will not meet the admittedly important need for cultivating the skills of deliberative democracy. These needs can be quite adequately met within separate schools. Indeed, they can be better met within the context of a system of educational pluralism which does justice to the demands of a politics of recognition.

SOME FINAL PROBLEMS WITH GUTMANN

To her credit, Amy Gutmann submits her defence of common schools as the best way of harmonizing universal and particular interests to a test, and it is a difficult test case – forbidding Muslim girls to wear chadors in a French school, referred to earlier in this chapter (Gutmann 1996, 162). Gutmann seems to be more liberal than most liberal theorists in that she would not force the girls to give up wearing chadors in class, but she is adamant in insisting that they be exposed to "a public culture of gender equality in public school" (169). If such an education will lessen the likelihood that such a cultural practice will be perpetuated, then so be it (169). We should boldly teach liberal principles, according to Gutmann, even though we know that this may lead to "a drastic weakening" of the hold that religious convictions have on a person (169; cf. Gutmann 1994, 4; 1995, 482). Various other liberal writers take a similar stand.[44]

Of course we are dealing here with the fundamental question of the limits of toleration. I quite agree that there must be limits. My concern, though, is that these limits are drawn too narrowly, thereby again creating an imbalance in the blend that Gutmann and I are trying to achieve. Here the contemporary debate surfaces concerning the thickness or thinness of liberal values. I would argue that common schools tend to have too thick a version of liberal values, thereby undermining the possibility of giving equal worth to particularist cultures and religions. Indeed, the common school finds itself in an impossible situation. If it adopts too thin a version of liberal values, if it tries to satisfy the most members of society by accepting "the lowest common denominator" of society's values, then both liberal and religious parents will find the moral diet too sparse.[45] If the common school adopts a thick version of liberal values, it will find itself at odds with various cultural and religious groups which reject some of these values. This further violates the liberal ideal of neutrality. In fact, this approach results in an arrogant imposition of a comprehensive version of liberal values.[46] Perhaps liberals, too, have got it wrong.

The problem of an imposition of liberal values also surfaces with regard to multicultural and multi-faith programs, which are often thought to accommodate particularity, as I have discussed earlier in this chapter. There is a widespread feeling that despite the efforts of public schools to introduce multicultural and multi-faith programs, these merely conceal "a subtle form of cultural domination" (Halstead 1992, 53).

Gutmann herself raises this point as an objection to her proposal. She worries that attempts to accommodate particularist interests in the common school via multicultural education are little more than a pretence of accommodation – "funny hat liberalism," as it is sometimes disparagingly called (Gutmann 1996, 169). Yes, indeed, and Gutmann admits the critics have a point! Olneck makes the point boldly, also introducing the additional problem of power and inequality that arises when there is one dominant cultural or religious group within a society:

Despite [the] ostensibly "pluralistic" features of much multicultural education rhetoric and theory, multiculturalism, in its more prevalent forms, fails ... to articulate an authentic ideology of pluralism, is fundamentally integrative and incorporative, and is possibly reproductive of prevailing relations of power and control ... Ironically, multicultural education reinterprets and re-presents minority culture and minority identity in the idioms of, from the perspectives of, and within constraints imposed by dominant cultural forms. (1992, 255, 259)

I have tried to show that any attempts by common schools to integrate universalist and particularist values will invariably be skewed towards the universalist pole of the continuum. This is ultimately because the common school represents the dominant cultural form of Western liberalism. The only way to avoid the oppression inherent in a system of state-maintained common schools is to introduce a pluralistic system of schools. Only this will do justice to particularity while at the same time acknowledging and cultivating the universal values that any society requires to live at peace.

I therefore conclude that Gutmann's support of state-maintained common schools as the best way of achieving her balance between universalist and particularist values is unwarranted. Indeed, there is a curious inconsistency in Gutmann's position that needs to be brought to the fore by way of concluding my argument. Gutmann undermines her position when applying her balance between particularist and universal values to the question of multinationalism and education. In a multinational society she allows for a division of the political as well as the educational system into national streams, "each of which tries to teach not only its own distinctive national values but also a shared set of civic values, including toleration and mutual respect for national (and other collective and individual) identities unlike their own" (Gutmann 1996, 172).

If such an arrangement is possible in a multinational society, then surely it should also be possible in a multicultural society. Gutmann really gives no reason for arguing so differently in the two cases, except perhaps by assuming that national differences are more important than cultural differences – a problematic assumption at best (173).

Indeed, in this same context Gutmann even goes beyond her requirement of a balance between particularity and universality when she gives several reasons why, in public schooling, one may rightly focus *more* on the history, culture, and politics of one's own country than on that of other countries (175). Her primary reason is that particular cultures and politics would not thrive if people were to take an equal interest in every other culture and politics on the face of the earth. She also argues that universality is best built on particularity. "Most people want to live their lives on a local, rather than global, level" (175). Yes, indeed! Here finally Gutmann is giving due regard to particularity –

perhaps even too much. But these reasons apply equally to the plurality of cultures and religious traditions within a country.

As Tamir has argued, cultural and religious traditions should be subsumed under the notion of nationality (1995a, 8, xvi). Tamir concludes, as Gutmann should: "National groups – minorities and majorities alike – should thus be given the freedom to have their own educational system" (Tamir 1995a, xxix).

MONOPOLY AND FREEDOM

Tamir's conclusion, like the conclusion of this book, grows out of an attempt to take pluralism seriously. In the preface to her book *Liberal Nationalism*, Tamir points to the now widely accepted understanding that "most states are not, never have been, and are unlikely to become nationally (or culturally) homogeneous" (1995a, xvii). What this transformation in the self-image of the state calls for, according to Tamir, is "a redefinition of the role of most political institutions, and especially of schools" (xvii). No more can schooling be seen primarily as a means of assimilating a plurality of peoples into one nation. We must somehow also do justice to the politics of recognition, and this calls for a radical restructuring of schooling.

I believe that monolithic state-maintained systems of education are a mistake. *Indeed, they have always been a mistake.* They might be expected in totalitarian regimes. It is no surprise that they are advocated in Plato's "ideal" republic. And we expect communist states to have state-maintained systems of education (cf. Glenn 1995). However, they are completely inappropriate for liberal democracies.

I object to all monopolies – whether political, religious, or economic. But I am especially concerned about monopolies in the realm of ideas. I fail to understand why there is not growing alarm about the scandal of ever-increasing monopolies in the media – newspapers, radio, television. I simply cannot comprehend why, in liberal democracies that place so much value on freedom of thought, state-maintained systems of education are considered to be appropriate. I take comfort in the fact that none other than John Stuart Mill clearly pointed to the dangers inherent in educational monopolies.

All that has been said of the importance of individuality of character, and diversity of opinion and mode of conduct, involves, as of the same unspeakable importance, diversity of education. A general State education is a mere contrivance for moulding people to be exactly like one another; and as the mould in which it casts them is that which pleases the predominant power in the government, whether this be a monarch, a priesthood, an aristocracy, or the majority of the existing generation – in proportion as it is efficient and successful, it establishes a despotism over the mind, leading by natural tendency to one over the body. (1978, 104–5)

Schooling, no matter how liberal, no matter to what extent it incorporates the ideal of liberal education, nevertheless involves the transmission of culture. Schooling never was, never is, and never can be value-free. Therefore the question of who controls the education of the young in schools is of crucial importance. A state-controlled system of education is inherently illiberal and undemocratic. Coupled with the principle of compulsory education, it is an expression of the worst kind of totalitarianism. Arons has quite rightly described the culture of American schooling in terms of "compelling belief," and the school system as "a suppressor of dissent and a manipulator of political consciousness" (1986, 190).

As Arons so ably shows, it is precisely because of their significance in shaping the minds of the young that there are growing battles over who controls what orthodoxies are taught in our public schools. Sadly, by stifling dissent, state-controlled systems of education also stifle "the vitality and regenerative ability of both culture and politics" (Arons 1986, 195–6). Indeed, in the repression of dissenting values, "seeds of future consensus and social cohesion are destroyed," which is the very goal that is often used to defend state-maintained and controlled schools (196). Such educational monopolies are in fact counterproductive in uniting a state. "The dead hand of orthodoxy not only deprives substantial numbers of families of the ability to participate in culture and public life, it threatens to end the process of growth altogether and to replace it with what Jung called 'the spiritual and moral darkness of State Absolutism'" (197).

State-maintained systems of education are a violation of the most basic freedoms of liberal democracies. Arons goes so far as to suggest that the present political and financial structure of American schooling is unconstitutional in that it violates the First Amendment clauses which establish the freedom of religion, speech, press, and assembly (1986, 198–214). The same could be said about Canadian schooling – to the extent that it is monolithic and state-maintained, it violates the Canadian Charter of Rights and Freedoms. While these democratic freedoms have been thought of primarily in terms of the *expression* of belief and opinion, they are equally applicable to the *formation* of belief and opinion (Arons 1986, 205). Arons therefore would like a reformulation of the First Amendment, making the formation of belief and opinion free from government coercion through schooling (206, 212). Unfortunately, Arons carries his argument too far here, because, as I have argued in various places in this book, the government does have *some* legitimate concerns with regard to the formation of *some* beliefs. However, I agree entirely with Arons that a government monopoly in education is a violation of some of the fundamental freedoms of liberal democracies.

I would also argue more specifically that a government monopoly of schooling entails a violation of religious freedom. Education is inextricably intertwined with religion, as I have argued in chapter 10. I would agree with Arons that we have been so preoccupied with preventing religious impositions in publicly supported schools in America (and Canada) that we have virtually ignored the equally significant imposition of ideology (1986, 198). A case can be made that the ideology underlying North American education is in fact religious in character (see Thiessen 1982b). Hence, the oft-made claim that the public school system of the United States is the established church of America.[47] It is precisely because state-maintained schools of the United States are used to reinforce its civil religion that McCarthy calls for "disestablishment a second time" (McCarthy et al. 1982).

Finally, an educational monopoly is harmful to the cause of education itself. Here again John Stuart Mill is instructive: "An education established and controlled by the State should only exist, if it exist at all, as one among many competing experiments, carried on for the purpose of example and stimulus, to keep the others up to a certain standard of excellence" (Mill 1978, 105). It is here that I am in partial agreement with contemporary calls for more competition in education. Educational plurality will foster competition and that in turn will promote excellence in education.

THE POLITICS OF RECOGNITION AND EDUCATION

My analysis of the dangers inherent in any educational monopoly should not be interpreted as rejecting entirely some of the original goals underlying the idea of a state-maintained system of education. There is a need to foster unity and harmony within a pluralistic society. Schools can make a significant contribution to achieving these goals. Nor do I wish to minimize the traditional liberal agenda of attempting to overcome the conflict that seems to be engendered by radically differing religious convictions. Indeed, it would seem that some of the conflicts over orthodoxy in our public schools are "the modern equivalent of the war over state religions fought in the seventeenth and eighteenth centuries" (Arons 1986, 20). The agenda of liberalism is as important now as it was in days gone by.

But traditional liberalism has not fulfilled its promise. State-maintained common schools seem to be failing to bring about that level of unity and harmony that is necessary for any pluralistic society.

As Glenn has amply demonstrated, the notion that a state system of education can create common loyalties and values among its citizens in the interest of national unity is a "myth," though a deeply engrained one (1988). Indeed, such schools only seem to be exacerbating the problem, as I have already pointed out earlier in this chapter.

Singh has correctly argued that the failure to recognize the equal worth of other cultural/religious traditions only serves to build resentment and create further alienation (1995, 17). Gutmann herself acknowledges that social injustice towards African-Americans generates a far more separatist sense of identity than would be the case if they were treated equally.[48]

Allowing for schools which are an expression of cultural/religious traditions, while at the same time ensuring that these schools teach liberal/democratic values, will do much more to create harmony within a pluralistic society than the imposition of liberal values and multicultural programs within an environment that is alien to students from minority cultural or religious traditions. Lois Sweet provides an illustration from the Netherlands, where Muslims are allowed to have their own schools (1997, 129–36). One official argues that separate schools actually stimulate integration. Sweet concurs and suggests there is a paradox here: "by emphasizing religious differences we may actually minimize their social impact." Skillen argues that just as ecclesiastical disestablishment brought about unity, so will the disestablishment of educational state monopolies (1994, 92). Educational pluralism will in fact solidify support of the state on the part of all citizens (129). Again, the works of Charles Glenn provide extensive documentation of the positive effects of educational pluralism for pluralistic societies (1988; 1989; 1995).

Gutmann and Callan correctly stress the importance of dialogue and democratic deliberation in teaching liberal/democratic values. Here again, dialogue that is forced and unequal is counter-productive. Equal recognition of cultural/religious traditions by allowing them to have schools which are an expression of their culture and religion will do more to create good will and foster genuine dialogue than any amount of multicultural and civic education forced on students in common schools. Minority cultures need to reclaim their voices within the context of supporting institutions. Or, in the words of Sue Jansen, we need "reflexive power talk" so as to be able to democratize dialogic opportunities, thereby fulfilling the unkept promises of the liberal Enlightenment (Jansen 1988, ch. 10). It is only if people are allowed to express their desires on equal terms that people will be (or will become) reasonable and decent and tolerant.

Applying the politics of recognition will also avoid the coercion implicit in a state-maintained system of education, and thereby again do more to achieve the traditional goals of liberalism. Here we have something to learn from pacifist writers who maintain that in order to achieve peace we need to relinquish positions of privilege and power.[49] Those who find themselves in such a position need to voluntarily make themselves vulnerable. This is particularly important for majority groups within a society and for any sort of liberal establishment that might exist within a society. I would suggest that it is precisely the coercive mentality stemming from arrogant attitudes of superiority on the part of majorities, or the liberal establishment, or the Christian Right, that is the primary roadblock to harmony and peace in our societies.[50] As various writers have noted, coercion is always counter-productive – genuine unity cannot be built on coercion.[51]

RESISTANCE AND REFORM

No doubt the overall argument of this book will be greeted by many readers with a good degree of scepticism, and even hostility and derision. I must confess that it is not easy to take a position which goes against conventional wisdom and which at times even seems counter-intuitive. I want to think that my arguments are sound, and yet I know there will be many who will disagree, and will disagree strongly. This raises the additional question: why should there be such strong opposition to what I hope are sound arguments?

My argument calls for radical reform in the educational realm. To move from a system of educational near-monopoly to a system of educational pluralism involves not only a paradigm shift in our thinking but also a major upheaval in the way in which we deliver education in practice. Sadly, a good deal of educational theory still proceeds as if the Enlightenment project had not failed. Educational practice lags behind even further in adjusting to the paradigm shift in philosophical ideas which I have argued for in this book. This again raises the interesting question – why this resistance to change in thinking and practice with regard to education? Why is there such strong opposition to accepting a system of educational pluralism?

Michael Wagner, a Canadian political scientist, addresses these questions, in a recent thesis based on a study of the debate regarding private versus public education in Alberta (1995). He dares to suggest that there might be vested interests behind the opposition to religious schools. Using "public choice theory," which suggests that virtually all political action is motivated by interest, Wagner explores to what extent state-maintained public education was established, and is still maintained even now, in the interest of education producers, i.e. teachers, school board officials, and other government education bureaucrats.

An examination of the origins of public education in North America suggests that there must have been some vested interests involved because a widespread and effective private school system was already in place. While the arguments of the "prime movers" (mainly professional educators) in the establishment of free common schools were couched in terms of the public interest, "much of the support of teachers and administrators for the public school movement derived from a narrow self-interest" – in particular, these private school educators "expected to enjoy greater certainty of employment, greater assurance that their salaries would be paid, and a greater degree of control if government rather than parents were the immediate paymasters" (Friedman and Friedman 1981, 143). Similar self-interest was also at stake in the support for compulsory attendance legislation and the campaigns for public funding (Wagner 1995, 86–7).

The same kind of self-interest can also be shown to underlie the current defence of the public system against any inroads by private education, a defence very often made by the well-organized and well-entrenched educational establishment – public teachers' unions, public school boards, and ministries of education. Wagner carefully documents how the strength of the opposition to religious separate schools by the educational establishment in Alberta in the 1980s varied in direct proportion to the perceived interest of the establishment.[52]

Although we must be careful not to exaggerate the extent to which self-interest influences the opposition to religious schools, I would concur with Wagner that self-interest by the educational establishment plays a "very significant" role in such opposition (1995, 99). We therefore need to be on guard when we encounter objections to religious schools. Perhaps the high-sounding arguments serve merely as rationalizations of narrow self-interest (2). We must be careful, however, not to get carried away with conspiracy theories. For one thing, as Holmes correctly observes, a powerful establishment has no need to conspire (1998, 242). Furthermore, given the epistemological theory I have defended in this book, all arguments are coloured to some extent by subjective factors such as self-interest. This includes arguments in defence of religious schools as well! We must therefore do our best to take arguments at face value, as I have tried to do in this book. Whatever the motivation that might lie behind arguments, they deserve to be treated fairly and as objectively as is humanly possible. Of course, all arguments also need to be examined critically.

Arguments can be characterized not only by their logic, but also by their tone. Here I want to express some concern about the vehemence with which opposition to religious schools is often stated. Then there is the emotionalism, rancour, extremism, bias, distortions, and extreme claims that often accompany objections to religious schools and colleges. Here again, I would be the first to admit that arguments in support of religious schools also do not always display a tone that is conducive to objective and critical analysis. In part this may be a response to the rhetoric often found behind the opposition, but that is no excuse. On controversial matters, we need dispassionate argument, careful reasoning, and appeal to accurate information. Whether I have succeeded in accomplishing this is for the reader to decide. That has certainly been my intent, though I must confess that it has been difficult to do, at times, because of the rhetoric that is sometimes found on the other side. Let me provide just a few examples.

The first is from a paper originally given at the International Conference on Education for Democracy in a Multicultural Society in Jerusalem in 1993. The quotation at the head of the previous chapter was taken from this paper by British philosopher Colin Wringe, in which he raises concerns about giving educational rights to so-called "illiberal societies" (1995). The paper begins by citing the Amish as an "obvious" example of "traditional groups" (285). Traditional cultural groups are described as "profoundly anti-democratic," and as "prepared to shed blood" over their beliefs.[53] What these groups need, according to Wringe, is an "enabling education" which will help individuals "to escape a life of drudgery, ill-health or fear of violence and abuse," a life "blighted by unnecessary suffering, oppression, isolation or restricted opportunity" (286, 291).

This is caricaturing at its worst. To generalize in this way about traditional cultural groups and to lump the Amish into such a characterization borders on the absurd. Wringe specifically argues against "sensitive democrats" who might want to acknowledge that there are "humane and thoughtful representatives of many established cultural communities." Against such generosity, Wringe argues that, philosophically, it is difficult to make distinctions (290). Surely, philosophy is all about making careful distinctions!

But the absurdity doesn't end there. The liberal-minded are described as "enlightened educators," and "good democrats" (Wringe 1995, 285, 288). How generous! I have encountered some educators, liberals, and democrats who are not good, who are narrow, dogmatic, intolerant, and whose thinking seems to be very much subject to "liberal group think." Wringe further seems to be completely oblivious to the fact that the individualism inherent in liberal theory is subject to the very same problems that he attaches to his caricature of traditional cultural groups.[54] Why this strange incongruity between the ability to see problems in the opponent's position and the inability to see that the same problems apply to one's own position? "Why do you look at the speck of sawdust in your brother's eye and pay no attention to the plank in your own eye" (Matthew 6:3)? Is it ideologically induced blindness? Or, is it perhaps prejudice? Even anti-religious prejudice?

American writer David Berliner is very frank in admitting his "animosity" toward fundamentalists (1997, 383). In a book seeking to expose the myths and frauds behind the attacks on America's public schools, Berliner admits that "This book was written in outrage" (1995, xiii). Animosity and outrage aren't exactly conducive to dispassionate argument.

Various writers have explored the politics behind efforts to get tax support for religious schools, and refer to the "lobbying" and "pressure group politics" that are used by religious groups (Doerr and Menendez 1991; Walford 1995). These same writers seem to be oblivious to the pressure-group politics behind establishment support for state-maintained common schools. It does not help to use emotively loaded language. Doerr and Menendez, for example, suggest that a pluralistic educational system would lead to "horrendous fragmentation," even while admitting that the Netherlands has had a pluralistic system for many years (1991, 139). Many other examples could be provided, but this must suffice to illustrate the tendencies to replace dispassionate argument with rhetoric among opponents of religious schools and colleges.[55]

Despite the strong feelings that often underlie opposition to religious schools and colleges, and despite the strong resistance to any suggestions that we need to restructure our educational systems so as to be more accommodating to pluralism, I want to believe that truth will win out in the end, and that change will eventually occur. We need to be patient in waiting for change, even though the establishment is tenaciously resisting such change. Change in established folkways, as William Sumner taught us long ago, can only come about slowly and gradually.

There is reason for optimism. Chester E. Finn Jr, who served as assistant U.S. secretary of education from 1985 to 1988, suggests in a recent essay reviewing a number of books dealing with educational reform that, at least outside the educational establishment's citadels, "an important breakthrough can be seen: widening awareness that the American educational system as we know it not only needs radical improvement but also needs its ground rules rewritten, its assumptions replaced, its structures overturned, and its power relationships transformed" (1997, 34). "We are, in fact, seeing signs of a whole new paradigm of education" emerging, according to Finn (34).

Eamonn Callan suggests, as "one of the most significant shifts" in educational thought during the twentieth century, "our collective loss of faith in the common school" (1997, 162). There is a growing realization that the present school enterprise is doing poorly, and, according to Finn, "it is incapable of doing much better because it is intellectually misguided, ideologically wrongheaded, and organizationally dysfunctional" (1997, 34). Hence the gradual emergence of a new paradigm, expressed in experiments with independent "charter" or "opt-out" schools, "contract schools," and "choice programs" (34). We are also seeing significant growth in home-schooling and independent religious schools. As with all paradigm shifts, there is controversy and fierce competition between the old and the new paradigms.

> To be sure, the old edifice of public education is large, but it is growing shaky. Today that shakiness is more intellectual than political. The teachers' unions still wield great clout in many statehouses and – especially when they team up with school boards and superintendents – they can still limit the impact of reforms they dislike. Yet they are starting to find themselves playing more defense than offense in the policy arena. More remarkably, they seem to be losing the war of ideas. (Finn 1997, 37)

Various other writers are similarly pointing to the inevitability of change.[56] I hope that they are right in their optimism.

CONCLUDING IDEAL

I have, in this chapter, been defending a system of educational pluralism. The overall thrust of this book has been to defend religious schools and colleges generally. As I have stated previously, this should not be taken to mean that I would be prepared to defend each and every religious school. Just as believers in a state-maintained system of education can defend such a system while at the same time admitting that there are very weak schools within the system, so I should be allowed to admit that there are weaknesses in specific religious schools even though I believe in educational pluralism.

It is all too easy to focus on the negative. I will admit that much of the argument of this book has been negative and critical. It is therefore perhaps fitting to conclude on a more positive note. "Our world today is a world of failed ideals," Wolterstorff reminds us in a book seeking to offer hope for our troubled times (1983, 113). Let me conclude with a brief description of what I consider to be the ideal in education, both structurally and specifically.

I dream of a society in which justice prevails, a society in which various intermediate institutions like the family, the church, and the school are each given a clear identity and are allowed to function in terms of that identity. There are a variety of schools in my ideal society, each reflecting differing cultural, ideological, and religious communities – Marxists and Buddhists, African-American and Hispanic-American, gypsies and Jews, anabaptist Christians and Roman Catholic Christians, and even liberal humanists.

Within each of these schools every effort will be made to maintain a careful balance between what are so often posited as polarized extremes: a balance between particularity and universality; between appreciating ethnicity and emphasizing a universal humanity; between seeing education as initiation into the present and the particular and as liberation from the present and the particular; between teaching for commitment and teaching for openness; between passing on the traditions of a culture and learning to think critically about those traditions; between confident affirmation of the truth and humility in admitting the possibility of error in this affirmation; between stressing freedom and appreciating the inevitable limits of freedom.

What do we do with those schools that do not maintain the above balances? What do we do with illiberal communities who will establish schools in which children will simply be indoctrinated into illiberal ways of life? And what do we do with the quite legitimate fear that these illiberal communities might themselves become a majority or gain enough power to impose an illiberal way of life on all of society? My answer will no doubt appear simplistic to many – we need to have faith and hope that these illiberal communities will eventually come to see the truth. Above all, we need to ensure that we ourselves don't become illiberal in our treatment of that which we see as narrow, confining, and illiberal.

Here another very important question arises, which Conrad Brunk raises in the context of a discussion on unilateral disarmament (1987). Is it even rational to act in accord with ideals or principles that put one at serious disadvantage *vis-à-vis* others if they cannot be counted on to act reciprocally? Hobbes believed that it was not rational except where the performance of others could be guaranteed by coercive sanctions. It is this same kind of Hobbesian thinking that lies behind the tendency of liberals to argue for state-imposed liberal education via common schools.

We need more faith and hope that good will ultimately prevail. For some, such faith and hope are found within a religious tradition. For those who don't appreciate this source, Annette Baier has suggested that they need a "secular faith" in the eventual reciprocation of others to one's own moral actions (1980). A civilized community is not possible unless there is some faith – not necessarily faith that others are essentially good, but only that they are not absolutely and unconditionally evil, ready to take full advantage of every vulnerability of their contemporaries. Even Hobbes had to appeal to such a faith in order to get out of a state of nature.

Without good will inspired by faith and hope, a liberal society is impossible, and, as Hobbes saw so clearly, we will find ourselves increasingly in a "state of nature" where life is "solitary, poor, nasty, brutish, and short."

Notes

PROLOGUE

1 "The existence of high-quality national public education school systems for the first dozen or so years of training is the key to a democracy where legitimacy lies with the citizen," says John Ralston Saul in the 1995 Massey Lectures (1995, 65).

2 However, it should be noted that sometimes it is Christians themselves who are opposed to the existence of Christian schools. In 1986, for example, David Jenkins, Bishop of Durham, maintained that church schools were inappropriate in the pluralistic society of Great Britain, and should be phased out (quoted in Hughes 1992, 25). A study of Catholic schools in Quebec reported that some Catholics saw the Catholic school as an "anachronism" (Catholic Committee 1989, 21). See also Hill (1982; 1990) and Smith (1988). Some of the objections coming from these Christian writers arise out of their Christian beliefs, and it is not my intent to answer these more specific theological objections in this work. Many of their objections, however, are the same as those coming from a secular context, and it is these with which I will be concerned.

3 For a theological defence of religious schools see, for example, Gangel (1988); Maffet (1987); Perks (1992); and Weeks (1988).

4 That this is possible from a Christian perspective rests on the Christian doctrine of general revelation or common grace. The Catholic doctrine of natural law also suggests the possibility of common ground between Christian and non-Christian. This possibility will be explored more carefully in chapter 10.

5 My objective is stronger than McLaughlin's (1992a), who is only concerned to show that the arguments against separate schools are not as strong as is generally assumed. For a booklet making a philosophical case for Muslim schools in England, see Halstead (1986). A special issue of *Ethics in Education* (1990), "The Ethics of Religiously Based Schools," which I edited, provides short article treatments of some of the objections that I will be dealing with in this book.

6 Mark Holmes has, I believe correctly, suggested that the restructuring of school systems "is the single most important policy issue facing western education" (1992, 31).

CHAPTER ONE

1 Some recent significant studies from which I will be drawing for my summaries include the following:

   *International or national comparative studies – Blair (1986); Cibulka and Boyd (1989); Glenn (1989); Tulasiewicz and Brock (1988); Walford (1989).

   *United States – Bryk et al. (1993); Cookson (1989); Doerr and Menendez (1991); Menendez (1993); Parsons (1987); Peshkin (1986); Rose (1988); Wagner (1990).

   *United Kingdom – Lambert (1993); MacKenzie (1994); O'Keeffe (1986; 1988); Walford (1991b; 1994a; 1994b; 1995).

   *Canada: Bergen (1989); Holmes (1990; 1998); McKim (1988); Matthews (1990); Peters (1996); Sweet (1997); Van Brummelen (1996; see also entire issue); Wilson and Lazerson (1982).

   *A new journal has also been launched recently from the Netherlands, *The International Journal of Education and Religion*, focusing on religiously affiliated schools, colleges, and universities.

2 My account of the status of church schools in Newfoundland and the ensuing controversy regarding the province's attempt to make changes to this status draws on the following sources: Blair (1986); Royal Commission (1992); McKim (1988); and a number of articles found in two of Canada's leading weekly magazines and newspapers, *Maclean's* and the *Globe and Mail* (see especially issues from July to September of 1997).

3 The British North America Act of 1867 made education the responsibility of the provinces, subject to four provisos which protected the rights and privileges enjoyed by people belonging to certain denominations at the time of entry into Confederation. These rights and privileges have been preserved in section 29 of the more recent Canadian Charter of Rights and Freedoms, which is part of the Constitution Act of 1982. The first of the aforementioned provisos states: "Nothing in any such Law (passed by the Province to regulate education) shall prejudicially

affect any Right or Privilege with respect to Denominational Schools which any Class of Persons have by Law in the Province at the Union" (Blair 1986, 8).

4 *Globe and Mail,* 3 Sept. 1997, A4.

5 *Globe and Mail,* 3 Sept. 1997, A1.

6 *Globe and Mail,* 30 Aug. 1997, A1.

7 *Globe and Mail,* 4 Sept. 1997, A4.

8 For example, Harold Flynn, president of the Newfoundland and Labrador Catholic Association, had this to say after the referendum: "If they can take a minority right out of Newfoundland at the federal level, I guess they can take it out of every other province or territory" (*Globe and Mail,* 4 Sept. 1997, A4). Liberal MP Joseph Fontana, the chairman of the federal Liberal caucus, allowed that there had been a concern, particularly among Ontario MPs, that Catholic schools might be threatened. "Once you get on the slippery slope, what's to stop Mike Harris [the premier of Ontario] from attacking separate schools" (*Globe and Mail,* 4 Sept. 1997, A4). See also Frank Peters, who in a review of the changing face of denominational education in Canada suggests that constitutional protection of denominational schools "may be far flimsier" than many supporters of such schools might wish to believe (1996, 255).

9 Though confessional in theory, Protestant schools have been more pluralist than confessional, serving people of diverse religions, including Jews and other non-Christians. Protestant schools have also not always enforced their own regulations with regard to religious instruction (Blair 1986, 22). A report of the Catholic Committee in Quebec (1989) stated that many of the people surveyed admitted "that they hesitate to say they are Catholic or to qualify their school as Catholic ... it does not seem realistic to believe that a Catholic public school today should attempt to educate students in Christianity" (Catholic Committee 1989, 26, 20).

10 On 10 Sept. 1997, the Quebec National Assembly, in a unanimous vote, passed a motion calling on the federal government to amend the Canadian Constitution to allow the province to replace Catholic and Protestant school boards with French and English ones (*Globe and Mail,* 10 Sept. 1997, A6). These amendments received approval of the Canadian Parliament and Senate in November and December of 1997 (*Globe and Mail,* 20 Dec. 1997, A16).

11 Quoted in *Christian Week,* 9 July 1996, 1, 4.

12 See Marcel-R. Fox, "The Quebec School System: Twenty-Five Years of Evolution," *CSSE News* 16(8) (1989): 10–14.

13 It should be pointed out that I am using the term "independent" rather than "private" or "non-public" because the latter terms are misleading in that they suggest that schools which are not operated directly by government decree do not serve the public interest or that they are in some way

operating as private enterprises when in fact they are usually run by non-profit organizations (Van Brummelen 1996, 5n1).

14 Van Brummelen points out that these figures understate the actual growth because of a reclassification of secondary Catholic schools in Ontario in the mid-1980s (1996, 1). If we take into account these changes in Ontario, independent school enrolment in 1992–3 is really much higher and should stand at about 5.4 per cent of total school enrolment in Canada, Van Brummelen estimates.

15 A 1985 report of the Commission on Private Schools in Ontario states that in the period 1973–83 elementary and secondary private school enrolment increased by 60 per cent and 90 per cent respectively (Shapiro 1985, 6). About 80 per cent of these schools were religiously defined. In the province of British Columbia, the proportion of children being educated outside the public school system rose by two-thirds, from 4.3 per cent in 1977/8 to 7.3 per cent in 1990/1. The number of non-public educational institutions also grew by two-thirds, from about 167 in 1977/8 to 279 by 1989–90. These figures do not include children who are being home-schooled, often for religious reasons (Barman 1991, 18).

16 Callan (1985, 118; cf. Callan 1988). Callan's opposition to religious schools has been softening in his later writings (1995; 1997; 2000).

17 *Toronto Star* carried a five-part series of lengthy articles (14–18 Sept. 1996). In conjunction with this series, CBC television also broadcast a two-part special on religious education, 16 and 17 Sept. 1996, on the National Magazine.

18 *Toronto Star,* 14 Sept. 1996, A28.

19 See Magsino (1986, 249–50); Shapiro (1986, 265); Alberta Private Schools Funding Task Force (1997, 28).

20 See *Adler and Elgersma v. Ontario, Minister of Education* (1996). But, in a dissenting opinion, Supreme Court Justice L'Heureux-Dubé argued that the plaintiffs were indeed victims of discrimination, arguing that the equality guarantees of the Charter were meant to protect vulnerable religious minorities against majority tyranny. This case, and the dissenting opinion, are reviewed in Callan (2000). Here it also should be noted that Canadian law is not constrained by a doctrine of strict separation of church and state as is the case in the United States, and hence there is the possibility of government funding of separate schools (Holmes 1985, 113).

21 In 1988, the Ontario Court of Appeal struck down a law which had compelled Ontario schools to hold daily religious exercises consisting of reading the Scriptures and repeating the Lord's Prayer (*Zylberberg v. Sudbury Board of Education*). In 1990 the same court struck down a long-standing regulation requiring that religious education (i.e. Christian education) be included in Ontario public school curricula (*Canadian Civil Liberties Assn. v. Ontario Minister of Education*). This case resulted in the government issu-

ing a memorandum and regulations on "Education and Religion in Schools" which stated that teaching about religion was to be non-indoctrinational and must not give primacy to any particular religious faith (see Sweet 1997, 218–19). A group of parents representing a number of faith communities (Sikh, Hindu, Muslim, Mennonite, and Christian Reformed) initiated a court challenge, arguing that the regulations and memorandum violated their freedom of religion. The Ontario Court, however, ruled that there was no infringement of religious freedom, since the secularism espoused by the public school system was non-coercive and neutral (*Bal v. Ontario*, 1994).

22 Funding for independent schools in the remaining provinces is as follows: Quebec – 60 per cent of the rate for public schools; Manitoba – 46.25 per cent of net operating expenses per student; Saskatchewan – most of the forty-eight private schools are not funded; only a few private schools receive some funding. These figures are based on a recent study done by the Alberta Private Schools Funding Task Force (1997, 28).

23 From a letter sent to all board chairs and superintendents by Jim Rivait, government affairs coordinator, 29 April 1997.

24 From a letter sent to the minister of education by Dick Chamney, president of the Public School Boards' Association of Alberta, 6 May 1997.

25 Kelly Torrance, "Attack on Independent Schools," *Alberta Report*, 10 Nov. 1997, 10–1.

26 The Edmonton public system has also had a Hebrew-language school with a religious component operating under its jurisdiction since 1975. "The Edmonton board side-stepped the thorny legal problem presented by the religious aspect of the school by calling it a language school" (Sweet 1997, 241)

27 Ontario has had a similar policy in place since 1984, though not excluding the possibility of religious schools becoming alternate public schools. Two Mennonite schools have been operating under this arrangement, though both have had to adjust their programs radically in the light of changes to government guidelines with regard to religion in public schools adopted in 1990. These guidelines specify that a public school may not give "primacy to ... any particular religion," and may not permit religious exercises or "provide instruction that includes indoctrination into a particular religion" (Vriend 1996, 26; cf. Sweet 1997, ch. 2; cf. 119).

28 Michael Jenkinson, "Shadows on the 'City of Light,'" *Alberta Report*, 26 Aug. 1996, 42–3.

29 Wagner (1990, 18; cf. Dwyer 1998, 16). Rose cites estimates as of 1984/5 suggesting that there are between fifteen and eighteen thousand Christian schools in the USA, with a student population of approximately one million (Rose 1988, 34–9; Carper 1984; Reese 1985). Cookson (1989) estimates that there are a total of twenty-eight thousand elementary and

secondary private schools in the United States, enrolling 5.6 million students. Most of these schools are religious, with the largest group being Roman Catholic and the next largest being evangelical Christian day schools (see also Dwyer 1998, 15–16). Private schools constitute 25 per cent of all elementary and secondary schools and educate 12% of the student population in the USA.

A recent article in the *Atlantic Monthly* (1999, 284(4):21–2) highlights the dramatic increase of children attending full-time Jewish schools in the USA. The numbers have more than tripled since the early 1960s, to about two hundred thousand. Of the current population of Jewish school-age children – roughly a million – the proportion enrolled in public schools has declined from more than 90 per cent in 1962 to about 65 per cent in 1999.

30 It should be noted that the majority of "voluntary" schools in Great Britain have a special "voluntary-aided" status, which gives the church significant control over them. O'Keeffe reports that five pupils in every hundred are in Church of England voluntary-aided schools and nine pupils in every hundred are in Roman Catholic voluntary-aided schools (1986, 14). See also Bell (1991); Deakin (1989); Walford (1991b, 1994a).

31 *Hansard*, vol. 526, no. 52, 4 March 1991, col. 1281.

32 See *Wesken Daily Press*, 31 Dec. 1993; and *Times Educational Supplement*, 22 Sept. 1995 and 26 Jan. 1996.

33 See article by Geraldine Hackett, "Adventist Secondary Wins Funding," in *Times Educational Supplement*, no. 4263, 13 March 1998, 11.

34 Dale Eisler, "Domestic Lessons," *Maclean's*, 1 Sept. 1997, 64.

35 From a document entitled "Home Education across the United States," published by Brian D. Ray and Home School Legal Defense Association, 1997.

36 *Times Educational Supplement*, no. 4219, 9 May 1997, supplement no. 2, 3. This figure comes from Roland Meighan, a founding member of Education Otherwise and researcher on home-schooling at the University of Nottingham. It is difficult to get an exact figure of home schools in Great Britain because only those students who have been in state schools and have been removed to be home-schooled have to register. Education Otherwise, a self-help organization run by and for families practising or interested in home-based education in the UK, has grown steadily from a small group of parents in 1977 to its current membership of about 2,500 (Bendell 1994, 151).

37 The *UK Christian Handbook – 1998/99 Silver Jubilee Edition* (Carlisle: Paternoster, 1997) lists ninety-one residential theological colleges and Bible schools, 37 per cent of which are inter- or non-denominational, ecumenical, or evangelical. Then there are another fifty-six non-residential theological colleges and Bible schools, of which 53 per cent are inter- or

non-denominational, ecumenical, or evangelical. Some of these may receive some government funding, however, and students will often be eligible for grants.

38 There are sixteen church-related universities (including university colleges and federated universities), fourteen religious liberal arts colleges, fifty-seven Bible colleges, forty-one seminaries or theological graduate schools, and twenty-one other schools (Rae 1995, 1, 21, 29–31). Of these, ten are free-standing institutions and fifty-two are affiliated with public universities, most often located on the same campus, a "distinctive Canadian arrangement" (30, 5). Rae's 1995 paper was based on research which eventually led to his Ph.D. dissertation entitled "Unholy Alliance? The Church and Higher Education in Canada" (1998).

39 For example, there are four Christian university colleges in Alberta which receive direct government funding for arts and science programs only, in the amount of about 75 per cent of the equivalent operating costs at the public universities. Then there are two religious colleges affiliated with the University of Alberta which get some indirect per pupil/course funding from the government (like Saskatchewan and Ontario). A third independent but affiliated college receives no funding. This information was culled from information supplied by Harald Zinner, Business Planning and Evaluation Branch, Department of Advanced Education, Alberta. See also a recent study of higher education in Canada organized around provincial jurisdictions, which includes short treatments of religious colleges and universities (Jones 1997).

40 As reported in *Alberta Report*, 12 Jan. 1987, 28.

CHAPTER TWO

1 For example, the Alberta School Boards Association recently argued the following in a submission presented to the Alberta Private Schools Funding Task Force: "While we strive to respect diversity, we must resist the temptation to segregate our children and reinforce our differences. Wherever possible we must encourage shared experiences among the diverse population in our public schools. A strong, open and diverse public education system is the best way to promote common understanding of Alberta's diversity and it is our best defense against intolerance" ("Our Children – Our Future: Submission to the Government of Alberta's Private Schools Funding Task Force," 12 Nov. 1997).

2 See *Hansard*, 4 March 1991, vol. 526, no. 52, cols. 1253, 1276, 1281, 1284. See also Walford (1995, ch. 5).

3 Shapiro, commenting on the 1985 Ontario report on private schools already referred to, defends state-maintained schools as a means of ensuring that "in a pluralistic and multicultural society, schools can contribute to

strengthening the social fabric by providing a common acculturation experience for children" (1986, 274).

The Public School Boards' Association of Alberta, in a letter to the minister of education, expressed opposition to an amendment to the school act which would have increased funding to independent religious schools and argued the following: "Public funding for private schools promotes fragmentation of the community and weakens the cohesion of the community" (letter to the Honourable Gary Mar, minister of education, 6 May 1997). In the 1997 Newfoundland debate regarding the restructuring of the denominational school system, one opponent suggested that those supporting it were in fact endorsing "a system of religious apartheid" (*Globe and Mail*, 2 Sept. 1997, A5).

4 See West (1970) for a treatment of the social cohesion justification for public education in Great Britain; see Sweet (1997, ch. 3) on Canada, and Wagner (1995, ch. 3) on Alberta. See also Tamir (1995a, Preface) on France, America, and Israel.

5 The same can be said about the origins of the Canadian public school system. Wagner refers to a study maintaining that "the overriding mission of the public school is not academic but social; it is to be a symbol of cohesion in society, an instrument of community, and to this end it seeks to make all students publicly useful by socializing them" (quoted in Wagner 1995, 55).

6 Hence the frequent reference to the public school system as the established church of America (Wagner 1995, 58; Rose 1988, 29; Illich, quoted in Arons 1986, 49; Skillen 1994, 126).

7 Kymlicka (1989, 162). Kymlicka does try to give some value to a plurality of cultures, but only in so far as cultural membership provides a context within which an individual can make choices (166).

8 Marshall (1989) makes this point, and refers to the early writings of Rawls, where Rawls admits that in his liberal society not all conceptions of the good will thrive. "If a conception of the good is unable to endure and gain adherents under conditions of equal freedom and mutual toleration, one must question whether it is a viable conception of the good and whether its passing is to be regretted" (Rawls 1975, 549).

9 See, for example, Marshall (1989) and various essays in Horton (1993) and Power and Lapsley (1993).

10 See Tamir (1995a, xxix). Goodenow (1988, 206–7) lists some other of these writers. Even Rawls, in his later writings, gives more explicit recognition to minority groups and gives them the freedom to establish their own educational system, or even to withdraw from the modern world in accordance with the injunctions of their religion, so long as they "acknowledge the principles of the political conception of justice and appreciate its political ideals of person and society" (1993, 200).

11 This is suggested by a statement of the former British secretary of state for education, John Patten: "Modern Britain has plenty of room for diversity and variety. But there cannot be room for separation or segregation" (quoted in Cumper 1994, 164). The recent Proulx Report in Quebec objects to a system of separate denominational schools for all religions because it would be "particularly incompatible with the social goal of promoting social cohesion by teaching students to live together" (1999, 185). At times it would seem that this equation of separation and divisiveness also lay behind the push for public education in Western societies – civic education was meant to rid students of all divisive features such as family affiliations, religious allegiances, and ethnic ties (Tamir 1995a, xxiii).

12 Writers affirming mediating structures include Berger and Neuhaus 1977; Mouw and Griffioen 1993, 115–16, 121–8, 168–71).

13 Mouw and Griffioen (1993, 173–7; cf. 1 Corinthians 13:9–12). American pragmatist William James captures the implications of a dual perspective on truth when he describes the absolutely true as "that ideal vanishing point towards which we imagine that all our temporary truths will someday converge" (1968, 170). Mouw and Griffioen maintain that only if we acknowledge a source of unity that transcends the bounds of human society, a point that is in fact acknowledged by various secular writers, does it become possible to promote unity without destroying plurality (1993, 168).

14 Several of the participants in the debate in the British House of Lords make this same point – Baroness Cox and Viscount Buckmaster, *Hansard*, vol. 536, no. 52, 4 March 1991, cols. 1253, 1287.

15 See also the study of the Netherlands' experiment in accommodating pluralism by Robert Tash (1991) and Glenn (1989, 47–78; cf. 1989).

16 Indeed, it can be argued that a system of educational pluralism contributed to overcoming the religious tensions that existed in Newfoundland when their system of denominational schools was first established. Sweet quotes Newfoundland psychologist Bill McKim, who points to the earlier religious tensions in Newfoundland, but both writers fail to acknowledge the possibility that denominational schools were successful in overcoming these tensions (Sweet 1997, 50–7; cf. McKim 1988).

17 Again Sweet provides a good description of the conflict between Catholics and Protestants in early Canada, but fails to entertain seriously the possibility that separate school systems have fostered the tolerance and unity that we now enjoy (1997, chs. 1–3).

18 Greeley and Rossi further argue that even if a separate school system had a divisive influence, this would be overcome by the homogenizing forces within an industrial culture – the mass media, common life-styles, and the frequent interaction in the work environment (1966, 116, 114). See also the results of a major American study reviewed in Greene (1998).

19 Dunn similarly maintains that there "is no hard evidence in the Northern Ireland context that 'togetherness' has any important effect on community relations." Indeed, Dunn goes on to say that because of the complexity of social problems, it is very difficult to demonstrate any conclusions in scientific terms (1986, 239). In a survey of the response of nine principals of denominational schools in Ireland to a local integrated school that had been established within the last two years, all of them "referred to the importance of links between Protestant and Catholic schools as a means of lessening community division, and saw this as a more realistic approach than integrated education" (Morgan et al. 1992, 172). Morgan treats the attitudes of these principals as a problem that must somehow be overcome. "Integration is about the destruction of myths," Morgan concludes (176). But surely the testimony of practitioners in the field must be taken seriously. Perhaps Morgan is guilty of some myth-making herself.

20 Holmes (1992, 147). Holmes argues further that "the most divisive social lines in contemporary western democracy are no longer those of religion and ethnicity but those of economic standing (and associated social class." He then goes on to suggest that an advantage of school choice based on religion is that it cuts across socio-economic lines (47, 105, 150).

21 Swann (1985, 508, 5). Patricia White similarly recognizes the need for a delicate balance between unity and diversity in a society, and then goes on to argue that schools themselves must embody this principle of unity and diversity (1988, 197). Common schools are better able to develop bonds of mutuality between a diversity of students, and help them to develop attitudes and skills necessary for negotiation and compromise (White 1994, 88–9; cf. Gutmann 1996).

22 On Feuerstein's work, see Sharron (1987). See also Rutter (1972), Bronfenbrenner (1979), and De Ruyter and Miedema (2000). For a similar argument concerning the development of autonomy, see Thiessen (1993, 140–3).

CHAPTER THREE

1 R. Ghitter, "Tolerance," Address to the Alberta School Trustees Association, unpublished paper, 28 Nov. 1983, 33.

2 This statement comes from the Committee's Interim Report, *Private Education in Alberta: Discussion Paper 1* (Edmonton: Government of Alberta, Department of Education, 1984), 15.

3 As was already noted in the previous chapter, an Ontario study on the question of funding religious schools found that the charges of divisiveness and intolerance are probably the two most frequently made charges against religious schools (Shapiro 1986, 270). See Van Brummelen (1990, 9) for some other examples of this charge.

4 Swann (1985, 510). The committee argues that the establishment of separate schools for ethnic minority communities "might exacerbate the very feelings of rejection which they are seeking to overcome" (519). The report clearly suggests that the narrow confessional approach to education which characterizes religious schools does not cultivate attitudes of appreciation and respect towards all faiths and belief systems (518–19, 474–5, 496–7).

5 For other recent writings on tolerance see, for example, Gaede (1993); Groffier and Paradis (1991); Horton (1993); Horton and Nicholson (1992); Horton and Mendus (1985); Mendus (1988; 1989); Mendus and Edwards (1987); Walzer (1997).

6 Newman therefore describes tolerance as "half-hearted; it is the acceptance in one sense of something one does not accept in another sense" (1982, 5). Newman's description in fact points the way to resolving the apparent paradox inherent in the notion of tolerance in that the item being tolerated is rejected and accepted in two quite different senses. Although we reject the item in question, we refrain from any strong reaction in the light of some other priorities such as the value of persons.

7 *Private Education in Alberta: Discussion Paper 1* (Edmonton: Government of Alberta, Department of Education, 1984), 15.

8 We do at times talk of tolerating ourselves, but we are then objectifying one aspect of ourselves that is less than ideal, i.e. we are distancing ourselves from what needs tolerance in ourselves.

9 Dewey (1966, 21–2). The Alberta Report includes a quote from the Citizens of Public Justice which describes the same tendency in Canada. "However, we must recognize that Canada has a long history of using its educational system not for the creation of a tolerant society, but to assimilate immigrants and native peoples into the majority's way of thinking and acting" (Committee 1984, 107).

10 Committee (1984, 111–12); see also the Swann Report (1985, 474–5, 496–7).

11 In fact, the Alberta Report acknowledges this point in places when it suggests that "intolerance is not the disagreement of one person with another" (Committee 1984, 3, 92).

12 Jesus clearly respects the right of people to refuse his message, and condemns his disciples for wanting to call down judgment on those who reject it (Luke 9:5, 55).

13 Locke (1968, 59). Sadly, tolerance has not always been characteristic of the Christian church and even Locke did not see the full implications of the teachings of Jesus when he excluded Roman Catholics and atheists from his call for tolerance.

14 Two of the criteria the Alberta Committee used in its curriculum audit reveal a relativistic standpoint. Programs and supporting materials were

evaluated in terms of whether they took "an essentially positive approach to human similarities and differences," and, further, in terms of whether they conveyed the idea "that excellence in human endeavour may be found in different ways in all human groups" (Committee 1984, 69). The Committee is enamoured of "the give and take in the marketplace of ideas," but is concerned about those who are "blinded by partisanship" to their own belief system (109, 113). We find the same kind of emphasis in the Swann Report: it states a preference for the phenomenological approach to religious education, which eliminates categorization of religions as true or false, superior or inferior (Swann 1985, 474–5, 496–7; see also an essay of Paul Hirst's [1985]), who was one of the members of the committee preparing the Swann Report).

15 This same error is also found in representations of certain religions such as Hinduism as more tolerant because of their inclusive approach to other religious traditions. But as Coward has argued, inclusivism is still exclusive in a certain sense. "The Hindu approach to other religions is to absolutize the relativism implied in the viewpoint that the various religions are simply different manifestations of the one Divine" (Coward 1985, 80). Thus Coward concludes that Hinduism is not really as open and tolerant in its view of other religions as it might seem.

16 For a critique of Hull's attack on religionism see Thompson (1993) and Barnes (1997).

17 For example, Whitehouse, in a review of two proposals for educational reform in Northern Ireland, points out that although both proposals claim that there is a connection between intolerance and physical isolation in separate schools, neither argues the point or refers to studies that might support this view (1990, 495). And both proposals simply assume that education in common schools can contribute in an important way to bridging division and to removing inter-group suspicions.

18 The Bryk et al. study confirms the results of an earlier study by Greeley and Rossi which actually found graduates from Catholic schools to be more tolerant in certain respects than graduates from non-Catholic schools (Greeley and Rossi 1966, 130, 136–7).

Erickson et al., in a 1979 survey of public and private schools in British Columbia, found that students in religiously based schools displayed less prejudice than their public school counterparts. Erickson also documented other research studies which confirmed his own findings (1979, 148–9, 170). This result has been confirmed more recently by Peshkin, in his sociological analysis and critique of Bethany Baptist Academy. Peshkin compared the attitudes of students at BBA with their secular counterparts on a number of issues relating to pluralism, and was forced to concede that the Bethany students' racial attitudes were equally or more positive, except on the issue of interracial marriage (1986, 186). BBA students and their secular counterparts were roughly equal in supporting the right to free speech for those who don't believe in God (333). They also gave equal support to the claim that belief in God is not a condition for being a good American (334). A more recent American study provides further confirmation of the same conclusion (see review in Greene 1998).

19 Greer's conclusions seem to be supported by Gallup and Jones (1992), who, based on a survey of ten thousand urban and rural Americans, conclude that devout Christians, regardless of denomination, are more tolerant than the spiritually uncommitted – 84 per cent of the spiritually committed would not object to a person of another race moving in next door, a score that was twenty points better than that of the spiritually uncommitted. Barnes, in a review of various studies for and against the connection between religion and intolerance, concludes that no clear causal connection between the two has been established (1997, 19–20). However, there are several studies suggesting that those who value religion for its own sake are more tolerant (Barnes 1997, 20). See also Lewy (1997) for a review of evidence that devoutly religious persons are more likely to lead lives we can agree are good in secular terms – including a life of tolerance.

20 Again, see Whitehouse (1990). Occasionally claims on behalf of common schools are put to the test. For example, Homan and King, although they stress the tentative nature of their work, nevertheless do refer to a "compelling" result of one study showing that multi-faith religious education (presumably in common schools) does foster tolerance (1993). But are we really justified in drawing this conclusion on the basis of a small-scale, short-term, qualitative research project?

21 See, for example, "Heat on the Christian Schools," *Alberta Report*, 12 March 1984, 26–32.

22 Committee (1984, 69). See, for example, Vitz (1986); Van Brummelen (1990); Bryan (1984); De Moor (1994, ch. 2); and Nord (1995, ch. 4).

23 Aronson et al. (1994, 530–3). In fact, in one careful analysis of the research on desegregated schools, 53 per cent of the studies showed that prejudice actually increased; in 34 per cent of the studies, no change in prejudice occurred (530).

24 Banks (1985, 138). Sociologist Peter Berger (1977, 1974) warns against the dangers of anomie and homelessness which result from our modern failure to take into account the need for a primary culture and to provide for institutions which satisfy this need. Berger sees education as providing some possibility of resisting these results of modernity. "Public policy, especially in the area of education, has tended to be indifferent if not hostile to the racial, ethnic and religious diversity of American society," argues Berger (1977, 177). One example of this is the American experiment with integration via a busing program, which Berger describes as "sociological folly" (177). Berger argues instead for a voucher system in education which

would respect the pluralism of American life by enabling children to attend schools which reflect the primary cultures of their homes (178). It is evidence such as this which is no doubt behind Michael Sandel's argument against liberalism to the effect that "intolerance flourishes most where forms of life are dislocated, roots unsettled, traditions undone" (1984b, 17).

25 Erickson et al. suggest the following as explaining why students in religiously based schools displayed less prejudice than their public school counterparts: non-public school students are educated "in more consistent social environments" and therefore "develop more sense of security, and thus are less threatened by people 'not like them'" (1979, 148–9, 170).

26 Aronson et al. (1994, 531–3).

27 The Alberta Committee Report admits that "one of the lessons of history is that repression of minority groups can most readily be found in societies where the educational system is taken over by authoritarian power structures which impose rigid philosophies and closed attitudes upon the educational system" (Committee 1984, 20). The United States, with its long history of prejudice and intolerance against blacks, has also had a long history of public education which served to reinforce public attitudes. There are some blatant examples of prejudice and intolerance in Canadian history as well, some of which the Alberta Committee found to be reinforced in the textbooks used in Alberta public schools (73–4). The Swann Report also reports on the problem of common schools reinforcing existing racism (Swann 1985, ch. 5).

28 Yancey, in his bold critique of evangelical Christianity, points out that evangelicals mostly sat on the sidelines during the emergence of the civil rights movement in the United States in the mid-1960s, and in fact resisted government action against private schools which were often the bastions of segregation (1997, 248). Marsden (1987) has reviewed the sad story of intolerance on the part of fundamentalism, particularly as it worked itself out at Fuller Seminary, an evangelical seminary in the United States. Edward Carnell, in his 1955 presidential inaugural address at Fuller Seminary, courageously defended a spirit of tolerance as the crowning glory of a seminary. The logic of intolerance, he argued, was founded on spiritual and intellectual arrogance. This address led to a deep internal division of faculty and eventually led to Carnell's resignation four years later (Marsden 1987, 148–9).

29 I would therefore defend the Independent School Acts of British Columbia, which explicitly prohibit all schools from offering programs that foster religious intolerance (Barman 1991, 15–16).

30 Richard John Neuhaus, "Why We Can Get Along," *First Things* 60 (1996):31. It is here that I am in agreement with the Alberta Committee's concerns about the damning of a person or a group because of what they

267 Notes to pages 59–64

believe (Committee 1984, 3, 92). The Committee had some difficulty identifying specific examples of this in the curricula used in Alberta religious
schools. They did find one example: a curriculum that "refers to Islam,
Buddhism and Hinduism as 'false transcendent' religions, and implies that
those who follow those religions or those who may be humanistic in their
philosophy of life are 'godless, wicked and satanical'" (111). In fact, the
terms "godless, wicked and satanical" were only applied to atheistic and
agnostic philosophies, not to persons, and not to the religions listed. And
there is surely something right about calling an atheistic *philosophy* godless!
There is clearly a danger in using language such as this, however, and one
of the authors of the textbook referred to expressed his own dissatisfaction
with the wording of the offensive passage. It further needs to be pointed
out that this same curriculum went on to encourage students to study other
religious groups and to consider inviting people of different races and faith
communities to the class ("The Goof on the Godless: The Committee's
Prize Case of Intolerance Caves In," *Alberta Report*, 21 May 1984, 23).

31 The Talmud, Lorberbaum argues, not only provides a range of acceptable
and authoritative argumentation and discourse, but also embodies diversity, conflicting opinion, and argumentative discourse. The Jewish tradition
can therefore serve as a model for tolerance by acknowledging authority
and at the same time allowing for an "epistemology of mistakes"
(Lorberbaum 1995, 275).

32 The same point needs to be made with regard to Islam. At times the Muslim
religion is portrayed as the most tolerant of the world's major religions
(Halstead 1986, 27; cf. Ayubi 1991). Much has been made of the millet system of the Ottoman Empire as an example of Muslim tolerance (Kymlicka
1995, 156–8; Halstead 1995, 264). But there is another side to this history,
as has been carefully documented recently by Ye'or (1996). Muslim schools
need to encourage careful and critical reflection on both stories.

33 For example, Ball and Troyna have documented the resistance of some
church-controlled schools in England to introducing multicultural education (1987). To give as an excuse for such an omission that there are few
non-European students in the school is simply not good enough for any
school situated in a society or world that is multicultural (20).

CHAPTER FOUR

1 *Alberta Hansard*, 13 June 1988, col. 1666.
2 *Alberta Hansard*, 28 June 1988, col. 2109.
3 *Alberta Hansard*, 28 June 1988, col. 2119.
4 Tamir refers to the first major modern proposal for state education, written in
1763 by the attorney-general of the Parliament of Brittany. The children of
the state, he argued, "should be educated by the state" (Tamir 1995a, xviii).

5 The U.S. Supreme Court has generally adhered to its 1925 pronouncement in *Pierce v. Society of Sisters* that parents have a constitutional right to direct and control the education of their children (Gilles 1996, 937). Further, a surprising number of school choice arrangements have recently emerged in the United States (and elsewhere) which would seem to acknowledge parental rights over education (Biggs and Porter 1994; cf. Raywid 1985). For a survey of the history of parental choice in education in Britain, see Stillman (1994). The theme of parental choice runs throughout the 1992 White Paper, *Choice and Diversity*, which became the basis for the 1993 Education Act of Great Britain (Department for Education 1992).

6 Gilles points out, for example, that the Supreme Court in the USA has never developed a broader theory to explain its long-standing adherence to the principle of parental rights. "Nor has it clarified the terms on which this right coexists with what the Court has also declared to be the state's fundamental interest in ensuring that children are educated to be productive individuals and responsible citizens" (1996, 937). Similar confusion would seem to exist in Great Britain. McLaughlin, for example, complains that all too often parental rights in education are simply assumed and not defended (1992a, 121). Hence his criticism of Cox et al. (1986) and Flew (1987) for failing to provide convincing justification for parental rights.

7 The question of the rights of parents with regard to education has received much attention from philosophers since the publication of McLaughlin's 1984 essay. McLaughlin's paper prompted several responses: Callan (1985; 1988) and Gardner (1988; 1991). See also, Bigelow et al. (1988), Bridges (1984), Cohen (1981), Cox et al. (1986), Flew (1987), Hobson (1984), and White (1988). Of particular significance is Brian Crittenden's book-length treatment of the topic, *Parents, the State and the Right to Educate* (1988). Much is also being written about the topic from a legal perspective, e.g. Gilles (1996; 1997).

8 Wagner (1995, 27–32). Jones is not alone in thinking of parental authority in exclusive terms. Amy Gutmann lists some writers who subscribe to what she calls "the state of families," in which educational authority is placed exclusively in the hands of parents (1987, 28–33; cf. Oppewal 1981, 363–5).

9 Wagner (1995, 27–8). The Alberta Department of Education finally laid charges against Jones and so the case went to court; indeed, all the way to the Supreme Court of Canada, where Jones finally lost. Jones still refused to comply, but in the end, after spending ten days in jail, and after renewed negotiations with a government that had demonstrated its commitment to parental rights, Jones agreed to voluntarily submit information about his students to the department. In return, he was able to continue operating the school without getting a licence (Wagner 1995, 32, 45).

10 I would argue that this position is quite in keeping with biblical authority, which gives to the state the right to punish the evil-doer, suggesting that the

state has every right, and even an obligation, to step in when parents abuse or blatantly neglect their children (Romans 13:1–5).

11 A forceful and bold defence of state rights in education is made by Joseph Tussman in a book entitled *Government and the Mind* (1977). Tussman admits that it was "surprisingly difficult" to write this book because his thesis that the government has "a serious and legitimate concern with the mind of the citizen" seems to require a defence against charges of advocating a totalitarian government (13). Tussman himself is opposed to government monopoly in education, and describes his inclinations in this field as "strongly pluralistic" (14, cf. 56, 163). Here is only one example of someone who defends government rights in education without claiming exclusive rights and without carrying this position to an extreme.

12 With Locke, I would argue that parental authority over children is in a large measure grounded in parental obligations to children (Locke 1980, no. 56). It is unfortunate that discussions about authority over education tend to be expressed in the language of rights. As various writers have noted, the language of rights tends to be absolutist, and therefore not helpful when conflicting rights emerge (Shapiro 1986, 273; cf. McLaughlin 1992a, 130n22). A greater focus on responsibilities to the child in the area of education would, I suggest, ameliorate some of the apparent conflicts that now dominate discussions.

13 Dwyer's position on religious schools is somewhat ambiguous. He is not opposed to religious schools as such. His main concern is with the failure of governments to regulate such schools (1998, 2). He admits, though, that his proposals would "so radically alter" the nature of religious schools "as to make them unrecognizable" as fundamentalist or Catholic schools (180). He declares this to be "cause for celebration, because any form of schooling that systematically violates the rights of children should not exist" (180). For a careful critical review of Dwyer's book, see Gilles (1999).

14 Though perhaps not quite as radical as Holt and Dwyer, many philosophers of education today challenge parental rights on much the same grounds. Bruce Ackermann, for example, though sensitive to parental rights in the *home*, claims that parents have no "basic right" to shape the education of their children. What is basic instead is the right of the *child* to receive a liberal education which will enable him or her to grow towards autonomy (1980, 160). Interestingly, Ackermann goes on to object to religious schools, calling them "petty tyrannies in which like-minded parents club together to force-feed their children without restraint" (160; cf. Patricia White 1983, 3, 87, 146). For other works of a similar kind see Aiken and La Follette (1980); Archard (1993); Wringe (1981).

15 There is, of course, considerable debate about the level of autonomy that should be aimed at, and the conditions under which the appropriate level of autonomy can be developed. Many liberal writers demand a very high

ideal of autonomy, while others would argue for a minimal level of autonomy, critical rationality, and independence. I have argued elsewhere for an
ideal of "normal autonomy" (Thiessen 1993, ch. 5).

16 Dwyer is forced to admit that the vast majority of parents do genuinely love
their children and will therefore take care of their fundamental needs
(1998, 89, 81, 86). Crittenden further argues that there is something
counter-intuitive about the claim that for many centuries parents were generally indifferent if not harsh to their children. From the viewpoint of biological survival, adults must care for their young. Even animals do the same
(Crittenden 1988, 32–3).

17 Crittenden, at one point, grants that historically there might have been a
tendency to regard children as property (1988, 92). This, however, seems
to contradict his earlier claims about a natural instinct to care for children
and his warnings about the dangers of claims about the neglect of children
being grossly exaggerated (32–3).

18 *Alberta Hansard*, 13 June 1988, col. 1671; Dwyer (1998, 72, cf. 5, 100, 143).

19 Dwyer underscores as a basic assumption of his analysis "that children are
persons and that morally they are equal persons" (1998, 67, 121). But
Dwyer's argument plays on an ambiguity in this claim. While he is quite
right in insisting that children ought to be treated as persons, and that they
are equal to adults in terms of having rights as moral persons, they are *not*
equal to *adults* in terms of their ability to be self-determining and to take on
certain responsibilities. Yet his whole argument hinges on treating them as
adults. For example, he repeatedly stresses that no person has the right to
control the lives of other persons (67–8, 100). But while this principle
might apply to adults – though even here it is problematic, since many relationships quite legitimately involve some degree of control over the other
person, as Dwyer is forced to admit (72) – this principle simply cannot apply to children, since they are not *adults*, as again Dwyer is forced on occasion to admit (64, 73, 85, 107). Indeed, to treat children as adults is to beg
the question from the start. Further, there is a vagueness inherent in the
very notion of "control," and Dwyer's failure to define the term more precisely undermines his entire argument.

20 Gilles makes this point most forcefully. To deny parental rights in the name
of children's rights merely shifts the locus of adult control from the family to
the collective or the state (1997, 15; cf. 1999, 19). See also Purdy (1992) for
a sustained argument against those who argue for equal rights for children.

21 Callan, for example, has recently argued for a strict equality of parental
and children's rights (1997, 144–5). He quite correctly points out that to
appeal only to the interests of parents is despotic. But to maintain that it is
only the interests of children that really count merely inverts the despotism. Like me, Callan wants to avoid exclusive claims with regard to educational rights. We need to affirm both parental and children's rights.

I would, however, disagree with the egalitarianism of Callan's treatment, because parental rights need to be given primacy.

22 Despite Dwyer's impassioned defence of children's rights, he is forced to admit that children cannot exercise these rights and that they are dependent on adults (1998, 81, 85). At times he grudgingly allows parents the "privilege" of acting in children's interest, or of being their "agent" (6, 64, 85–6, 92). But the predominant emphasis is on the state, which *in fact* is given the right to act on behalf of children's interests. For example, Dwyer suggests that it is the state that "confers on parents rights to control certain child-rearing matters" (45). On certain educational matters, the state has "presumptive authority" to decide (87). He further quotes with approval a Supreme Court decision which suggests that "education is perhaps the most important function of state and local governments" (134). And the final two chapters of Dwyer's book are preoccupied with the state's control of education (chs. 5 and 6).

23 There is one further option that could be considered, that parental authority ought to yield to that of experts, i.e. teachers. Since many of the considerations regarding the latter option are very similar to the option involving the primacy of state authority, I will not provide a separate treatment of the position which gives primacy to teacher authority. I will, however, touch on the question of teacher authority from time to time.

24 Crittenden (1988, 68). Crittenden devotes a section to reviewing writers, both ancient and modern, who have used the biological relationship itself to confer certain moral rights on parents over their children (55–61). Various writers have also extended the biological argument by appealing to maternal and paternal instincts (Crittenden 1988, 73; cf. Locke, 1980, no. 56, 67).

25 Hobson (1984, 64) agrees with Wringe (1981, 100–1) in objecting to the biological argument, maintaining that the mere fact of giving birth to a child does not give a parent moral rights over it. But in the next paragraph Hobson argues that "[t]he only rights that parents have by virtue of giving birth to a child flow from duties that this gives rise to" (64). This is to concede the very point he seems to be arguing against!

26 Crittenden (1988, 71). There are other problems with transferring parental rights to other adults. How would decisions on the placements of children be made? What criteria would be used to decide when a child should be put into the care of others? Can we measure adequacy of care accurately enough to make decisions like this? Administrative problems such as these lead Gilles to conclude that the rejection of special custodial rights for biological parents is not only unjust but imprudent (1996, 961).

27 Gilles draws a useful analogy pointing out that we don't abandon the principle of adult self-governance just because many adults mistreat, abuse, or even kill themselves (1996, 954).

28 Dwyer (1998, 4–5, 47, 92, 119). This privilege, which in fact sounds suspiciously like a right, Dwyer's claims to the contrary notwithstanding (46–7),
is based on the fact that it is in the best interests of children to give this
right to parents. Dwyer raises one important objection to this argument:
There is no self-evident connection between parents' religious beliefs and
children's temporal interests (82). But this rests on Dwyer's grossly exaggerated assessment of the harm that religion does to children, and on an
arbitrary limitation to temporal interests. There are studies to show that religion has temporal benefits (Gallup and Jones 1992).

29 Crittenden refers to research by Brigitte and Peter Berger (1984, 178)
showing that the family was regarded as the most important personal value
by 92 per cent of the adults surveyed. See also Callan (1997, 144) and
Randall (1994, ch. 5).

30 Patricia White, for example, stresses children's rights, but admits that becoming a parent and bringing up a family is something to which most people want to devote a good part of their lives and which gives them
considerable satisfaction (1994, 85). White stops at using the language of
rights here, however, though she gives no reason for doing so. Gutmann
similarly writes that "an essential part of our good life is imparting an understanding of our values to our children," although in the end she places
more weight on citizenship and public life (1987, 26).

31 On the child's need for the family, Crittenden refers to Fraiburg (1977), as
well as to a study by Rossi (1977) summarizing research showing the difficulties in communal child rearing. I have already referred to research
showing the need for a primary culture in chapter 3 (see also Ackerman
1980; McLaughlin 1984; and De Ruyter and Miedema 2000). Even Dwyer,
despite his strong attack on parental rights, concedes that "optimal upbringing for a child involves an intimate, continuous relationship with a
single set of parents that is largely insulated from interference by third parties" (1998, 81). In another place, however, he suggests there is no empirical evidence for the need of a primary culture (145). The facts are
otherwise and this contradicts his earlier claim.

32 Bronfenbrenner, in his review of the research regarding the child's need
for a stable and secure home environment, specifically raises the question
of the age of the child who has such a need. His reply: "The matter is debatable, but I would suggest anyone under the age of, say, 89" (1980, 1).

33 Another simpler variant of this argument involves an appeal to the liberal/
democratic value of freedom and personal autonomy. Patricia White reviews several writers who have defended parental rights simply in terms of
the democratic right of citizens to personal autonomy (1994, 84–5).
Crittenden similarly argues that the right "to direct the upbringing of one's
children is a distinct moral right that derives from a more general right
protecting freedom of action" (1988, 66).

34 There are many people today who would object to any appeal to nature, with or without its theological overtones. The family is viewed as an artificial construct, just as the state is most often seen as a product of a social contract. Crittenden himself, though defending a position similar to mine, explicitly rejects an appeal to nature when he maintains that "marriage and the family are cultural and social designs, not natural necessities" (1988, 48). But Crittenden contradicts himself when he goes on to say that marriage and the family "are anchored in human dispositions and needs that are fundamental in the life of individuals and the species: sexual relations between male and female, the conception and procreation of human life, the care of helpless infants, the socialization and education of children, the companionship of a man and woman, membership of an intimate and personal community that has identity over generations" (48). Crittenden fails to see that to appeal to universal dispositions and needs is to appeal to nature.

   To those who claim that the nuclear family is a passing phenomenon, I would suggest that historical evidence is against them. Crittenden reviews the evidence and concludes that the institutions of marriage and the family "have proved to be remarkably enduring and resilient" (1988, 48). Such continuity provides some justification for claiming that the nuclear family is a natural institution, and that education as a parental responsibility is also natural.

35 Gilles proposes an experiment to put his position on educational emancipation to the test – give adolescents the financial means to make educational choices entirely on their own. He suggests that few defenders of child rights would really be willing to do this, because of their fear that it would result in significant harm to adolescents (1997, 43–4). Therefore parental educational rights should be extended even to adolescence.

36 For example, see Dwyer (1998), as described in note 22.

37 E.G. West in his critique of state authority in education suggests that the main argument of nineteenth-century liberal economists for state education had to do with the need to protect infants from incompetent parents. (1970, 7).

38 Gutmann uses Plato's *Crito* to illustrate this theory of "the family state." The Laws and the Constitution of Athens speak of their right to rule Socrates: "Did we not give you life in the first place? Was it not through us that your father married your mother and begot you? … [S]ince you have been born and brought up and educated, can you deny, in the first place, that you were our child and servant, both you and your ancestors?" (Gutmann 1987, 24).

39 In the 1972 *Wisconsin v. Yoder* case, the state's objection to a traditional Amish education was that it deprives Amish adolescents of the knowledge and skills needed to "make an intelligent choice between the Amish way of

life and that of the outside world," and to flourish if they should choose the latter (Gilles 1997, 20–1). Coleman and Hoffer (1987) show how this same assumption is related to the statist orientation towards schooling which has been so influential in North American history. This orientation "sees schools as society's instrument for releasing a child from the blinders imposed by accident of birth into this family or that family. Schools have been designed to open broad horizons to the child, transcending the limitations of the parents, and have taken children from disparate cultural backgrounds into the mainstream of American culture" (Coleman and Hoffer 1987, 3).

Sometimes this argument is expressed in terms of an emphasis on children's rights to an open future (e.g. Ackerman 1980, 159; Callan 1997, ch. 6; see also Sweet 1997, 178 and Dwyer 1998, 27–33, 164, 168–9).

40 Crittenden draws attention to a similar assumption underlying Hegel's influential statist view of education. Hegel saw the role of schools as leading children from the personal and affective moral relationships of the family to an impersonal and ethical standpoint required for participation in the political life (Crittenden 1988, 166).

41 See Randall (1994) for an excellent attempt at defining the balance between minimalist state regulation and the primacy of parental rights in education.

42 What this list of goods includes might be open to some dispute, but the following surely can be safely included: survival and healthy physical growth; affectionate care by their parents; a sense of identity and worth; and education (Crittenden 1988, 101, 116).

43 See Thiessen (1993, chs. 5 and 9), Crittenden (1988, 99, 116, 203), Galston (1991, 252), Gilles (1996, 945), and Callan (1997, 190).

44 Ackerman argues this point as one element of his liberal educational principles: "As the child gains increasing familiarity with the range of cultural models open to him in a liberal society, the choice of his curriculum should increasingly become his responsibility, rather than that of his educators" (1980, 158). See also Crittenden (1988, 98).

45 Crittenden (1988, 164); cf. Gilles (1996, 941) and Randall (1994, ch. 5).

46 Walford, for example, refers to some heads of independent schools in Britain who were fiercely opposed to the idea of government funding because they believed that no government should be allowed to interfere in the running of their schools (1995, 92). A British Columbia provincial inspector of private schools commented that some non-funded independent schools were deeply opposed to a new School Act which offered partial funding of such schools in return for mandatory registration, because they were afraid of government intervention (Barman 1991, 24). Peshkin similarly points out that schools in the American Association of Christian Schools struggle to stay free of all governmental ties, submitting only reluctantly even to the health and safety regulations (1986, 274).

47 Sweet notes that most Accelerated Christian Education schools operate out of church basements (1997, 89). Peshkin's Bethany Baptist Academy, for example, involves a large church-school complex, consonant with the belief that "the school is simply the academic expression of the church" (1986, 33). Although there is a separate administrative head, Headmaster McGraw, it is really Pastor Muller who is the spiritual and academic leader of BBA, and who regularly gives in-service instruction to the teachers (1, 48, 74). What we have here is a very hierarchical and authoritarian structure which gives the church primary educational rights. The governmental structure of Covenant School, an independent charismatic school in upstate New York, described by Rose (1988, 95), reveals a very similar pattern to that of BBA.

48 As quoted in Kevin Cox, "Newfoundland Referendum Second to Tackle Schools," *Globe and Mail*, 2 Aug. 1997, A5.

49 See, for example, Rose (1988, ch. 7); Bryk et al. (1993, 201, 306–8). Rose makes the following interesting observation: "This contrasts with much of the literature on public schools which reports the negative, hostile, distrustful, alienating and defensive relationships that often characterize relationships between parents and teachers" (1988, 147). In this kind of hostile environment, talk of rights invariably becomes important.

50 What Pastor Muller fails to appreciate is that he might have too much power at BBA. Sweet further notes that many ACE schools prefer not to have certified teachers lest they usurp the authority of the pastor and the Bible (1997, 88–9). Both of these examples fail to do justice to teachers' rights and responsibilities.

51 Peshkin admits that "coercion seems only to apply to the 10 of the 114 students who said that their parents made them attend BBA and that if they could, they would leave and attend a public school" (1986, 264). Peshkin gives no indication of the criteria used to single out only these 10 students as being subject to coercive measures. Clearly he is unwilling to apply the coercive description to all 114 students who would rather be elsewhere.

CHAPTER FIVE

1 See, for example, Magsino and Covert (1984) and Woodhouse (1990). Sweet describes the problem of a lack of academic freedom at religious schools in terms of a failure to uphold teachers' rights. She gives several examples of such a failure (Sweet 1997, 180–7).

2 See Hamilton (1995, 160); Russell (1993, 2); Tierney (1993, 145). For the main sources of the Canadian concept of academic freedom, see Horn (1999, 7–10).

3 See McConnell (1993, 303). Here it should be noted that the McConnell article provides a useful review of some of the recent legal literature on this

topic, and is taken from an anthology, edited by Van Alstyne (1993), previously published as volume 53, no. 3 of the journal *Law and Contemporary Problems*. For another helpful and more detailed treatment of the typical principles inherent in the historic, American conception of academic freedom over the past seventy-five to one hundred years, see Horner (1992, 36–7). For a history of academic freedom in Canada, see Horn (1999).

4 See appendix B in Van Alstyne (1993, 407–9).

5 Marsden (1993, 232). Metzger (1993, 38) and McConnell (1993, 309) correctly point out that more recent developments in the Roman Catholic church and evangelical denominations cast doubt on the empirical basis for this Interpretive Comment. McConnell also points out that organized academia has never articulated any principled justification for the limitations clause accommodating religious colleges and universities. It would seem that its earlier acceptance was mainly a concession made because of the large percentage of institutions which were then under denominational control (McConnell 1993, 311).

Similar controversy surrounded a recent attempt by the Association of Universities and Colleges of Canada (AUCC) to revise its Statement on Academic Freedom and Institutional Autonomy, which includes a limitations clause similar to that of the American 1940 statement. The proposed revision suggested, among other changes, that "most church-related colleges in Canada do not now require a modification of the above-described principles on academic freedom." In the end (in 1994), the revisions were not adopted because of disagreement on appropriate and inappropriate limits on academic freedom owing to controversy over political correctness (from a letter from Justin Cooper, president of Redeemer College, to the author, 5 June 1997).

6 McConnell (1993, 311). Many examples of this purely secular interpretation of academic freedom can be found in the reports of AAUP's Committee A on Academic Freedom and Tenure as published in *Academe: Bulletin of the AAUP*. McConnell (1993) and Marsden (1993) also cite a good number of cases of censure against religious institutions.

7 The minutes of the Annual Meeting of the Canadian Philosophical Association, 12 June 1984, report that an *ad hoc* committee of the association had investigated alleged violations of academic freedom at St Thomas More College, affiliated with the University of Saskatchewan.

More recently Trinity Western University was a victim of the imposition of a secular ideal of academic freedom when the British Columbia College of Teachers denied its application to operate the final year of its elementary teacher education program because of some Christian behavioural standards imposed on its students (*Financial Post*, 20–2, July 1996, 16). This case is going all the way to the Supreme Court of Canada and will be heard in the fall of 2000 or the winter of 2001.

In another case occurring in the USA in 1979, a small group of
students from the Graduate School of Psychology at Fuller Theological
Seminary registered formal charges against the school with the American
Psychological Association (APA). They accused the school of violating the
principle of academic freedom by requiring that faculty sign a statement of
faith and take a specific stand on sexual behaviour. Dean Neil Warren gave
leadership in a difficult one-and-a-half-year struggle to uphold Fuller's position that its creedal boundaries in no way undermined its academic standing (Marsden 1987, 268). In the end, APA renewed accreditation of the
school, though it did so only by adding an "Exclusion Clause" in the accreditation procedures. This clause allows programs to be accredited which
do not meet the APA standards for inclusiveness (in race, and religion, for
example), if they can demonstrate that their exclusive guidelines are directly related to their curricular goals (from a letter to the author from
H. Newton Malony, senior professor, dated 7 July 1994).

8 Minutes of the Annual General Meeting of the Canadian Society for the
Study of Religion, 9 June 1993, as reported in the Oct. 1993 issue of the
CSSR Bulletin, 17(1):16.

9 As stated by the 1988 subcommittee of the AAUP's Committee A on
Academic Freedom and Tenure, cited in McConnell (1993, 309). As another example of this bias against religiously based schools, the prestigious
Phi Beta Kappa Society has denied membership to even the best of the
many liberal arts colleges of the Christian College Coalition, as well as to
the overwhelming majority of the hundreds of Catholic colleges and universities, on the grounds that any religiously defined standards for teaching
are incompatible with academic freedom (Marsden 1993, 233).

10 The secularization of many former Protestant schools can be linked to the
acceptance of a secular ideal of full academic freedom (cf. Curran 1990,
79). By contrast, David Horner, president of evangelical North Park
College and Theological Seminary, argues that Christian colleges can only
have limited freedom because of their hiring policies and their lack of neutrality with regard to truth (Horner 1992, 36, 38, 39). Others, like Hardy
(1995) and Marsden (1993), argue for equal status between religious
and secular institutions, though based on a revised notion of academic
freedom.

11 For example, this statement on academic freedom is found in the Educational Creed of the Institute for Christian Studies in Toronto: "Academic
Freedom: That scholarly pursuits are to be undertaken in the God-given
freedom of a complete and voluntary submission to the Word of God and
the divine laws that govern human life. The responsible freedom of the
scholar must be protected against any constraint or domination of the
church, state, industry, or other societal structure." This statement was reaffirmed by the ICS Board in 1994 after controversies surrounding state-

ments made by some senior members of the institution about positions held concerning certain ethical questions (from a letter sent to members and friends of ICS, dated 16 Dec. 1994, and signed by Hilda Buisman and Rudy De Groot). See also Calvin College (Diekema 2000).

12 Louis Menand, in a recent essay discussing the future of academic freedom, admits that "the concept of academic freedom has always been problematic. It is *inherently* problematic" (1996, 6). Interestingly, although Menand admits that a reconsideration of the concept of academic freedom is needed, he goes on to say that it is impossible to provide a restatement of the philosophical foundations of academic freedom such that everyone will be happy with its practical consequences all the time (1993, 11, 12). But, surely we must not give up too soon.

13 Marsden cites this as an early criticism of the 1940 AAUP statement of academic freedom (1993, 229). Curran points out that this is a criticism frequently made by Roman Catholics (1990, 26, 39, 58, 116, 158). Of course, disciplinary, professional, and ethical constraints are at times acknowledged, but the ideal still seems to be that of full freedom.

14 Cited in Curran (1990, 39).

15 Kennedy has recently urged us to balance the call for academic freedom with an equal emphasis on "academic duty" (1997; cf. Hamilton 1995, chs. 4, 10; Horner 1992, 35–6).

16 Marsden (1993, 226–31). In its earlier 1915 Declaration of Principles, AAUP argued for freedom also in the domain of theology. "Such freedom is the breath in the nostrils of all scientific activity" (cited in McConnell 1993, 318). This drawing on the imagery from Genesis 2:7, which states that God "breathed into [Adam's] nostrils the breath of life," cannot help but contribute to a feeling that science is here being deified. See also Hamilton (1995, 160–1) for a further analysis of the liberal intellectual system underlying the American statement of academic freedom.

17 See, for example, Kuhn (1970); Young (1971); MacIntyre (1988); Clouser (1991); Middleton and Walsh (1995); and Garry and Pearsall (1989).

18 See also Marsden (1993, 232), Curran (1990, 21), Ericson (1991, 185), and Menand (1993, 11–12), for other calls for an updated statement of academic freedom in the light of recent epistemological developments.

19 McConnell refers, for example, to a statement made by the 1988 subcommittee of AAUP's Committee A on Academic Freedom and Tenure with regard to a possible alternative rationale for the accommodation of religious schools: "many of these institutions usefully function as 'decompression chambers' that ease the passage into the larger world for the religiously provincial." McConnell continues: "The condescension – indeed bigotry – of this suggestion seems to have passed unnoticed" (1993, 312).

20 A reply to Menand's response to the call to revise the concept of academic freedom in the light of the postmodernist challenge would seem to be un-

necessary, because Menand relativizes the meaning of academic freedom, and ultimately concedes that there is no need for academic freedom if you think that universities are sites for social indoctrination (Menand 1993).

21 See Bloom (1987); Kimball (1990); D'Souza (1991); Rauch (1993).

22 The qualifier "normal" is added to follow a paradigm I have adopted in an earlier work (Thiessen 1993).

23 See Marsden (1993, 233). This is not at all to suggest that religious institutions cannot also serve the public good. See Bryk et al., *Catholic Schools and the Common Good* (1993) for a strong argument to this effect (see quotation from Bryk et al. in chapter 13, p. 378).

24 To gain an awareness of the boundaries to academic freedom that do in fact exist at secular institutions, I would recommend Hamilton's excellent summary of seven waves of ideological zealotry that have swept American universities over the past 125 years, and which have threatened, and continue to threaten, the ideal of academic freedom as typically understood (1995, chs.1 and 2). For a description of widespread violations of academic freedom during the McCarthy era, see Schrecker (1986). For a description of violations of academic freedom in Canadian universities, see Horn (1999). Of course, as was pointed out earlier in this chapter, these violations will sometimes have been rationalized in some way, thus leading to revised notions of academic freedom – limited academic freedom.

25 See, for example, the call for academics to submit to the Word of God at the Institute for Christian Studies in Toronto (see note 11).

26 McConnell (1993, 312). This, of course, raises the additional question whether it can be shown that the religious model of truth seeking is better than the scientific model. McConnell suggests that there is no way of proving the correctness of either (314). Thomson and Finkin, in their critique of McConnell, are forced to concede this point, though they go on to object to the "coercion" that exists at religiously based schools (1993, 429). What they forget, though, is that secular institutions are similarly coercive in limiting academic freedom to a particular model of truth seeking. Unfortunately, all too often the secular academic community displays bad faith in not admitting to the same.

27 Karl Popper, for example, while stressing the need for critical thought, also stresses the need for some dogmatism in science: "the dogmatic scientist has an important role to play. If we give in to criticism too easily, we shall never find out where the real power of our theories lies" (1970, 55).

28 Horner, for example, sees this institutional neutrality as a key ingredient in the American conception of academic freedom (1992, 36).

29 Marsden does make a suggestion regarding educational pluralism at the end of his careful historical study of the secularization of the American university, though this suggestion seems to be only tentatively made, given the section title, "Concluding Unscientific Postscript" (1994, 436–40).

30 The basic thrust of Curran's book is to argue for full academic freedom at Catholic institutions of higher education. Towards the end of his book, however, when he discusses the role of Catholic theologians, he maintains that they should theologize within the parameters of the Catholic faith, and that any Catholic theologian who does not accept Jesus' divinity, for example, could be dismissed for incompetence (1990, 181–8). But surely, as Kliever (1988) has pointed out, this is to adopt a position of limited academic freedom. A rose by any other name! Curran tries to cover up this inconsistency by talking about "competence" – a professional criterion. A Catholic theologian who adopts this position is professionally incompetent. I agree that this doctrinal position might raise questions about competence within a Catholic seminary, but the fact remains that we are no longer talking about *full* academic freedom, which is what Curran is defending.

31 According to Hardy, the confessional boundaries would be too narrow if, at a Christian College or a Reformed University, it was required that one be a Dooyeweerdian or an analytic philosopher in philosophy, a new critic or a deconstructionist in literary studies, or a neo-institutionalist in economics (1995, 23).

32 Marsden provides the historical example of Lafayette College, where the literature defining the identity of the college was so ambiguous that it was impossible to determine when doctrinal boundaries had been violated (1994, 301–5).

33 See Burtchaell (1998), and Gleason (1995).

34 Mouw cites the example of a respected professor at Brigham Young University, D. Michael Quinn, who was dismissed from his position because of a book he wrote on Mormonism that portrayed Joseph Smith and other early Mormon leaders as being immersed in the beliefs and practices of folk magic (Mouw 1994, 43–4). What is significant in this case is that Quinn did not see the link between early Mormonism and folk magic as a matter for embarrassment. He maintained that it is extremely difficult to draw sensible boundaries between religion and magic, and therefore it is better to be honest about such links. Given Quinn's apparent continuing allegiance to Mormonism, he should have been given the freedom to explore these issues within the context of BYU.

35 MacIntyre describes vital traditions and the institutions that bear these traditions as being constituted by a "continuous argument," and as embodying "continuities of conflict." "A living tradition then is an historically extended, socially embodied argument" (1984, 222). Mill, although too individualistic in his approach, nevertheless is quite justified in warning that however strongly a person holds an opinion, however true an opinion may be, "if it is not fully, frequently, and fearlessly discussed, it will be held as a dead dogma, not a living truth" (1978, 34).

36 Unfortunately, Thomson, in a response to various complaints that faculty selection cannot help but be ideologically tainted, skirts the central problem by restricting her treatment to making some admittedly useful distinctions. But she herself admits that she "will not even try to assess the correctness of these complaints" (1993, 156).

37 Hardy (1995, 10). It is this voluntary dimension of a faculty member's joining a religious educational institution that undermines the central objection which Thomson and Finkin make against such schools, namely their allegedly coercive nature (1993).

38 McConnell cites a number of examples of the biases inherent in the secular ideal of academic freedom (1993, 314–15). Marsden too suggests that the refusal to accept religious schools as equal partners in the pursuit of truth can only be described as "sheer prejudice" on the part of the secular establishment (1993, 234).

CHAPTER SIX

1 See also Must (1992) for a collection of essays defending public schools and opposing public support of religious schools based on the SCS principle.

2 For example, support for parochial busing is said to have reached "scandalous" proportions (Doerr and Menendez 1991, 61). Different types of parochiaid are described as "nothing if not ingenious" (64). Parochiaiders are described as having been "extraordinarily clever and successful in circumventing both state constitutions and federal court rulings to achieve many of their objectives" (67). The results of various parochiaid referenda are seen as "the parochiaiders' horrendous losing streak" (85). The word "horrendous" comes up again in speculating about the fragmentation that would occur in education if the USA followed the Netherlands' example of educational pluralism (139). The parochiaid issue is described as having divided US religious groups into "warring camps," and of course the supporters of parochiaid are to blame (135). Unfortunately, such language detracts from reasoned argument.

3 Shapiro, in his 1985 report on private schools in Ontario, also found public school boards objecting to the use of public funds for the inculcation of a particular faith stance in a private school (23). Interestingly, the Roman Catholic separate school system was deemed to be "legally excepted" from this argument! See also Long and Magsino (1993) for an analysis of early Charter cases concerning religion and education which would suggest that Canadian legal reasoning is going in the direction of the American constitutional tradition of maintaining a wall between church and state.

4 *Hansard*, vol. 526, no. 52, 4 March 1991, cols. 1281, 1268–9, cf. 1295.

5 Doerr and Menendez are forced to concede that there is considerable dis-

pute concerning the original and present meaning of the SCS principle (1991, 16, 126–30).

6 Viteritti (1996); Carter (1993, ch. 6); See also McConnell (1990; 1992), Laycock (1986; 1990), and Smith (1989).

7 While Jefferson refused to proclaim a day of religious thanksgiving in 1802, he did just that as governor some twenty years earlier. Indeed, his gubernatorial proclamation was very religious, calling for "a day of public and solemn thanksgiving and prayer to Almighty God" (Carter 1993, 117). Further, Jefferson, as president, authorized funds for the construction of a church and the support of a Roman Catholic priest on a mission to the Kaskaskia Indians (127).

8 Doerr and Menendez argue against the non-preferential interpretation of the First Amendment by pointing out that there was no establishment of a single church in America as there was in Europe (1991, 128–9). They forget, however, that American settlers were from Europe, and that they took steps to avoid the problems of establishment churches which they hoped they had left behind (Viteritti 1996, 118–20). Doerr and Menendez also seem to contradict themselves when they approvingly quote Justice Rutledge, who explicitly states that Jefferson and Madison were trying to guard against the strife caused between established religion and dissident groups (1991, 135). They also cite Chief Justice Rehnquist as supporting the view that the real intent of the First Amendment was to ensure that the government would be non-preferential in its treatment of religions. In his dissenting opinion in *Wallace v. Jaffree* (1985), Rehnquist referred to the separationist view as "an historically faulty doctrine," and insisted that the First Amendment framers sought only "to prohibit the designation of any church as a 'national' one" and to "stop the Federal Government from asserting a preference for one religious denomination or sect over others" (Doerr and Menendez 1991, 128; cf. Viteritti 1996, 137n147).

9 It should be noted, in passing, that Australia has a very similar Establishment Clause in its constitution, which yet is interpreted as allowing for tax support for religious schools (Bryk et al. 1993, 343). The Netherlands has also traditionally separated church and state and yet recognizes a state responsibility "to create the conditions under which the religious or humanist situation can take place" (Sweet 1997, 128). These examples again suggest that the adoption of the SCS principle is open to varied interpretations, some of which seem to allow for state support of religious schools.

10 Miller (1986, 284). This point was also clearly made by Chief Justice Berger: "Our prior holdings do not call for total separation between church and state; total separation is not possible in an absolute sense. Some relationship between government and religious organizations is inevitable" (quoted in Viteritti 1996, 133n89).

11 See Viteritti (1996, 140, 186); McConnell (1992, 115–17; 168–9); Neuhaus (1984); Carter (1993, 113).

12 Viteritti (1996, 184). See, for example, Lewy (1997).

13 Viteritti (1996, 137). McCarthy, in her comprehensive survey of the history of legal developments pertaining to church-state-school relations in America, concludes that "conceptual chaos" seems to pervade the entire history (1983, 171).

14 From a letter sent to Gary Mar, the minister of education in Alberta, and copied to all board chairs and superintendents, written by Jim Rivait, government affairs coordinator, Alberta School Boards Association, 29 April 1997. This was in response to private member's Bill 209, calling for more funding for private (religious) schools in Alberta.

15 Letter to Gary Mar, minister of education, from L.J. Roy Wilson, president of the Alberta School Boards Association, 6 March 1998.

16 See Lord Peston, giving expression to the Labour party policy in Great Britain (*Hansard*, vol. 526, no. 52, 4 March 1991, col. 1295). Mr Chumir, in debating the earlier Bill 27 in the Alberta legislature, which explicitly referred to parental rights in education, made it clear that he was not opposed to the right of parents to send their children to private schools: "But I believe that is a private obligation. It does not serve public interests – indeed, it is contrary to the public interest" (*Alberta Hansard*, 13 June 1988, col. 1670).

17 For example, Mill is forced to admit that his so-called "self-regarding faults" are in fact other-regarding, and do have an effect on the public (1978, ch. 4).

18 See evidence in Chapter 3.

19 Ravitch and Viteritti use these criteria in order to correct the common association of charter schools with privatization (1997, 7).

20 On these positive dimensions of the SCS principle see Carter (1993, 16, 106, 115–21, 124) and Viteritti (1996, 189).

21 This phrase comes from the 1988 Education Reform Act, which still defines current practices in religious education in British schools. John Hull has been an opponent of this legislation from the beginning, and although I would disagree with some aspects of his critique, I would certainly concur with his concerns about the imposition of one faith via a public school system that serves a religiously pluralistic society (see Hull 1989).

22 The Christian Right in Britain, for example, has been lobbying to have the religion clause tightened even further so that not only worship but religious education will be mainly Christian, instead of the multi-faith approach that now tends to predominate. The lobbyists are very specific: "Parliament should amend the present Education Reform Bill in such a way that Religious Instruction is defined as being predominantly the study of the Christian religion, including its scriptures, its significance in history, and its relevance to contemporary society" (Burn and Hart 1988, 29).

In support of such legislative changes, the Christian Right appeals to the Christian cultural inheritance of Britain, which allegedly is still adhered to by the majority of the population (Burn and Hart, 1988, 24–5). Clearly Christianity has been a major contributor to the cultures of Western societies. This inheritance will inevitably be reflected in a society's institutions. But such reflection will and should occur as a natural process. There are further other principles that should be taken into account when dealing with the character of a society as a whole, one of which is the principle of freedom. Christians should be at the forefront of defending religious freedom. British evangelicals need to be reminded that in discussions of the "religious difficulty" which was being addressed prior to the passing of the 1870 Education Act, the option of an Act of Parliament to enforce the teaching of one religion in all schools was condemned by the Victorians as illiberal (West 1970, 77).

For a powerful critique of the constantinianism of the Christian Right in America by an evangelical Christian, see Yancey (1997, chs. 17 and 18). Yancey refers to C.S. Lewis who correctly observed that almost all crimes of Christian history have come about when religion is confused with politics (233). In keeping with the central theme of his book, grace, Yancey astutely points out that when the church joins with the state, it tends to wield power rather than dispense grace (233).

23 This is the point of George Marsden's recent study of "the soul of the American university," subtitled "rom Protestant Establishment to Established Nonbelief" (1994). It is also the central concern of Sweet (1997), although she does not support religious schools as a solution to the problem. See also Baer (1987), McCarthy (1983, 89–92), Nord (1995), and Viteritti (1996, 179–82).

24 Marsden comes to a very similar conclusion in his "Concluding Unscientific Postcript" where he suggests that a proper understanding of the SCS principle might even entail institutional pluralism in the realm of education (1994, 435–40). Similar considerations are also behind a book by McCarthy et al. with the intriguing title *Disestablishment a Second Time: Genuine Pluralism for American Schools* (1982). This book traces the place of civil religion in the founding of the republic (ch. 1). The authors then show how this civil religion is central to the public school system of America. Hence, public education is committed to an "established civil religion" (48). And hence also the need to disestablish this religion in the name of genuine religious freedom (48–51).

25 Again it is interesting to note that Doerr and Menendez, when they grudgingly concede at least peripheral support to religious schools, argue that as long as *all* children get this aid in all schools, the SCS principle has not been violated (1991, 119).

26 This is the central argument made by Magsino in his excellent article entitled "Human Rights, Fair Treatment, and Funding of Private Schools in

285 Notes to pages 110–11

Canada" (1986). Shapiro also identifies this as the most common argument put forward in support of the public funding of private schools, based on his work as a commissioner for the 1985 Commission on Private Schools in Ontario: "It is discriminatory and, therefore, inappropriate for Ontario to continue to offer to its Roman Catholic community an educational option not offered to all other Ontario communities – at least to all other Ontario communities that are religiously defined" (Shapiro 1986, 266). This point is also made repeatedly in the recent Quebec Proulx Report (1999), though the solution to unfairness is seen as secularization.

27 This principle of fairness is appealed to several times in the House of Lords debate concerning an amendment to the Education Act which would have allowed for independent religious schools to opt in to the state-maintained sector and get full financial support (*Hansard* vol. 526, no. 52, 4 March 1991, cols. 1250, 1287, 1289, 1290). Indeed, Viscount Brentford carries the argument one step further by suggesting that if the principle of fairness were consistently applied so that Muslim schools got government support in Britain, then "it would put us in a much stronger position in this country in arguing for similar treatment for Christian schools in Islamic-governed countries" (col. 1289). How true, but sadly, all too often, many people, including Christians, fail to see the inconsistency.

28 This is difficult in Canada where support for Catholic schools is constitutionally guaranteed, but it might be argued that we should at least recognize "that a publicly supported denominational school system was an unfortunate historical mistake, one which may have to be supported or tolerated but which certainly should not be repeated" (Shapiro 1986, 270). But, as Shapiro points out, the appropriateness of this response is undermined, at least for Ontario, because the government extended full public funding for Roman Catholic schools to the secondary-school level in 1984, which would suggest that this was an act of political will rather than a fulfilment of a constitutional obligation. "The government is, of course, clearly entitled to exercise this political will but not on a discriminatory basis" (269–70). And of course, as was observed in chapter 1, recent Canadian history has demonstrated that constitutions can be modified.

29 See, for example, the Swann Report (1985, 520, 774). Lord Dormand of Easington, in responding to the amendment referred to in note 27, above, argued for "a phased withdrawal of all state subsidies to religious foundations" (*Hansard*, vol. 526, no. 52, 4 March 1991, col. 1281; cf. Walford 1995, 124–5; Ball and Troyna 1987, 23–4).

30 Viteritti (1996, 116, 142, 165, 187). Interestingly, Doerr and Menendez also defend peripheral aid to religious schools based on the child benefit theory. As long as the intent of parochiaid is to benefit the child, not the school, the SCS principle is not being violated, according to Doerr and Menendez (1991, 114).

31 Monsignor Thomas J. Curry expresses this concern from a Catholic perspective: "There is simply no possibility that Catholic education can receive substantial public assistance and that the church can at the same time maintain complete control and direction of its schools. The reception of public monies must inevitably involve public supervision or control" (quoted in Doerr and Menendez 1991, 140). See also examples listed in 274n46.

32 Bryk and associates have highlighted the market metaphors, the radical individualism, the sense of purpose organized around competition, and the pursuit of individual economic rewards that dominate the contemporary rhetoric of public schooling in America, Canada, and Great Britain (Bryk, et al. 1993, 11). Neil Postman too describes a variety of narratives that compete for dominance in the educational arena today. He gives them names such as the god of Consumership, the god of Technology, and the god of Economic Utility (Postman 1995). These destructive values, I believe, are seriously undermining education and the fostering of the common good.

33 Again, Monsignor Thomas J. Curry expresses this concern: "The greatest danger for Catholic schools is [not] that they may fail to secure public assistance, but in order to receive such aid they may secularize themselves piecemeal in the process" (quoted in Doerr and Menendez 1991, 141). See also Burtchaell (1998), Marsden (1994), and Gleason (1995).

34 For example, Barman points out that British Columbia's Independent School Act of 1989 began with the same preamble as did its companion School Act governing the public system: "The purpose of the British Columbia school system is to enable learners to develop their individual potential and to acquire the knowledge, skills and attitudes needed to contribute to a healthy society" (1991, 26). Although such a broad mission statement can and should be accepted by religious schools, the state must be very careful not to go on to mandate *how* that mission statement is to be accomplished within a religious school. It is here that religious schools have a legitimate concern about government regulations.

35 "Presentation to Private Schools Funding Task Force," by the Medicine Hat Catholic Board of Education, 3 Oct. 1997, 1–5.

36 This is the point argued by Renton Patterson in his little pamphlet "Not Carved in Stone: Public Funding of Separate Schools in Ontario" (referred to in Sweet 1997, 56–7).

37 Evidently, some evangelical Christians in Britain, while lobbying for state support of evangelical religious schools, have difficulty extending the same right to Muslims (Walford 1995, 69, 74, 75). It would seem, though, that the evangelical community is divided on this question, as there are some who are "grieved by this attitude," and have openly supported equal rights for Muslim schools (74, 72).

CHAPTER SEVEN

1 Quoted in Fernhout (1990, 6).
2 Alberta Private Schools Funding Task Force (1997, 2).
3 From a brief submitted to the Alberta Private Schools Funding Task Force, by the Medicine Hat School District no. 76, entitled "Public Funding for Private Schools" (3 Oct. 1997, 4). The same concern about finances was stated in a brief submitted by the Medicine Hat Catholic Board of Education: "Any increase to support private schools would undermine the public school system in this province and its ability to recover from the damage done by budget cuts" (3 Oct. 1997, 5).
4 From a brief submitted by the Medicine Hat Catholic Board of Education to the Alberta Private Schools Funding Task Force (3 Oct. 1997, 4). Similar concerns were expressed in the brief submitted by the Medicine Hat School District no. 76: "Public education is more than a curriculum of subjects. It is the creation of a civil society. It is the creation of a 'no caste,' 'no class' society … [I]f private education were to receive the same funding as public education, we believe it should have to … serve all children without the usual discrimination based on family wealth, ability, social status, religion or some other form of elite discriminator" (2, 5).
5 Walford (1995, 120; cf. 1994a, 148–9). Very early in the Swann Report, this same egalitarian ideal emerges in a discussion of the nature of society, where it is argued that the enforced separate development of different groups would be unlikely to offer equality or justice to all groups, especially minorities (1985, 5).
6 Kai Nielsen does grapple explicitly with the problem of defending egalitarianism, but in the end suggests that it is an intrinsic good which is recognized as such pre-theoretically (1985, 8). It is clear that not all people share this intuitive hunch. As John White points out, though we might agree with the need to help the disadvantaged, this is a quite different matter from wanting an equal society (1994, 174).
7 John White (1994) provides a helpful brief critique of three fairly recent egalitarian texts: Nagel (1991), Nielsen (1985), and Norman (1987). See also West (1970, 53–4) for a summary critique of attempts to defend egalitarianism.
8 Rawls (1971, 74). See also Narveson (1993, 2) and Gutmann (1987, 131).
9 Quoted in West (1970, xxxviii).
10 Gutmann (1987, 135). See also Robert Nozick's argument that "the foundations of desert needn't themselves be *deserved all the way down*" (quoted in Gutmann 1987, 135n13; cf. Sandel 1982, 82–95). Cooper (1982), in a delightful essay exploring the possible connection between "equality and envy," challenges the argument of Rawls and other egalitarians that inequality produces envy. He argues the opposite, drawing on psychological

studies which show that envy is more likely to arise among people at very similar levels of income, status, and education (35–6). Cooper reminds us that egalitarianism is a fairly recent idea, and he is surely right in suggesting that the notion that some should have less because others have less is a rather "extraordinary" idea, and one which can only be explained by making some reference to "the darker side of human motivation" (45). It might seem like an *ad hominem* fallacy to attribute envy to those who appeal to elitism in their opposition to independent schools, but some self-examination is advisable.

11 See Gutmann (1987, 134). Rawls allows for some inequality in his defence of the "difference principle" (1971, 75–80).

12 Gutmann (1987, 132). See also Holmes, who points out that it "is impractical and probably immoral and undemocratic, for the state to intervene within the family for the purpose of disadvantaging the advantaged" (1992, 131).

13 I base my more moderate egalitarianism on a Christian metaphysics. See Pojman for an outline of a Christian defence of such egalitarianism (1991, 496–500). Indeed, after criticizing various secular attempts to defend egalitarianism, Pojman concludes by suggesting that, at best, secular egalitarians have made it "a posit of faith," and that historically this ideal rests on "the borrowed interest of a religious metaphysic" (501).

14 See John White (1994) for a review of some of these writers. Hence also Nagel's attraction to the ideal of a society with an increasingly high social minimum (1991, 128).

15 Peter Mueller, in the *Medicine Hat News*, 2 June 1997, B3.

16 The recent Task Force in Alberta reported that tuition fees charged by independent religious schools range from a low of less than $1,000 per year to over $6,000 per year. In 1995, just over half the parents paid between $2,000 and $4,000 tuition each year. "Most private schools provide special arrangements for families with more than one child and many offer a subsidy program for parents who are unable to pay" (Alberta Private Schools Funding Task Force 1998, 17).

17 Bernadette O'Keeffe, in a study of some eighty Christian schools in Britain, reports that the majority of these schools are financed by a combination of standard tuition fees, which are substantially lower than the per capita cost of state-maintained education, ability-to-pay schemes, and voluntary donations. Compared with state-maintained schools, these schools "are considerably under-resourced financially" (O'Keeffe 1992, 93; cf. Lambert 1993, 326).

In an important recent study of Catholic schools in America, it was found that the average level of income of parents sending their children to these schools was only marginally higher than that of public school parents (Bryk et al. 1993, 71). It is also noteworthy that over the years there has been a significant increase in the number of blacks and other ethnic minority groups represented in Catholic schools in America (7, 69–70). Indeed, the typical Catholic school is more internally diverse with regard to race and income than the typical public school (73). Some Catholic schools have shut down, or are in serious danger of shutting down, because of financial difficulties – hardly an indication of wealth (333, 336–8). And, if greater levels of public financial support were available for the education of the disadvantaged, all available evidence suggests that Catholic schools would welcome the opportunity to educate more of these students (340).

18 Hirsch, for example, makes this confession: "It is a bitter irony that the egalitarian rhetoric of American educational orthodoxy has fostered inequality" (1996, 4). Shapiro, though opposed to the funding of private religious schools, is forced to admit that a system of state-maintained schools has not always achieved one of the historic missions of the public school, namely that of acting "as a kind of social mobility ladder for young people who do not bring to schooling special advantages of background, experience and/or wealth" (Shapiro 1986, 272).

West, in a chapter dealing specifically with "equality of opportunity" as a goal of education, suggests that to treat this goal as one which can inevitably be fostered by state education "is unwarranted and unproven since it overlooks the probability that such a cure makes things worse than before" (West 1970, 69). See also Carter (1993, 195), Rose (1988, 221), Holmes (1998, 271), and Viteritti (1996, 170).

19 Miller (1982, 114). Gutmann makes the same point: "Having taken their children out of public schools, the most affluent parents – who also tend to be the most politically influential – will oppose increased spending on public schools. The quality of public schooling will therefore decline even further" (1987, 116; cf. Callan 1997, 186).

20 For example, see a study referred to in Holmes (1998, 175–7). See also Schneider et al. (1997).

21 Jefferson (1988). Shapiro cites this as one of the most common arguments against the funding of private education in Ontario: "that, whatever one's view in principle, the current financial constraint on the Ontario treasury and, consequently, on the funding of public schools makes any extension of public funding to private schools inappropriate – at least at this time" (1986, 267). Doerr and Menendez, arguing against parochiaid in the United States, similarly suggest that "including nonpublic schools in tax-funded school choice plans will entail extremely high costs for taxpayers" (1991, 130).

22 This statement is found in the "Summary Report" of the Royal Commission of Inquiry into the Delivery of Programs (1992, 10). Interestingly, I could not find this same statement in the parallel pages of the full report (Royal Commission 1992, 195–8)!

23 Instead of an estimated saving of $21.3 million with the introduction of a non-denominational system of education (and this figure often was inflated in media discussions), the Commission estimated that the saving would only be $14.5 million if the proposed system was compared to a streamlined denominational system. Sweet must be relying on inflated media reports when she suggests that an estimated $25 to $30 million a year could be saved by eliminating separate denominational bureaucracies in Newfoundland (1997, 50).

24 Holmes (1992, 40). The Netherlands has also had a variety of competing school systems, and yet educationalists there claim that their approach does not cost appreciably more than a system like Canada's (Holmes 1992, 40; Lois Sweet, "Dutch Offer 'Integration' Model," *Toronto Star*, 17 Sept. 1997, A19). Then we must not forget the arguments of the neo-liberals who favour educational vouchers as a cost-effective way of improving the educational system (Halstead 1994, 12; e.g. Chubb and Moe, 1990).

25 Walford (1991b, 118–19).

26 See, for example, Miller (1982, 113; cf. Aspin 1983, 238). Interestingly, Miller seems to have softened his position in a subsequent article, where he concedes that it is unlikely that each religious group would want its own school (1986, 286).

27 This would be in keeping with Holmes's suggestion of a majoritarian system of public schools with alternative religious schools allowed, though not encouraged (1992, 156). In a later book, Holmes estimates that, given a pluralistic educational system in Canada, the area public school would still attract between 30 and 50 per cent of the population, once these schools have been reformed to reflect more closely the public will (1998, 253).

28 See a booklet prepared by the Denominational Educational Committees of Newfoundland entitled *The School Board*, St John's Newfoundland, 1976. See also Sweet (1997, 50).

29 This is operative in part, in Britain, with their voluntary-aided or controlled schools. Canada also exemplifies this approach in part, with Catholic schools being viewed as part of the public school system in some provinces. Then, of course, there was a brief experiment with the Logos school in Calgary (Miller 1986, 287). More recently, religious schools have been incorporated into the public system of Alberta as charter schools (Sweet 1997, 241–5).

30 For example, Shapiro reports that defenders of the funding of independent religious schools "suggested that the current near-monopoly of the state in elementary and secondary schooling reduces competition, raises costs, lowers efficiency, and degrades the quality of the product delivered" (1986, 267). Two classic applications of the market model to education include West (1970) and Coons and Sugarman (1978). More recent defences include Livingstone (1985), Chubb and Moe (1990), and Coulson (1999).

31 Brown, like Walford, merely assumes that there is a link between an emphasis on parental rights and the agenda of the Right with its market policies with regard to education. There is very little by way of empirical support for making this link. In this chapter I have deliberately distanced myself from the agenda of the Right and its market approach to education. Here again we must be careful not to succumb to conspiracy theories.

32 This is the central criticism that Walzer makes in his review of Nagel (Walzer 1992).

33 Galston (1991, 252; cf. Holmes 1992, 132). Walford, despite his opposition to religious schools based on their alleged elitism, is forced to concede, after a comparative study of private schools in ten countries, that "the extent to which particular schools act to reproduce patterns of inequality and privilege in a society" is a function of government regulation (1989, 222).

34 See, for example, Deut. 10:17–18; Luke 14:12–14. For a helpful exposition of a biblical perspective on the poor and possessions see Sider (1977, part 2). See also Wolterstorff (1983) and Goudzwaard and de Lange (1994).

35 There are some Christians who preach a distorted "Health and Wealth Gospel" (see Barron 1987).

CHAPTER EIGHT

1 See also two summary articles of mine (Thiessen 1984a; 1991).

2 For two important earlier works on indoctrination within the strictly analytic tradition, see Snook (1972a; 1972b). For some more recent works that still take an analytical approach, see Barrow and Woods (1988), several of the essays in Spiecker and Straughan (1991), and Kazepides (1983; 1989; 1994).

3 Spiecker (1991, 16). Snook, who, in his earlier writings, defended the intention criterion as both necessary and sufficient, argues that a person indoctrinates if he teaches with the intention that the pupil or pupils believe what is taught, regardless of the evidence (1972b, 47).

4 McLaughlin, for example, draws on White in stressing intention (1984, 77–9).

5 See, for example, Halstead (1986, ch. 5); Hull (1984, ch. 18); and Siegel (1988, 80, 165n8).

6 This is from an older essay by Dunlop (1976, 39).

7 Sweet, for example, admits that scholars can't agree on what constitutes indoctrination, and yet she objects to religious schools because they indoctrinate (1997, 149, ch. 8).

8 This is the central criticism of Nielsen in his response to a paper of mine in which I develop an earlier version of my argument (Thiessen 1984a; Nielsen 1984). For my response to Nielsen, see Thiessen (1984b).

9 Nielsen, for example, while an outspoken atheist, nevertheless maintains that some of the characteristic practices of mainline Protestant and Catholic churches should *not* be described as indoctrination. He also maintains that the teachings of Cardinal Newman should *not* be described as indoctrination (1984, 70). Yet, Newman's model of liberal education no doubt inspires the Catholic schools that Barrow and Woods cite as paradigm cases of indoctrination.

10 See, for example, Stolzenberg's careful analysis of the litigation surrounding *Mozert v. Hawkins County Board of Education* (1993). See also Sweet (1997, 34–5, 222); Deakin (1989, 6–8); Nord (1995, ch. 5); and Walford (1995, 41–8).

11 Nieman (1989, 53). Nieman goes so far as to suggest that because of the sterility of conceptual analysis, "nothing qualitatively new has occurred in the debate" on indoctrination since Snook's writings (i.e. from 1972 to 1989) (Nieman 1989, 60n4). Sadly, Nieman's time-line needs to be extended even further, since some philosophers of education still function as though logical positivism were alive and well.

12 Page (1980, 162–73). Noam Chomsky provides a careful analysis and empirical documentation of thought control in liberal democracies, particularly via the media (1988a; 1988b; 1992).

13 This description of education is taken from Oakeshott's essay, "Education: The Engagement and Its Frustration" (1972). See also R.S. Peters's classic description of "Education as Initiation" (1965).

14 In his defence of rationality and critical thinking as essential components to education, Siegel devotes an entire chapter to the problem of the inevitability of non-rational teaching methods (1988, ch. 5). He concedes the problem, but, like me, refuses to say that some indoctrination is good, because this leads to confusion. Instead, he argues that if non-rational methods eventually lead to rationality, then such methods should not be labelled as indoctrination, understood pejoratively.

15 Here it should be noted that Kazepides has provided some reasons for not linking initiation with education in an earlier essay (1983), but these reasons are all inadequate, as I have argued elsewhere (see Thiessen 1985b; 1993, 228–31).

16 Sweet (1997, 17). See also Dwyer, who makes the same error with regard to the autonomous status of children (1998). See chapter 4, note 19 for some commentary on Dwyer's treatment.

17 For a detailed treatment of the problem of institutional indoctrination and an argument concerning indoctrination in public schools, see Thiessen (1993, ch. 7). For an argument that British state-maintained schools are guilty of political indoctrination, see Scruton et al. (1985).

18 See Wagner (1990) and Thiessen (1993, ch. 7) for responses to Peshkin, arguing that Christian schools are far from all-encompassing total institutions.

19 Behind this concern for liberation is, of course, the perception that parents (especially religious parents, and also religious schools) give children a limiting and restrictive outlook from which they need to be liberated. See also Ackerman, who describes voucher schools as "petty tyrannies in which like-minded parents club together to force-feed their children without restraint" (quoted in Gilles 1996, 949n46). More recently, Dwyer has suggested that it is imperative for the state to try to prevent religious traditionalists from passing their beliefs on to their children by guaranteeing those children "an education that counteracts this effort, that makes it possible for [them] to choose and live successfully within other ways of life and systems of belief" (1998, 168).

20 See Bronfenbrenner (1980); McLaughlin (1984); Rutter (1980); Sharron (1987); Taylor (1989); De Ruyter and Miedema (2000).

21 My reconstructed definition of indoctrination comes fairly close to the suggestion of Ralph Page, who in turn draws on John Dewey for his analysis (Page 1980). Watson also comes very close to my position when she describes indoctrination as nurture which is conducted without due regard and sensitivity to the awakening maturity of the child (1987, 13). Sweet sometimes gets the distinction between education and indoctrination right when, for example, she stresses "that young people be taught the value of autonomous thinking as they age and mature" (1997, 159). Unfortunately, she makes the mistake of associating initiation with indoctrination (13, 149).

22 For example, various studies have shown that the Accelerated Christian Education (ACE) curriculum, which is used in many evangelical schools, is oriented towards information recall and discourages discussion and questioning (Rose 1988; Van Brummelen 1989; Alberta Education 1985). I would suggest that ACE materials are weak in fostering growth towards normal rational autonomy and hence schools using these materials should be charged with a degree of indoctrination.

23 Contemporary philosopher Linda Zagzebski describes her religion teacher at an all-girls Catholic school as "both open-minded and smart. She seemed genuinely delighted that I was able to come up with a continuous stream of rebuttals to her defenses of Christianity" (Zagzebski 1993, 242).

24 I agree entirely with Sweet when she argues that "if schooling doesn't enable people to move confidently in a world larger than the one in which they were brought up, then to my mind it's failed the interests of both the student and the larger society" (1997, 152). But Sweet does not do justice to the fact that religious schools have graduated many students who are able to do precisely that, a point that she herself is forced to admit.

25 For a more detailed critique of Peshkin's position, see Thiessen (1990; 1993, ch. 7).

CHAPTER NINE

1 Cf. Barrow (1991, 101); Nodelman (1992, 121).

2 Statements of intellectual freedom of library associations in other countries are very similar (see, for example, the Canadian Library Association 1985).

3 For an excellent critique of this statement of intellectual freedom, see an essay by Leo Flanagan, which has unfortunately been largely ignored in the literature, provocatively entitled "Defending the Indefensible: The Limits of Intellectual Freedom" (1975). Johnson (1986; 1990) provides a good critique from a Christian perspective.

4 Swan (1979, 2042–5). Swan is careful to qualify this admission by arguing that in some sense the librarian should also be opposed to censorship – the paradox is that the librarian is a censor who must at the same time oppose censorship (2042). I agree. But we need to face up to this paradox, and this will lead to a more "enlightened" and more realistic ideal of intellectual freedom. The tension between a purist and a more realistic approach to intellectual freedom is already evident in the Introduction to the Intellectual Freedom Manual of the American Library Association (1989, xvii). But despite the admission that in practice the purist position gives way to compromises by individual librarians, the manual goes on to commend its statements as providing help for individual librarians in combatting library censorship.

5 For a helpful overview of attempts to make this distinction, see Schrader (1995, ch. 2, 13–17). See also Asheim's classic defence of the distinction (1953), and his reappraisal of the distinction written thirty years later (1983).

6 Swan cites the example of a librarian who simply didn't replace her library's copy of *Joy of Sex* after it was stolen. This was done in order to avoid further complaints from patron (1979, 2043). Berry admits that most librarians don't stock X-rated movies or *Penthouse*, but in so doing they are in fact censoring (1982, 839). Schrader, in his survey of Canadian librarians, reports that some respondents admitted that their staff probably do engage in self-censorship during the selection process (1995, 117). In the Introduction to the same book, he describes Canada as a nation of "quiet censors" (11).

7 "Power-knowledge" is a term Jansen borrows from Foucault, though she modifies the meaning somewhat in order to accommodate insights from the long-established tradition of the sociology of knowledge which draws on Nietzsche, Marx, and others (Jansen 1988, 6–7; 219–20).

8 There are other attempts to make the distinction between selection and censorship. For example, some would maintain that selection is an activity governed by professional standards, and censorship is a rejection of materials for non-professional reasons (Schrader 1995, 13). The fundamental problem here is that professional standards are themselves ideologically loaded.

9 Jansen (1988, 181–2). See Jansen (1988, 219n1 and 246n1) for a catalogue of the epistemological moorings of her position.

10 See Chomsky (1988b, 7; 1988a, xii; cf. Jansen 1988, 189). Chomsky goes
on to maintain that educational institutions and the media serve the interests of the state and corporate power, and he provides careful documentation to support these claims (1988a; 1988b; 1992).

11 Canavan provides a careful documentation of ways in which the US Supreme
Court has not accepted the absolutist theory of freedom of expression, however many Americans may assume that it has done so (1984, ch. 1).

12 See, for example, Canavan (1984, 4); Strike (1985, 240–1); Arons (1986,
55–6); Flanagan (1975, 1888); American Library Association (1989, 91).

13 In 1972, the National Council of Teachers of English first published the influential pamphlet "The Students' Right to Read." A more recent 1993
publication of this same body again objects to any infringement of intellectual freedom for all students in public schools (Simmons 1994, 168). For
repeated appeals to children's rights, see a special issue of *Canadian
Children's Literature* devoted to the matter of censorship (no. 68, 1992).
Strike points out that in the conventional view on censorship, the rights of
students take precedence over the rights of parents (1985, 241). Schrader
underscores the fact that the Canadian Library Association on Intellectual
Freedom makes no mention of age-related access restrictions in libraries,
and the American Library Association's Bill of Rights has prohibited discrimination on the basis of age since 1967 (Schrader 1995, 117).

14 Interestingly, one writer attempting to argue for complete intellectual freedom for children does acknowledge the developmental assumptions being
made by those who favour censorship. And this leads him to attempt to dis-
credit Piaget's research on child development (Nodelman 1992, 127–8).
However, Nodelman's criticisms focus on details concerning Piaget's theory, his appeal to "rigid" or "distinct" stages of development – specific criticisms which do nothing to undermine the general developmental theory,
which is all that is needed to suggest that children are not fully autonomous and should not be treated as such.

15 Susan Musgrave, a Canadian writer of children's books whose writings have
occasionally been on censors' lists, admits that she draws the line as to what
her children can watch on television, although, strangely, she doesn't call
this censorship (Davis 1992, 115–17). Nodelman is similarly inconsistent
when in one breath he prides himself on having allowed his children to
read anything they wanted, and then in the next breath admits that there
were times when he rejected a book or TV show on their behalf. He further
admits that his pleas for allowing children "more" freedom in their choices
come with one very important proviso: "that it take place within the context of active adult interest and involvement in children's lives in general
and their reading in particular" (Nodelman 1992, 130–1).

16 American Library Association (1989, 1923); cf. Schrader (1995, 67–81).

17 Comments taken from the American Library Association (1989, 94); Nodelman (1992, 128–32); Stanbridge (1992, 36); Schrader (1995, 120).

18 Quoted in Swan (1979, 2041).

19 See comments in note 15, above. It should also be noted that the American Library Association, in a clause interpreting its policies for minors, holds "that it is parents – and only parents – who may restrict their children – and only their children – from access to library materials and services" (American Library Association 1989, 22–3).

20 For comments on this, see Canavan (1984, 4); Peshkin (1986, 190); Strike (1985, 240); Arons (1986, 55–6).

21 For example, Johnson, a former librarian at Ontario Bible College and Seminary, says this about censorship and selection: "A censorious attitude thus tends to emphasize reasons for rejecting a publication as more important than reasons for accepting it. In contrast, an exemplary Christian approach evaluates the contribution a potential purchase would make in the learning process of the library's users (i.e. its educational value) and the significance of the item in representing the literature of the field in the library's collection (i.e. its documentation value), and in the case of highly controversial item, weighs its contribution against the likelihood that it will achieve its intended effect in the community being served (i.e. its functional value" (1990, 66).

22 For a defence of intellectual freedom from a Christian point of view, see Johnson (1990, esp. 64) and Jones (1994, esp. 125–43). Unfortunately, although Jones acknowledges that censorship "in some guises may be inevitable," he does not do justice to delineating between acceptable and non-acceptable uses of power in defining and distributing knowledge (133). For example, he maintains that "great care has to be taken to ensure that censorship does not degenerate into a means by which individuals exert power over others" (133). But all censorship involves the exertion of a degree of power.

23 Jansen (1988, 185–7). Unfortunately, Jansen does not fully appreciate this weakness of her position, although she does at one point maintain that her analysis does not surrender itself to relativism (203). Generally, however, she doesn't seem to be bothered by the relativism inherent in her postmodernist position.

24 Jansen argues that, like Bentham's Panoptican, there is control without the controllers being seen (1988, 16, 22). Church and state censorships were merely replaced by market censorship; the offices of the Censor were merely transferred from civic to private trust (4, 14–25, 202).

25 Indeed, we must not underestimate the role that state schools have played in keeping modern liberal societies enslaved to the Enlightenment narrative. It is not enough to call on individual citizens to reclaim their voices.

While individuals can begin to identify and criticize the socially structured silences which make arbitrary forms of censorship possible, this is not enough (Jansen 1988, 9). Jansen succumbs here to the very individualism that she criticizes. Individuals need the support of institutions.

26 Marsden identifies Charles W. Eliot, one-time president of Harvard, as one of the few founders of modern academia to recognize that universities might not be as free as they claimed. Speaking at a meeting of the Cornell Phi Beta Kappa Society in 1907, Eliot pointed to the subtle censorship that could exist even at places like Cornell (Marsden 1994, 314n25).

27 Rose (1988), in her critical study of two evangelical schools in America, gives us an example of one school where I believe it would be inappropriate to charge the school with excessive censorship. Rose is forced to admit that the educators of Covenant Christian School do expose students to a variety of secular materials, give them freedom to decide what books to read, and encourage them to develop critical discernment (75, 220).

Davis (1986, 5) provides us with one example of excessive censorship in the Christian publishing world. In 1984, as a result of pressure brought by Franky Schaeffer and his friends in the Christian Action Council, a campaign was mounted against InterVarsity Press for publishing Gareth Jones's *Brave New People: Ethical Issues at the Commencement of Life*, a book in which Jones, himself an evangelical, challenged some traditional evangelical assumptions concerning the topic in question. Despite the fact that the book had been competently refereed before publication and endorsed by eight leading evangelicals who understood the contribution Jones was making to current discussion on this topic, InterVarsity Press yielded to this pressure group and withdrew the book from publication. See also Jones (1994, ch. 1) for the author's own description of this sad event.

28 See Johnson (1981) for a rationale for censorship in Christian libraries. The qualification about religious schools taking their religious orientation seriously is necessary because, sadly, the history of religious schooling suggests a deeply entrenched slide towards secularity, as has been documented by George Marsden in his recent book, *The Soul of the American University: From Protestant Establishment to Established Nonbelief* (1994; see also Burtchaell 1998).

29 For an excellent expression of intellectual freedom within the library of a Christian school, see Johnson (1990), quoted in note 21, above.

30 Johnson (1986, 32). The librarian of a religious college will further see it as his or her function to stimulate thought about topics which the community he or she is serving might be uneasy with, by providing bibliographical coverage of a wide range of views (Davis 1986, 5). Asheim paraphrases eighteenth-century British leader Edmund Burke, applying his advice for elected representatives to librarians: "Your librarians owe you, not their industry only, but their judgment; and they betray, instead of serving you, if they sacrifice it to curry your favour" (Asheim 1983, 184).

31 American Library Association (1989, 51–4, 171–86). See Johnson (1990, 74n50) for a sample of a complaints policy at a Canadian Bible College and Seminary.

CHAPTER TEN

1 Marsden recounts an address he gave at the 1993 plenary session of the American Academy of Religion. His topic, "Religious Commitment in the Academy," created quite a stir, which even spilled over into the mainstream media. One scholar made this observation: "If a professor talks about studying something from a Marxist point of view, others might disagree but not dismiss the notion. But if a professor proposed to study something from a Catholic or Protestant point of view, it would be treated like proposing something from a Martian point of view" (quoted in Marsden 1997, 7). A leading American intellectual historian maintained that "the notion that scholars' personal beliefs are compatible with their academic interests is 'loony' and reflects 'a self-indulgent professoriate'" (Marsden 1997, 5).
2 My brief summary of this case draws upon the Alberta provincial court decision *Regina v. Wiebe*, 3 WWR 36 (1978), Joanne Levy (1979), and reports found in the *St. John's Edmonton Report*, 30 Jan. 1978, 27–30; and 13 Feb. 1978, 30–4. A detailed treatment of this case is found in Thiessen (1982b).
3 *Regina v. Wiebe* at 48.
4 In the end, Judge Oliver concluded that these Mennonites were not guilty, because the School Act of Alberta, which required attendance at public schools, involved an infringement of their religious freedom (*Regina v. Wiebe* at 62).
5 Halstead, for example, argues for a uniquely Muslim curriculum (1992, 50–1; 1986, 63, 54–5).
6 This section draws on an earlier response of mine to Hirst (Thiessen 1985a).
7 Hirst frequently lists religion as one of the seven or eight forms of knowledge (1974a, 44, 88, 137, 144). At times, however, he expresses doubts about this (1974a, 65, 180, 185). I have argued elsewhere that, on Hirst's own criteria, religion must be a form of knowledge (Thiessen and Wilson 1979, 16–20).
8 "The logical interrelations between the different forms of knowledge are manifestly many and complex" (Hirst 1974a, 90; cf. 89–90, 138, 145–6, 150–1).
9 Hirst (1974a, 52). Thus, for example, scientific knowledge is found to be relevant to the problems considered in other forms (Hirst 1974a, 170, 153, 137, 144–5, 161). Religion can "logically build on science," though, strangely, the reverse is impossible, according to Hirst (1976, 155).

10 Hirst (1974a, 91). Although sympathetic to this notion of a "logical hierarchy," Hirst feels that we have not done enough in the way of a "detailed
conceptual mapping of these areas," which would justify definite conclusions about the exact nature of the interrelations between the forms of
knowledge (1974a, 91). But, Hirst remains firm in his claim that there are
logical interrelations between them.

11 Lois Sweet, for example, admits that every area of human study is
grounded in theory or explanation which "inevitably involves a certain leap
of faith." Thus there is "an element of faith in every area of human study"
(1997, 212). Interestingly, when Sweet addresses the question of religious
schools, to which she is opposed, she seems to forget all about her earlier
concessions to the new epistemology and makes a sharp distinction between faith and knowledge: all students must "learn how personal faith differs from public reasonableness, and where to draw the line" (247).

12 Marsden tends to resort to vague terms such as these (1997, 10, 62, 65, 67,
70).

13 Hirst, for example, in defending the ideal of a religiously neutral school,
raises this as an additional problem for Christian thinkers who maintain
that "private" religious beliefs are inextricably interwoven with the rest of
the curriculum. He argues that "it is by no means clear *how* private beliefs
and values do enter, for instance, the teaching of science" (Hirst 1967,
332; my emphasis).

14 Reformed Epistemology can be traced back to John Calvin and other leaders of the sixteenth-century reformation. Key figures in its development are
Abraham Kuyper in the nineteenth century, and some contemporary
American philosophers such as Alvin Plantinga and Nicholas Wolterstorff.
For a collection of essays dealing with Reformed Epistemology, see Hart et
al. (1983). See Shortt (1991) for a recent account of this approach to epistemology and an analysis of its educational implications. Quite some time
ago, I responded at length to a book critiquing a Reformed approach to
the Christian mind by Barclay (1984; see Thiessen 1992). More recently
I have responded to a lively exchange on this topic in *Spectrum* (Allen 1993;
Velten 1994; Smith 1995; see Thiessen 1997). Even more recently I have
responded to an essay critical of my position (Wright 1998; see Thiessen
1999).

15 See Shortt on Kuyper and Van Til (1991, esp. chs. 1 and 5). Brummer
(1969) provides an excellent overview of some ambiguities that exist in
Dooyeweerd's analysis of the relation between faith and learning. (1) At
times Dooyeweerd understands the relation between religious presuppositions and the rest of knowledge to be a logical one. (2) Religious presuppositions can also be interpreted as serving a transcendental function, thus
providing a necessary condition of theoretical thought by giving us an
Archimedean point which unifies all our thinking. (3) Dooyeweerd's reli-

gious presuppositions can finally be interpreted as serving a regulative
function, thus providing a way in which to interpret experience.

16 Quoted in Heie and Wolfe (1987, 328n6).

17 The part that philosophical beliefs play in educational theory, Hirst maintains, is "not that of axioms in a deductive system," but rather "that in the
midst of a complex network of understanding which cannot be adequately
and formally expressed, we form our judgments and in the statements
which we use to express our reasons, draw attention to the bigger considerations which have influenced us" (Hirst 1969, 178).

18 Clouser argues: "What we want to say is that the influence of religious beliefs is much more a matter of a presupposed perspective guiding the direction of theorizing than of Scripture supplying specific truths for theories"
(1991, 104). Wolterstorff uses the notion of control beliefs to show how
these presuppositions function. "Control beliefs function in two ways. Because we hold them, we are led to *reject* certain sorts of theories – some because they are inconsistent with those beliefs; others because, though
consistent with our control beliefs, they do not comport well with those beliefs. On the other hand control beliefs also lead us to *devise* theories. We
want theories that are consistent with our control beliefs. Or, to put it more
stringently, we want theories which comport as well as possible with those
beliefs" (Wolterstorff 1984, 67–8).

19 Wolterstorff too suggests that for committed Christians, the Bible serves to
open our eyes to creation and its normative structure, thus encouraging us
to look for norms governing the political, economic, aesthetic, and other
spheres of life (1980, ch. 2). Marsden uses the notion of a Gestalt picture
to illustrate the commonality and differences between Christian and non-
Christian scholarship (1997, 61–2). Michael Polanyi argues that science
rests on some basic premises about the nature of reality and the process of
discovery and verification. "The influence of these premises on the pursuit
of discovery is great and indispensable." But they cannot be clearly defined
or transmitted in the form of definite precepts or explicit knowledge. They
influence belief systems subjectively, interpreting reality much as the
Gestalten of Gestalt psychology influence perception (Polanyi 1964,
10–11, 24–5, 42–3, 76).

20 In a way reminiscent of Quine, Shortt addresses the issue of varying degrees of influence of Christian presuppositions by introducing the notion
of a "hierarchy of perspectives" (1991, 70).

21 Marsden therefore quite correctly points out "that explicitly Christian convictions do not very often have substantial impact on the techniques used
in academic detective work, which make up the bulk of the technical, scientific side of academic inquiry" (1997, 47).

22 On the philosophy of mathematics, see Ernest (1991) and Clouser (1991,
ch. 7); on the history of science, see Matthews (1989).

301 Notes to pages 171–6

23 For a careful analysis of these doctrines and their implications, see Walsh and Middleton (1984, chs. 3, 4, 5) and Wolters (1985, chs. 2, 3, 4).

24 See essays by Nicholas Wolterstorff and Paul Helm on "The Scottish Common-Sense Tradition and Rationality," in Hart et al. (1983).

25 See Rorty (1987) for an exploration of this idea. Unfortunately, Rorty sees the notions of "intersubjective agreement" and objective truth as mutually exclusive. Surely one can distinguish between the human search for truth and objective truth as a goal. Intersubjective agreement at the human level can then be seen as a sign (though not infallible) of coming closer to transcendent truth.

26 Kuhn (1977). See Ratzsch (1986, 70–1); Cooling (1994, 81, 84); and Netland (1991, 183–6). Murphy and McClendon (1989) argue that postmodern epistemologies accept these criteria too.

27 Some Reformed writers seem to take this extreme position at times. Abraham Kuyper, for example, describes Christians and non-Christians as approaching science quite differently: "their activities run in opposite directions because they have different starting-points; and because of the difference in their nature they apply themselves differently to this work, and view things in a different way" (quoted in Shortt 1991, 8). Van Til similarly argues that "epistemologically the believer and non-believer have nothing in common" (quoted in Shortt 1991, 11). Another writer, Stephen Perks, a British Christian Reconstructionist, argues that Christian and humanist worldviews are "mutually exclusive." "They can never agree fundamentally on the interpretation of the facts of reality at *any* point if they are consistent with their presuppositions. For the Christian and the humanist, therefore, there can be no common ground" (Perks 1992, 28).

28 Perks, for example, is forced to admit that there is some common ground – he allows for God's "common grace" to mankind, which makes it possible for the non-believer to "understand to a degree the world in which he lives" and to "arrive at the truth concerning many aspects of reality" (1992, 28n7). He further admits that "the non-believer will teach the same subjects and the same facts that the Christian teaches" (27). Similar emphases are also found in Kuyper and Van Til (see Shortt 1991, ch. 1).

29 I have borrowed this diagram from a presentation that Trevor Cooling made at the International Seminar on Religious Education and Values, held at Banff in 1992. It also appears in an earlier essay of mine, "Curriculum after Babel" (Thiessen 1997, 174). See also Rawls (1987), who uses the idea of an "overlapping consensus" in his political liberalism.

30 Indeed, general revelation is the more immediate and normal source of much of our knowledge, even for Christians, a point stressed by Catholic theologians, but one to which evangelical and Reformed theologians have not always paid sufficient attention (Curtis 1994, 94).

31 Marsden (1997, 70). Elsewhere I have expanded on an analogy of an un-
finished Shakespeare play, drawn from Wright (1992, 140), that is very
helpful in understanding the challenge facing Christians in developing a
Christian curriculum, and in explaining the diversity of the results, as well
as the hope of an ultimately unified response to what a Christian curriculum or scholarship should look like (Thiessen 1997, 171–3).

32 Catholic Committee (1989, 20, 23, 27). These same trends also exist in
Catholic higher education (Gleason 1995). It was in response to the rapid
and distressing decline of a strong religious presence at Catholic universities that Pope John Paul II issued the apostolic constitution *Ex Corde
Ecclesia* (1990). Sadly this statement has met with strong resistance from
the Fellowship of Catholic Scholars. While there are complex issues here,
involving the relation between Catholic universities and the church, I
would suggest that the underlying problem is one of Catholic universities
forfeiting their identity as religious educational institutions. For a discussion of this ongoing dispute, see comments made by Richard John Neuhaus in *First Things* no. 70 (Feb. 1997): 62 and no. 92 (April 1999):71–2.
See also an essay by John Piderit, "The University at the Heart of the
Church," *First Things* no. 94 (June/July 1999):22–5.

33 Fisher's study is referred to in Marsden (1997, 104–5). Marsden general-
izes: "Often, even when schools retain a substantial church affiliation, most
of what is taught in their classrooms, except for Bible or theology courses,
is indistinguishable from what is taught in state universities" (1997, 104).
In another study, a review of church-related college catalogues in the USA
revealed that except for some historical comments at the beginning of the
catalogue, the justification for specific courses of study, departments, and
programs is based almost entirely on an appeal to secular ideals such as
personal self-fulfilment, autonomy, and vocational choices (Springsted
1991, 472–3). Similar results were found in a recent survey of an evangelical college in Canada. In a study of course syllabi which contained written
objectives, it was found that in about one-half of them, professors made no
explicit reference to the goal of providing biblical or Christian perspectives
in the course. An explicit Christian worldview component was totally absent
in 63 per cent of the exams surveyed. The authors conclude that most
courses at this Christian college were minimally different from those taught
at secular institutions (Faw and Van Brummelen 1993).

34 This study is referred to in Thatcher (1990, 171–2).

35 See Burtchaell (1998), Marsden (1994), and Gleason (1995) for excellent
analyses of this trend in the USA.

36 See Marsden (1997, 3, 7, 58, 102).

37 For two excellent books outlining the basic presuppositions of a Christian
worldview and exploring how they shape the various disciplines, see
Wolters (1985) and Walsh and Middleton (1984). The latter also includes

an excellent bibliography of books and resources related to a Christian perspective on each of the disciplines.

38 This superficial approach to a Christian curriculum would seem to characterize the PACE learning packets used by Accelerated Christian Education (ACE) schools, where each packet contains a Scripture verse, taken from the King James version (Rose 1988, 126). Carl Zylstra, president of Dordt College, confesses to another form of superficiality that he and his graduate school colleagues succumbed to when, in their study of educational theory, they "simply grabbed the latest research from human developmental psychology, laminated it onto issues of Christian faith maturity, and called it Christian scholarship" (1997, 5).

39 Paul can be seen as encouraging this approach in 1 Thessalonians 5:21: "Test everything. Hold on to the good."

CHAPTER ELEVEN

1 Several articles describing this event are found in *Time* 149(14) (1997): 16–35.

2 Newman draws on an earlier study of the Zealots of Jesus' time by S. Brandon for this example (Newman 1986, 70).

3 For an initial response to Spiecker's review of my book, see Thiessen (1996).

4 Alternatively, state-maintained public schools are often seen as a key to avoiding the dangers of fanaticism. In America, for example, Mann and the reformers were specifically worried about fanaticism (Glenn 1988, 8). Jefferson hoped that the changes brought about by a school system would include "a quiet euthanasia of the heresies of bigotry and fanaticism which have so long triumphed over human reason" (quoted in McCarthy et al. 1982, 43).

5 Paul Hirst similarly makes a sharp distinction between Christian nurture or catechesis and liberal religious education – they need to be distinguished in terms of both their starting points and their aims (1985, 14; 1981, 92). In religious education that is truly liberal, the educator seeks "from the stance of reason the development of reason in matters concerning religion," whereas in Christian catechesis "the aim is from the stance of faith, the development of faith" (Hirst 1981, 89). Commitment is clearly one essential element of faith. Hence, Christian nurture can be described as beginning from a position of commitment and aiming to foster commitment to the Christian faith. Such teaching Hirst associates with indoctrination and with a ghetto mentality; it is opposed to rationality and autonomy, and hence must be viewed as "inadequate," committed to goals that can only be described as "improper, even sub-human" (1981, 92; 1985, 7, 10, 15). Liberal education, by contrast, seeks to liberate students from the narrowness of religious commitments, the dogmatism of religious convictions, and

religious fanaticism. See also Blacker (1998) for a recent expression of worry about "fanatical schools."

6 Deuteronomy 6:4–9. Jesus also calls us to deny ourselves and follow him (Lk. 9:23). We are to lose ourselves in our commitment to Christ. Jesus stressed the cost of discipleship – no excuses are accepted (Lk. 9:57–62). If anyone loves father, mother, or children more than me, he is not worthy of me (Matt. 10:37). In Pauline language, a believer is called to be "a servant of Christ Jesus," or even a "slave to God" (Romans 1:1; 6:22).

7 Here I am rejecting the tendency of some Protestant theologians of the twentieth century who have treated commitment as ultimately irrational. Trigg has responded to this, suggesting that there is necessarily a propositional component to all commitment (1973, 43–9, 79).

8 Newman (1986, 12–13). Newman omits the behavioural ingredient, preferring a strictly dispositional analysis of commitment. However, he is forced to admit that there is a close relation between dispositions and behaviour, with respect to fanaticism (74–9).

9 Newman (1986, 46–7). Eric Hoffer describes the undercommitted person as "the gentle cynic" who simply doesn't care about God or about anything (1951, 54–5).

10 Blacker defines fanaticism in terms of two broad standards: comprehensiveness and single-mindedness (1998, 245–53). The first characteristic really introduces a content criterion (holding a worldview), which becomes problematic because this makes everyone a fanatic, a problem that Blacker himself hints at. Single-mindedness is already part of what I consider to be a more adequate analysis of fanaticism by Newman.

11 For some helpful discussions of needed distinctions between fundamentalism and evangelicalism, see Bebbington (1989); Marsden (1987); Balmer (1989, xi-xii); Smith (1998); and Stolzenberg (1993, 614–23).

12 Dekmejian helpfully distinguishes between passive and active Islamic fundamentalism (1985, 54–5). He raises the following caution: "The Western practice of placing Islamic fundamentalism under the rubric of 'fanaticism' is singularly dysfunctional to a balanced and dispassionate analysis of the subject" (7). Ayubi, in a similar vein, tries to refute the widely held view in the West that Islam is by its very nature a political religion (1991). For a contrasting interpretation of Islam, see Ye'or (1996).

13 We have already seen similar concerns emerge in considering the charge of indoctrination (ch. 8 – see especially the sections on the content and consequences criteria of indoctrination). Dwyer accuses Catholic and Fundamentalist schools of fostering in students dogmatic and inflexible modes of thought and expression (1998, 15). Peshkin, in his study of Bethany Baptist Academy, was particularly concerned about the doctrinal stance of the school: "I confess to seeing Bethany's doctrinal yardstick poised like a guillotine to lop off dissenting heads, mine and others" (1986, 290).

14 I would argue, for example, that the initial acceptance of revelation as a source of truth can be undertaken in a rational and critical manner, and in such a way as to satisfy the criteria of procedural independence, which are essential to autonomy (cf. Thiessen 1993, 133). It is further most important to distinguish between revealed truth, and the human understanding of revealed truth. The latter is fallible, and if such fallibility is admitted, fanaticism can be avoided. For some philosophical defences of the possibility of divine revelation, and some criteria to use in assessing such a revelation, see Mavrodes (1988), Abraham (1981), Swinburne (1981, ch. 7).

15 On the exclusivity of all commitments, see also Newman (1986, 67; 1982, ch. 6). For a critique of Hull's universalist outlook, see Barnes (1997) and Thompson (1993).

16 Newman (1986, 9–10). In fact, Newman is not entirely clear on this question. Later in the book he identifies, as one of three criteria of a healthy and socially constructive commitment, that "the content of the world view of which it is an 'acceptance' must be compatible with truth" (1986, 135).

17 Mill makes the following comment in the context of a defence of the importance of critical thinking: "Such negative criticism would indeed be poor enough as an ultimate result, but as a means to attaining any positive knowledge or conviction worthy of the name it cannot be valued too highly" (1978, 43). Mill underscores the importance of "living conviction," and having a "deep feeling" of the truth of an opinion (39, 44).

18 See, for example, Astley (1994, ch. 8; cf. Thiessen 1993, ch. 6).

19 See 1 Corinthians 13:9, 12. See also Gooch (1987).

20 This is a secondary conclusion drawn by Gallup and Jones (1992), referred to in the next note.

21 For example, Gallup and Jones (1992), based on a survey of 1,052 urban and rural Americans, conclude that devout Christians, regardless of denomination, are truly and overwhelmingly better and happier than the average citizen. See also Lewy (1997), referred to in more detail in note 25, below.

22 See Aristotle's *Ethics* (1109a; cf. Newman 1986, 138).

23 In the story of creation, man and women are not only to be in relation to God but are also told to take care of the Garden of Eden (Genesis 2:15). Jesus asked his disciples to remain firmly rooted in the world, while at the same time adhering to otherworldly values (John 17:6–19). Servants are asked to serve their masters wholeheartedly, "as if you were serving the Lord" (Ephesians 6:7).

24 For a helpful and careful analysis of how total devotion to God is compatible with other earthly interests, including loving one's neighbour, see Adams (1986).

25 This conclusion has also been supported recently by Guenter Lewy, in a book entitled *Why America Needs Religion* (1997). Interestingly, the

author's original intent was to argue against those who maintain that the real crisis of our age is a crisis of unbelief. In the end, though Lewy still believes there is no God, he makes a strong case for the benefits of traditional religious commitment for American society, particularly in the area of morality.

26 See Newman (1986, 116). Hoffer provides an explanation for this phenomenon by characterizing fanaticism as a form of self-assertion through attachment to a cause. "He embraces a cause not primarily because of its justice and holiness but because of his desperate need for something to hold on to" (1951, 83–4; cf. Newman 1986, 58–9). This idea is well expressed in a song by John Cougar Millencamp: "If you don't stand for something, you'll fall for anything."

27 Modern liberal education for many critics is seen as an initiation into a very particular ideal of critical rationality. It also involves a deification of the individual, and ultimately a trivialization of choice (Marshall 1989, 10–11; MacIntyre 1988, 399–400). Hence also the recurring criticism – that the so-called methodological neutrality of liberal education fosters a secular and relativistic mind-set. "Insofar as this education works, the pupil becomes trained in the dogmatics of liberalism," Marshall quips (1989, 10).

28 Again and again it is maintained that liberal education, and schools which seek to provide a liberal education, must be neutral with regard to substantive judgments about matters which are controversial or about which there is significant value diversity. John White, for example, maintains that teachers should develop and encourage what is necessary for informed and reflective choice, but they should not advertise or impose or have their own moral commitments treated as authoritative (1982, ch. 3). White is well aware of the dangers of carrying this caution about commitment to an extreme. He recognizes the danger of being, like Hamlet, "eternally reflecting but never committed to anything" (1982, 56–7, 60). But, the caution about teaching for commitment remains (see also Dearden 1984, ch. 7; Gardner 1989; Gutmann 1987, 34–43, 54–6; McLaughlin 1992b, 108–10).

29 Brenda Watson reviews some additional problems with neutral teaching: (a) The stance of neutrality may be professionally inappropriate, when countering prejudice, for example. (b) Neutral teaching undermines the quality of teaching, making it dull. (c) Neutrality is impossible because the selection of material, manner of presentation, and handling of questions and discussion all reflect a viewpoint (Watson 1987, 38–9; cf. Warnock 1988). These problems are simply an expression of a central theoretical problem highlighted by postmodernism, namely, that all thinking is theory-laden, and therefore neutral teaching is impossible (Crittenden 1988, 214; cf. Baer 1987).

30 Paul recognized this danger when he warned about being people who are "always learning but never able to acknowledge the truth" (2 Timothy 3:7).

CHAPTER TWELVE

1 Paul Marshall describes liberalism as a variable political philosophy that stresses some or all of the following: "individuality, freedom, autonomy, rights, the separation of religion and politics, reason, tolerance, the non-imposition of belief, and decent progressiveness" (1997, 47).

2 Kimball (1986, 218). In 1944, John Dewey, for example, noted, "Nothing is more striking in recent discussions of liberal education than the wide-spread and seemingly spontaneous use of *liberating* as a synonym for *liberal*" (Kimball 1986, 158).

3 See, for example, Goodin and Reeve (1989); Marshall (1997, 47); and Ackerman (1980, 11).

4 Coleman and Hoffer (1987, 3). Horace Mann, the single most important American founder of public education, saw public schools as a tool for cre-ating "national unity by reducing the power of the particularisms of creed or region" (Glenn 1988, 116; cf. Hunter 1991, 198). Crittenden illustrates this view by referring to Hegel, who saw the role of schools as leading chil-dren from the personal and affective moral relationships of the family to the impersonal ethical standpoint required for participation in the politi-cal life (1988, 166; cf. Carr 1995, 76; Tamir 1995a, 142).

5 Hirst (1981, 92; 1985, 7, 10, 15).

6 See also Jonathan, who talks about the "crisis of modernity" and suggests that it is high time "to problematise theoretical reliance on the central philosophical doctrines of modern neutralist liberalism," which have been the foundation of philosophy of education for too long (1995, 102, 93; cf. Bowers 1987, ch. 1).

7 Tamir (1995a, 3, xxvi). Juergensmeyer (1993) similarly documents the rise of religious nationalism throughout the world. Such religious nationalism is united by a common enemy, Western secular liberal nationalism, as well as by a common solution, the revival of religion in the public sphere.

8 See, for example, MacIntyre (1984), Hauerwas (1983), and Sandel (1982, 1984a; 1996). I am aware that Sandel might dispute the appropriateness of being labelled a communitarian (see, for example, Allen and Regan 1998).

9 See, for example, Bork (1997) and Gairdner (1998).

10 See, for example, Apple (1996); Toulmin (1990); Stout (1981); Rorty (1982; 1983). For some recent critiques of liberalism see Kekes (1997), who challenges liberalism's assumptions concerning human nature. Neal (1997) reviews some of the ferment in contemporary liberalism and then offers his own version of "vulgar liberalism."

11 Weinstein (1995, 378). Walter Anderson contrasts the differing views of re-ality and truth in modernism and postmodernism by telling the joke of three umpires having a beer after a baseball game. One says, "There's balls and there's strikes and I call 'em the way they are" (the Enlightenment view

of truth which assumes there is a real world out there). Another responds, "There's balls and there's strikes and I call 'em the way I see 'em" (the critical realist). The third says, "There's balls and there's strikes, and they ain't nothin' until I call 'em" (the postmodernist denial of truth and reality) (Anderson 1990, 75).

12 This becomes very apparent in the conflicting views expressed in the Canadian Supreme Court's ruling in *Adler v. Ontario* (1996). While the majority opinion emphasized individual rights, Justice L'Heureux-Dubé's dissenting opinion appealed to the principle of group recognition. For a careful analysis of this case, see Callan (2000).

13 Various writers have called for such a reconciliation. See, for example, the end of Toulmin's study of modernity (1990, ch. 5), as well as the final chapter of Huntington (1996). Stout repeatedly argues that we must go beyond the debate between liberalism and communitarianism, seeking a bridge between the two, which he finds in part in Rorty's pragmatic liberalism (Stout 1988, 220, 236). Bowers, in his *Elements of a Post-Liberal Theory of Education*, very deliberately uses the word "post-liberal" to show that his theory has some connection with the past (1987, vii). Carr (1995) appeals to Dewey as providing a way to reconcile the insights of modernism and postmodernism. Gray suggests that the key challenge facing liberal thought today is the pluralist challenge, and that it is "in the development of a postliberal political theory that addresses this challenge that the best hope lies for salvaging and renewing what remains of value in liberal thought and practice" (1995, 96).

14 Rawls's social contract, for example, requires that we hide behind a veil of ignorance that masks our particular ties and commitments (Tamir 1995a, 105, cf. 142). Nagel finds "solidarity which depends on racial, linguistic, or religious identification distasteful" (1991, 178).

15 This point is developed in McCarthy et al. (1982, chs. 2 and 3). Tamir points out that early American education emphasized civic education, which was expected to eliminate divisiveness. "Family affiliations, religious allegiances and ethnic ties all were viewed as private matters and hence unessential, even disturbing to civic life" (Tamir 1995a, xxiii).

16 I have been unable to trace this quotation to its original source. Richard John Neuhaus refers to this statement of Burke's in a treatment of ecumenical pluralism, *Freedom for Ministry* (Grand Rapids, Michigan: Wm. B. Eerdmans, 1979), 48. Schwehn, writing as a Christian, draws on what another writer describes as his own "hard-won achievement as a Jew." "Any authentic affirmation of one's humanity begins at home, moving out toward others in the form of a large-spirited hospitality which, in offering refuge or possible friendship to the stranger, can respect his inviolate being only if one honors one's own" (1993, xi).

17 Tracy (1990, 5–6). Or, in Richard Rorty's words, it is simply futile "to step outside our skins and compare ourselves with something absolute ... to

escape from the finitude of one's time and place, the 'merely conventional' and contingent aspects of one's life" (1982, 6).

18 Gutmann puts it well when she suggests that deconstructionists deconstruct themselves (1994, 19; cf. Siegel 1995).

19 For a defence of objective knowledge see Nagel (1986; 1997); Helm (1987); and Middleton and Walsh (1995). Similar emphases can be found in Kuhn and MacIntyre, who have mistakenly been thought to succumb to relativism. MacIntyre, for example, after reaffirming his central emphasis that all reasoning takes place within the context of some traditional mode of thought, goes on to talk about "transcending through criticism and invention the limitations of what had hitherto been reasoned in that tradition" (MacIntyre 1984, 222; cf. Kuhn 1977).

20 I am indebted to Hart (1995) for this account of Nagel's work.

21 Or, as Nagel puts it in his more recent work, the last word is not that this is justified "for me" or "for us." Instead, it is an affirmation of objective truth which any reasoner is obliged to recognize. The last word does not belong to human nature. "The idea of reason, by contrast, refers to nonlocal and nonrelative methods of justification – methods that distinguish universally legitimate from illegitimate inferences and that aim at reaching the truth in a nonrelative manner" (1997, 5).

22 It should be noted, however, as Middleton and Walsh show, that a socially constructed self, in the end, becomes a decentred self (1995, ch. 3). Gergen explains that "if identities are essentially forms of social construction, then one can be anything at any time so long as the roles, costumes, and settings have been commodiously arranged" (1991, 184). This explains the lack of rootedness that is felt so deeply by contemporary man and woman (cf. Taylor 1989).

23 Halstead (1995, 258). Two other characteristics might be added to this list – nationality and race – because, as Halstead suggests, there are compelling arguments that these should be considered cultural or ideological phenomena rather than biologically determined groupings. Thus too Tamir defines "nations" as "cultural communities demarcated by the imaginative power of their members" (1995a, 68).

24 See Singh (1995, 12–13, 21–2); Halstead (1995, 271); Gutmann 1994, 9); Tomasi (1995, 583); and Dwyer (1998, 99). For example, John Rawls, in his earlier work, does acknowledge the "collective activity of society," and the many associations within society, ranging "from families and friendships to much larger associations" (1971, 529, 520, 527). But his account has a strong voluntarist tone and he never really gives up the position of contracting individuals (Mouw and Griffioen 1993, 25).

25 Another way to illustrate the secondary status of cultural membership within traditional liberalism is to examine how a conflict between individual and group interests is handled. If individual interests conflict with the

interests of a group, then it is individual interests that must be given a priority (Wringe 1995, 287; Kymlicka 1989, 140).

26 Gray, for example, in his concluding section, subtitled "Postliberalism," considers a number of contemporary attempts at formulating a "communitarian liberalism" or a "postmodern liberalism," though he feels each has failed (1995, 85–96).

27 Taylor's essay is found in the highly acclaimed book *Multiculturalism and "The Politics of Recognition"* edited by Amy Gutmann, first published in 1992, and reissued in an expanded version in 1994. For other important discussions of liberalism's attempt to accommodate the politics of difference in relation to education, see the "Symposium on Citizenship, Democracy, and Education," in *Ethics* 105(3) (April 1995); and a special issue of the *Journal of Philosophy of Education*, edited by Yael Tamir, on "Democratic Education in a Multicultural State" 29(2) (1995). This work has been reissued as a separate monograph (see Tamir 1995c). The first issue of a new journal coming out of the Netherlands, *International Journal of Education and Religion*, is devoted to the topic of multiculturalism. The editor, Chris Hermans, in an introductory essay, points out that Taylor's "Politics of Recognition" is probably the most cited article in this issue. See also Kymlicka and Norman (2000), and Leicester and Taylor (1992).

28 Despite the risk in trying to make classifications, I will attempt to do so. While liberalism has always tried to accommodate difference, there would seem to be a progression towards more acceptance of cultural diversity. The early Rawls (1971) clearly stressed unity and the assimilation of all cultural differences. Less extreme is comprehensive liberalism, which, in addition to the basic civic virtues, demands also that all individuals and societies support autonomy. See, for example, Kymlicka (1989; 1995; 1998), Raz (1986; 1994), Gutmann (1996); and Callan (1997; 2000). Political liberalism is often described as attempting to do more by way of accommodating social diversity. See, for example, the later Rawls (1993) and Macedo (1990; 1995a; 1995b). Galston (1991; 1995), Tamir (1995a), Walzer (1983; 1994; 1995), Spinner-Halev (2000), and perhaps Taylor (1993; 1994) go even further in establishing the principle of maximum accommodation. At the extreme in accepting the politics of difference would be feminist writers such as Young (1990), Honig (1993), and Mouffe (1993).

29 In the Introduction to her *Liberal Nationalism*, Tamir states as her aim "placing national thinking within the boundaries of liberalism without losing sight of either" (1995a, 12). "Liberal nationalism attempts to capture what is essential to both schools of thought, drawing from liberalism a commitment to personal autonomy and individual rights, and from nationalism an appreciation of the importance of membership in human communities in general, and in national communities in particular" (35).

CHAPTER THIRTEEN

1 Callan provides a careful analysis of one example of this kind of defence of religious schools in the dissenting opinion of Justice L'Heureux-Dubé in the 1996 ruling of the Supreme Court in *Adler v. Ontario*. Callan correctly points out that the nerve of her dissenting argument was an appeal for equality based on group recognition – a very postmodernist emphasis (2000).

2 See especially Gutmann (1996), Callan (1995; 1997; 2000), Leicester and Taylor (1992), Snik and DeJong (1995), and Tamir (1995a). See also references in note 27 of chapter 12.

3 For some recent discussions of other problems with state-maintained common schools, see Emberley and Newell (1994); Finn (1991); Hirsch (1996); Holmes (1998); Kozol (1991); Lieberman (1993); Nikiforuk (1993); Perelman (1992); Steinberg et al. (1996); Stevenson and Stigler (1992); and Sykes (1995).

4 McCarthy et al. point to the academic tunnel vision that characterizes most of Anglo-American thinking about democracy, and its failure to see that majoritarian politics is not the only kind of democracy (1982, 108; cf. Tash 1991, 9).

5 Guinness's proposal for a rethinking of the role of religion in American public affairs is a response to the recent expansion of pluralism not only in America but as a worldwide phenomenon (1993, 246). Tamir's argument for a new kind of liberal nationalism is also a response to increasing pluralism: "The era of homogeneous and viable nation-states is over (or rather, the era of the illusion that homogeneous and viable nation-states are possible is over, since such states never existed), and the national vision must be redefined" (1995a, 3).

6 Rawls's more recent work gives explicit attention to what he calls "the fact of pluralism," and he now seems more serious in wanting to address the question of how social unity is possible in a society "marked by deep divisions between opposing and incommensurable conceptions of the good" (1987, 1; 1985, 251).

7 Guinness calls for a rediscovery of the vision of the 1776 Williamsburg Charter, which became the model for the Bill of Rights of the American Constitution: "It is a call to a vision of public life that will allow conflict to lead to consensus, religious commitment to reinforce political civility. In this way, diversity is not a point of weakness but a source of strength" (quoted in Guinness 1993, 255).

8 On pragmatic liberalism, see Rorty (1982; 1983; 1989; 1991), Walzer (1983), and Stout (1988). On consociational democracy, see Lijphart (1977), McCarthy et. al. (1981, ch. 2; 1982, ch. 7), and Tamir (1995a, ch. 7). On chartered pluralism, see Guinness (1993). On "liberal national-

ism," see Tamir (1995a). See also Cassity et al. (1990), Mouw and Griffioen (1993), and Spinner-Halev (2000). I regret not being able to take into account more fully the arguments of Spinner-Halev's excellent work, in which he defends a revised liberalism so as to better accommodate the interests of religious communities. My manuscript was already in press when I had opportunity to review this work.

9 For some other writers defending various aspects of structural and confessional pluralism, see Berger and Neuhaus (1977); Guinness (1993); McCarthy et al. (1981; 1982); Skillen (1994, ch. 6); Skillen et al. (1991); Tamir (1995a); Tash (1991).

10 Here I agree with Galston that the liberal state will "betray its own deepest and most defensible principles" if it seeks to "prescribe – as valid for, and binding on, all – a single debatable conception of how human beings should lead their lives" (Galston 1991, 256; cf. Gilles 1996, 984).

11 Tamir (1995a, xxix). Here I agree again with Galston, who argues that liberal societies may still use state power to promote thinner and more widely shared understandings of civic excellence and freedom (1991, 256). He identifies two general norms that the state can legitimately try to enforce: "normal development," which includes physical health and "the acquisition of basic linguistic and social skills," and a basic civic education (252, cf. Gilles 1996, 984).

12 My position here is close to that of Mark Holmes, who advocates a "pluralist majoritarian position" (1992, 122). Holmes estimates that between 30 and 50 per cent of the population in Canada would prefer area public schools if given a choice (1998, 253).

13 On the system of education in the Netherlands, see Tash (1991), De Ruyter and Miedema (2000), and Glenn (1989). Halstead gives some other examples – the "millet" system of the Ottoman Empire, and the current approach to education in Israel (1995, 264). The Canadian province of Newfoundland also had such a pluralistic system of education until it was dismantled in 1998. This dismantling was in part justified because it was too church-controlled, and it also did not take into account those parents who did not want a Christian education for their children.

14 Gutmann argues, for example, that if the government were to subsidize separate schooling, "then no group needs to compromise its particularist values for the sake of a common civic education" (1996, 164). She suggests that particularism displays a "relative silence" on the question of how many regulations government can impose on schools before they subsidize them (164). She also suggests that if particularism were "modified" so as to accommodate democratic principles, then "controversies" would emerge about the content of civic education within separate schools (164). The demands of separatist particularism with regard to schooling are such that they would expect "too little" by way of giving attention to the needs of

universal values (165). Finally, in discussing multinationalism and education, Gutmann argues that if differing nationalities were respectful of each
other's particularities, "they would probably feel less of a need to segregate
the education of their children by nationality" (173). All of these statements make it sound as though it is (nearly) impossible for religious
schools to do justice to the universal values of citizenship.

15 Michael Walzer, for example, who is very sympathetic to giving intrinsic
value to cultures, defends the need for democratic education in multicultural societies, and in so doing suggests that such education "is probably
best carried on in integrated schools, which anticipate the integration of
the political arena" (1995, 185). He does, in a more pragmatic vein, go on
to suggest that in a radically divided society like Israel, it might be difficult
to achieve anything like a full-scale integration (185).

Terry McLaughlin too is clearly trying to defend an approach to education which seeks to exert a balanced "combination of centripetal (unifying)
and centrifugal (diversifying) forces on pupils and on society itself" (1995,
242). In the light of this principle, he argues both that liberal arguments
against separate schools are not as strong as is generally assumed, and that
liberal arguments for common schools are not as strong as commonly assumed (1992a; 1995). But in both cases McLaughlin is rather cautious in
his conclusions – indeed, one doesn't quite know where he stands. I want
to argue that in each case, the arguments are stronger than he thinks, and
that he simply fails to carry his arguments to their logical conclusion.

Eamonn Callan also wants a learning environment that is "genuinely
hospitable to the credal and cultural diversity the society exhibits" (1995,
253). He wants an educational system that acknowledges "*both* the necessity
of some common education and the acceptability of at least certain kinds
of separate education for those who would choose them" (254). But in the
end, while he expresses some sympathies with a moderate separatist argument, he maintains that the need for common education creates "a presumptive case for common schooling" (268; see also Callan 1997, ch. 7).

16 Although Tamir specifically argues that national groups – minorities and majorities alike – should be free to have their own educational system, she goes
on to say that she *prefers* an arrangement, presumably within state schools,
which gives each nationality special hours or special days (1995a, xxix).

17 See also Berliner, who argues that many among the Christian Right are unable to engage in politics that would make a common school and common
values possible (1997). Callan, recognizing the transformative character of
religious presuppositions, seems to be suggesting that in a genuinely religious school, accommodating the ends of common education would be
difficult, if not impossible (1997, 168). The Proulx Report suggests that
there is something "paradoxical" about introducing students to other religions via Catholic or Protestant religious instruction programs (1999, 71).

18 David Smith has provided a helpful exposition of the biblical stories of the Tower of Babel and Pentecost as affirmations of plurality (1996).

19 Rawls (1987). See Cooling (1994, ch. 7) and Thiessen (1997, 173–6). See also the diagram of overlapping ellipses in chapter 10, p. 176 above.

20 A biography of G.K. Chesterton illustrates this well. Dale describes, as one "fascinatingly original aspect" of Chesterton's conversion, how he found that the roots of his liberalism were in fact orthodox creedal Christianity. Chesterton found that the classic principles of liberalism "were so intertwined in his thinking about Christianity that he himself seemed not to know where one began and the other ended" (Dale 1982, 103). See also Chaplin (1997).

21 Some items are easily identified as illiberal, though I find it curious that there is even a need to list such things as slavery, torture, murder, the sacrifice of children, and female circumcision as illiberal (Gutmann 1993, 189; 1996, 166).

22 To cite just one oft-repeated specific example, liberals differ on how to respond to the right of girls and women to wear a *hidjab* in French schools and universities (Tamir 1995b, 166–7; Gutmann 1996, 162–70). Tamir quite correctly points to the possibility of portraying the debate between French liberals and Muslims on this issue as a debate between French illiberalism and a legitimate Muslim way of life, or even as a debate between two illiberal cultures (1995b, 172n17)

23 Gutmann (1994, 23); Rawls (1993, xvii–xviii).

24 See also Callan (1995; 1997) and P. White (1994).

25 Arons (1986, 178). See also Hunter (1991, ch. 8) for a good description of irresolvable "culture wars" in American schools, including universities.

26 For these objections, see Gutmann (1993, 182–8); Cooling (1997, 79–81); Callan (1997, 132–3, 176), and Rorty (1995).

27 Feinberg (1995, 209–10). Callan too points to the problems inherent in "a nomadic curriculum" if that wrenches students abruptly away from all that gives meaning to their lives outside the school (1997, 132).

28 Gutmann herself admits this point in discussing the problem of multinationalism and education. A broadening of respect for others is best built on first learning to respect those close to you, especially in the early years of schooling (1996, 175). Developmental considerations can be used to argue for a lessening of the need for particularist schools as students mature (Callan 1997, 132–3, 176; Spinner-Halev 2000, 118). We must be careful, though, to avoid arbitrariness about when particularist schools are no longer necessary. Bronfenbrenner argues that the need for cultural continuity continues to some degree throughout every person's life (1980, 1).

29 The central thrust of my book *Teaching for Commitment* is to include religious nurture as an essential ingredient in a liberal education (Thiessen 1993; cf. Halstead 1992, 51).

30 Sweet, for example, quotes Joan Flood, who, though a Catholic, is chair of Essex (public) Board of Education, and who "adamantly maintains that the purpose of education isn't to make people 'distinct' " (1997, 49). Callan, in his defence of common schools within the parameters of keeping a balance between universalist and particularist values, calls on common schools to pay more attention to particularist education, and even suggests that this might be done by way of optional language programs or even specialized religious instruction (1995, 269–70, 253). But these suggestions remain vague, and in the main Callan simply skirts the issue of what is required for a genuinely particularist education. Indeed, he tends to belittle its importance – "separate schooling protects no vital interest of the students who attend or their parents" (266). This is hardly being "genuinely hospitable to the credal and cultural diversity" of a pluralistic society (253).

31 McLaughlin has attempted to stretch liberal non-partisanship with respect to differing ways of life by allowing common schools to reflect the cultural and religious context within which they are located (1995, 245–8). But this is surely a betrayal of the liberal principle of neutrality, which calls for a strict agnosticism with regard to differing concepts of the good life. McLaughlin fails to address the problems that arise given a truly multicultural context of a common school.

32 De Ruyter (1999) describes a Dutch experiment with multi-religious or interreligious schools which, in effect, house several separate schools, and in which students are initiated into a particular religious tradition and are also given a common civic education. De Ruyter's analysis of the problems of such schools would suggest that there is an inevitable slide towards the traditional agenda of common schools (cf. De Ruyter and Miedema 2000).

33 Gutmann's opposition to initiation also comes to the fore when she associates Afrocentrism with developing self-esteem by group identification, which she criticizes (1996, 159). She also lauds some Muslims who do not argue for their right to be religiously educated as Muslims, in public schools (170).

34 Feinberg is very frank in admitting this: "Ultimately what is involved in multicultural education is much the same as what is involved in the development of a democratic public. We are learning how to listen and how to discourse about our differences where the rules of discourse – both our own and others' rules – are part of what we are listening for" (1995, 209). This same emphasis also comes to the fore in Nord's attempt to resolve the problem of culture wars (1995). Nord's solution is to accommodate religion in the schools by studying religious controversy itself (235). While such a study might be helpful in overcoming our current culture wars, it belongs in the realm of civic education. It has nothing to do with particularist education, which in fact Nord specifically rejects (259, 374, 378–9).

35 See Gutmann (1996, 164, 165, 167; cf. 1987, 116). Susan Mendus refers to another writer who similarly argues that national identity must take priority over cultural loyalty, and who even dares to suggest that in the case of conflict between these two, political education should reinterpret cultural identity in the direction of common citizenship: "be selective or, if you like, biased" (Mendus 1995, 191). Callan, too, although he wants to accommodate plurality, focuses primarily on creating citizens (1997).

36 Liberal civic education, according to Macedo, will seek to "formulate and defend basic principles of justice by relying on public reasons that we can share while disagreeing about our ultimate commitments" (1995a, 478; cf. Rawls 1993, 191–4). At times Macedo seems to suggest that it would be acceptable for students to introduce religious interpretations into classroom discussions of civic education. He argues, for example, that his intent is not "to exclude religious speech from the public realm," or to "silence" religious people (1995a, 474–5; 1995b, 232). He cites, with approval, a judge's illustration of a student interpreting a reading assignment from a biblical perspective (1995a, 475). But reading assignments in literature are rather different from lessons in civics. Macedo does in fact ask children in the classroom "to forbear from asserting the truth of their own particular convictions, at least for political purposes" (1995a, 471). While he does not want to curtail the political speech of religious people, Macedo does want to curtail their *religious political speech*, at least in public places such as the classroom. So it would seem to be much more in keeping with Macedo's overall position that public schools "focus on shared public principles and leave the religious dimensions of the question aside" (1995a, 475; 1995b, 226).

37 "To demand 'neutral discourse' in public life, as some still do, should be recognized as a way of coercing people to speak publicly in someone else's language and thus never to be true to their own" (Guinness 1993, 243).

38 See Carter (1993, 8, 26–33, 56, 63, 230). Macedo repeatedly argues that Carter's complaint is unfair because liberalism in no way excludes religious citizens from the public realm (1995a, 475; 1995b, 227). But Macedo fails to acknowledge the real impact of requiring that religious citizens not be allowed to bring their religious reasons concerning political arrangements into the public arena. It is a denial of their full personhood (cf. Sandel 1996, 322). They are not allowed to bring their religious self into public arena. This approach does create a split self.

39 This statement comes from a review of a recent book edited by Power and Lapsley (1993). The reviewer suggests this as the unifying theme of all the essays of the book, thus leading also to a critique of the common school (review by A.J.S. in *Harvard Educational Review* 64(1) (1994):103–6).

40 Some important discussions on deliberative democracy include Fishkin (1992), Gutmann (1994), and Gutmann and Thompson (1996). See also a good summary of the notion of deliberative democracy in Callan (2000, 64).

41 See 280n35 for some quotations from MacIntyre and Mill.

42 Lorberbaum has made this point with regard to the teaching of tolerance, and illustrates how this can be done from within the context of the Jewish tradition (1995). Gutmann, in fact, concedes this point in her treatment of the problems of nationalism (1996, 175). Callan too admits that mutuality, recognition of fallibility, and recognition of the other can all begin in the home (1997, 181).

43 Callan's ideal of inclusive deliberation is also too demanding. Clearly Callan is worried about a religious school in which students might be taught that homosexuality is sinful (2000, 64). He requires that this view must itself be open to discussion and deliberation and possible revision. This surely violates the Rawlsian principle (which Callan accepts) that some disagreements between reasonable people about what is good and right are simply irreconcilable (Callan 1995, 261–2). The aim of deliberation is not to gain agreement about the differing "convictions" about what is good and right, or to assess the reasonableness of the convictions themselves (1995, 264). The aim is merely to find a sufficient degree of consensus concerning how to live together in peace and harmony despite our differing convictions. We are only interested in coming to a pragmatic consensus. As Rorty has reminded us, we are not held together primarily by shared beliefs, but by shared hopes (of getting along) and trust (again, a very practical matter) (Rorty 1991, 207, 210; 1989, 44).

44 Pring talks of a "non-negotiable curriculum content" (1992, 28). Callan supports "a limited tolerance of ways of life that repudiate the liberal virtues and the educational policies that go with them" (1995, 269). But he is rather vague as to how limited this tolerance is. In his later work he boldly says that liberal democratic education will not leave everything as it is (1997, 13).

45 Callan (1995, 257). Holmes struggles with this problem in terms of common schools accepting "low-doctrine" or "high-doctrine," and in the end settles for the latter option in order to satisfy the many parents who want more values taught in the schools (1992, 106–10; 145). In fact, Holmes's "high-doctrine" is very minimalist and still will not satisfy religious parents.

46 See Taylor (1994, 73). Indeed, in their pronouncements concerning allegedly universal values, liberals often sound very much like the religious fundamentalists they so roundly condemn. This seeming arrogance surfaces particularly when liberals advocate the imposition of their liberal values onto illiberal societies. Taylor describes liberalism as "a fighting creed" (1994, 62). Although Macedo defends Rawls's political liberalism as the best way of accommodating illiberal societies as far as is possible and of avoiding "declarations of holy war" on them, he is nonetheless concerned to portray this liberalism as "tough-minded," as having "sufficient spine" to stand up for liberal values, and in the end he reminds fundamentalists and

others "that they must pay a price for living in a free pluralistic society" (Macedo 1995a, 470, 496; cf. 1995b, 227; Callan 2000, 55). Indeed, as is noted by Spinner-Halev, "While liberals often say that religious freedom is a cardinal virtue of liberalism, it is hard to see that in much of today's liberalism (2000, 201)."

47 "[T]he public schools in the United States took over one of the basic responsibilities that traditionally was always assumed by an established church. In this sense the public school system of the United States *is* its established church" (Mead, quoted in McCarthy et al. 1982, 41; cf. Rose, 1988, 29; Illich, in Arons 1986, 49; Glenn 1988, 14, 85).

48 Gutmann (1993, 187). See also Halstead (1995, 265) on examples of Muslims in England moving towards greater group solidarity because of oppression.

49 There is abundant empirical evidence to suggest that a relinquishing of power and privilege is indeed very effective in overcoming violence, in disarming the enemy, and in bringing about peace. Conrad Brunk, for example, challenges the very prevalent assumption that one must always "negotiate from strength." "No theory," he argues, "has been more thoroughly discredited by empirical studies of conflict management than this one" (1987, 524). I believe the very same principles and approach would work for overcoming the "enemy" of illiberal societies. Liberal ideals cannot be imposed from without. There is no room for what has been rightly called a "militant liberalism" (Leicester 1992, 33). On pacifism, see the writings of Gene Sharp, the foremost researcher into pacifist methods (1973), and Sider and Taylor (1982). See also Lackey for a parallel argument on unilateral disarmament as a way of achieving peace (1985). Lackey defends his proposal on utilitarian grounds and also via a games theory analysis. For a defence of pacificism on theological grounds, see Wink (1992). Interestingly, Wink suggests that, ideally, "democracy is nonviolence institutionalized" (171).

50 Guinness provides a chilling example of a coercive mentality from a leading Christian reconstructionist, Garry North: "So let us be blunt about it: we must use the doctrine of religious liberty to gain independence for Christian schools until we train up a generation of people who know that there is no religious liberty, no neutral law, no neutral education, and no neutral civil government. Then they will get busy in constructing a Bible-based social, political, and religious order which finally denies the religious liberties of the enemies of God" (quoted in Guinness 1993, 261).

51 Attitudes of arrogance and the coercive tactics that follow them tend to lead to resentment and hardening of attitudes on the part of minority groups (Singh 1995, 17). Unity simply cannot be built on enforced moral conformity (McCarthy et al. 1982, 125). Nothing fragments a society more than public coercion of private beliefs (Arons 1986, 194). The suppression of cultural and religious identities only leads to civil strife (Galston 1995, 207).

52 Wagner (1995, 92–9; cf. Glenn 1989, 209). More recently (1995/6), the
   Alberta Teachers' Association again launched a well-funded and carefully
   orchestrated propaganda campaign under the banner "Public Education
   Works" to counter the possibility of the government becoming sympathetic
   with increasing funding for independent religious schools. Holmes identifies the legally enforced unionization of Canadian teachers as leading to
   enormous rigidity and one of the greatest barriers to reform in schools
   (1998, 186, cf. 194, 241). Hirsch similarly complains about institutional
   and intellectual monopoly in American education, which leads to resistance to criticism and change (1996, 63–8). Chubb and Moe (1990) offer
   a scathing indictment of the bureaucratic and political systems surrounding public schooling in America, particularly such organized interests as
   teachers' unions, which stand as a major obstacle to reform in education.
53 Wringe argues that some traditional groups are prepared to shed blood
   over such propositions as "morality and religious belief are not matters of
   autonomous judgement," or "error has no rights and may be summarily
   punished" (1995, 285–6). According to Wringe, we need to counteract traditional cultural identities which cause people to see their fellow citizens
   "as enemies and rivals for power and resources" (288).
54 If community loyalty is placed above justice, Wringe argues, then we are not
   a society at all, "but a collection of separate, mutually hostile societies, jock-
   eying for position, waiting for the moment when we shall have the advantage and may legislate our rivals into subjection or be rid of them
   altogether" (1995, 288). The very same thing can be said about the individualism inherent in liberalism. There are illiberal individuals! Perhaps liberals like Wringe need to read Hobbes once more so they can appreciate that
   the danger of seeing fellow citizens as "enemies and rivals for power and resources" also applies to the individualism that they see as so essential to liberal theory (288).
55 Peshkin is very frank in stating his biases: "total institutions and absolute
   Truth are nonetheless anathema to me" (1986, 276). He goes on to describe the doctrinal yardstick of Bethany Baptist Academy as "poised like a
   guillotine to lop off dissenting heads, mine and others" (290). Canadian
   philosopher Tasos Kazepides resorts to similar inflammatory language,
   which I have analysed in my earlier work (Thiessen 1993, 228). Gilles
   (1999) provides a careful analysis of rhetoric and bias in Dwyer's critique
   of religious schools (1998).
56 Mark Holmes, struggling with the problems of educational policy for pluralist democracies, begins with the bold suggestion that it is impossible to
   return to the past: "the genie is truly out of the bottle" (1992, 6). Ravitch
   and Viteritti, in their analysis of "new schools for a new century," similarly
   suggest that "the signs of change are apparent," and these signs point to "a
   fundamental restructuring of public education" (1997, 12).

Bibliography

Abraham, William J. 1981. *The Divine Inspiration of Holy Scripture*. Oxford: Oxford University Press.

Ackerman, Bruce. 1980. *Social Justice in the Liberal State*. New Haven: Yale University Press.

Adams, Robert Merrihew. 1986. "The Problem of Total Devotion." In *Rationality, Religious Belief and Moral Commitment: New Essays in the Philosophy of Religion*, ed. Robert Audi and William J. Wainwright, 169–94. Ithaca and London: Cornell University Press.

Aiken, W., and H. La Follette, eds. 1980. *Whose Child? Children's Rights, Parental Authority and State Power*. New York: Littlefield Adams.

Alberta Education. 1985. *An Audit of Selected Private School Programs*. Edmonton: Alberta Education.

Alberta Private Schools Funding Task Force. 1997. *Funding Private Schools in Alberta*. Edmonton: Government of Alberta.

– 1998. *Setting a New Framework: Report and Recommendations of the Private Schools Funding Task Force*. Edmonton: Government of Alberta.

Allen, Anita L., and Milton C. Regan Jr, eds, 1998. *Debating Democracy's Discontent: Essays on American Politics, Law & Public Philosophy*. Oxford New York: Oxford University Press.

Allen, R.T. 1982. "Rational Autonomy: The Destruction of Freedom." *Journal of Philosophy of Education* 16(2): 199–207.

– 1993. "Christian Thinking about Education." *Spectrum* 25(1): 17–24.

Allport, Gordon. 1954. *The Nature of Prejudice*. Reading, Mass.: Addison-Wesley.

American Library Association. 1989. *Intellectual Freedom Manual*. 3rd ed. Chicago and London: American Library Association.

Anderson, Walter Truett. 1990. *Reality Isn't What It Used to Be: Theatrical Politics, Ready-to-Wear Religion, Global Myths, Primitive Chic, and Other Wonders of the Postmodern World*. San Francisco: Harper and Row.

Apple, Michael W. 1990. *Ideology and Curriculum*. 2nd ed. New York: Routledge.

– 1993. *Official Knowledge: Democratic Education in a Conservative Age*. New York: Routledge.

– 1996. *Cultural Politics and Education*. New York: Teachers College Press.

Archard, David. 1993. *Children: Rights and Childhood*. London and New York: Routledge.

Arons, Stephen. 1986. *Compelling Belief: The Culture of American Schooling*. Amherst: University of Massachusetts Press.

Aronson, Elliot, Timothy D. Wilson, and Robin M. Akert, eds. 1994. *Social Psychology: The Heart and the Mind*. New York: HarperCollins College Publishers.

Asheim, Lester. 1953. "Not Censorship but Selection." *Wilson Library Bulletin* 28: 63–7.

– 1954. "The Librarian's Responsibility: Not Censorship but Selection." In *Freedom of Book Selection*, ed. Frederic Mosher, 90–9. Chicago: American Library Association.

– 1983. "Selection and Censorship: A Reappraisal." *Wilson Library Bulletin* 58: 180–4.

Aspin, D.N. 1983. "Church Schools, Religious Education and the Multi-ethnic Community." *Journal of Philosophy of Education* 17(2): 229–39. Reprinted in Francis and Lankshear (1993, 84–101).

Astley, Jeff. 1994. *The Philosophy of Christian Religious Education*. Birmingham, Ala.: Religious Education Press.

Astley, Jeff, and David Day, eds. 1992. *The Contours of Christian Education*. Great Wakering, Essex: McCrimmons.

Astley, Jeff, and Leslie J. Francis, eds. 1994. *Critical Perspectives on Christian Education: A Reader on the Aims, Principles and Philosophy of Christian Education*. Leominster: Gracewing.

Ayubi, Nazih. 1991. *Political Islam: Religion and Politics in the Arab World*. London and New York: Routledge.

Baer, Richard A., Jr. 1987. "American Public Education and the Myth of Value Neutrality." In *Democracy and the Renewal of Public Education*, ed. Richard John Neuhaus, 1–24. Grand Rapids, Mich.: Eerdmans.

Baier, Annette. 1980. "Secular Faith." *Canadian Journal of Philosophy* 10: 131–48.

Bailey, C. 1984. *Beyond the Present and the Particular: A Theory of Liberal Education*. London: Routledge and Kegan Paul.

Ball, Wendy, and Barry Troyna. 1987. "Resistance, Rights and Rituals: Denominational Schools and Multicultural Education." *Journal of Education Policy* 2(1): 15–25. Reprinted in Francis and Lankshear (1993, 397–409).

Balmer, Randall. 1989. *Mine Eyes Have Seen the Glory: A Journey into the Evangelical Subculture in America.* New York and Oxford: Oxford University Press.

Banks, J.A. 1985. "Ethnic Revitalization Movements and Education." *Educational Review* 37(2): 131–9.

Barclay, Oliver R. 1984. *Developing a Christian Mind.* Leicester: Inter-Varsity Press.

Barman, Jean. 1991. "Deprivatizing Private Education: The British Columbia Experience." *Canadian Journal of Education* 16(1): 12–31.

Barnes, L. Philip. 1997. "Religion, Religionism and Religious Education: Fostering Tolerance and Truth in Schools." *Journal of Education and Christian Belief* 1(1): 7–23.

Barron, Bruce. 1987. *The Health and Wealth Gospel.* Downers Grove, Ill.: Inter-Varsity Press.

Barrow, Robin. 1991. "Censorship and Schooling." In *Freedom and Indoctrination in Education: International Perspectives*, ed. Ben Spiecker and Roger Straughan, 94–102. London: Cassell Educational.

Barrow, Robin, and Ronald Woods. 1988. *An Introduction to Philosophy of Education.* 3rd ed. London and New York: Routledge.

Bebbington, D.W. 1989. *Evangelicalism in Modern Britain: A History from the 1730s to the 1980s.* London: Unwin Hyman.

Bell, Robert. 1991. *The Right to Be Different: Becoming a Voluntary School.* Bristol: Regius Press.

Bellah, Robert, Richard Madsen, William M. Sullivan, Ann Swidler, and Steven Tipton. 1985. *Habits of the Heart: Individualism and Commitment in American Life.* Berkeley: University of California Press.

Bendell, Jean. 1994. "Parents Who Choose to Educate Their Children at Home." In *Parental Choice and Education: Principles, Policy and Practice*, ed. J. Mark Halstead, 151–63. London: Kogan Page.

Bergen, J. 1989. "Canada: Private Schools." In *Private Schools in Ten Countries: Policy and Practice*, ed. Geoffrey Walford, 85–104. London and New York: Routledge.

Berger, Brigitte and Peter. 1984. *The War over the Family: Capturing the Middle Ground.* Harmondsworth: Penguin Books.

Berger, Peter L. 1969. *The Sacred Canopy: Elements of a Sociological Theory of Religion*, Garden City, NJ: Anchor.

– 1974. *Pyramids of Sacrifice: Political Ethics and Social Change.* New York: Penguin Books.

– 1977. *Facing Up to Modernity: Excursions in Society, Politics and Religion.* New York: Penguin Books.

Berger, Peter L., and Richard John Neuhaus. 1977. *To Empower People: The Role of Mediating Structures in Public Policy.* Washington, DC: American Enterprise Institute.

Berliner, David C. 1997. "Educational Psychology Meets the Christian Right: Differing Views of Children, Schooling, Teaching, and Learning."*Teachers College Record* 98(3): 381–415.

Berliner, David C., and B.J. Biddle. 1995. *The Manufactured Crisis*. Reading, Mass.: Addison-Wesley.

Berry, John. 1978. "Censorship and Ideology." *Library Journal* 103:15.

– 1982. "From Theory to Practice." *Library Journal* 107:9.

Bibby, Reginald W. 1990. *Mosaic Madness: The Poverty and Potential of Life in Canda*. Toronto: Stoddart.

Bigelow, John, et al. 1988. "Parental Autonomy." *Journal of Applied Philosophy* 5 (2):183–96.

Biggs, Donald, and Gerald Porter. 1994. "Parental Choice in the USA." In *Parental Choice and Education: Principles, Policy and Practice*, ed. J. Mark Halstead, 36–50. London: Kogan Page.

Blacker, David. 1998. "Fanaticism and Schooling in the Democrate State." *American Journal of Education* 106(2):241–72.

Blair, Andrew G. 1986. *The Policy and Practice of Religious Education in Publicly-Funded Elementary and Secondary Schools in Canada and Elsewhere: A Search of the Literature*. Toronto: Queen's Printer for Ontario.

Bloom, Allan. 1987. *The Closing of the American Mind*. New York: Simon and Schuster.

Bork, Robert H. 1997. *Slouching towards Gomorrah: Modern Liberalism and American Decline*. New York: HarperCollins.

Bowers, C.A. 1987. *Elements of a Post-Liberal Theory of Education*. New York and London: Teachers College Press.

Brenton, H., and D. Hare. 1985. *Pravda: A Fleet Street Comedy*. London and New York: Methuen.

Bridges, D. 1984. "Non-Paternalistic Arguments in Support of Parents' Rights." *Journal of Philosophy of Education* 18(1):55–61.

Bronfenbrenner, Urie. 1979. *The Ecology of Human Development: Experiments by Nature and Design*. Cambridge, Mass.: Harvard University Press.

– 1980. "On Making Human Beings Human." *Character: A Periodical about the Public and Private Policies Shaping American Youth* 2(2):1–7.

Brown, Phillip. 1994. "Education and the Ideology of Parentocracy." In *Parental Choice and Education: Principles, Policy and Practice*, ed. J. Mark Halstead, 51–67. London: Kogan Page.

Brummer, Vincent. 1969. "The Function of Religion in Philosophy." *Themelious* 6(3/4): 1–11.

Brunk, Conrad. 1987. "Realism, Deterrence, and the Nuclear Arms Race." In *Contemporary Moral Issues*, 2nd ed., ed. Wesley Cragg, 511–28. Toronto: McGraw-Hill Ryerson.

Bryan, Robert. 1984. *History, Pseudo-History, Anti-History: How Public School Textbooks Treat Religion*. Washington, DC: Learn. Education Foundation.

Bryk, Anthony, Valerie E. Lee, and Peter B. Holland. 1993. *Catholic Schools and the Common Good.* Cambridge, Mass.: Harvard University Press.

Burn, John, and Colin Hart. 1988. *The Crisis in Religious Education.* London: Educational Research Trust.

Burtchaell, James Tunstead. 1998. *The Dying of the Light: The Disengagement of Colleges and Universities from Their Christian Churches.* Grand Rapids, Mich.: Eerdmans.

Callan, Eamonn. 1985. "McLaughlin on Parental Rights." *Journal of Philosophy of Education* 19(1):111–18.

– 1988. *Autonomy and Schooling.* Kingston and Montreal: McGill-Queen's University Press.

– 1992. "Tradition and Integrity in Moral Education." *American Journal of Education* 101:1–28.

– 1995. "Common Schools for Common Education." *Canadian Journal of Education* 20(3): 251–71.

– 1997. *Creating Citizens: Political Education and Liberal Citizenship.* Oxford: Clarendon Press.

– 2000. "Discrimination and Religious Schooling." In *Citizenship in Diverse Societies,* ed. Will Kymlicka and Wayne Norman, 45–67. New York: Oxford University Press.

Canadian Library Association. 1985. "Statement on Intellectual Freedom." Canadian Library Association.

Canavan, Francis. 1984. *Freedom of Expression: Purpose as Limit.* Durham, NC: Carolina Academic Press.

Carper, James C. 1984. "The Christian Day School." In *Religious Schooling in America,* ed. J.C. Carper and T.C. Hunt, 110–29. Birmingham, Ala: Religious Education Press.

Carr, Wilfred. 1995. "Education and Democracy: Confronting the Postmodernist Challenge." *Journal of Philosophy of Education* 29(1):75–91.

Carter, Stephen L. 1993. *Culture of Disbelief: How American Law and Politics Trivialize Religious Devotion.* New York: Doubleday.

Cassity, Michael D., et al. 1990. *Living with Our Deepest Differences: Religious Liberty in a Pluralistic Society.* Fairfax, Va.: First Liberty Institute and Learning Connections Publishers.

Caston, G. 1989. "Academic Freedom: The Third World Context." *Oxford Review of Education* 15(3):305–38.

Catholic Committee. 1989. *The Catholic School: Challenge of Its Educational Project.* Government of Quebec: Ministry of Education.

Chaplin, Jonathan. 1997. "Christians and the Public Realm." In *Agenda for Educational Change,* ed. John Shortt and Trevor Cooling, 57–75. Leicester: Apollos.

Chomsky, Noam, 1988a. *Manufacturing Consent: The Political Economy of the Mass Media.* New York: Pantheon Books.

– 1988b. *Necessary Illusions: Thought Control in Democratic Societies.* CBC Enterprises.

– 1992. *Chronicles of Dissent.* Vancouver: New Star Books.

Chubb, J., and T. Moe. 1990. *Politics, Markets and America's Schools.* Washington, DC: Brookings Institution.

Cibulka, J.G., and W.L. Boyd, eds. 1989. *Private Schools and Public Policy: International Perspectives.* Falmer Press.

Clarke, Robert A., and S.D. Gaede. 1987. "Knowing Together: Reflections on a Holistic Sociology of Knowledge."In *The Reality of Christian Learning: Strategies for Faith -Discipline Integration,* ed. Harold Heie and David L. Wolfe, 55–86. Grand Rapids, Mich.: Christian University Press.

Clouser, Roy A. 1991. *The Myth of Religious Neutrality: An Essay on the Hidden Role of Religious Belief in Theories.* Notre Dame, Ind.: University of Notre Dame Press.

Cohen, Brenda. 1981. *Education and the Individual,* London: George Allen and Unwin.

Coleman, J.S., and T. Hoffer. 1987. *Public and Private High Schools: The Impact of Communities.* New York: Basic Books.

Committee on Tolerance and Understanding. 1984. *Final Report of the Committee on Tolerance and Understanding.* Edmonton: Government of Alberta, Department of Education.

Cookson, Peter W., Jr. 1989. "United States of America: Contours of Continuity and Controversy in Private Schools." In *Private Schools in Ten Countries: Policy and Practice,* ed. Geoffrey Walford, 57–84. London: Routledge.

Cooling, Trevor. 1994. *A Christian Vision for State Education: Reflections on Theology and Education.* London: SPCK.

– 1997. "In Defense of the Common School." In *Agenda for Educational Change,* ed. John Shortt and Trevor Cooling, 76–86. Leicester: Apollos.

Coons, John E., and Stephen A. Sugarman. 1978. *Education by Choice: The Case for Family Control.* Berkeley: University of California Press.

Cooper, David E. 1982. "Equality and Envy." *Journal of Philosophy of Education* 16(1):35–47.

Cors, Paul B. 1989. "Academic Libraries and Intellectual Freedom." In *Intellectual Freedom Manual,* 3rd ed. American Library Association, 130–3. Chicago and London: American Library Association.

Coulson, Andrew J. 1999. *Market Education: The Unknown History.* New Brunswick (USA) and London: Transaction Publishers.

Coward, Harold. 1985. *Pluralism: Challenge to World Religions.* Maryknoll, NY: Orbis Books.

Cox, Caroline, et al. 1986. *Whose Schools? A Radical Manifesto.* London: Hillgate Group.

Crittenden, Brian. 1988. *Parents, the State and the Right to Educate.* Melbourne University Press.

Cumper, Peter. 1994. "Racism, Parental Choice and the Law." In *Parental Choice and Education: Principles, Policy and Practice*, ed. J. Mark Halstead, 164–79. London: Kogan Page.

Curran, Charles. E. 1990. *Catholic Higher Education, Theology, and Academic Freedom*. Notre Dame and London: University of Notre Dame Press.

Curtis, Edward M. 1994. "Some Biblical Contributions to a Philosophy of Education." *Faculty Dialogue* 21:91–110.

Dale, A.S. 1982. *The Outline of Sanity: A Life of G.K. Chesterton*. Grand Rapids, Mich.: Eerdmans.

Davis, Donald G. 1986. "Intellectual Freedom and Evangelical Faith." *Christian Librarian* 29(1/2): 3–6.

Davis, Marie. 1992. "Susan Musgrave: An Interview." *Canadian Children's Literature* no. 68:114–20.

Deakin, Ruth. 1989. *New Christian Schools: The Case for Public Funding*. Bristol: Regius Press.

Dearden, R.F. 1984. *Theory and Practice in Education*. London: Routledge and Kegan Paul.

Dekmejian, R. Hrair. 1985. *Islamic Revolution: Fundamentalism in the Arab World*. New York: Syracuse University Press.

De Moor, Ary. 1994. "Tolerance in Religious Education: Three Dissenting Worldviews in Canadian Education." M.Ed. thesis. Department of Educational Foundations, University of Alberta.

De Ruyter, Doret J. 1999. "Christian Schools in a Pluralistic Society?" *Interchange* 30(2):213–33.

De Ruyter, Doret J., and Siebren Miedema. 2000. "Denominational Schools in the Netherlands." In *Spiritual and Religious Education*, ed. Mal Leicester, Celia Modgil, and Sohan Modgil, 133–41. London and New York: Falmer Press.

Department for Education. 1992. *Choice and Diversity – A New Framework for Schools*. London: HMSO.

Dewey, John. 1966. *Democracy and Education*. New York: Free Press.

Diekema, Anthony J. 2000. *Academic Freedom and Christian Scholarship*. Grand Rapids, Mich.: Eerdmans.

Doerr, Edd., and Albert J. Menendez. 1991. *Church Schools and Public Money: The Politics of Parochiaid*. New York: Prometheus Books.

Douglas, Mary. 1986. *How Institutions Think*. Syracuse: Syracuse University Press.

D'Souza, Dinesh. 1991. *Illiberal Education: The Politics of Race and Sex on Campus*. New York: Free Press.

Dunlop, Francis. 1976. "Indoctrination as Morally Undesirable Teaching." *Education for Teaching* 100:39–42.

Dunn, Seamus. 1986. "The Role of Education in the Northern Ireland Conflict." *Oxford Review of Education* 12(3):233–42.

Dwyer, James G. 1998. *Religious Schools v. Children's Rights*. Ithaca: Cornell University Press.

Ellul, Jacques. 1969. *Propaganda: The Formation of Men's Attitudes*, trans. Konrad Kellen and Jean Lerner. New York: Knopf.

Emberley, Peter C. 1996. *Zero Tolerance: Hot Button Politics in Canada's Universities.* Toronto: Penguin Books.

Emberley, Peter C., and W.R. Newell. 1994. *Bankrupt Education: The Decline of Liberal Education in Canada.* Toronto: University of Toronto Press.

Erickson, Donald A., Lloyd MacDonald, and Michael E. Manley-Casimir. 1979. *Characteristics and Relationships in Public and Independent Schools: The Consequences of Funding Independent Schools – Interim Report.* Vancouver: Educational Research Institute of British Columbia.

Ericson, Edward E., Jr. 1991. "Academic Freedom: Keeping It Complex – a Response to Samuel Logan."*Christian Scholars Review* 21(2):182–190.

Ernest, Paul. 1991. *The Philosophy of Mathematics Education.* London: Falmer Press.

Faw, Harold, and Harro Van Brummelen. 1993. "Staying on Course or Straying off Course? Final Examinations and the Mission of a Christian College." In *A Vision with a Task: Christian Schooling for Responsible Discipleship*, ed. D. John Lee and Gloria Goris Stronks, 157–77. Grand Rapids, Mich.: Baker Book House.

Feinberg, Walter. 1995. "Liberalism and the Aims of Multicultural Education." *Journal of Philosophy of Education* 29(2):203–16.

Fernhout, Harry. 1990. "Dragon or Partner? Public Funding for Religiously Based Schools." *Ethics in Education* 8(4):6–8.

Finn, Chester E., Jr. 1991. *We Must Take Charge: Our Schools and Our Future.* New York: Free Press.

– 1997. "Reforming Education: A Whole New World." *First Things* 73:33–8.

Fishkin, James. 1992. *The Dialogue of Justice: Toward a Self-Reflective Society.* New Haven: Yale University Press.

Flanagan, Leo N. 1975. "Defending the Indefensible: The Limits of Intellectual Freedom." *Library Journal* 100: 1887–91.

Flew, Antony. 1987. *Power to Parents: Reversing Educational Decline.* London: Sherwood Press.

Fraiberg, Selma. 1977. *Every Child's Birthright: In Defense of Mothering.* New York: Basic Books.

Francis, Leslie, and David W. Lankshear, eds. 1993. *Christian Perspectives on Church Schools: A Reader.* Leominster: Gracewing.

Francis, Leslie, and Adrian Thatcher, eds. 1990. *Christian Perspectives for Education: A Reader in the Theology of Education.* Leominster: Gracewing.

Friedman, Milton, and Rose Friedman. 1981. *Free to Choose.* New York: Avon Books.

Gaede, S.D. 1993. *When Tolerance Is No Virtue: Political Correctness, Multiculturalism and the Future of Truth and Justice.* Downers Grove, Ill.: InterVarsity Press.

329   Bibliography

Gairdner, William, ed. 1998. *After Liberalism: Essays in Search of Freedom, Virtue and Order.* Don Mills, Ont.: Stoddart.

Gallup, G.H., and T.K. Jones. 1992. *The Saints among Us.* Ridgefield, Conn.: Morehouse Publishers.

Galston, William A. 1991. *Liberal Purposes: Goods, Virtues and Diversity in the Liberal State.* New York: Cambridge University Press.

– 1995. "Two Concepts of Liberalism." *Ethics* 105(3):516–34.

Gangel, Kenneth. 1988. "Christian School Education." In *Schooling Choices: An Examination of Private, Public, and Home Education,* ed. H. Wayne House, 89–151. Portland, Oreg.: Multnomah Press.

Gardner, Peter. 1988. "Religious Upbringing and the Liberal Ideal of Religious Autonomy."*Journal of Philosophy of Education* 22 (1):89–105.

– 1989. "Neutrality in Education." In *Liberal Neutrality,* ed. R. E. Goodin and A. Reeve, 106–29. London and New York: Routledge.

– 1991. "Personal Autonomy and Religious Upbringing: The 'Problem.'" *Journal of Philosophy of Education* 25 (1):69–81.

Garry, Anne, and Marilyn Pearsall. 1989. *Women, Knowledge and Reality.* Boston: Unwin Hyman.

Geiger, Roger L. 1986. *Private Sectors in Higher Education: Structure, Function and Change in Eight Countries.* Ann Arbor, Mich.: University of Michigan Press.

Gergen, Kenneth J. 1991. *The Saturated Self: Dilemmas of Identity in Contemporary Life.* New York: Basic Books.

Gilles, Stephen G. 1996. "On Educating Children: A Parentalist Manifesto." *University of Chicago Law Review* 63(3):937–1034.

– 1997. "Liberal Parentalism and Children's Educational Rights." *Capital University Law Review* 26(1):9–44.

– 1999. "Hey, Christians, Leave Your Kids Alone!" Review of James Dwyer, *Religious Schools v. Children's Rights* (Cornell University Press, 1998). *Constitutional Commentary* 16(1):149–211.

Gleason, Philip. 1995. *Contending with Modernity: Catholic Higher Education in Twentieth Century America.* New York: Oxford University Press.

Glenn, Charles Leslie. 1988. *The Myth of the Common School.* Amherst: University of Massachusetts Press.

– 1989. *Choice of Schools in Six Nations.* Washington, DC: US Department of Education.

– 1995. *Educational Freedom in Eastern Europe.* Washington, DC: Cato Institute.

Gooch, P.W. 1987. *Partial Knowledge: Philosophical Studies in Paul.* Notre Dame, Ind.: University of Notre Dame Press.

Goodenow, Ron K. 1988. "Schooling, Identity and Denominationalism: The American Experience." In *Christianity and Educational Provision in International Perspective,* ed. Witold Tulasiewicz and Colin Brock, 192–216. London and New York: Routledge.

Goodin, R.E., and A. Reeve, eds. 1989. *Liberal Neutrality.* London and New York: Routledge.

Goudzwaard, Bob, and Harry de Lange. 1994. *Beyond Poverty and Affluence: Towards a Canadian Economy of Care.* Toronto: University of Toronto Press.

Gray, John. 1995. *Liberalism.* 2nd ed. Minneapolis: University of Minnesota Press.

Greeley, A.M., and P.H. Rossi. 1966. *The Education of Catholic Americans.* Chicago: Aldine Press.

Greene, Jay P. 1998. "Civic Values in Public and Private Schools." In *Lessons from School Choice,* ed. Paul C. Peterson and Bryan C. Hassel, 83–106. Washington, DC: Brookings Institution Press.

Greer, J.E. 1985. "Viewing 'the Other Side' in Northern Ireland: Openness and Attitudes to Religion among Catholic and Protestant Adolescents." *Journal for the Scientific Study of Religion* 24(3):275–92. Reprinted in Francis and Lankshear (1993, 444–63).

Greer, J.E., and E.P. McElhinney. 1984. "The Project on 'Religion in Ireland': an Experiment in Reconstruction." *Lumen Vitae* 39(3):331–42.

– 1985. *Irish Christianity: A Guide for Teachers.* Goldenbridge, Dublin: Gill and Macmillan.

Groffier, Ethel, and Michel Paradis, eds. 1991. *The Notion of Tolerance and Human Rights: Essays in Honour of Raymond Klibansky.* Ottawa: Carleton University Press.

Guinness, Os. 1993. *The American Hour: A Time of Reckoning and the Once and Future Role of Faith.* New York: Free Press.

Gutmann, Amy. 1985. "Communitarian Critics of Liberalism." *Philosophy and Public Affairs* 14(3):308–22.

– 1987. *Democratic Education.* Princeton: Princeton University Press.

– 1993. "The Challenge of Multiculturalism." *Philosophy and Public Affairs.* 22(3):171–206.

– ed. 1994. *Multiculturalism: Examining the Politics of Recognition.* Princeton: Princeton University Press.

– 1995. "Civic Education and Social Diversity." *Ethics: An International Journal of Social, Political and Legal Philosophy* 105(3):557–79.

– 1996. "Challenges of Multiculturalism in Democratic Education." In *Public Education in a Multi-cultural Society: Policy, Theory, Critique,* ed. Robert K. Fullinwider, 156–79. New York: Cambridge University Press.

Gutmann, Amy, and Dennis Thompson. 1996. *Democracy and Disagreement.* Cambridge, Mass.: Belknap Press of Harvard University Press.

Halstead, J.M. 1986. *The Case for Muslim Voluntary-Aided Schools: Some Philosophical Reflections.* Cambridge: Islamic Academy.

– 1992. "Ethical Dimensions of Controversial Events in Multicultural Education." In *Ethics, Ethnicity and Education,* ed. Mal Leicester and Monica Taylor, 39–56. London: Kogan Page.

– ed. 1994. *Parental Choice and Education: Principles, Policy and Practice.* London: Kogan Page.

– 1995. "Voluntary Apartheid? Problems of Schooling for Religious and Other Minorities in Democratic Societies." *Journal of Philosophy of Education* 29(2):257–72.

– 1996. "Liberalism, Multiculturalism and Toleration." *Journal of Philosophy of Education* 30(2):307–13.

Hamilton, Neil W. 1995. *Zealotry and Academic Freedom: A Legal and Historical Perspective.* New Brunswick (USA) and London: Transaction Publishers.

Hanus, Jerome J., and Peter W. Cookson, Jr. 1996. *Choosing Schools: Vouchers and American Education.* Lanham, Md: American University Press.

Hardy, Lee. 1995. "Between Inculcation and Inquiry: The Virtue of Tolerance in the Liberal Arts Tradition." Presented at the RUNA (Reformed University in North America) Conference, Grand Rapids, Michigan, 24–25 March, 1995. Pamphlet, 5–26.

Hare, William. 1979. *Open-Mindedness and Education.* Kingston and Montreal: McGill-Queen's University Press.

– 1985. *In Defence of Open-Mindedness.* Kingston and Montreal: McGill-Queen's University Press.

Hart, Hendrik, Johan van der Hoeven, and Nicholas Wolterstorff, eds. 1983. *Rationality in the Calvinian Tradition.* Lanham, Md.: University Press of America.

Hart, Trevor. 1995. *Faith Thinking: The Dynamics of Christian Theology.* London: SPCK.

Hauerwas, S. 1983. *The Peaceable Kingdom: A Primer in Christian Ethics.* Notre Dame, Ind.: University of Notre Dame Press.

Haworth, Lawrence. 1986. *Autonomy: An Essay in Philosophical Psychology and Ethics.* Notre Dame, Ind.: University of Notre Dame Press.

Heie, Harold, and David L. Wolfe, eds. 1987. *The Reality of Christian Learning: Strategies for Faith-Discipline Integration.* Grand Rapids, Mich.: Christian University Press.

Helm, Paul. 1987. *Objective Knowledge: A Christian Perspective.* Leicester: Inter-Varsity Press.

Heyd, David, ed. 1996. *Toleration: An Elusive Virtue.* Princeton: Princeton University Press.

Hill, Brian V. 1982. *Faith at the Blackboard.* Grand Rapids, Mich.: Eerdmans.

– 1990. "Is It Time We Deschooled Christianity?" In *Christian Perspectives for Education: A Reader in the Theology of Education,* ed. Leslie Francis and Adrian Thatcher, 119–33. Leominster: Fowler Wright Books.

Hirsch, E.D., Jr. 1996. *The Schools We Need and Why We Don't Have Them.* New York: Doubleday.

Hirst, Paul H. 1967. "Public and Private Values and Religious Educational Content." In *Religion and Public Education,* ed. Theodore R. Sizer, 329–39. Boston: Houghton Mifflin Co.

- 1969. "Philosophy and Educational Theory." In *What Is Philosophy of Education*, ed. C.J. Lucas, 175–87. London: Macmillan.
- 1972. "Christian Education: A Contradiction in Terms?" *Learning for Living* 11: 6–11. Reprinted in Astley and Francis (1994, 305–13).
- 1974a. *Knowledge and the Curriculum*. London: Routledge and Kegan Paul.
- 1974b. *Moral Education in a Secular Society*. London: University of London Press.
- 1976. "Religious Beliefs and Educational Principles." *Learning for Living* 15(4): 155–7.
- 1981. "Education, Catechesis and the Church School." *British Journal of Religious Education* 3(3):85–93. Reprinted in Francis and Lankshear (1993, 2–16).
- 1985. "Education and Diversity of Belief." In *Religious Education in a Pluralistic Society*, ed. M.C. Felderhof, 5–17. London: Hodder and Stoughton.
- 1993. "Education, Knowledge and Practices." In *Beyond Liberal Education*, ed. R. Barrow and P. White, 184–99. London: Routledge.

Hobson, Peter. 1984. "Some Reflections on Parents' Rights in the Upbringing of Their Children." *Journal of Philosophy of Education* 18(1):63–74.

Hoffer, Eric. 1951. *The True Believer.* New York: Harper and Row.

Holmes, Mark. 1985. "The Funding of Private Schools in Ontario: Philosophy, Values and Implications for Funding."In *The Report of the Commission of Private Schools in Ontario*, by B.J. Shapiro, 109–52. Toronto: Department of Education, Government of Ontario.

- 1990. "The Funding of Independent Schools." In *Canadian Public Education System: Issues and Prospects*, ed. Y.L. Jack Lam, 229–59. Calgary: Detselig Enterprises.
- 1992. *Educational Policy for the Pluralist Democracy: The Common School, Choice and Diversity*. Washington, DC and London: Falmer Press.
- 1998. *The Reformation of Canada's Schools: Breaking the Barriers to Parental Choice*. Montreal and Kingston: McGill-Queen's University Press.

Holt, John. 1975. *Escape from Childhood: The Needs and Rights of Children*. Harmondsworth: Penguin Books.

Homan, R., and L. King. 1993. "Mishmash and Its Effects upon Learning in the Primary School." *British Journal of Religious Education* 15(3):8–13.

Honig, Bonnie. 1993. *Political Theory and the Displacement of Politics*. Ithaca: Cornell University Press.

Horn, Michiel. 1999. *Academic Freedom in Canada: A History*. Toronto: University of Toronto Press.

Horner, David G. 1992. "Academic Freedom." *Faculty Dialogue* Winter, 17:35–41.

Horton, John, ed. 1993. *Liberalism, Multiculturalism and Toleration*. London: Macmillan.

Horton, John, and Susan Mendus, eds. 1985. *Aspects of Toleration: Philosophical Studies*. London and New York: Methuen.

Horton, John, and Peter Nicholson, eds. 1992. *Toleration: Philosophy and Practice*. Aldershot: Avebury.

Hughes, F. 1992. *What Do You Mean – Christian Education?* Carlisle: Paternoster Press.

Hull, John. 1984. *Studies in Religion and Education.* London: Falmer Press.

– 1989. "School Worship and the 1988 Education Reform Act." *British Journal of Religious Education* 11(3):119–25.

– 1992. "The Transmission of Religious Prejudice." *British Journal of Religious Education* 14(2):69–72.

Hulmes, Edward. 1979. *Commitment and Neutrality in Religious Education.* London: Geoffrey Chapman.

Hunter, James Davison. 1991. *Culture Wars: The Struggle to Define America.* New York: Basic Books.

Huntington, Samuel P. 1996. *The Clash of Civilizations and the Remaking of World Order.* New York: Simon and Schuster.

James, William. 1968. *Essays in Pragmatism.* New York: Hafner.

Jansen, Sue Curry. 1988. *Censorship: The Knot That Binds Power and Knowledge.* Oxford: Oxford University Press.

Jefferson, Anne L. 1988. "The Unknown Consequence of Public Support for Private Schools."*Canadian Journal of Education* 13(3):441–8.

Johnson, James R. 1981. "A Rationale for Censorship in Christian Libraries." *Christian Librarian* 24(2):28–34.

– 1986. "Censoriousness vs. Censorship." *Christian Librarian* 29(1–2):7–10.

– 1990. "A Christian Approach to Intellectual Freedom in Libraries." *Christian Librarian* 33(3):61–74.

Jonathan, Ruth. 1995. "Liberal Philosophy of Education: A Paradigm under Strain."*Journal of Philosophy of Education* 29(1):93–107.

Jones, D. Gareth. 1984. *Brave New People: Ethical Issues at the Commencement of Life.* Downers Grove, Ill.: InterVarsity Press.

– 1994. *Coping with Controversy: Conflict, Censorship and Freedom within Christian Circles.* Dunedin, New Zealand: Visjon Publications.

Jones, Glen. A., ed. 1997. *Higher Education in Canada: Different Systems, Different Perspectives.* New York and London: Garland Publishing.

Juergensmeyer, Mark. 1993. *The New Cold War? Religious Nationalism Confronts the Secular State.* Berkeley and Los Angeles: University of California Press.

Kazepides, Tasos. 1983. "Socialization, Initiation and Indoctrination." In *Philosophy of Education 1982: Proceedings of the 38th Annual Meeting of the Philosophy of Education Society,* ed. Donna H. Kerr, 309–18. Normal, Ill.: Philosophy of Education Society, Illinois State University.

– 1989. "Programmatic Definitions in Education: The Case of Indoctrination." *Canadian Journal of Education* 13(3):387–96.

– 1994. "Indoctrination, Doctrines and the Foundations of Rationality." In *Critical Perspectives on Christian Education,* ed. Jeff Astley and Leslie Francis, 397–407. Leominster: Gracewing.

Kekes, John. 1997. *Against Liberalism.* Ithaca: Cornell University Press.

Kennedy, Donald. 1997. *Academic Duty.* Cambridge, Mass.: Harvard University Press.

Kimball, Bruce A. 1986. *Orators and Philosophers: A History of the Idea of Liberal Education.* New York: Teachers College Press.

Kimball, R. 1990. *Tenured Radicals.* New York: Harper and Row.

Kliever, Lonnie, 1988. "Academic Freedom and Church-Affiliated Universities." *Texas Law Review* 66(7):1477–80.

Kors, Alan Charles, and Harvey Silverglate. 1999. *The Shadow University: The Betrayal of Liberty on America's Campuses.* New York: Free Press.

Kozol, Jonathan. 1991. *Savage Inequalities: Children in America's Schools.* New York: Crown.

Kuhn, Thomas S. 1970. *The Structure of Scientific Revolutions.* 2nd ed. Chicago: University of Chicago Press.

– 1977. "Objectivity, Value Judgement and Theory Choice." In *The Essential Tension,* ed. Thomas S. Kuhn, 320–39. Chicago: University of Chicago Press.

Kymlicka, Will. 1989. *Liberalism, Community and Culture.* Oxford: Clarendon Press.

– 1995. *Multicultural Citizenship: A Liberal Theory of Minority Rights.* Oxford: Clarendon Press.

– 1998. *Finding Our Way: Rethinking Ethnocultural Relations in Canada.* Toronto: Oxford University Press.

Kymlicka, Will, and Wayne Norman. 2000. *Citizenship in Diverse Societies.* New York: Oxford University Press.

Lackey, Douglas. 1985. "Ethics and Nuclear Deterrence." In *Moral Dilemmas: Readings in Ethics and Social Philosophy,* ed. Richard L. Purtill, 36–46. Belmont, Calif.: Wadsworth.

Lambert, I. 1993. "The New Christian Schools Movement in Britain – A Case Study." Ph.D. diss., Department of Education, Cambridge University.

Laycock, Douglas. 1986. "'Nonpreferential' Aid to Religion: A False Claim about Original Intent." *William and Mary Law Review* 27:875–923.

– 1990. "Text, Intent and the Religion Clauses." *Notre Dame Journal of Law, Ethics and Public Policy* 4:683–97.

Leahy, Michael. 1990. "Indoctrination, Evangelization, Catechesis and Religious Education." *British Journal of Religious Education* 12(3):137–44. Reprinted in Astley and Francis (1994, 426–36).

Leahy, Michael, and Ronald S. Laura. 1997. "Religious 'Doctrines' and the Closure of Minds." *Journal of Philosophy of Religion* 31(2):329–43.

Leicester, Mal. 1992. "Values, Cultural Conflict and Education." In *Ethics, Ethnicity and Education,* ed. Mal Leicester and Monica Taylor, 31–8. London: Kogan Page.

Leicester, Mal, and Monica Taylor, eds. 1992. *Ethics, Ethnicity and Education.* London: Kogan Page.

Lewy, Guenter. 1997. *Why America Needs Religion: Secular Modernity and Its Discontents.* Grand Rapids, Mich.: Eerdmans.

Levy, Joanne. 1979. "In Search of Isolation: The Holdeman Mennonites of Linden, Alberta, and Their School." *Canadian Ethnic Studies* 11(1):115–30.

Lieberman, Myron. 1993. *Public Education: An Autopsy.* Harvard University Press.

Lijphart, A. 1977. *Democracy in Plural Societies.* New Haven: Yale University Press.

Livingstone, D.W. 1985. *Social Crisis and Schooling.* Toronto: Garamond Press.

Locke, John. 1968. *A Letter Concerning Toleration*, ed. Raymond Klibansky, tr. J.W. Gough. Oxford: Clarendon Press.

– 1980. *Second Treatise of Government*, ed. C.B. Macpherson. Indianapolis: Hackett.

Long, J.C., and R.F. Magsino. 1993. "Legal Issues in Religion and Education." *Education and Law Journal* 4:189–215.

Lorberbaum, Menachem. 1995. "Learning from Mistakes: Resources of Tolerance in the Jewish Tradition." *Journal of Philosophy of Education* 29(2):273–84.

McCarthy, Martha M. 1983. *A Delicate Balance: Church, State, and the Schools.* Bloomington, Ind.: Phi Delta Kappan Educational Foundation.

McCarthy, Rockne, Donald Oppewal, Walfred Peterson, and Gordon Spykman. 1981. *Society, State and Schools*, Grand Rapids, Mich.: Eerdmans.

McCarthy, Rockne, James W. Skillen, and William A. Harper. 1982. *Disestablishment a Second Time: Genuine Pluralism for American Schools.* Grand Rapids, Mich.: Christian University Press.

McClellan, B. Edward. 1985. "Public Education and Social Harmony: The Roots of an American Dream." *Educational Theory* 35(1):33–42.

McConnell, Michael W. 1990. "The Origins and Historical Understanding of Free Exercise of Religion." *Harvard Law Review* 103:1410–1517.

– 1992. "Religious Freedom at a Crossroads." *University of Chicago Law Review* 59:115–94.

– 1993. "Academic Freedom in Religious Colleges and Universities." In *Freedom and Tenure in the Academy*, ed. William W. Van Alstyne, 303–24. Durham, NC, and London: Duke University Press.

Macedo, Stephen. 1990. *Liberal Values: Citizenship, Virtue and Community in Liberal Constitutionalism.* Oxford: Clarendon Press.

– 1995a. "Liberal Civic Education and Religious Fundamentalism: The Case of God v. John Rawls." *Ethics* 105(3):468–96.

– 1995b. "Multiculturalism for the Religious Right: Defending Liberal Civic Education." *Journal of Philosophy of Education* 29(2):223–38.

MacIntyre, Alistair. 1984. *After Virtue.* 2nd ed. Notre Dame, Ind.: University of Notre Dame Press.

– 1988. *Whose Justice? Which Rationality?* Notre Dame, Ind.: University of Notre Dame Press.

MacKenzie, Pamela J. 1994. "A Critical Analysis of the Christian School Movement in England and Wales." Ph.D. diss., Faculty of Education, Reading University.

McKim, William A., ed. 1988. *The Vexed Question: Denominational Education in a Secular Age.* St John's, Nfld: Breakwater Books.

McLaughlin, T.H. 1984. "Parental Rights and the Religious Upbringing of Children." *Journal of Philosophy of Education* 18(1):75–83. Reprinted in Astley and Francis (1994, 171–83).

– 1985. "Religion, Upbringing and Liberal Values: A Rejoinder to Eamonn Callan." *Journal of Philosophy of Education* 19(1):119–27.

– 1992a. "The Ethics of Separate Schools." In *Ethics, Ethnicity and Education,* ed. Mal Leicester and Monica Taylor, 114–36. London: Kogan Page.

– 1992b. "Fairness, Controversiality and the Common School." *Spectrum* 24(2):105–118. Reprinted in Astley and Francis (1994, 331–42).

– 1994. "The Scope of Parents' Educational Rights." In *Parental Choice and Education: Principles, Policy and Practice,* ed. J. Mark Halstead, 94–107. London: Kogan Page.

– 1995. "Liberalism, Education and the Common School." *Journal of Philosophy of Education* 29(2):239–55.

Maffet, Gregory J. 1987. *Biblical Schools for Covenant Children.* Middleburg Heights, Ohio: Signal Reformed Educational Publishing.

Magsino, Romulo F. 1986. "Human Rights, Fair Treatment, and Funding of Private Schools in Canada." *Canadian Journal of Education* 11(3):245–63.

Magsino, Romulo F., and James R. Covert. 1984. "Denominational Thrust in Education: Some Issues Affecting Canadian Teachers." *Canadian Journal of Education* 9(3):243–60.

Manley, Will. 1986a. "Facing the Public." *Wilson Library Bulletin* 60(5):40–1.

– 1986b. "Facing the Public." *Wilson Library Bulletin* 60(7):42–3.

Manley-Casimir, Michael E., ed. 1982. *Family Choice in Schooling: Issues and Dilemmas.* Lexington, Mass.: Lexington Books.

Marsden, George M. 1987. *Reforming Fundamentalism: Fuller Seminary and the New Evangelicalism.* Grand Rapids, Mich.: Eerdmans.

– 1993. "The Ambiguities of Academic Freedom." *Church History* 62:221–36.

– 1994. *The Soul of the American University: From Protestant Establishment to Established Nonbelief.* New York: Oxford University Press.

– 1997. *The Outrageous Idea of Christian Scholarship.* New York: Oxford University Press.

Marshall, Paul. 1989. "Liberalism, Pluralism and Christianity: A Reconceptualization." *Fides et Historia* 23(3):4–17.

– 1997. "Liberalism, Pluralism and Education." In *Agenda for Educational Change,* ed. John Shortt and Trevor Cooling, 45–56. Leicester: Apollos.

Matthews, Carl J. 1990. *Catholic School Systems across Canada.* Willowdale, Ont.: Canadian Catholic School Trustees' Association.

Matthews, Michael R., ed. 1989. *The Scientific Background of Modern Philosophy: Selected Readings*. Indianapolis: Hackett.

Mavrodes, George, I. 1988. *Revelation in Religious Belief*. Philadelphia: Temple University Press.

Mayberry, Maralee, J. Gary Knowles, Brian Ray, and Stacey Marlow. 1995. *Homeschooling: Parents as Educators*. Thousand Oaks, Calif.: Corwin Press.

Menand, Louis. 1993. "The Future of Academic Freedom." *Academe: Bulletin of the AAUP* 79:11–17.

– ed. 1996. *The Future of Academic Freedom*. Chicago: University of Chicago Press.

Mendus, Susan. 1988. *Justifying Toleration: Conceptual and Historical Perspectives*. Cambridge: Cambridge University Press.

– 1989. *Toleration and the Limits of Liberalism*. Atlantic Highlands, NJ: Humanities Press.

– 1995. "Tolerance and Recognition: Education in a Multicultural Society." *Journal of Philosophy of Education* 29(2):191–201.

Mendus, Susan, and D. Edwards. 1987. *On Toleration*. Oxford: Clarendon Press.

Menendez, Albert J. 1993. *Visions of Reality: What Fundamentalist Schools Teach*. Buffalo, NY: Prometheus Books.

Metzger, Walter P. 1993. "The 1940 Statement of Principles on Academic Freedom and Tenure." In *Freedom and Tenure in the Academy*, ed. William W. Van Alstyne, 3–77. Durham, NC, and London: Duke University Press.

Middleton, J. Richard, and Brian J. Walsh. 1995. *Truth Is Stranger Than It Used to Be: Biblical Faith in a Postmodern Age*. Downers Grove, Ill.: InterVarsity Press.

Mill, John Stuart. 1978. *On Liberty*. Indianapolis: Hackett.

Miller, Ralph. 1982. "Is the Religious Alternative School Useful in the Public School?" *Journal of Educational Thought* 16(2):113–15.

– 1986. "Should There Be Religious Alternative Schools within the Public School System?" *Canadian Journal of Education* 11(3):278–92. Reprinted in Francis and Lankshear (1993, 328–41).

Morgan, Valerie, Grace Fraser, Seamus Dunn, and Ed Cairns. 1992. "Views from Outside – Other Professionals' Views of the Religiously Integrated Schools in Northern Ireland." *British Journal of Religious Education* 14(3):169–77.

Mouffe, Chantal. 1993. *The Return of the Political*. London: Verso.

Mouw, Richard J. 1994. *Consulting the Faithful: What Christian Intellectuals Can Learn from Popular Religion*. Grand Rapids, Mich.: Eerdmans.

Mouw, Richard J., and Sander Griffioen. 1993. *Pluralisms and Horizons: An Essay in Christian Public Philosophy*. Grand Rapids, Mich.: Eerdmans.

Murphey, Archibald D. 1914. *The Papers of Archibald D. Murphey*. Raleigh, NC: University of North Carolina Press.

Murphy, Nancey, and James Wm. McClendon. 1989. "Distinguishing Modern and Postmodern Theologies." *Modern Theology* 5(3):191–214.

Must, Art, Jr. 1992. *Why We Still Need Public Schools: Church/State Relations, and Visions of Democracy.* Buffalo, NY: Prometheus Press.

Nagel, Thomas. 1986. *The View from Nowhere.* New York: Oxford University Press.

— 1991. *Equality and Partiality.* New York and Oxford: Oxford University Press.

— 1997. *The Last Word.* New York and Oxford: Oxford University Press.

Narveson, Jan. 1993. "On Recent Arguments for Egalitarianism." Unpublished paper presented at the annual meeting of the Canadian Philosophical Association, June 1993.

Neal, Patrick. 1997. *Liberalism and Its Discontents.* New York: New York University Press.

Netland, Harold. 1991. *Dissonant Voices: Religious Pluralism and the Question of Truth.* Leicester: Apollos.

Neuhaus, Richard John. 1984. *The Naked Public Square: Religion and Democracy in America.* Grand Rapids, Mich.: Eerdmans.

— 1997. "We Hold These Truths: A Statement of Christian Conscience and Citizenship." *First Things* 76:51–4.

Newbigin, Lesslie. 1995. *Proper Confidence: Faith, Doubt and Certainty in Christian Discipleship.* Grand Rapids, Mich.: Eerdmans.

Newman, Jay. 1982. *Foundations of Religious Tolerance.* Toronto: University of Toronto Press.

— 1986. *Fanatics and Hypocrites.* Buffalo, NY: Prometheus Books.

Nicholson, Peter. 1985. "Toleration as a Moral Ideal." In *Aspects of Toleration: Philosophical Studies,* ed. J. Horton and S. Mendus, 158–73. London and New York: Methuen.

Nielsen, Kai. 1984. "On Not Being at Sea about Indoctrination." *Interchange: A Quarterly Review of Education* 15(4):68–73.

— 1985. *Equality and Liberty: A Defense of Radical Egalitarianism.* Totowa, NJ: Rowman and Allanheld.

Nieman, Alven M. 1989. "Indoctrination: A Contextualist Approach." *Educational Philosophy and Theory* 21(1):53–65.

Nikiforuk, Andrew. 1993. *School's Out: The Catastrophe in Public Education and What We Can Do about It.* Toronto: Macfarlane Walter and Ross.

Nodelman, Perry. 1992. "We Are All Censors." *Canadian Children's Literature* 68:121–33.

Nord, Warren. 1995. *Religion and American Education: Rethinking a National Dilemma.* Chapel Hill, NC: University of North Carolina Press.

Norman, R. 1987. *Free and Equal.* Oxford: Oxford University Press.

Oakeshott, M. 1972. "Education: The Engagement and its Frustration." In *Education and the Development of Reason,* 19–49. ed. R.F. Dearden, P.H. Hirst, and R.S. Peters. London: Routledge and Kegan Paul.

O'Keeffe, Bernadette. 1986. *Faith, Culture and the Dual System: A Comparative Study of Church and County Schools.* London, New York and Philadelphia: Falmer Press.

– ed. 1988. *Schools for Tomorrow: Building Walls or Building Bridges.* London: Falmer Press.

– 1992. "A Look at the Christian Schools Movement." In *Priorities in Religious Education: A Model for the 1990s and Beyond,* ed. Brenda Watson, 92–112. London: Falmer Press.

Olneck, Michael. 1992. "Is Pluralism Possible in American Public Education?" In *The Challenge of Pluralism: Education, Politics and Values,* ed. F. Clark Power and Daniel K. Lapsley, 251–71. Notre Dame, Ind.: University of Notre Dame Press.

Oppewal, Donald. 1981. "Competing Views of Educational Authority." *Educational Forum,* March 1981, 361–74.

Page, Ralph C. 1980. "Some Requirements for a Theory of Indoctrination." Dissertation, University of Illinois at Urbana-Champaign.

Parsons, Paul F. 1987. *Inside America's Christian Schools.* Macon, Ga.: Mercer University Press.

Perelman, Lewis J. 1992. *School's Out: A Radical Formula for Revitalization of America's Educational System.* New York: Avon Books.

Perks, Stephen C. 1992. *The Christian Philosophy of Education Explained.* Whitby: Avant Books.

Peshkin, Alan. 1986. *God's Choice: The Total World of a Fundamentalist Christian School.* Chicago and London: University of Chicago Press.

Peters, Frank. 1996. "The Changing Face of Denominational Education in Canada." *Education and Law Journal* 7(3):229–56.

Peters, R.S. 1965. "Education as Initiation." In *Philosophical Analysis and Education,* ed. R.D. Archambault, 87–111. London: Routledge and Kegan Paul.

Plunkett, Dudley. 1990. *Secular and Spiritual Values: Grounds for Hope in Education.* London and New York: Routledge.

Pojman, Louis P. 1991. "A Critique of Contemporary Egalitarianism: A Christian Perspective." *Faith and Philosophy: Journal of the Society of Christian Philosophers* 8(4):481–504.

Polanyi, Michael. 1964. *Science, Faith and Society.* Chicago and London: University of Chicago Press.

Popper, Karl. 1970. "Normal Science and Its Dangers." In *Criticism and the Growth of Knowledge,* ed. I. Lakatos and A. Musgrove, 51–8. Cambridge: Cambridge University Press.

Postman, Neil. 1995. *The End of Education.* New York: Vintage Books.

Power, F. Clark, and Daniel K. Lapsley. 1993. *The Challenge of Pluralism: Education, Politics and Values.* Notre Dame, Ind.: University of Notre Dame Press.

Pring, Richard. 1992. "Education for a Pluralist Society." In *Ethics, Ethnicity and Education,* ed. Mal Leicester and Monica Taylor, 19–30. London: Kogan Page.

Proulx Task Force. 1999. *Religion in Secular Schools: A New Perspective for Quebec.* Government of Quebec: Ministry of Education.

Purdy, Laura M. 1992. *In Their Best Interest: The Case against Equal Rights for Children.* Ithaca and London: Cornell University Press.

Quine, W.V. 1961. *From a Logical Point of View.* 2nd ed. Cambridge, Mass.: Harvard University Press.

Quine, W.V., and J.S. Ullian. 1978. *The Web of Belief.* 2nd ed. New York: Random House.

Rae, Peter. 1995. "Clearly Canadian: Church-Related Higher Education." Paper presented at the "With Heart and Mind Conference," Canadian Bible College, Regina, Sask., May 1995.

– 1998. "Unholy Alliance? The Church and Higher Education in Canada." Ph.D. Thesis. Faculty of Education: University of Manitoba.

Randall, E. Vance. 1994. *Private Schools and Public Power: A Case for Pluralism.* New York and London: Teachers College Press.

Ratzsch, Del. 1986. *Philosophy of Science: The Natural Science in Christian Perspective.* Downers Grove, Ill.: InterVarsity Press.

Rauch, Jonathan. 1993. *Kindly Inquisitors: The New Attacks on Free Thought.* Chicago: University of Chicago Press.

Ravitch, Diane, and Joseph P. Viteritti, eds. 1997. *New Schools for a New Century: The Redesign of Urban Education.* New Haven and London: Yale University Press.

Rawls, John. 1971. *A Theory of Justice.* Cambridge, Mass.: Harvard University Press.

– 1975. "Fairness to Goodness." *Philosophical Review* 84: 536–54.

– 1985. "Justice as Fairness: Political Not Metaphysical." *Philosophy and Public Affairs* 14(3):223–51.

– 1987. "The Idea of an Overlapping Consensus." *Oxford Journal of Legal Studies* 7(1):1–25.

– 1993. *Political Liberalism.* New York: Columbia University Press.

Raywid, M.A. 1985. "Family Choice Arrangements in Public Schools: A Review of the Literature." *Review of Educational Research* 55:435–67.

Raz, J. 1986. *The Morality of Freedom.* Oxford: Clarendon Press.

– 1994. *Ethics in the Public Domain.* Oxford: Oxford University Press.

Reese, William J. 1985. "Soldiers for Christ in the Army of God: The Christian School Movement in America." *Educational Theory* 35(2):175–94.

Rorty, Richard. 1982. *Consequences of Pragmatism.* Minneapolis: University of Minnesota Press.

– 1983. "Postmodern Bourgeois Liberalism." *Journal of Philosophy* 80:583–9.

– 1987. "Science and Solidarity." In *Rhetoric of the Human Sciences: Language and Arguments in Scholarship and Public Affairs*, ed. John S. Nelson, Allan Megill, and Donald N. McCloskey. Madison: University of Wisconson Press.

– 1989. *Contingency, Irony, and Solidarity.* Cambridge: Cambridge University Press.

– 1991. *Objectivity, Relativism and Truth.* Cambridge: Cambridge University Press.

– 1995. "Runes and Ruins: Teaching Reading Cultures." *Journal of Philosophy of Education* 29(2):217–22.

Rose, Susan D. 1988. *Keeping Them Out of the Hands of Satan: Evangelical Schooling in America.* New York and London: Routledge.

Rossi, Alice. 1977. "A Biosocial Perspective on Parenting." *Daedalus* 106(2):1–31.

Rothbard, M.N. 1972. *Education, Free and Compulsory.* Wichita, Kans.: Center for Independent Education.

Royal Commission of Inquiry into the Delivery of Programs and Services in Primary, Elementary, Secondary Education. 1992. *Our Children, Our Future* St. John's: Government of Newfoundland and Labrador.

Russell, Conrad. 1993. *Academic Freedom.* London: Routledge.

Rutter, Michael. 1972. *Maternal Deprivation Reassessed.* Harmondsworth, Middlesex: Penguin Books.

Rutter, Michael, ed. 1980. *Developmental Psychiatry.* Washington, DC: American Psychiatric Press.

Sandel, Michael. 1982. *Liberalism and the Limits of Justice.* New York: Cambridge University Press.

– 1984a. *Liberalism and Its Critics.* New York: New York University Press.

– 1984b. "Morality and the Liberal Ideal." *New Republic,* 7 May, 15–17.

– 1996. *Democracy's Discontent: America in Search of a Public Philosophy.* Cambridge, Mass.: Harvard University Press.

Saul, John Ralston. 1995. *The Unconscious Civilization.* Concord, Ont.: Anansi.

Schneider, M., P. Teske, M. Marschall, M. Mintrom, and C. Roch. 1997. "Institutional Arrangements and the Creation of Social Capital: The Effects of School Choice." *American Political Science Review* 91:82–93.

Schrader, Alvin M. 1995. *Fear of Words: Censorship and the Public Libraries of Canada.* Ottawa: Canadian Library Association.

Schrecker, Ellen W. 1986. *No Ivory Tower: McCarthyism and the Universities.* New York: Oxford University Press.

Schumacher, E.F. 1973. *Small Is Beautiful: Economics As If People Mattered.* New York: Harper and Row.

Schwehn, Mark R. 1993. *Exiles from Eden: Religion and the Academic Vocation in America.* New York and Oxford: Oxford University Press.

Scruton, Roger, Angela Ellis-Jones, and Dennis O'Keeffe. 1985. *Education and Indoctrination: An Attempt at Definition and a Review of Social and Political Implications.* Harrow, Middx: Education Research Centre.

Shapiro, Bernard J. (Commissioner) 1985. *The Report of the Commissioner on Private Schools in Ontario.* Toronto: Department of Education, Government of Ontario.

– 1986. "The Public Funding of Private Schools in Ontario: The Setting, Some Arguments, and Some Matters of Belief." *Canadian Journal of Education* 11(3):264–77. Reprinted in Francis and Lankshear (1993, 316–27).

Sharp, Gene. 1973. *The Politics of Nonviolent Action.* Boston: Porter Sargent.

Sharron, H. 1987. *Changing Children's Minds: Feuerstein's Revolution in the Teaching of Intelligence.* London: Souvenir Press.

Shortt, John. 1991. "Reformed Epistemology and Education." Ph.D. thesis. University of London Institute of Education.

Sider, Ronald J. 1977. *Rich Christians in an Age of Hunger: A Biblical Study.* Downers Grove, Ill.: InterVarsity Press.

Sider, Ronald J., and Richard K. Taylor. 1982. *Nuclear Holocaust and Christian Hope.* Downers Grove, Ill: InterVarsity Press.

Siegel, Harvey. 1988. *Educating Reason: Rationality, Critical Thinking, and Education.* New York and London: Routledge.

– 1995. " 'Radical' Pedagogy Requires 'Conservative' Epistemology." *Journal of Philosophy of Education* 29(1):33–46.

Simmons, John S., ed. 1994. *Censorship: A Threat to Reading, Learning, Thinking.* Newark, Del.: International Reading Association.

Singh, Basil R. 1995. "Shared Values, Particular Values, and Education for a Multicultural Society." *Educational Review* 47(1):11–23.

Skillen, James W. 1994. *Recharging the American Experiment: Principled Pluralism for Genuine Civic Community.* Grand Rapids, Mich.: Baker Books.

Skillen, James W., and Rockne M. McCarthy, eds. 1991. *Political Order and the Plural Structure of Society.* Atlanta: Scholars Press.

Smedes, Lewis B. 1988. *Caring and Commitment: Learning to Live the Love We Promise.* San Fransisco: Harper and Row.

Smith, Christian. 1998. *American Evangelicalism: Embattled and Thriving.* Chicago: University of Chicago Press.

Smith, David. 1995. "Christian Thinking in Education Reconsidered." *Spectrum* 27(1): Spring, 9–24.

– 1996. "What Hope after Babel? Diversity and Community in Genesis 11:1–9, Exodus 1:1–14, Zephaniah 3:1–13 and Acts 2:1–13." *Horizons in Biblical Theology* 18(2):69–91.

Smith, David W. 1988. "Public School Education." In *Schooling Choices: An Examination of Private, Public, and Home Education,* ed. H. Wayne House, 19–72, 153–9. Portland, Oreg.: Multnomah Press.

Smith, Steven D. 1989. "Separation and the 'Secular': Reconstructing the Disestablishment Decision." *Texas Law Review* 67:955–1031.

Snik, Ger, and Johan De Jong. 1995. "Liberalism and Denominational Schools." *Journal of Moral Education* 24(4):395–407.

Snook, I.A., ed. 1972a. *Concepts of Indoctrination: Philosophical Essays.* London: Routledge and Kegan Paul

– 1972b. *Indoctrination and Education.* London: Routledge and Kegan Paul.

Spiecker, Ben. 1991. "Indoctrination: The Suppression of Critical Dispositions." In *Freedom and Indoctrination in Education: International Perspectives,* ed. Ben Spiecker and Roger Straughan, 1–14. London: Cassell Educational.

– 1996. "Review Article: Commitment to Liberal Education." *Studies in Philosophy and Education* 15(3):281–91.

Spiecker, Ben, and Roger Straughan, eds. 1991. *Freedom and Indoctrination in Education: International Perspectives*. London: Cassell Educational.

Spinner-Halev, Jeff. 2000. *Surviving Diversity: Religion and Democratic Citizenship*. Baltimore and London: Johns Hopkins University Press.

Springsted, E.O. 1991. "Liberal Individuals and Liberal Education." *Religious Education* 86:467–78.

Stanbridge, Joanne. 1992. "Out of the Blue: Coping with the Book-Banners." *Canadian Children's Literature* no. 68:36–42.

Steinberg, Laurence D., B.B. Brown, and S.M. Dornbusch. 1996. *Beyond the Classroom: Why School Reform Has Failed and What Parents Need to Know*. New York: Simon and Schuster.

Stevenson, Harold W., and James W. Stigler. 1992. *The Learning Gap: Why Our Schools Are Failing and What We Can Learn from Japanese and Chinese Education*. New York: Simon and Schuster.

Stillman, Andy. 1994. "The Scope of Parents' Educational Rights." In *Parental Choice and Education: Principles, Policy and Practice*, ed. J. Mark Halstead, 19–35. London: Kogan Page.

Stolzenberg, Nomi Maya. 1993. " 'He Drew a Circle That Shut Me Out': Assimilation, Indoctrination, and the Paradox of Liberal Education." *Harvard Law Review* 106:581–667.

Stout, Jeffrey. 1981. *The Flight from Authority: Religion, Morality and the Quest for Autonomy*. Notre Dame, Ind.: University of Notre Dame Press.

– 1988. *Ethics after Babel: The Languages of Morals and Their Discourses*. Boston: Beacon Press.

Strike, Kenneth A. 1985. "A Field Guide of Censors: Toward a Concept of Censorship in Public Schools." *Teachers College Record* 87:239–58.

Sutherland, Margaret. 1988. "Religious Dichotomy and Schooling in Northern Ireland." In *Christianity and Educational Provision in International Perspective*, ed. Witold Tulasiewicz and Colin Brock, 38–60. London: Routledge.

Swan, John C. 1979. "Librarianship is Censorship." *Library Journal* 104(17):2040–3.

Swann, Lord, and Committee of Inquiry into the Education of Children from Ethnic Minority Groups. 1985. *Education for All: The Report of the Committee of Inquiry into the Education of Children from Ethnic Minority Groups*. London: Her Majesty's Stationery Office.

Sweet, Lois. 1997. *God in the Classroom: The Controversial Issue of Religion in Canada's Schools*. Toronto: McClelland and Stewart.

Swinburne, Richard. 1981. *Faith and Reason*. Oxford: Clarendon Press.

Sykes, Charles. 1995. *Dumbing Down Our Kids: Why American Children Feel Good about Themselves But Can't Read, Write, or Add*. New York: St Martin's Press.

Tamir, Yael. 1995a. *Liberal Nationalism*. Princeton: Princeton University Press.

– 1995b. "Two Concepts of Multiculturalism." *Journal of Philosophy of Education* 29(2):161–72.

– ed. 1995c. *Democratic Education in a Multicultural State*. Oxford: Blackwell Publishers and Journal of Philosophy of Education.

Tash, Robert C. 1991. *Dutch Pluralism: A Model in Tolerance for Developing Democracies*. New York: Peter Lang.

Taylor, Charles. 1989. *Sources of the Self: The Taking of the Modern Identity*. Cambridge: Harvard University Press.

– 1993. *Reconciling the Solitudes: Essays on Canadian Federalism and Nationalism*. Montreal and Kingston: McGill-Queen's University Press.

– 1994. "The Politics of Recognition." In *Multiculturalism: Examining the Politics of Recognition*, ed. Amy Gutmann, 25–73. Princeton: Princeton University Press.

Teilhard de Chardin, Pierre. 1964. *The Future of Man*; tr. Norman Denny. St. James Place, London: Collins.

Thatcher, Adrian. 1990. "The Distinctiveness of the Church Colleges." In *Christian Perspectives for Education*, ed. Leslie Francis and Adrian Thatcher, 168–73. Leominster: Fowler Wright Books.

Thiessen, Elmer John. 1982a. "Indoctrination and Doctrines." *Journal of Philosophy of Education* 16(1):3–17. Reprinted in Astley and Francis (1994, 376–96).

– 1982b. "Religious Freedom and Educational Pluralism." In *Family Choice in Schooling: Issues and Dilemmas*, ed. Michael E. Manley-Casimir, 57–69. Lexington, Mass.: Lexington Books.

– 1984a. "Indoctrination and Religious Education." *Interchange* 15(3):27–43. Reprinted in Francis and Thatcher (1990, 215–30).

– 1984b. "Paradigms of Religious Indoctrination: A Response to McLean and Nielson." *Interchange* 15(4):74–9.

– 1985a. "A Defense of a Distinctively Christian Curriculum." *Religious Education* 80(1):37–50. Reprinted in Francis and Thatcher (1990, 83–92).

– 1985b. "Initiation, Indoctrination and Education." *Canadian Journal of Education* 10(3):229–49.

– 1987. "Two Concepts or Two Phases of Liberal Education." *Journal of Philosophy of Education* 21(2):223–34. Reprinted in Francis and Lankshear (1993, 17–32).

– 1989. "R.S. Peters on Liberal Education." *Interchange* 20(4):1–8.

– 1990. Review of *God's Choice: The Total World of a Fundamentalist Christian School*, by Alan Peshkin (Chicago and London: University of Chicago Press, 1986), *Ethics in Education* 9(4):13–15.

– 1991. "Christian Nurture, Indoctrination and Liberal Education." *Spectrum* 23(2):105–24. Reprinted in Astley and Day (1992, 66–86).

– 1992. "In Defence of Developing a Theoretical Christian Mind: A Response to Oliver R. Barclay." *Evangelical Quarterly: An International Review of Bible and Theology* 64(1):37–54.

– 1993. *Teaching for Commitment: Liberal Education, Indoctrination and Christian Nurture*. Montreal: McGill-Queen's University Press; and Leominster: Gracewing.

– 1996. "Fanaticism and Christian Liberal Education: A Response to Ben Spiecker's 'Commitment to Liberal Education.'" *Studies in Philosophy and Education* 15(3):293–300.

– 1997. "Curriculum after Babel." In *Agenda for Educational Change*, ed. John Shortt and Trevor Cooling, 165–80. Leicester: Apollos.

– 1999. "Transformative Christian Education: A Response to Andrew Wright." *Journal of Education and Christian Belief* 3(1):23–9.

Thiessen, Elmer John, and L.J. Roy Wilson. 1979. "Curriculum in the Church-State Controversy: Are the Mennonites Justified in Rejecting the Public School Curriculum?" *Salt: Journal of the Religious Studies and Moral Education Council* (Spring): 16–20.

Thompson, Penny. 1993. "Religionism: A Response to John Hull." *British Journal of Religious Education* 16(1):47–50.

Thomson, Judith Jarvis. 1993. "Ideology and Faculty Selection." In *Freedom and Tenure in the Academy*, ed. William W. Van Alstyne, 155–76. Durham, NC, and London: Duke University Press.

Thomson, Judith Jarvis, and Matthew W. Finkin. 1993. "Academic Freedom and Church-Related Higher Education: A Reply to Professor McConnell." In *Freedom and Tenure in the Academy*, ed. William W. Van Alstyne, 419–29. Durham, NC, and London: Duke University Press.

Tierney, W.G. 1993. "Academic Freedom and the Parameters of Knowledge." *Harvard Educational Review* 63(2):143–60.

Tomasi, John. 1995. "Kymlicka, Liberalism, and Respect for Cultural Minorities." *Ethics: An International Journal of Social, Political, and Legal Philosophy* 105(3):580–603.

Toulmin, Stephen. 1990. *Cosmopolis: The Hidden Agenda of Modernity.* New York: Free Press.

Tracy, David. 1990. *Dialogue with the Other.* Grand Rapids, Mich.: Peeters Press/ Eerdmans.

Trigg, Roger. 1973. *Reason and Commitment.* London: Cambridge University Press.

Tulasiewicz, Witold, and Colin Brock, eds. 1988. *Christianity and Educational Provision in International Perspective.* London and New York: Routledge.

Tussman, J. 1977. *Government and the Mind.* New York: Oxford University Press.

Van Alstyne, William W. 1993. *Freedom and Tenure in the Academy.* Durham, NC, London: Duke University Press.

Van Brummelen, Harro. 1989. *Curriculum: Implementation in Three Christian Schools.* Grand Rapids, Mich.: A Calvin College Monograph.

– 1990. "Tolerance in Public and Religiously Based Schools." *Ethics in Education* 9(4):8–11.

– 1996. "Independent Schools in Canada: An Overview." *Private School Monitor* 17(2):1–6.

Velten, Dieter. 1994. "Christian Thinking in Education." *Spectrum* 26(1):59–70.

Viteritti, Joseph P. 1996. "Choosing Equality: Religious Freedom and Educational Opportunity under Constitutional Federalism." *Yale Law and Policy Review* 15(113):113–92.

Vitz, Paul C. 1986. *Censorship: Evidence of Bias in Our Children's Textbooks.* Ann Arbor, Mich.: Servant Books.

Vriend, John. 1996. "Public 'Umbrellas' for Independent Schools: Canadian Examples and Reflections." *Private School Monitor* 17(2):24–8.

Wagner, Melinda, B. 1990. *God's Schools: Choice and Compromise in American Society.* London: Rutgers University Press.

Wagner, Michael G. 1995. "Private versus Public Education: The Alberta Debate." MA thesis: Department of Political Science, University of Alberta.

Walford, Geoffrey, ed. 1989. *Private Schools in Ten Countries: Policy and Practice.* London: Routledge.

– ed. 1991a. *Private Schooling: Tradition, Change and Diversity,* London: Paul Chapman Pub.

– 1991b. "The Reluctant Private Sector: Of Small Schools, People and Politics." In *Private Schooling: Tradition, Change and Diversity,* ed. G. Walford, 115–32. London: Paul Chapman Pub.

– 1994a. "Weak Choice, Strong Choice and the New Christian Schools." In *Parental Choice and Education,* ed. M. Halstead, 139–50. London: Kogan Page.

– 1994b. "The New Religious Grant-Maintained Schools." *Educational Management and Administration* 22(2):123–30.

– 1994c. "Ethics and Power in a Study of Pressure Groups Politics." In *Researching the Powerful in Education,* ed. Geoffrey Walford, 81–93. London: UCL Press.

– 1995. *Educational Politics: Pressure Groups and Faith-Based Schools.* Aldershot: Avebury.

Walsh, Brian J., and J. Richard Middleton. 1984. *The Transforming Vision: Shaping a Christian World View.* Downers Grove, Ill.: InterVarsity Press.

Walzer, Michael. 1983. *Spheres of Justice: A Defense of Pluralism and Equality.* New York: Basic Books.

– 1992. "The View from Somewhere." *New Republic,* 17 Feb. 30–2.

– 1994. *Thick and Thin: Moral Argument at Home and Abroad.* Notre Dame, Ind.: University of Notre Dame Press.

– 1995. "Education, Democratic Citzenship and Multiculturalism." *Journal of Philosophy of Education* 29(2):181–9.

– 1997. *On Toleration.* New Haven: Yale University Press.

Warnock, Mary. 1988. "The Neutral Teacher." In *Philosophy of Education,* ed. Wm Hare and J.P. Portelli, 177–86. Calgary: Detselig.

Watson, Brenda. 1987. *Education and Belief.* Oxford: Blackwell.

Weaver, R.M. 1971. *Ideas Have Consequences.* Chicago: University of Chicago Press.

Weeks, Noel. 1988. *The Christian School: An Introduction* Edinburgh: Banner of Truth Trust.

Weinstein, Mark. 1995. "Social Justice, Epistemology and Educational Reform." *Journal of Philosophy of Education* 29(3):369–86.

West, E.G. 1970. *Education and the State: A Study in Political Economy.* 2nd ed. London: Institute of Economic Affairs.

West, Mark I. 1988. *Trust Your Children: Voices against Censorship in Children's Literature.* New York: Schuman Publishers.

White, John. 1982. *The Aims of Education Restated.* London: Routledge and Kegan Paul.

– 1994. "The Dishwasher's Child: Education and the End of Egalitarianism." *Journal of Philosophy of Education* 28(2):173–81.

White, Patricia. 1983. *Beyond Domination.* London: Routledge and Kegan Paul.

– 1988. "The New Right and Parental Choice." *Journal of Philosophy of Education* 22(2):195–9.

– 1994. "Parental Choice and Education for Citizenship." In *Parental Choice and Education: Principles, Policy and Practice,* ed. J. Mark Halstead, 83–93. London: Kogan Page.

Whitehouse, Peter. 1990. "Education for Mutual Understanding: A Guide." *Journal of Curriculum Studies.* 22(5):493–9.

Wilson, J. Donald. 1970. "Education in Upper Canada: Sixty Years of Change." In *Canadian Education: A History,* ed. J. Donald Wilson, Robert M. Stamp, and Louis-Philippe Audet, 190–213. Scarborough, Ont.: Prentice-Hall of Canada.

Wilson, J. Donald, and Marvin Lazerson. 1982. "Historical and Constitutional Perspectives on Family Choice in Schooling: The Canadian Case." In *Family Choice in Schooling: Issues and Dilemmas,* ed. Michael E. Manley-Casimir, 1–19. Lexington, Mass.: Lexington Books.

Wink, Walter. 1992. *Engaging the Powers: Discernment and Resistance in a World of Domination.* Minneapolis: Fortress Press.

Wolters, Albert M. 1985. *Creation Regained: Biblical Basics for a Reformational Worldview.* Grand Rapids, Mich.: Eerdmans.

Wolterstorff, Nicholas. 1980. *Educating for Responsible Action.* Grand Rapids, Mich.: Eerdmans.

– 1983. *Until Justice and Peace Embrace.* Grand Rapids, Mich.: Eerdmans.

– 1984. *Reason within the Bounds of Religion.* 2nd ed. Grand Rapids, Mich.: Eerdmans.

Woodhouse, Howard. 1990. "Teacher Autonomy: A Professional Hazard?" *Paideusis* 4(1):32–8.

Woods Gordon Management Consultants. 1984. *A Study of Private Schools in Alberta.* Edmonton: Alberta Education.

Wright, Andrew. 1998. "Transformative Christian Education: New Covenant, New Creation. An Essay in Constructive Theology." *Journal of Education and Christian Belief* 2(2):93–108.

Wright, N.T. 1992. *The New Testament and the People of God.* London: SPCK.

Wringe, C.A. 1981. *Children's Rights: A Philosophical Study,* London: Routledge and Kegan Paul.

Wringe, Colin. 1995. "Educational Rights in Multicultural Democracies." *Journal of Philosophy of Education* 29(2):285–92.

Yancey, Philip. 1997. *What's So Amazing about Grace?* Grand Rapids, Mich.: Zondervan Publishing House.

Ye'or, Bat. 1996. *The Decline of Eastern Christianity under Islam: From Jihad to Dhimmitude.* Fairleigh Dickinson University Press.

Young, Iris Marion. 1990. *Justice and the Politics of Difference.* Princeton: Princeton University Press.

Young, Michael F.D., ed. 1971. *Knowledge and Control: New Directions for the Sociology of Education.* London: Collier-Macmillan.

Young, R.E. 1988. "Critical Teaching and Learning." *Educational Theory* 38(1):47–59.

Zagzebski, Linda Trinkaus. 1993. "Vocatio Philosophiae." In *Philosophers Who Believe,* ed. Kelly James Clark, 237–57. Downers Grove, Ill.: InterVarsity Press.

Zylstra, Carl E. 1997. "Faith-Based Learning: The Conjunction in Christian Scholarship." *Pro Rege* 26(1):1–5.

Index

Abraham, William J., 188
academic freedom, ch. 5; calls for
  updating, 86, 90, 96, 278nn18, 20;
  controversies surrounding, 83–4;
  and duties, 278n15; as expressed in
  primary and secondary schools, 80,
  275n1; history of, 81–3; and limitations clause, 81–2, 89, 90–1, 95,
  276n5; limitations of, in secular institutions, 85, 87–8, 91, 92, 95, 96,
  278n13, 279nn24, 26; problems
  with traditional ideal of, 23–4, 84–
  90, 278n12; reconstructed definition of, 90, 94
academic freedom and religious
  schools/colleges, ch. 5; arguments
  against possibility, 81–3, 91–2; arguments for possibility, 84, 90–2;
  charges regarding, 81–3, 93,
  276nn5, 6, 7, 277n9, 278n19,
  280n34, 281n38; limitations clause
  as qualifying, 81–2, 89, 90–1, 93,
  95, 275n1, 276n5, 277n10; positive
  and negative examples of, 84, 93–

4, 280n34, 277n11; in relation to
  hiring and firing, 94–6, 281nn36,
  37; restrictions of, 91, 93–5,
  279n25, 280nn30, 31, 32; statements of, 277n11
Accelerated Christian Education
  schools. *See under* religious schools
Ackermann, Bruce, 41, 71, 141,
  269n14, 274n44, 293n19
Adams, Robert Merrihew, 305n24
Adler v. Ontario, Minister of Education,
  17, 256n20, 308n12, 311n1
Alberta Committee on Tolerance and
  Understanding, 30, 39, 44–5, 48–
  50, 53–4, 55, 263nn9, 10, 265n22,
  266nn27, 30
Alberta Education, 293n22
Alberta Private Schools Funding Task
  Force, 18, 114, 256n19, 257n22,
  259n1, 288n16
Allen, R.T., 140, 299n14
Allport, Gordon, 57
American Library Association, 144,
  296nn16, 17, 19, 298n31

273n39, 293n19; and parental
rights, 66–70, 72, 79
Chomsky, Noam, 148, 149, 292n12,
295n10
Christian curriculum and scholarship. *See* curriculum, Christian; curriculum and religious schools;
curriculum theory
Chubb, J., and T. Moe, 319n52
church-related schools. *See* religious
schools
church rights in education, 78, 111,
225, 275n47
church-state separation. *See* separation of church and state
civic and universal values education,
235–8; arguments that religious
schools can do justice to, 226–30,
235–8; best accomplished within
particularist context, 238, 317n42;
charge that religious schools cannot do justice to, 226–8, 312n14,
313nn15, 17; foundations of, 236;
implications of the new epistemology for, 236; as initiation, 233–4;
mandate for religious schools, 43;
need for religious support for, 104;
overemphasis on, in state common
schools, 234–5, 240, 316n35
Clarke, Robert A., and S.D. Gaede,
173
closed-mindedness. *See* open-mindedness
Clouser, Roy A., 169, 212, 300n18
Coleman, J.S., and T. Hoffer, 206,
273n39, 307n4
colleges. *See* post-secondary schools
Commission on Private Schools in
Ontario, 29
commitment, religious: as emphasized in Christianity, 182–3, 188–
91, 304n6, 305nn23, 24; fanaticism as a perversion of healthy,

183–5; healthy, 183–8, 304n8,
305n16, 25; need to balance with
tolerance, 52; need to balance with
uncertainty, 58; need for healthy,
191–2, 197–8, 306n26; need to
teach for, 58, 197, 250; origins of
suspicion about teaching for,
192–4; rationality of, 304n7; tendency to equate with fanaticism,
183; undercommitment as a perversion of healthy, 189, 192,
304n9. *See also* fanaticism
Committee on Tolerance and Understanding. *See* Alberta Committee on
Tolerance and Understanding
common schools. *See* state common
schools
communities and communitarianism, 208–10, 211–12; Amish as
example of, 247; character formation requires, 236; critique of, 215;
and defence of religious schools,
219, 311n1; definition of, 211,
216, 309n23; growing emphasis
on, 208, 217, 222, 311n5; need
for balance with individualism,
214, 216–17, 222, 230–1, 310n29;
universality grows out of, 212.
See also liberalism, and cultural
membership
constantinianism, 108, 113, 283n22
Cookson, Peter W., Jr, 20, 21, 254n1,
257n29
Cooling, Trevor, 58, 175, 301n29
Cooper, David E., 287n10
Cors, Paul B., 158, 159
court cases, 17, 100, 163–4, 256nn20,
21, 268n5, 273n39, 281n3, 282n8,
292n10, 298n2, 308n12, 311n1
Coward, Harold, 264n15
Cox, Caroline, et al., 268nn6, 7
critical thinking: and indoctrination,
134; need to teach, 160, 197, 250;

and liberal education, 204,
306n27; limitations of, in science,
279n27; as parasitic on initiation,
140, 151, 195; in relation to commitment, 305n17

Crittenden, Brian, 64, 67, 68, 69, 73,
77, 270n16, 270n17, 271nn24, 26,
272n33, 273n34, 274nn40, 42, 45,
307n4

cultural communities. *See* communities and communitarianism

culture wars, 208, 230, 242–3,
314n25, 315n34. *See also* Arons,
Stephen

Cumper, Peter, 37, 261n11

Curran, Charles. E., 82, 94, 278nn13,
14, 280n30

curriculum, Christian, ch. 10;
charges of impossibility of, 163,
298n1; and common ground with
other belief systems, 174–6,
301nn27, 28, 29; disagreement
concerning nature of, 176–7; how a
faith perspective affects, 107, 167–
72, 299nn13, 15, 300nn17, 18; figure of overlapping ellipses, 176;
and the problem of incommensurability and relativism, 172–6,
301nn27, 28. *See also* epistemology,
presuppositions; epistemology,
worldviews

curriculum and religious schools:
charge that distinct curriculum is
impossible, 163, 164; danger of
compartmentalization, 167, 178–9;
danger of superficial integration of
faith and, 179; defence of distinctiveness of, ch. 10; examples of secularization, 177–8, 302nn32, 33,
35; importance of relating to scholarship of other religious traditions,
179–80; importance of unique
Christian perspective in entire,

177–8; in Muslim schools, 298n5;
positive examples of, 179. *See also*
curriculum, Christian; forms of
knowledge; curriculum theory

curriculum theory, ch. 10; belief systems, 170–2; figure of belief systems, 172; Hirst's forms of
knowledge, 164–5, 298nn7, 8, 9,
299n10; how religion affects, 167–
72, 300nn18, 20

Dale, A.S., 314n20
Davis, Donald G., 297nn27, 30
Davis, Marie, 295n15
Deakin, Ruth, 258n30
Dekmejian, R. Hrair, 304n12
deliberative skills and democracy:
best context for development, 221,
237–8, 244, 262n21; need for, 43,
74, 236–8, 316n40
democracy: as institutionalized nonviolence, 318n49; kinds of, 222,
311nn4, 8; need for deliberative
skills, 236–8; state common schools
essential for, 3, 31–2, 219, 220–2,
253n1. *See also* deliberative skills
and democracy
Department for Education, Great
Britain, 268n5
De Ruyter, Doret J., 315n32
Dewey, John, 29–30, 49, 81, 263n21,
307n2
diagrams. *See* figures
Diekema, Anthony, 277n11
disestablishment of religion, 101–4,
108–9, 284n24
diversity. *See* unity and diversity. *See
also* pluralism
divisiveness and religious schools,
ch. 2; charge relating to, 17, 18, 19,
23, 29–31, 259n3, 261n11; coun-
terbalancing forces to, 261n18,
281n2; economic status as more

critical to, 262n20; empirical
evidence related to, 37–40,
261nn16, 17; logical relation between, 36–7; practical suggestions
on how to avoid, 43
doctrines. *See* religious doctrines
Doerr, Edd., and Albert J. Menendez,
20, 30–1, 99, 100, 103, 104, 105,
116, 119–20, 122, 125, 248,
281nn2, 5, 282n8, 284n25,
285n30, 286nn31, 33, 289n21
Dooyeweerd, Herman, 168, 299n15
Douglas, Mary, 138
D'Souza, Dinesh, 83
Dunlop, Francis, 291n6
Dunn, Seamus, 262n19
Dwyer, James G., 21, 44, 67–8, 70, 72,
133, 163, 257n29, 269n13,
270nn16, 18, 19, 271n22, 272nn,
28, 31, 292n16, 293, 19, 304n13,
319n55

economics and religious schools, chs.
6 and 7; charge that funding of
leads to underfunding of state common schools, 115, 124–7, 287n3,
289nn19, 21; charge that cost of a
multi-tiered school system is excessive, 116, 124–7, 290n27; need for
cooperation, 130; parents responsible for costs of religious education,
115. *See also* elitism and religious
schools; funding of religious
schools; separation of church and
state and religious schools
education. *See* liberal education. *See
also* schools
educational pluralism, a system of,
92–3, 112, 124, 157, 196, 218, 220,
ch. 13; arguments in support of,
226–45, 284n24; central aim of defending, 5, 7, 35, 77, 92–3, 218,
220; constraints on, 225; examples

of, 225, 244, 312n13; growing acceptance of, 248–9, 269n11,
279n29, 319n56; model of, 222–6,
249–50, 312n12; opposition to,
225–6, 245–9; prejudice underlying opposition to, 246–8; vested interests underlying opposition to,
245–6; as a way of fostering social
cohesion, 38, 243–5, 261nn16, 17;
as a way of fostering tolerance, 57;
as a way of overcoming power-
knowledge, 157
egalitarianism. *See* equality
elitism and religious schools, ch. 7;
academic kind of, 121–3; charges
of, 17, 115, 116, 119, 121–2, 123,
287nn4, 5; defence of elitism, 117–
18, 121; empirical evidence countering charges of, 119–20, 129–30,
288nn16, 17; as expressed in parental commitment, 123–4; values
instruction regarding, 129
Ellul, Jacques, 148
Emberley, Peter C., 84
Enlightenment: censorship during,
156; evolutionary assumptions inherent in, 206; as origin of ideals
connected with education, 8, 81,
85, 86, 144, 147, 148, 165–6, 203,
204; as origin of objections to religious schools, 217; as origin of suspicions about teaching for
commitment, 192–4; postmodernism as a reaction to, 88, 209; and
universalism, 211–12. *See also* modernism
epistemology: belief systems, 170–2;
common-sense knowledge, 173,
301n24; criteria of theory choice,
174, 301n26; feminist, 212; foundationalism, 137, 140; knowledge
and power, 156, 240, 244, 294n7;
Marxist, 212; need for balance

Hunter, James Davison, 208, 314n25
Huntington, Samuel P., 208, 308n13

illiberal religious traditions, 227–8,
239, 250–1, 260n8
Illich, Ivan, 260n6
illustrations. *See* figures
independent Christian schools: vs. private schools, definition of, 255n13.
See religious schools, evangelical or
independent Christian schools
individualism: as central value of liberalism, 202, 230, 241, 247; as inherent in secular colleges and
universities, 92–3; and liberal education, 204; need for balance with
community, 216–17, 222; and traditional ideal of academic freedom,
87–8
indoctrination, ch. 8; author's definition of, 141, 293n19; charge, as
growing out of the traditional ideal
of liberal education, 136, 139–41;
controversy over meaning of, 133–
6, 291n7; critique of analytical approach to defining, 136; developmental approach to defining, 141;
inevitability of, 137, 292n14; institutional, 139, 196, 292n17,
295n10; in liberal democracies,
147, 148, 292n12; need for developmental approach to defining,
141; non-propositional ways of,
136; Ontario guidelines to avoid, in
religious education, 256n21,
257n27; paradigm cases of, 133,
135; and total institutions, 133,
134, 139, 292n18, 319n55
indoctrination and religious schools,
ch. 8; charges of, 17, 22, 26, 133,
135, 291n7, 293n19, 303n5,
304n13; examples, positive and
negative, 142, 293nn22, 23; re-

sponse to charges, 135–6, 139,
141–2, 292n8
initiation: as a component of liberal
education, 68, 137–8, 140–1, 195–
6, 206, 233, 250, 292nn13, 21,
293n21; education into particularity, 230–3; inconsistency regarding, in liberal education, 233–4. *See
also* liberal education
intellectual freedom, ch. 9; and assumption of absolute freedom,
148–50, 295nn11, 13; based on
search for truth, 152–3, 296n23; as
a Christian ideal, 294n3, 296n22;
definition of, 143, 294n2; educational pluralism as an expression
of, 157, 158; limitations of, 147–8;
and moral concerns, 151–2; origins
of ideal of, 143–4; revised and realistic ideal of, 155–7, 294n4
intermediate institutions. *See* mediating institutions
intolerance, ch. 3; and certainty, 58;
definition of, 45–8; Enlightenment
suspicion of, 193; and fundamentalism, 186, 187; increases in desegregated schools, 265n23; increases
when cultural identities not respected, 265n24; misconceptions
regarding, 48–52; and state common schools, 57, 266n27
intolerance and religious schools,
ch. 3; charges of, 17, 23, 29, 44–5,
50–2, 182, 187; empirical evidence
relating to, 52–6, 264n18, 265n19,
266nn25, 28, 30; and exclusive
claims to truth, 50–2, 262n3,
263n4, 264n15; on how to avoid,
56–9; positive and negative examples, 57, 266nn28, 30, 267n33. *See
also* tolerance
Ireland, Northern: effects of religious
schools on divisiveness, 39–40,

with liberalism, 209–11, 219–20,
310n26
postmodernism, 149, 155, 172,
207–10, 306n29; as challenge to
traditional ideal of academic
freedom, 88–9; and constructivism, 172–3; core idea of, 88,
166, 208–9; critique of, 173,
209–10, 309n22; and defence
of religious schools, 219,
311n1; and knowledge, 88–90,
165–6; and need for reconciliaion
with modernism, 194, 209–11,
219–20; and particularity,
209, 211
Postman, Neil, 286n32
Pojman, Louis P., 117
post-secondary schools: in Canada,
25, 259nn38, 39; in Great Britain,
25, 258n37; in the US, 25
Power, F. Clark, and Daniel K. Lapsley, 260n9, 316n39
practical suggestions for religious
schools, 43, 57–9, 77–9, 93–6,
112–14, 128–30, 142, 158–60,
177–80, 196–8
presuppositions. See epistemology:
presuppositions
primary culture, 41, 56–7, 195, 231,
237; as foundation for parental
rights in education, 70–1,
272nn31, 32; state common
schools as undermining, 228–33,
234–5, 265n24
Pring, Richard, 317n44
private schools, 11–12, 18, 25, 119,
255n13
privatization of schooling, 7, 127,
128, 243, 283n19, 290nn30, 31. See
also free market
propaganda, 148
Proulx Task Force, 15, 177, 261n11,
284n26, 313n17

public/private distinction, 18, 64, 99,
105–7, 178, 216, 236, 205. See also
liberalism
public schools. See state common
schools
Purdy, Laura M., 270n20

Quebec, schooling in, 14–15,
255n10. See also Proulx Task Force
Quine, W.V., 170–2, 300n20

Rae, Peter, 25, 259n38
Randall, E. Vance, 74, 272n29,
274nn41, 45
rationality: development of, as essential aim in education, 77, 79, 141,
197, 204; Enlightment conception
of, 86–7, 212–14; and fundamentalism, 187; neutral public reason,
235, 316nn36, 37; lack of, as key to
meaning of indoctrination, 136–7;
postmodernist conception of,
88–9, 212–14; soft, 188; universal
and/or particularist reason, 173,
212–14, 235. See also epistemology
Rauch, Jonathan, 83
Ravitch, Diane, and Joseph P.
Viteritti, 126, 283n19, 319n56
Rawls, John, 117–18, 187, 214, 227,
228, 235, 260nn8, 10, 288n11,
301n29, 308n14, 309n24, 310n28,
314n19, 317n43
Raywid, M.A., 268n5
Regina v. Wiebe, 163–4, 298nn2, 3, 4
Reid, Thomas, 173
relativism, epistemological: as inherent in postmodernism, 88–9, 209;
need to balance relativism of human search for truth and absolutism of the goal of Truth, 213–14,
309n19; in relation to intellectual
freedom, 152–3, 156; in relation to
tolerance, 50–1; solutions to the